disturbing
attachments

*A series edited by
Lauren Berlant and
Lee Edelman*

disturbing
attachments

Genet, Modern Pederasty, and Queer History

KADJI AMIN

DUKE UNIVERSITY PRESS · DURHAM AND LONDON · 2017

© 2017 Duke University Press
All rights reserved

Designed by Amy Ruth Buchanan
Typeset in Arno Pro by Copperline Books

Library of Congress Cataloging-in-Publication Data
Names: Amin, Kadji, [date–] author.
Title: Disturbing attachments [electronic resource] :
Genet, modern pederasty, and queer history / Kadji Amin.
Description: Durham : Duke University Press, 2017. | Series:
Theory Q | Includes bibliographical references and index. |
Description based on print version record and CIP data
provided by publisher; resource not viewed. Identifiers:
LCCN 2017009234 (print) | LCCN 2017015463 (ebook)
ISBN 9780822368892 (hardcover)
ISBN 9780822369172 (pbk.)
ISBN 9780822372592 (e-book)
Subjects: LCSH: Genet, Jean, 1910–1986. |
Homosexuality in literature. | Queer theory. Classification:
LCC PQ2613.E53 (ebook) | LCC PQ2613.E53 Z539 2017 (print) |
DDC 842/.912—dc23
LC record available at https://lccn.loc.gov/2017009234

Cover art: Felipe Baeza, *Fogata*, 2013. Woodblock, silkscreen,
and monoprint on varnished paper. Courtesy of the artist.

contents

ACKNOWLEDGMENTS · ix

INTRODUCTION · 1

CHAPTER 1 · 19
Attachment Genealogies
of Pederastic Modernity

CHAPTER 2 · 45
Light of a Dead Star: The Nostalgic
Modernity of Prison Pederasty

CHAPTER 3 · 76
Racial Fetishism, Gay Liberation,
and the Temporalities of the Erotic

CHAPTER 4 · 109
Pederastic Kinship

CHAPTER 5 · 141
Enemies of the State: Terrorism,
Violence, and the Affective Politics
of Transnational Coalition

EPILOGUE · 176
Haunted by the 1990s:
Queer Theory's Affective Histories

NOTES · 191

BIBLIOGRAPHY · 235

INDEX · 249

Solange: S'aimer dans le dégoût, ce n'est pas s'aimer.

Claire: C'est trop s'aimer.

Solange: To love each other in disgust isn't love.

Claire: It's too much love.

—Jean Genet, *The Maids*

acknowledgments

This book is the product of a long process of sitting with my graduate research on Genet and considering (and reconsidering) where I might go with it. I am fortunate to have received help at various stages of this process from a series of generous mentors. The book would never have been written without Robyn Wiegman. I was ready to drop this project after defending my dissertation. It was she who read between the lines of my dissertation and into my crisis of faith with Genet. She convinced me that, rather than moving on in search of a better object, I might write a good book by thinking through Genet's disappointment of my scholarly ideals. The publication of her book *Object Lessons* was a major catalyst in my thinking about how to do this. I am as grateful to her for the example of her rigorous and searching inquiry into the affective life of field formation as I am for her continually pushing me to make this book the most interesting possible version of itself. I thank my dissertation director, Marc Schachter, for allowing me to stretch the boundaries of a dissertation in French literature. Heather Love's use of literature to think the historical experience of sex and gender deviance and attentiveness to texts that do not go where critics might want to push them in *Feeling Backward* was a major influence on this project. I am indebted to her for writing this book and for her intensive and insightful engagement with my manuscript. At a critical juncture, Tavia Nyong'o took the time to help me understand the genre of the book and find the center of what was then a more dispersed project. I am grateful to Lauren Berlant and Lee Edelman for believing in this book's potential as a contribution to queer theory and championing it for inclusion in Theory Q. Elizabeth Freeman and Todd Reeser have been important supporters of my scholarly endeavors. The book benefited enormously from the astute suggestions and generative critiques of Heather Love, Todd Shepard, Lauren Berlant, Abbie Boggs, and an anonymous reader, all of whom read the manuscript in its entirety. I thank Stephanie Clare, Lisa Duggan, Jack Halberstam, Christina Handhardt, Sharon Holland, Denis Provencher, Jordy Rosenberg, Valerie Traub, and Elizabeth Wilson for their comments and suggestions on earlier version of chapters and on portions of the book developed as talks.

Sections of this book have benefited greatly from workshopping and from the feedback of audiences. Fellow members of the Sexual Politics / Sexual Poetics Collective—Katherine Brewer Ball, Ramzi Fawaz, Zakiyyah Imam Jackson, Uri McMillan, Amber Jamilla Musser, Roy Pérez, Jennifer Row, Shanté Paradigm Smalls, Jordan Alexander Stein, and Damon Young—provided smart and generative feedback on chapter drafts and injected a crucial sense of solidarity and energy into my endeavors as an early-career queer scholar. I particularly want to thank Amber and Damon for their friendship and their generous engagement with this project. Members of the 2015–16 Penn Humanities "Sex" Forum offered crucial suggestions on a section of chapter 1. I am particularly grateful to Heather Love and Jim English, who convened the seminar, and to Nguyen Tan Hoang, Durba Mitra, Sima Shakhsari, and Hsiao-wen Cheng, who have become insightful interlocutors and fast friends. Abbie Boggs and the graduate students in her seminar on Queer Temporality helped me to understand what was coming across in the manuscript and what still needed clarification. The book has benefited from the insights of audiences at Wesleyan University, Emory University, the University of Madison–Wisconsin, the University of Minnesota, the Adult Contemporary Reading series, and the Humanities Institute at Stony Brook.

I have been gifted with warm, ethical, and supportive colleagues conversant in Queer Studies at Stony Brook University. I particularly want to thank Victoria Hesford, Lisa Diedrich, Jeffrey Santa Ana, Kathleen Wilson, Liz Montegary, Lena Burgos-Lafuente, Joseph Pierce, Nerissa Balce, and Tracey Walters for their engagement with and support of my research and for making it a pleasure to work at Stony Brook.

Ken Wissoker has been a wonderfully supportive, encouraging, and efficient editor; and the staff at Duke University Press, particularly Maryam Arain, have been responsive and helpful in shepherding the book to its completion.

This book was completed with the generous help of a Mellon Postdoctoral Fellowship in "Sex" at the University of Pennsylvania Penn Humanities Forum and a Faculty Fellowship at the Humanities Institute at Stony Brook University. I thank Albert Dichy for providing me with access to the Genet archives at the Institut Mémoires de l'Édition Contemporaine (IMEC), which proved crucial to the completion of chapter 5.

Earlier versions of portions of chapter 2 were developed as articles: "Anachronizing the Penitentiary, Queering the History of Sexuality," GLQ: A Journal of Lesbian and Gay Studies 19, no. 3 (2013): 301–40; and "Spectral Mourning and Carceral Masculinities: Jean Genet's *Miracle de la rose*," *French Studies: A Quarterly Review* 65, no. 2 (2011): 200–211. I thank *Women's Studies Quarterly* for allowing me to reprint, in the epilogue, "Haunted by the 1990s: Queer Theory's Affective Histories," in "Queer Methods," special issue, *Women's Studies Quarterly* 44, nos. 3–4 (2016).

introduction

A truck with a spray-painted "Genet" tag in mauve is spotted in New York City, a queer British pop-punk duo takes the name "Jean Genet" (2004), the U.S. artist David Woynarowitz produces a lithograph in which angels carry weapons, Jesus Christ is shooting up, and a haloed Genet occupies the foreground (1978–79), the Canadian band CocoRosie writes a song narrating Genet's mythic life story with, as its melancholy chorus, "Oh those beautiful boyz / pimps and queens and criminal queers / Oh those beautiful boyz / tattoos of ships and tattoos of tears" (2004), a queer/transgender couple, one of them a sex worker, gets tattoos representing the street queen Divine and her pimp Darling from Genet's 1946 novel *Our Lady of the Flowers* to commemorate their love (2009).[1] These anecdotes are suggestive not only of French author and activist Jean Genet's (1910–86) contemporary subcultural iconicity,[2] but also of the impassioned identification he inspires in many of his queer admirers. Genet is capable of sparking such passionate attachment because he resonates, more than any other canonical queer author from the pre-gay liberation past, with contemporary queer sensibilities attuned to a defiant nonnormativity. Genet, after all, was not only sexually queer; he was also a criminal, hated France, and therefore, all nationalisms, famously "chose" abjection, taking up the position of the social pariah by begging, tramping, and prostituting himself, and allied himself, late in life, with the revolutionary anticolonial movements of the Black Panthers and the Palestinian Liberation Organization (PLO). From the vantage point of a "homonationalist"[3] present in which gays and lesbians, as avatars of sexual modernity, have become assets to liberal states, Genet seems to exemplify a prior historical formation of queerness as politically potent outsiderhood. *Genet embodies the queer romance of the alternative.*

Queers are not the first to have found, in Genet, the quintessential romantic outlaw. Indeed, "outlaw" and "antihero" were performances he first honed as a scrappy thief trying to get out of prison and into the French literary canon. In 1943, the psychiatrist Dr. Henri Claude was charged with determining the extent of Genet's responsibility for stealing a rare edition of Verlaine's *Fêtes galantes*. Having already undergone numerous convictions for theft, Genet was eligible for life in prison if sentenced in excess of three months. On realizing that Claude idolized Romantic poets, Genet strove to embody his fantasies, posing as an amoral "noble savage" and vagabond poet in search of "absolute freedom."[4] Claude responded by pronouncing him "morally mad" but not insane. This diagnosis attenuated his responsibility for his crime without, for that matter, mandating institutionalization in an asylum for the criminally insane. As a result, Genet was sentenced to exactly three months in prison, one day shy of what would have meant a life conviction.

Performing outsiderhood was Genet's way into the exclusive world of French letters. Introduced to Parisian high society as a criminal-poet, Genet pilfered his hosts' valuables as a parlor trick to thrill the *haute bourgeoisie*.[5] The fascination he exerted on Jean-Paul Sartre was so great that the latter prematurely canonized him. The first volume of Genet's complete works, published in 1952 when he was still a relatively young author, was composed not of his own writing but of Sartre's mammoth existentialist biography of him, *Saint Genet: An Actor and a Martyr* (*Saint Genet: Comédien et martyre*). In it, Sartre details Genet's heroic journey from dependence and inauthenticity—as a foster child, thief, prisoner, and "passive" homosexual—to existential freedom as an author. In the process, he at once redeems Genet of his outsider past and resuscitates that past as the insignia of all that he has overcome.

Like many minoritarian subjects, Genet had to learn to perform other people's exotic fantasies about him in order to achieve recognition and success. Rather than stripping away the mask, Genet's writing sets the stage for his live performances. His texts give us, as their most fascinating spectacle, Genet "himself," frozen in a series of obscene postures designed to solicit the reader's hatred, pity, and disgust. This is Genet, fantasizing that he is orally tunneling into his dead lover, Jean Decarnin, via the latter's asshole, Genet, luring gay men with the promise of sex only to beat and rob them, Genet, ogling the strong thighs of policemen violently repressing protests at the 1968 U.S. Democratic convention.[6] This, Leo Bersani tells us, is the Genet we know best, "willfully offering transgressive spectacles to others, making himself into a gaudy performer of their most lurid views of him."[7] By deliberately seeking to coincide with the positions of abjection and evil, positions that, he repeatedly assures us, are the consequence of his pederasty, Genet forces the reader to take up extreme positions. Do we critique and reject him, given his efforts to spoil every political program and ethical ideal? To do so would be to inscribe ourselves within a tradition of scandalized critics, humorless defenders of the bastion of French letters. The only other option appears to be to follow in Sartre's footsteps, sanctifying him *despite* and *because of* the morally abhorrent, socially marginal experience he represents.

Genet's writing predicts this bifurcated reception. The moral universe of his literary work is one of extreme polarization, emblematized by "the eternal couple of the criminal and the saint."[8] Informed at once by a Catholic mysticism and a modernist ethic of transvaluation, it is a universe in which moral poles dizzyingly invert. The high are brought low, guillotined murderers become saints, and sexual humiliation is transfigured into a sign of election. Writing during a moment in which transgression, marginality, and the destruction of bourgeois social values has been claimed as the tenets of high modernism, Genet issues a dare: *"Canonize me. I'm so bad I'm good."*[9] Literary critics have enthusiastically responded, awarding Genet his paradoxical position as "an officially sanctioned representative of marginality within French literature."[10]

Just when he has forced the reader into an extreme position of idolization or disgust, however, Genet deflates and renders risible his demons and saints, exposing his moral universe of good and evil, his erotic universe of phallic power and its worshippers, as a sham. This, after all, is the author who refused to take seriously the role of author, forging his own manuscripts for money, telling an interviewer that he might be "an impostor who never wrote any books," and famously declaring that poetry was the art "of using shit and making you eat it."[11] Genet is playing with us, soliciting our hatred, daring us to invert it into idolatry, then, once his status is secure, assuring us that he never meant a word he said. This play is part of his seduction.

Genet's seduction routine worked for Sartre; it worked for modernist literary critics; and it is working for a new generation of queer readers. If the latter is the case, it is because Genet's moral universe and games of seduction are uncannily familiar within queer culture. Like Genet in his role as seductive performer, queer sensibilities[12] *polarize*—into transgressive versus normative, utopian versus antisocial;[13] they *invert*—the badder, the better and more radically queer; and they aggressively and lovingly *deflate* their own ideals. Queer Studies' paradoxical position as an institutionalized site for the study of sexual and social marginality in the academy rhymes with Genet's position in the literary canon. This placement requires of queer scholars some of the *same* seduction routines—*"What we study is so bad it's good"*—that Genet was so adept at performing. Such parallels explain why Genet, more so than any other canonized queer pre-gay liberation author, extends such a seductive mirror to contemporary queers.

Rather than luxuriate in the narcissism of idealized reflections, *Disturbing Attachments* exploits Genet's queer exemplarity as a diagnostic of Queer Studies. The book's method is to investigate what his exemplarity obscures by homing in on the mismatches between Genet's historical attachments and those of contemporary scholarship. However seductive, polarization and idealization distort and omit more than they reveal. Specifically, I will argue that they cannot adequately account for the textures of racial, historical, and geographical difference—precisely those differences marginalized across the history of queer inquiry. *Disturbing Attachments* wagers, nevertheless, that a Queer Studies without idealization would not be Queer Studies at all. Rather than presuming the possibility of a neutral objectivity within this field (and rather than pretending that my claiming of Genet will be the definitive or true one), I explore how, *in the moment of an ideal's deflation*, disturbing attachments— to race, history, and geopolitics—may be revealed.

THE IDEALIZING ENGINE OF QUEER STUDIES

I arrived at this method as Genet spoiled my own investments in him. Initially, I approached Genet as an ideal object for Queer Studies in its utopian, coalitional mode. As a prisoner, juvenile delinquent, homosexual, and prostitute, he incarnates one understanding of *queer* as a term that brings together a range of forms of social marginality.[14] The political dimension of this understanding has been the hope that, in addition to naming miscellaneous modes of social deviance, *queer* might carve out the space for a coalition politics based not on identity, but on a shared relation of distance from normativity.[15] Again, Genet fulfills this ideal, drawing from his multiple forms of marginalization the affective, erotic, and political energy that powered his transnational radical activism with the German Red Army Faction, the Black Panther Party, and the PLO. It would have been possible to write a book celebrating Genet as the realization of precisely this queer coalitional project, and indeed, this is the book I originally hoped to write. However, as I set about the painstaking labor of research, I grew increasingly disturbed by aspects of Genet's queer relations that would not fit this utopian narrative. Writing such a book would have meant smoothing over or redeeming, as so many Genet critics do, the centrality of racial fetishism not only to Genet's early novels, but also to his late activism with the Panthers and the Palestinians. It would have meant ignoring, as have so many critics, the structuration of Genet's relations by the politically and historically "backward" form of age-differentiated pederasty, with its constitutive inegalitarianism and fraught colonial history. Disaffected and uneasy with Genet, I came very close to abandoning him in the hopes of writing a more utopian book on *truly* marginalized and alternative queer socialities. I eventually realized that the failure was not, as I initially thought, Genet's alone. Granted, Genet is well suited to force such a revelation by taking up extreme positions that he cannot fully inhabit, then turning around and puncturing them. But even if I had chosen a more unambiguously politically "good" figure or group—one better positioned to contest the multiple modes of power that go by the names of colonialism, white supremacy, and patriarchal heteronormativity—I would have had to contend with other complicities, other failures, though these may have been easier than Genet's to redeem or to ignore.

Avery Gordon's reflections on how those forms of politicized scholarship that are, in theory, *the most concerned* with denigrated forms of subjectivity so often sacrifice "complex personhood" might be addressed, with particular pertinence, to work in Queer Studies. Gordon reflects:

> Even those who live in the most dire circumstances possess a complex and oftentimes contradictory humanity and subjectivity that is never adequately glimpsed by viewing them as victims or, on the other hand, as superhuman agents. It has always baffled me why those most interested in understanding and changing the barbaric domination that characterizes our modernity often—not always—withhold from the very people they are most concerned with the right to complex personhood.[16]

Insofar as Queer Studies' institutionalization, the measure of its mettle as a field, has depended on its capacity to *extract theoretical and political value* from the most transgressive objects of study, complex personhood—the ways in which we are all, even the "queerest" or most subaltern among us, both good and bad subjects, imperfect, contradictory, and "ordinary"—risks being the fallout of the field's institutional norms.[17] The failure of my object of study to behave in the ways that I hoped he would, his failure to consistently and routinely secrete political value was, I eventually concluded, not his alone. It was a failure endemic to the project of revalorizing deviance.

Genet's failures lay bare a methodological dilemma within queer scholarship as well as politicized criticism as a whole: how to counter the pathologization of denigrated groups without reacting by idealizing them. In Western modernity, sexual and racialized deviance has been pathologized, violently policed, and subjected to normalizing discipline in prisons, hospitals, and schools. As a result, the cultures, knowledges, and life-worlds of denigrated groups have been stigmatized and rendered monstrously unintelligible. A powerful tendency within scholarship has been to respond to this damaging legacy of shame and stigma by loudly idealizing the alternatives that emerge from deviance. The result has been a strain of romantic antinomianism in queer culture and scholarship.[18] Our sex, because outlawed, is hotter; our love, because uninstitutionalized, is truer; our families, because freely chosen, are uniquely supportive and antihierarchical; our political movements, because unbound by narrow social identities, are coalitional and capable of fighting oppression on all fronts. In short, because we are forced to invent relations outside of tired old blueprints, our socialities are not only better, more authentic, and more pleasurable; they also actualize real-life alternatives to existing relations of oppression. This idealism, which neatly inverts the historical denigration of queer bonds, has been one of the powerful redemptive impulses of Queer Studies.[19]

Queer Studies in this redemptive mode has seized the resources of scholarship for the project of stressing the viability, the political potency, and the world-building potential of queer life-worlds violently represented as unintelligible in the hope of enlarging the capacity for imagining and practicing alternatives in the present. Such a project, however laudable, puts an idealizing strain on the relationship between scholarship and culture. One refrain in queer scholarship is that theory lags behind culture.[20] What scholars mean by this assertion is that queer cultures abundantly generate alternative imaginaries and political potentialities that it is the theorist's humble work to recognize, document, and translate into the idiom of scholarship. Such faith orients scholars to the circular project of locating queer possibility, positioned as what theory both wants and lacks, in the social.[21] This places a great burden on queer social forms. *What happens when culture fails the expectations with which theory ap-*

proaches it? The narrator of Genet's *Our Lady of the Flowers* (*Notre-Dame-des-Fleurs*) (1943) explains to the hetero-bourgeois reader, "Our domestic life and the laws of our Homes do not resemble your Homes." The reason, however, is not that queer households are more loving, ethical, and sex positive, but that "we love each other without love."[22] This simultaneously idealizing *and* deidealizing assertion prefaces the announcement of the pimp Darling's sudden and remorseless decision to abandon the street queen, Divine, who has been lovingly supporting him by prostituting herself. Queer intimacies, taxed with the burdens of pathologization, criminalization, and social abjection and with the precarity and psychic duress these conditions engender, are as likely to produce abuse, exploitation, and the renunciation of care as more loving, sexually liberated, and just alternatives to heteronormative social forms.

The Darling/Divine example—rooted in an early twentieth-century subculture of street queens, pimps, and petty criminals—suggests that *some* queer cultures may be more amenable to idealization and, thus, more translatable into queer theory than others. We might get a sense of which by examining the ethics of queer culture outlined in Michael Warner's "Normal and Normaller" (1999). At the high point in the essay, Warner lists twelve points, each of which reinforces the others in what amounts to a strong case for queer culture as the site for a theoretical and political production of thought that affirms the value of "nonstandard" intimacies and alternative sexualities while leveling a cogent critique of the hierarchies of value that would denigrate them.[23] This essay demonstrates that, in 1999, it is still possible to position queer theory as founded on an articulable list of basic ethical values expressed consistently by an identifiably queer political culture that extends, in a heartening show of historical continuity, from gay liberation through AIDS activism and into the present. To its credit, the essay frankly exposes the grounding of its halcyon unity of queer theory, culture, and politics in a nongeneralizable post-Stonewall U.S. historical context. The epistemological foundation of queer theory on a politicized post-Stonewall gay, lesbian, and/or queer culture continues to delimit the terms under which nonnormative social formations in other historical moments and geopolitical areas might enter the purview of queer scholarship (see the epilogue).

At this juncture, however, the historical continuity of queer culture and its seamless expression in queer theory can no longer be taken for granted. Queer of color critique, transnational, and area studies scholarship have critically interrogated *which* versions of queer culture, *which* histories may serve as not only the object but also the very epistemological foundation of queer theorization.[24] Yet even as the social formations claimable as queer are multiplied, the fundamental problem of idealization persists and, indeed, grows ever more acute. For if the subjects of queer culture are no longer out-and-proud gay and lesbian activists fighting to destigmatize and diversify sexual practices and intimate forms, but rather nineteenth-century Chinese immigrants forced to live in residentially segregated, crowded, and insalubrious conditions,[25] refugees and undocumented migrants struggling under conditions of debility and "slow death," and drug addicts,[26] then to what extent can scholars ethically celebrate the alternatives they innovate? This dilemma is a function not only of focusing on ever more marginalized populations with fewer resources for collective and self reinvention, but also, in some cases, of accounting for prepolitical forms of agency that have not yet and might never articulate a coherent ethical and political platform. Queer Studies has become the name of an effort to amplify the ethics, politics, and inventiveness of marginalized cultures. In setting it this task, however, we risk subscribing to a romance of the alternative whereby even as we refuse to silence the transgressive aspects of marginalized cultures in the name of respectability or assimilation, we may be tempted to idealize their political and cultural effects.

Queer Studies in the present inherits the problem of the persistent idealization of queer culture, however that culture is defined. But what exactly is idealization? We might look back to the 1990s debate about lesbian butch/femme for a relevant anatomization of idealization's operations. In her afterword to *Butch/Femme*, a 1998 volume edited by Sally Munt, Judith Butler notes that the desire to claim lesbian butch/femme sex and gender practices as irreducible to heteronormativity too often leads to the idealization and polarization of each term. She defines idealization as a *purification* of one's object that relies on the *repudiation* of its relationship to normative social forms. Both operations are driven by the "oblique work of shame," which responds to the denigration of the queer object, its status as a failed copy, with an effort to redeem it by disavowing its bedevilment by normativity.[27] Idealization, I would add, tends to be ahistorical, since history, in the Foucauldian sense, is nothing if not the strategic mobility of shifting relational networks within which no one entity can occupy the position of resistance for very long.[28] The fact that U.S. butch/femme lesbian culture is no longer the object of queer theoretical idealization, as it was in the 1990s, should alert us to the ways in which idealization binds us to the circular process, which Robyn Wiegman analyzes in *Object Lessons*, of idealization, disappointment, and the search for a new object thought to be better able to fulfill the aspirations of the field.

What I find most energizing about Queer Studies is that it provides a site within the academy for theoretically informed and nonpathologizing work on deviant sexuality and sociality. However, this focus on social deviance cannot, ultimately, survive the turn to more richly situated queer cultures without checking the field's impulse of idealization. As it becomes more diversified and responsive to its objects of study, Queer Studies stands positioned to offer more textured accounts of the distinct cultural and historical modalities of deviance, its precise relation to multiple forms of power, and the (un)ethical and (a)political visions it fosters. To do so, however, means navigating the contradictions between deviance, with its complex and variable politics, and the idealized polarities that often go by the name of *queer*.

THE HEURISTIC OF DEIDEALIZATION

Genet is well positioned to illuminate the methodological dilemmas at the heart of Queer Studies specifically and left criticism in general. As a paradigmatic figure for the romance of the alternative, Genet virtually *demands* idealization as a saint or antihero, adeptly setting the trap that criticism will fall into. Eventually, however, he spoils every ideal. When we want to claim him as a precursor for today's queer and transgender prison abolition movement, he insists that the penal colony of Mettray was a "paradise," when we want to celebrate his transnational coalitions with the Panthers and the Palestinians, he confesses that a sexual desire for Arab and black men drew him toward these movements, and when we want to honor his queer bonds, we are confronted with their pederastic inegalitarianism. Genet has the virtue of making critics feel uneasy about the ideals we make him represent.

The experience of *unease* tends to lead to a limited and rather defensive range of scholarly strategies. When a "promising" object fails to deliver, scholars too often compensate by switching gears from idealization to critique, flaying the object for its failure to be sufficiently transgressive or consistently radical. If this occurs early on in a research project, it can initiate the wholesale abandonment of the object that has failed to live up to its promise. Otherwise, we might either sidestep the source of unease, the better to celebrate the object's truly radical aspects, or use it to hone the ego-enhancing aggression of critique, thereby shoring up the critic's position of mastery and political unassailability. Genet taught me that politicized scholarship needs to cultivate a wider set of methods and tactics with which to negotiate what disturbs and disappoints and a wider range of scholarly moods than utopian hope, on the one hand, and critique, on the other. Scholars might *inhabit unease*, rather than seeking to quickly rid themselves of it to restore the mastery of the critic, the unassailability of her politics, and the legitimacy of her trained field expectations.

The experience of unease, *Disturbing Attachments* proposes, can serve as a generative heuristic for politicized scholarship. It might herald not only something heroically counterhegemonic that ruptures the rationalities of the present, but also a shape of the alternative that rubs against the grain of trained scholarly expectations. It might reveal that field dispositions that sanction some objects of study while rendering others illegible and ignored are neither neutral nor inherently just; rather, they reflect the field's historical inheritance. *Disturbing Attachments* responds to the crisis of Genet's spoilage of the ideal of queer sociality by centering moments when nonnormative attachments and uninstitutionalized relations from the queer past disturb not only the rationality of the gay/lesbian liberal present, but also the field habitus of Queer Studies itself.[29] Its paradigmatic disturbing attachment is *modern pederasty*—an age-structured male same-sex form, practiced by Genet and many others, that, despite its commonality, has been undertheorized within queer scholarship. The problem of pederasty is its inegalitarianism—its impolite and impolitic admission that it gets off on power, including but not limited to that most righteously reproved form of power between an adult and a minor.

Since objects, such as modern pederasty, that inspire scholarly nausea and unease will not further all of the field's aspirations (this is precisely why they cause unease) and I am arguing that we should not be so quick to critique them, they require another scholarly mood, one I term *deidealization*. *Disturbing Attachments* contends that deidealization is the condition of taking deviance, nonnormativity, and minoritarian cultures seriously in scholarship. Deidealization deexceptionalizes queerness in order to analyze queer possibility as inextricable from relations of power, queer deviance as intertwined with normativity, and queer alternatives as not necessarily just alternatives. In centering deidealization, I draw inspiration from another queer tradition, one Genet again exemplifies—that of living with damage in a damaged world. For if queers have become, by necessity, adept at imagining unlikely utopias "somewhere over the rainbow," we have also honed the skill of acerbically puncturing one another's claims to mastery, of making art out of the darkest and most traumatic aspects of queer experience, and of eroticizing not only the successes but also the inadequacies of failed genders and unconventional embodiments. My thinking on deidealization is ethically and tonally inspired by a body of Queer and Critical Race Studies work by scholars such as Sharon Holland, Heather Love, Antonio Viegas, and Darieck Scott that embraces irreparability.[30] Nevertheless, as I argue in chapter 3, negativity can be idealized as well. While reparation, a term that originates in Eve Sedgwick's reading of Melanie Klein, is often glossed in queer scholarship as the optimistic will to repair and ameliorate a damaged world, I position deidealization within an expanded understanding of reparation that stays close to the latter's origin in the "depressive" position.[31] Deidealization is not the wholesale destruction of cherished ideals, but a form of the reparative that acknowledges messiness and damage, refuses the repudiating operations of idealization, and acknowledges the ways in which complicity is sometimes necessary for survival. It names a form of queer inquiry, which I understand to be already under way, that offers a less binary, less repudiating account of the constitutive entanglement of queer and deviant cultures within a range of modes of social power. It offers an interdisciplinary means to connect scholarship more affiliated with queer theory to empirical and area studies scholarship on sexuality that has tended to be marginalized within Queer Studies, in part because it rarely follows into the terrain of idealization and utopianism promoted by queer humanities scholarship.[32]

Deidealization may not immediately enable a muscular and decisive politics, but it does have consequences for politicized thought. On the most basic level, it calls for an acknowledgment of the "complex personhood" of queer, racialized, and subaltern persons too often assigned the psychically flat role of righting the ills of an unjust social order and denied the right to be damaged, psychically complex, or merely otherwise occupied. Deidealization does, however, require scholars to acknowledge a break between scholarly and political practice. Whereas politicized fields of scholarship too often seek to make scholarship the scene of political practice by critiquing all that is bad and idealizing all that might be good, deidealization acknowledges that the politics of scholarship are only a small part, rather than the full realization, of political activism in a complex world.

THE DIAGNOSTIC OF ATTACHMENT

Idealization is, in itself, a mode of often impassioned attachment. It tends, however, to preempt a range of other attachments—to objects that defy idealization, as well as to complex conditions that complicate moral polarities, such as history, racialization, and geography. By deidealizing Genet's queer relations, *Disturbing Attachments* foregrounds their structuration by histories of race, colonialism, crime, and biopolitics. Genet charts a surprise course through queer history, leaping from the criminal and male prostitute subcultures of the 1920s and 1930s directly to the Third World liberation movements of the 1970s and 1980s while skipping over the familiar landmarks of gay identity and community formation—homophile organizations, the gay liberation movement, and the building of gay urban business districts. I argue that a pederastic sexuality formed in Third Republic French prisons is at the origin of Genet's passionate cross-racial and transnational activism with the Black Panther Party and the PLO during the moment of revolutionary decolonization. Animated by eroticized differentials of age, sexuality, and sometimes race, pederasty is among a series of problematic and outmoded queer attachments *Disturbing Attachments* uses to deidealize and historicize queer theory.

Genet offers the opportunity to study queer attachments during a moment, which chapter 1 identifies as that of *pederastic modernity*, in which they were *constituted by* and *experientially inseparable from* criminalization, colonial histories of racialization, and eroticized differentials of age and power. Rather than seeking sex, relationships, community, and political solidarity with "other" gay men, Genet actually made a show of disdaining them, bragging, for instance, about luring them with the promise of sex or prostitution only to beat and rob them in his youth.[33] A queer erotics *did*, nevertheless, propel Genet's political affinities and imagined belongings—particularly with French prisoners, decolonizing Arabs, and black Americans. One sense of *queer*, championed by Eve Sedgwick, is of a transitive and transversal *movement athwart or across*.[34] Genet's attractions illuminate queer movements and impulses across social categories that will increasingly be erased by the identity-based notion of political belonging that the gay rights movement, in its bid for liberal inclusion, will use with some success from the late 1970s onward to redefine the imaginable vectors of queer attachment. Perversely elaborated from within *multiple* regimes of power, these queer erotics, relations, and affinities would be *made retrograde* during the rights-based gay and lesbian movement of the 1970s and 1980s, so that an identity and political constituency based exclusively on "the one fact of privately experienced and conducted sexual desire and practice" could emerge by separating itself from other, less easily privatized, forms of social difference, and, therefore, from alternative vectors that might otherwise organize belonging, identity, and desire.[35] By focusing on the transversal attachments of pederastic modernity, this book interrogates the separations between contemporary categories of social difference, including race, nationality, and sexuality. At the same time, it works against the scholarly tendency to idealize movements across categories by attending to the political and ethical trouble they often foment.

Disturbing Attachments deidealizes Genet's transversal movements by foregrounding their animation by unsavory and outdated modes of attachment, including pederastic kinship, racial fetishism, nostalgia for prison, and fantasies of queer terrorism. I understand *attachment* as a diagnostic that looks *beneath* relation to the affective and imaginary processes of identification, attraction, and belonging that structure and bind any given relation. As Lauren Berlant proposes, "Attachment is a *structure* of relationality. But the experience of affect and emotion that attaches to those relations is as extremely varied as the contexts of life in which they emerge."[36] Attachment's analytical purchase inheres in its capacity to mark all that is passive, needy, historically overdetermined, compulsive, phantasmatic, and nonvolitional about interpersonal relations. While, in some strains of Queer Studies, the injunction that queer collectivities, kinship, coalitions, and counterpublics operate as a utopian model of more just, egalitarian, and caring social forms implicitly poses queer relations as a practice of justice, the analytic of attachment critically interrogates the unstated assumption that a heroic and even ascetic agency animates queer relations—that is, that autonomous queer subjects can and do choose to participate in just ways of relating and to refrain from dominating, racist, and coercive ones. The reliance of certain models of queer relation on such assumptions of autonomous choice minimizes the nonrational, socially constituted, and historically contingent aspects of queer subjectivity, as well the ways in which feelings of attraction, belonging, identification, and affinity prove resistant to conscious manipulation. *Disturbing Attachments* seeks to move beyond both the injunction that queer relations be *exceptional*—exceptionally just, oppositional, and distant from heterosexual and homonationalist modes of belonging—and the model of autonomous choice that undergirds this injunction by using a focus on attachment to discern how power, race, and history come together to produce queer relations with politically unpredictable effects.[37]

Disturbing Attachments investigates what happens when queer attachments fail to live up to the inverted ideals of politicized scholarship. It analyzes forms of transgression with dire material consequences—including imprisonment, social death, and bodily harm—while at the same time investigating how and why they do not necessarily provide the payoff of either utopian world making or progressive politics that scholars might desire. The book proceeds by setting its sights squarely on modes of queer relation that go just beyond the pale of what has been deemed reclaimable by queer theory. Asking why Daddy/ Boy, but not intergenerational pederasty, why the black submissive's embrace of "extravagant abjection" in an interracial scene but not the white bottom's racial fetishism, why incarcerated queers' calls for prison abolition, but not their quieter moments of pleasure in incarceration, *Disturbing Attachments* brings unsavory, complicit, and politically problematic modes of queer relation to bear on queer theory.[38] The result is an interrogation of the political imperative of *queer* and the disavowed historical imaginaries that inform the term's contemporary use, and a reorientation of *queer* toward unsavory and historically dated modes of attachment.

The project's focus on the defamiliarizing torque of outmoded queer attachments owes a great debt to the emergent body of work on queer temporality, exemplified by Carolyn Dinshaw's *Getting Medieval: Sexualities and Communities, Pre- and Postmodern* (1999), Carla Freccero's *Queer/Early/Modern* (2005), J. Halberstam's *In a Queer Time and Place: Transgender Bodies, Subcultural Lives* (2005), Heather Love's *Feeling Backward: Loss and the Politics of Queer History* (2007), and Elizabeth Freeman's *Time Binds: Queer Temporalities, Queer Histories* (2010). I remain critical, nevertheless, of the ways in which queer time is often idealized. Despite scholars' caveats that time experienced as nonchronological or out of step with national timing is not necessarily resistant, politically progressive, or even nonheteronormative, they most often choose to focus on those moments, pregnant with possibility, when an alignment between queer erotic practices, nonchronological time, and historically distant periods opens alternate possibilities for the flourishing of queer erotic subjects and communities.[39]

I intervene in this conversation by proposing that, before it can explore cross-historical and nonchronological queer desires, queer scholarship on temporality must first historicize the desires encoded within the term *queer* itself. To do this, I develop a new method, *attachment genealogy*—fully explicated in chapter 1 and carried out in each of the chapters—that excavates earlier and more transnational modes of queer attachment to both historicize and expand *queer*'s current affective orientations. Each time an *analytically* queer form of nonnormative sociality clashes with *queer*'s current affective and political connotations, producing the scholarly experience of unease, I perform an attachment genealogy to excavate the attachments that inform *queer*'s aversion to this particular object. In this way, the book explores how disavowed and undertheorized attachments to gay liberalism, gay liberationism, the 1980s–90s

Anglophone discourse of "chosen family," and 1990s queer activism inform *queer*'s attractions and aversions, delimiting what forms of deviance qualify as properly *queer*. By centering relations from the queer past that disturb these recent historical attachments, I seek to expand the affective orientations of Queer Studies. The ambition of this method is to both bring into view and multiply the historical and geographical conditions that shape what is possible, imaginable, and sensible under the sign of *queer*. This enables historical, transnational, and area studies scholarship not only to expand the range of objects that *queer* describes, but also to impact the epistemologies and feeling states of Queer Studies itself.

If Genet's queer exemplarity is my problem, his practice of deidealization is my heuristic. Each chapter is organized around Genet's failure of a contemporary political ideal. In the moment of deidealization, I zero in on one of Genet's disturbing attachments—nostalgia for prison, racialized attraction, pederastic kinship, hatred of the state—and excavate it for the obscured histories and theoretical questions it indexes. The chapters analyze the uneasy tension between these attachment genealogies and pressing issues in contemporary queer politics and scholarship—from prison abolition to homonationalism and pinkwashing to feminist reevaluations of the Black Power movement. By studying "archaic" modes of queer attachment that resist the ideals of the present, *Disturbing Attachments* challenges Queer Studies to avow the history of its affective tendencies and to allow them to be unsettled and transformed by earlier modes of queer feeling.

Queer theory has embraced Michel Foucault's interview "Friendship as a Way of Life" as being about the utopian potential of uninstitutionalized relations to generate reconfigured and antidisciplinary bodies, selves, and collectivities. In the process, it has forgotten that a central topic of this interview, and the blueprint for the uninstitutionalized relations Foucault has in mind, is *pederasty*, not the Ancient Greek kind, but that practiced contemporaneously by French men in the 1980s. Chapter 1, "Attachment Genealogies of Pederastic Modernity," uses the book's method of *attachment genealogy* to examine why, despite its centrality to the history of sexuality, what I term modern pederasty—that is, an age-structured coupling between either adult men, boys of different ages, or an adult man and a youth—remains an inconvenient and embarrassing object for queer inquiry. It closes by theorizing *pederastic modernity* as a generative analytic of the erotic life of modern Western (post) colonial power.

Chapter 2, "Light of a Dead Star: The Nostalgic Modernity of Prison Pederasty," plumbs a politically retrograde feeling—Genet's perverse nostalgia for the silenced pleasures of the pederastic culture of the boys' penal colony of Mettray, in which he was incarcerated as an adolescent. It contrasts Genet's nostalgia with reform-oriented narratives of the boys' penal colonies published during the 1920s–50s, in which pederasty is rejected as a figure for perversely racialized masculine hierarchies incoherent with the French social contract. I critically modify Elizabeth Freeman's concept of erotohistoriography to argue that Genet's 1946 memoir-novel *Miracle of the Rose* theorizes pederastic subject formation as a state of continued woundedness and haunting by a traumatic past that one does not want to repress or forget, for it also contains prohibited pleasures. I argue that *Miracle* models a queer disposition toward the past that would neither turn away in horror and distaste from its commingled affects of pleasure and trauma nor recuperate them through a progress narrative of sexual or penal emancipation, but rather allow their haunting to disturb the certainties of the present.

Chapter 3, "Racial Fetishism, Gay Liberation, and the Temporalities of the Erotic," moves between Genet's writings and two censored journal issues of a French gay liberation group, the FHAR, that position the black or Arab sexual penetrator as the fetishized instrument through which the white bottom may enjoy his temporary release from the burdens of identity via self-shattering. These FHAR texts exemplify the understudied tradition I term *liberationist negativity*, to which psychoanalytic queer negativity, with its celebration of self-shattering and jouissance, is indebted. This chapter deidealizes both psychoanalytic and liberationist negativity by examining how practices of racial fetishism can intensify sexual self-shattering. I seek to shift queer work on desire onto common ground with scholarship on race by theorizing the history and temporality of erotic life.

Chapter 4, "Pederastic Kinship," draws attention to the kinship function of many modern pederastic relationships and theorizes the complex interrelations between pederasty's kinship forms and those of the heterosexual family. I trace the shape of pederastic kinship within Genet's life practices of affiliation, including his habit of introducing himself into the domesticities of heterosexual couples, his practice of financing the heterosexual households of his younger male lovers, and his fantasy of himself as the adopted foundling of the Black Panther Party. By making the argument that Genet's passionate attachment to the Black Panther Party was structured by an erotics of pederastic intergenerationality, this chapter reveals, as Angela Davis wrote regarding Genet's posthumously published memoir *Prisoner of Love*, "suppressed moments of the history of sixties nationalism" and of sexual politics alike.[40] Ultimately, I position pederastic kinship as a forgotten and uncomfortable attachment genealogy of gay and lesbian "chosen" and nuclear family that restores power and inequality to overly idealized imaginaries of queer kinship.

Through archival research, chapter 5, "Enemies of the State: Terrorism, Violence, and the Affective Politics of Transnational Coalition," reads "The Language of the Wall," Genet's unpublished 1981–82 film manuscript on the imperialist utility of the boys' penal colony of Mettray, and "Violence and Brutality," his almost universally excoriated 1977 newspaper article in support of the German Red Army Faction, as windows into a crucial shift between the 1940s, in which Genet imagines himself a pederast and a criminal, and therefore, an enemy of the French state, and the 1970s, in which he identifies passionately with nonnational revolutionary groups that defend the use of political violence against liberal states. I argue that both texts contribute to homonationalist critique a window into the affective and intellectual labor required to shift affective *landscapes of queer revolt* so that they might sensually apprehend the scale of the global. The chapter's afterword uses the example of Genet's late activism to deidealize the aspirations that animate the utopian queer imaginary of an oppositional antinormative coalition.

I conclude by considering how this book's method of attachment genealogy and heuristic of deidealization might open the way toward an interdisciplinary future, grounded in the specificities of *multiple* racial, geographical, and historical contexts, for the field of Queer Studies. The epilogue, "Haunted by the 1990s: Queer Theory's Affective Histories," proposes that the future of the field of Queer Studies — as well as its relevance for scholarship on prior historical periods, racialized populations, and areas outside the United States — requires a reckoning with the field's affective haunting by the inaugural moment of the U.S. 1990s. This reckoning might take the form of a *rehistoricization*. That is, by engaging *queer*'s *multiple* pasts — including those prior to its explicit deployment as a political and theoretical term in the 1990s — scholars might expand and multiply the affective histories that give *queer* meaning. I frame the book's chapters, which excavate historical attachments that clash with the affective histories of queer theory, as modeling such a version of queer inquiry.

Disturbing Attachments contributes to an ongoing conversation in Queer Studies about the history and the futures of *queer* as both method and analytic.

It wagers that when practitioners attend to how *queer* functions in queer scholarship—to what it is taken to mean and expected to do, as well as to what happens when its critical capacities fall short or break down—we can critically and rigorously reorient the field's future. My hope is that this future will be one in which Queer Studies can be more attentive to the opacities of its objects of study, less zealous about the radicalism, reach, and portability of its methods and analytics, and more capacious in acknowledging the historical, racial, and geopolitical multiplicity of feelings and moods that might yet interact with the histories that inform queer inquiry.

chapter 1

ATTACHMENT GENEALOGIES
OF PEDERASTIC MODERNITY

At the heart of this book is the question of how queer theory selects its historical examples. What historical forms of relation must be forgotten, overlooked, or suppressed so that contemporary queer theory can sustain its key critical and political commitments and imaginaries? To illustrate the stakes of this question and the book's method of *attachment genealogy*, this chapter restores the centrality of pederasty to Genet's contemporary, Michel Foucault, in his interview "Friendship as a Way of Life" ("De l'amitié comme mode de vie"). It goes on to theorize the centrality of modern pederasty to the history of sexuality as well as to modern Western (post)colonial power.

Queer theory has embraced "Friendship as a Way of Life" as being about the utopian potential of uninstitutionalized relations to generate reconfigured and antidisciplinary bodies, selves, and collectivities.[1] We might therefore look back at this interview—given before the advent of an activism or scholarship that names itself "queer"—to get a sense of what has been left behind in the canonization of *queer* as a conjunction between alternative futurity, uninstitutionalized relations, and a utopian world-making project. One underappreciated element of the interview, Heather Love has argued, is Foucault's point that a position outside sanctioned social and familial relations might be terrifying or even anguishing as well as exhilarating. "What is it," Foucault wonders, "to be 'naked' among men, outside institutional relations, family, profession, and obligatory camaraderie? It's a desire, an uneasiness, a desire-in-uneasiness that exists among a lot of people."[2] Love uses this passage to critique the ways in which sustaining "the stabilizing role" of a positive and caring version of friendship in imagining queer community depends on ignoring the "unease" that Foucault associates with uninstitutionalized relations, along with all that might be disturbing, terrifying, and destructive about lives lived outside widely held values and intelligible codes of conduct.[3] It is, after all, a banal observation that queer communities and relationships have nurtured addiction, abuse, and outsized sentimental longings for marital normalcy as well as alternative and resistant world-building possibilities.

"Unease," however, might also describe the feeling underlying the neglect within Queer Studies of a theme fundamental to Foucault's reflections in this interview. To the interviewer's question, "Can you say that desire and pleasure, and the relationships one can have, are dependent on one's age?" Foucault responds, with apparent enthusiasm:

> Yes, very profoundly. Between a man and a younger woman, the marriage institution makes it easier: she accepts it and makes it work. But two men of noticeably different ages—what code would allow them to communicate? They face each other without terms or convenient words, with nothing to assure them about the meaning of the movement that carries them toward each other. They have to invent, from A to Z, a relationship that is still formless, which is friendship: that is to say, the sum of everything through which they can give each other pleasure.[4]

Age differences between two men not only come readily to the mind of the interviewer, but are enthusiastically affirmed by Foucault as central to the theme of exhilaratingly uninstitutionalized queer friendship for which this interview is remembered.[5] Why was modern pederasty—by which I mean an erotic relation structured by a difference of age and generation between two men, two boys, or a man and a boy, rather than the more rigid Ancient Greek relation between a pubescent boy and an adult man—such an obvious referent for the interviewer as well as Foucault? Why, despite David Halperin's acknowledgment of its importance, has its presence in this interview been ignored by subsequent work in Queer Studies? Finally, what difference would it make to the idealization of friendship and uninstitutionalized relations within queer theory to remark that "Friendship as a Way of Life" is largely about *pederasty*?

The pederastic referent lends a different meaning to Foucault's critique, immediately afterward, of a certain increasingly popular idea of homosexuality: "two young men meeting in the street, seducing each other with a look, grabbing each other's asses and getting each other off in a quarter of an hour. There you have a kind of neat image of homosexuality without any possibility of generating unease."[6] This passage is normally read as a critique of the notion that homosexual sex, in and of itself, is either oppositional or world building and as a node in Foucault's thesis that what is potentially interesting about same-sex practices are the *relations* that can be invented around them. When the referent of pederasty is restored, however, the passage might simultaneously be read as a critique of the emergent norm, which historian Scott Gunther has located as solidifying in *Gai pied hebdo*, the 1982 incarnation of the French gay magazine in which Foucault is being interviewed, of homosexuality as a relationship between two gay-identified adult men of roughly the same age.[7] This norm emerged as part of a concerted effort by French gay rights activists, beginning around 1979, to combat the discriminatory 1942 law that fixed a higher age of consent for homosexual than for heterosexual sex.[8] The political stakes of this strategy would have been a matter for public debate at the time of Foucault's interview, given that, during the late 1970s, more radical activists and intellectuals, including Foucault himself, had been active in a campaign to decriminalize noncoercive adult-child sexual relations entirely rather than merely equalizing the heterosexual and homosexual ages of consent.[9] This campaign to decriminalize noncoercive adult-child sex overlapped with a veritable discursive explosion—in well-regarded novels, journal special issues, and letters and editorials published in the national newspaper *Libération*—proclaiming pedophilia and child sexuality the last frontier of the movement for (homo)sexual liberation and the leftist cultural issue of the day. I am proposing, therefore, that "Friendship as a Way of Life" can be read as a commentary on same-age male homosexuality, not as the natural essence of homosexuality once freed of pre-gay liberation social strictures, but as an ambivalent *historical achievement* in the contentious process of being secured in France during the very moment of Foucault's interview.

Foucault goes on to elaborate two reasons why the popular image of a sexual pickup of two young men on the street might be incapable of provoking the *unease* that functions, in this interview, as the affective symptom of all that is potentially disturbing about queer relations. His first remark, that such a pickup responds to a "reassuring canon of beauty," might be understood in implicit contrast to the "ugly" pederastic image of the older man seducing a youth, or, as Gayle Rubin wrote in 1981, "drooling old sickies corrupting or harming sweet innocent children."[10] During this time period, both Rubin and Foucault comment on the recent media fervor, in the United States and France, respectively, around the dangers of child pornography and pedophilia and the imperative to protect the sexual innocence of children from predatory pedophiliac monsters.[11] Resituating Foucault's remarks in this discursive context suggests that he is not only critiquing a familiar gay male obsession with youth and beauty; he is also, more interestingly, reflecting on the ways in which the gay male canon of beauty is coming into line with that of the mainstream by disavowing cross-generational relations, increasingly, though not exclusively portrayed as monstrous and ugly in the French popular press. Second, Foucault claims that the sexual pickup of two young men "cancels everything that can be troubling in affection, tenderness, friendship, fidelity, camaraderie, and companionship, things that our rather sanitized society can't allow a place for without fearing the formation of new alliances and the tying together of unforeseen lines of force."[12] Foucault's emphasis on "new alliances" and "unforeseen lines of force" in this quote suggests that the kinds of relations he values as having the potential to disturb the social order have more to do with the differences, inequalities, and dissymmetries of pederasty than with a friendship between two young, white, gay men of the same class status. Indeed, Foucault notes that the homosexual "way of life" that gives rise to uninstitutionalized and affectively intense relations "can be shared among individuals *of different age, status, and social activity*."[13] Foucault's repeated returns, throughout the interview, to the dissymmetry of age differences suggests that "Friendship as a Way of Life" is better read as a speculation on the potential of *pederastic relations that cross one or more significant social differences* to create "diagonal lines" in the social fabric that allow "virtualities to come to light" than as a more general case for the world-building potential of uninstitutionalized queer friendship.[14] Foucault ascribes to pederasty the same capacity to move transitively *athwart or across* social categories that Eve Sedgwick will later champion as distinctively queer.[15]

In his reading of the interview, David Halperin relates Foucault's discussion of age differences to differences of class and race that may also produce imbalances of power. He goes on, importantly, to connect the issue of inegalitarian erotic relations to Foucault's better-known interest in S/M as a means of using power to produce pleasure.[16] Subsequent queer critics, however, have "forgotten" the centrality of cross-generational sexual relations to Foucault's thinking in this interview. If Queer Studies has enthusiastically picked up on Foucault's suggestive statements, in his late interviews and essays, regarding the potential of both BDSM and uninstitutionalized relations to produce new pleasures, remapped bodies and selves, and transformative social alliances, while "forgetting" the centrality of modern (as opposed to Ancient Greek) pederasty to these reflections, this is not a chance oversight. In Rubin's "Thinking Sex," a landmark 1984 essay often credited with founding Sexuality Studies as a field and inaugurating the queer theoretical commitment to the critical analysis of sexual hierarchies and oppressions of all kinds,[17] Rubin predicts that, twenty years hence, the sad and practically unquestioned persecution of boy-lovers, who lack "defenders for their civil liberties, let alone for their erotic orientation," will become visible to all as the injustice it is, leaving many ashamed of their complicity with the current "witch hunt." Reflecting on this prediction upon the essay's reprint in 2011, Rubin admits that "this assessment was, to say the least, overly optimistic" and alludes to ways in which the context had "changed beyond all recognition" since the time she wrote the essay.[18] Again, while Rubin's comments in this essay on the politically motivated persecution of consensual gay BDSM have had an extensive and largely favorable afterlife in Queer/Feminist/Sexuality Studies scholarship, her parallel and equivalently weighted arguments about boy-love have received far less attention, tinged as they now are with untouchability and taboo.[19]

I will take a moment to briefly sketch some of the ways, explored in greater detail in chapter 4, in which the historical context of politics of pederasty "changed beyond all recognition" during the 1970s and 1980s in France. During the French gay liberation moment of the early 1970s, male "homosexual revolutionaries" widely accepted that the liberation of pederasts would be the cutting edge of the sexual revolution agenda. As the Groupe de Libération Homosexuelle 14 writes in a 1976 publication, "The fight for the liberation of pederasts ... is essential, perhaps, more fundamental than that of homosexuals, perhaps even more than that of women. It radically questions all of society; subversion *par excellence*."[20] French gay liberationists valued pederasty as a radical challenge to the bourgeois nuclear family, understood to be the fundamental disciplinary unit of a society founded on repressive sex and gender normalization. They theorized pederasty/pedophilia as a crucial means of contesting parents' possessive investment in their children and of championing minors' free exercise of their sexuality.[21] The 1970s saw, more broadly, a coalition of leftist intellectuals and cultural producers reclaiming pedophilia—a pathologizing but barely used late nineteenth-century term—as, variously, a legitimate form of love, a potentially ethical means of relating to children as agential erotic beings, a vanguard cause sure to shock the bourgeoisie, and an increasingly critical node in the changing landscape of disciplinary, pathologizing, and securitizing power.[22] However, during the late 1970s, as French gay activists increasingly embraced a rights-oriented strategy and sought to win legitimacy in terms of existing legal and cultural norms, they gradually muted the longstanding connection between homosexuality and pederasty. When testimonies of adult survivors of incest and a series of horrific rapes and murders of girls were spectacularly mediatized during the late 1980s, comparatively few voices were willing to defend the 1970s vision of pedophilia as an erotic love for children with no necessary relation to child sexual abuse.[23] The "sex panics" that have raged since then have durably installed the pedophile as a figure of fear and loathing and an alibi for the extralegal extension of neoliberal surveillance, control, and regulation.[24] As a result, it is now difficult to remember modern pederasty, within gay counterpublics, except as the sad remnant of a less liberated past, if not a homophobic invention altogether. Nevertheless, as is suggested by the existence of Quintes Feuilles, a French press dedicated primarily to the theme of pederasty, and the publication of a critique of efforts to categorically separate pedophilia from homosexuality in *Gay pied hebdo* as late as 1991, pederasty remains a living, though largely silenced, cultural practice.[25]

The story of pederasty is thus, in part, the history of how age-differentiated sex went from being, within the span of the twentieth century in France, a dominant male same-sex relational form, to an avant-garde sexual practice containing the shape of a liberationist future, to the dusty and sad relic of a sexual past imagined as both distant and repressive. The twentieth-century career of pederasty is illustrative of one of the central questions of this book: how do queer relations *become historical*, in the sense of being *made retrograde* and forced to signify earlier historical periods? I posit that it is only when queer relations *become political*—in the sense of being seen as pregnant with the shape of a utopian future to come—that they are permitted to *become theoretical*—to be taken up as something of interest to politically and temporally avant-garde queer theory—rather than being left to the domain, implicitly dismissed as "merely documentary," of gay and lesbian history. Remembered, due to the vicissitudes of history, as irredeemably old-school, inegalitarian, abusive, and without any bearing on political futurity, modern pederasty does not appear to constitute a promising object for contemporary queer theory.

EVERY QUEER LOVES A DADDY: PEDERASTIC BDSM

Age-differentiated sex was, until as recently as the mid-twentieth century, both a dominant and a common form of male same-sex practice, one documented and analyzed by historians and anthropologists alike.[26] For scholars of literature, it should be striking that virtually all late nineteenth- and early twentieth-century canonical authors now remembered as "gay"—including Walt Whitman, Oscar Wilde (whose famous "love that dare not speak its name" was pederasty), Marcel Proust, Jean Cocteau, André Gide, Jean Genet, and even James Baldwin—participated in and, in some cases, wrote about age-differentiated same-sex erotic relations.[27] This fact has not received the critical or theoretical attention it warrants, even within queer scholarship.[28] In his 2013 book, *Brown Boys and Rice Queens*, Eng-Beng Lim characterizes the native boy/white man dyad as at once ubiquitous and yet curiously "under the critical radar."[29] Alan Sinfield titles his chapter on the modern and contemporary literature of age-differentiated sex "Boys and Embarrassment," asserting that the improbable pairing of the age-differentiated couple has proven embarrassing even to queer theorists.[30] But why should pederasty be considered embarrassing within Queer Studies, a field attuned to sexual nonnormativity in all its forms, skeptically critical of all claims about the harmfulness of consensual sexual practices, and particularly responsive to the functions Foucault and gay liberationists associated with pederasty: affronting the nuclear family, challenging sanctioned forms of kinship, association, and relation, and potentially tracing "unforeseen lines of force"? The response to this question reveals much about the field norms of Queer Studies, its unacknowledged historical imaginaries, and its continued indebtedness to a liberal egalitarian tradition it nonetheless continually sets itself against.

If, for Rubin, both intergenerational sex and BDSM are crucial sites of struggle against the persecution of sexual minorities and, for Foucault, both pederasty and BDSM are critical practices through which to think the ethics of power in asymmetrical and "diagonal" social relations, it is instructive that *only* BDSM has been taken up, within queer theory, for the potentially radical ways in which it negotiates power, gender, and history in and through sex. There is, nonetheless, an inscription of pederasty within BDSM that we might bring into focus in order to disaggregate what we think we know about queer sex radicalism in the present; namely, Daddy/Boy play. If it seems counterintuitive to connect Daddy/Boy play to pederasty, it is because since the 1980s, Daddy/Boy has been embraced as part of a sex radical queer culture and rendered synonymous with the "now." By contrast, pederasty is more likely to be associated with homosexual self-loathing than with contemporary sex radicalism and is assimilated to the "then" of a vaguely defined pre-Stonewall history and the "there" of an equally vaguely defined Arab-Islamic culture. With their presumably antagonistic politics and alleged locations in distant time periods and geographical spaces, it seems certain that pederasty and Daddy/Boy will never meet.

One might protest, however, that there are significant formal differences between pederasty and Daddy/Boy. As elaborated within BDSM cultures, Daddy/Boy is a contractual means of playing with both intergenerational power differentials and the incest taboo to create erotic scenarios with a particularly intense sexual and affective charge. These power differentials, however, need not be based on real world differences in social power. In other words, the "boy" need not be literally younger than the "Daddy," neither need be male, and the "Daddy" need not have greater social, economic, or racial capital than the "boy." Pederasty, on the other hand, would appear unseemly in its exuberant attachment to the scene of social power, uncritically adopting its patriarchal homoerotics of hierarchy between men and youths or older and younger men, and even intensifying it with inequalities of race, class, and geopolitical power. As a form that is not associated with kinship, pederasty, moreover, appears to be distant from both the incest taboo's erotic charge and Daddy/Boy's self-conscious manipulation of that charge. In short, if BDSM play, including Daddy/Boy, has been understood within queer theory as a distinctively *queer* method of responsibly, consensually, and self-consciously playing with social power, assuming pleasurable agency over sexual trauma,[31] exploring new female, genderqueer, and transgender masculinities,[32] and challenging "the racial and gendered hierarchies that undergird the disciplinary paternalism of the state,"[33] pederasty would appear, uninterestingly, to do none of the above. What does it mean, then, that a "modernized" and recognizably queer pederasty might take the shape of a contractual Daddy/Boy BDSM relation, in which the Daddy *really is* old enough to be the Boy's father and *really does* provide material support and pedagogical instruction, and the Boy *really is* dependent, in various psychic, emotional, and material ways, upon the Daddy? If Daddy/Boy play can come so vertiginously close to reality, then the time has come to interrogate the valorizing and modernizing separation between retrograde pederasty and queer radical Daddy/Boy by theorizing *both* as inegalitarian erotic dependencies that cannot be adequately held within the liberal form of contractual consent.[34]

We might use the queer cultural memory of Foucault to question the valorizing separation of Daddy/Boy—the modern, sexually radical, inventively queer, and critically self-conscious form—from retrograde pederasty. One starting place is the title of Bersani's important essay critiquing Foucault's redemption of BDSM as a means of playing with social power for its ejection of fantasy from sexuality, "The Gay Daddy." Bersani's title plays on the various meanings of "Daddy" to perform a deft substitution. Foucault as queer theory's generationally removed progenitor—"Daddy" in the "straight" sense—flickers for a moment only to settle into the more acceptably "queer" image: Foucault as sexy leather Daddy producing Theory from the dungeons of the queer underground. In its play of meanings, the title offers a witty commentary on the ways in which, in Queer Studies, we would rather replace the figure of Foucault as Daddy of the field—along with the suspect Oedipal and unqueer overtones of the metaphor of fatherhood—with the iconic figure of Foucault as leather Daddy, that is, sex radical intellectual. What the latter figure also absorbs, however, is the proximate, though less redeemable, figure of the pederast. Foucault was famously discreet about his sexual practices and preferences, and, while we know both that Foucault's life partner, Daniel Defert, was a decade younger than he and that Foucault participated in the San Francisco gay leather scene of the 1970s and 1980s, there is no more evidence that Foucault was a pederast than that his specific BDSM position was Daddy. Rather, I read Bersani's title as a playful figuration of some of the fantasy positions of contemporary queer scholars *in relation* to Foucault. While pederasty might name the position of desirous learning and angry revolt we assume before Foucault just as well as Daddy/Boy or Girl, Daddy appears in Bersani's title and BDSM as the topic of his essay, whereas pederasty is only a haunting phantom. We might plumb the valorizing absorption of Foucault-as-pederast-and-thinker-of-pederasty by the proximate fantasy construction, Foucault-as-leather-Daddy-and-thinker-of-BDSM for what it suggests about the historical supersession of pederasty by Daddy/Boy. After all, Daddy is by now not only a BDSM specific sexual term. It has "gone mainstream," so to speak, in vanilla gay and straight bedrooms alike.[35] "Daddy" is one of the few rubrics under which older men might be eroticized within a gay male culture that valorizes youth and beauty. Intergenerational sex and relationships continue to be practiced within North American gay male cultures, but under the linguistic rubric of "Daddy/Boy" (or "twink") rather than "pederasty," that is, if they name age differences at all.[36] Moreover, many of these relations resemble less the self-conscious contract and stylized theatrics of BDSM than the more literal eroticization of actually existing asymmetries of the "forgotten" form of pederasty. Is it any coincidence, then, that Daddy/Boy emerges into cultural and theoretical prominence during the 1980s, the very moment when, in both the United States and France, man-boy love and pederasty cease to be recognizable as either erotic orientations or politically resonant sexual practices?[37]

DISTURBING GENEALOGIES

What difference would it make to Queer Studies if we thought modern pederasty as a *recent*, albeit foreclosed genealogy of Daddy/Boy and understood contemporary practitioners of Daddy/Boy play as implicated in this genealogy? *Disturbing Attachments* uses Genet, whom I argue we have misread as a gay man rather than a pederast, to bring disturbing, unsavory, and retrograde modes of queer attachment to bear on Queer Studies. This approach exemplifies my method of *attachment genealogy*, which excavates earlier and more transnational modes of queer attachment to both historicize and expand *queer*'s current affective orientations. Attachment genealogy, so named in homage to Christopher Nealon's evocatively underdeveloped term *affect-genealogies*, seeks to produce a synergy between the recent attention to affective attachment in work loosely affiliated with Affect Studies and the Foucauldian method of genealogy.[38]

In "Nietzsche, Genealogy, History," Foucault describes genealogy as "the systematic dissociation of identity" through historical inquiry. Rather than excavating the historical foundations of the identities of the present, genealogy "disturbs what was previously considered immobile; it fragments what was thought unified; it shows the heterogeneity of what was imagined consistent with itself."[39] Critical historians of sexuality have wielded genealogy to reveal the residues of past understandings of same-sex behavior that persist, though incoherently, under the cover of modern notions of sexual identity. According to Halperin:

> A genealogical analysis of homosexuality begins with our contemporary notion of homosexuality, incoherent though it may be, not only because such a notion inevitably frames all inquiry into same-sex sexual expression in the past but also because its very incoherence registers the genetic traces of its own historical evolution. In fact, it is this incoherence at the core of the modern notion of homosexuality that furnishes the most eloquent indication of the historical accumulation of discontinuous notions that shelter

within its specious unity. The genealogist attempts to disaggregate those notions by tracing their separate histories as well as the process of the interrelations, their crossings, and, eventually, their unstable convergence in the present day.[40]

Genealogical analysis might demonstrate that pederasty is not, in itself, backward; that is, it does not merely originate from and belong within a prior epoch. Rather, its "backwardness" is an overdetermined historical production in which the emergent gay rights movement of the late 1970s and early 1980s expended a certain labor, a production that then required the forgetting of that labor and the concomitant erasure of the alternative visions of queer affiliation, politics, and kinship that age-differentiated relations might foster. Pederasty's apparent foreignness to both "modern homosexuality" and Daddy/Boy is, in fact, produced through temporal and geographic displacements that at once secure the modernity, knowability, and coherence of "modern homosexuality" and demarcate earlier historical epochs and non-Western geographical regions as fields of difference. Genealogy is a critical method of analysis, as it reveals the ongoingness of pasts usually thought to be quite distant, the temporal incoherence of a present fragmented by the survival of prior historical practices, and the political motivation of all attempts to definitively separate "present" from "past," "radical" from "retrograde" modes of sexuality.

Disturbing Attachments therefore makes three complementary moves. Rather than use pederasty to divide historical periods and geographic regions, it understands pederasty as marking the *genealogical connection* between modern and premodern sexualities as well as the charged *interrelation* of European and Arab-Islamic sexualities. Second, it claims pederasty as a *modern* form of sexual relation, focusing specifically on the function and form of cross-generational same-sex erotic relations during the twentieth century. At the same time, it strategically deploys pederasty's association with the backward, the retrograde, and the politically regressive in order to both foreground and trouble contemporary queer orientations toward novelty and futury. In this way, it keeps alive Foucault's attunement, in "Friendship as a Way of Life," to all that is affectively, politically, and conceptually "disturbing [*inquiétant*]" about uninstitutionalized queer relations. At the present juncture, queer relations most likely to disturb are those, like pederasty, that are at once marked as retrograde and presumed to be politically useless, if not counterproductive.

Attachment genealogy approaches genealogical analysis as a method that is not only historical *but also affective*. Indeed, I propose that genealogy *must* have an affective valence if it is to operate with the critical charge that Foucault attributed to it. Foucault writes, "History becomes 'effective' to the degree that it introduces discontinuity into our very being—as it divides our emotions, dramatizes our instincts, multiplies our body and sets it against itself."[41] Although genealogy has been understood as an ascetic method, one which resists "the consoling play of recognitions" and the comforting desire to identify with the past, Carolyn Dinshaw and Heather Love have both noted that Foucault's language belies this reading.[42] In the passage above, for example, Foucault describes genealogy as an *affectively intense* multiplication, cleaving, and swarming of the sensate, embodied self. The objective of such a genealogical swarming is to open a space for a potential recomposition of the bits of presentist unities, such as "the homosexual" or "gay politics," into new virtualities or lines of force that, without being either egalitarian or liberated from power, redeploy power in unforeseen and transformative ways.

But how might effective genealogical analysis *actually* feel? While Foucault uses dramatic metaphors reminiscent of the self-shattering, beyond pleasure and pain, that has been celebrated within much psychoanalytic queer theory, I would argue that the affects of genealogy are often more mundane. Genealogy often feels discomfiting or, to take up one of Foucault's favorite terms again, *disturbing*. The ground seems to shift beneath our feet as the taken-for-granted bases of identification and political agency fracture and realign. This description still risks sounding all too desirable and even thrilling to those of us trained within Queer Studies, a field that values anti-identitarian critique and that encourages, in José Esteban Muñoz's words, "the rejection of a here and now and an insistence on potentiality or concrete possibility for another world."[43] But the other world glimpsed through the breaking apart of the present by the genealogical project is not necessarily queerer, more nurturing, more pleasurable, or more just. It might exacerbate particular inequalities and exercise alternate techniques of regulation, even as it traces potentially radical connections between populations and social categories now cordoned off from one another and considered ontologically distinct, with divergent histories and separate political "interests," such as criminals and homosexuals, or pederasts and decolonizing revolutionaries. Queer Studies embraces and, indeed, *prescribes* the fragmentation of contemporary identities and ideologies; but as it has become partially institutionalized as a field, it has increasingly promised a payoff to this queer fragmentation of identity and unsettling of the present. Anti-identitarian fragmentation is "supposed to" give way to the alternative, which is taken to describe *at once* that which is unimaginable within the rigid epistemologies of the present *and* that which promotes more nurturing, more pleasurable, and more just queer life-worlds. In short, Queer Studies teaches us that it is permissible to feel temporarily destabilized by the critical and dissociative aspects of queer scholarship, because we can legitimately expect that this dissociation is of terms that are constraining, pernicious, and intolerable, and that they will give way to something at once more politically radical, more just, and more affectively rich and erotically pleasurable.

But the alternative and the nonnormative—those terms most valued within Queer Studies—*need not be politically desirable or affectively pleasurable*; at times they might be experienced as barely tolerable, or more likely, as nauseating in the ways in which they twist the valued terms of the present to an unrecognizable state. Genealogy is truly disturbing when it fragments the categories and rationalities of the present, not to outline a more utopian and hopeful scene for the thriving of queer life, but to offer a version of queerness that, however compelling, is equally or *more* politically problematic, equally or *less* egalitarian than the world we now know. Such unease, *Disturbing Attachments* proposes, can serve a generative heuristic for Queer Studies scholarship. It might herald not only something heroically counterhegemonic that ruptures the rationalities of the present, but also a shape of the queer alternative that rubs against the grain of scholarly orientations trained by the field norms of Queer Studies. It might reveal that field dispositions that sanction some objects of study while rendering others illegible and ignored are neither neutral nor inherently just; rather, they reflect the field's historical inheritance. Taking seriously that which disturbs this inheritance requires a shift in the frame and the tenor of inquiry. Such a shift would allow a new range of objects to materialize before the critical and theoretical gaze.

PEDERASTY AS AN ATTACHMENT GENEALOGY OF QUEER STUDIES

The object that inspires unease is frequently one, like modern pederasty, so suffused with pastness that it is all but invisible and inaudible in the present. Confronting this object means interrogating the scholarly inheritances that would render it ignored. For the field of Queer Studies, an object that produces unease is one that exposes, fragments, and reworks *queer*'s own affective histories. Rather than reject the bad object, we might take our own unease as the sign that we would benefit from performing an attachment genealogy. The first step is to locate the source of the rub—what field disposition does the object fail to satisfy? Attachment genealogy traces backward to locate and fill out the specific geographic and historical context from which that field disposition emerged. The scholar is then freed to perform the final step of attachment genealogy, that of elaborating the alternative scholarly priorities and feeling states the object generates. In this way, rather than seeking out objects that resonate with the feeling states of queer scholarship, historical, geographical, and racial difference might conceptually and affectively reorient queer inquiry.

Pederasty is a rich object through which to perform such an attachment genealogy. It is suffused with pastness, associated with distant historical periods and geographical spaces, and difficult to recognize as a part of white Western modernity. It is, in itself, nauseating, breaching the contemporary taboo on sex between adults and minors and triggering panic, loathing, survivor trauma, and disgust. It appears politically nefarious, sexualizing social hierarchy rather than striving for more egalitarian erotic relations. This section performs the first step of attachment genealogy, tracing backward from the field dispositions unsettled by modern pederasty to the historical inheritances that pederasty disturbs and in disturbing, reveals.

As Martin Manalansan has argued, the consolidation of "modern" homosexuality in the West has cast same-sex partnerships based on age or gender dissymmetries as nonmodern and not-yet-liberated, regardless of their continued contemporary practice, particularly in non-Western, racialized, and prison cultures.[44] As a putatively nonmodern and not-yet-liberated practice, pederasty remains indissociably associated with internalized homophobia, social violence, and sexual exploitation. This is particularly true since pederasty's age differences have often been compounded by class, race, and status differences. Pederasty evokes the image of the pitiful old queer paying younger working-class straight men, who may well beat, rob, and blackmail him, for sex, the predatory pervert lurking in the schoolyard, and the privileged Western sexual tourist buying boys in Thailand, Cuba, and Cameroon . . . that is, if it evokes any images at all. The recent historical memory of pederasty as a common and even dominant male same-sex practice has become almost entirely blotted out by the historically novel figure of the pedophile. According to Gillian Harkins, "In 1978, the idea that all adults who have sex with children are pædophiles and that all pædophiles are moral predators, was barely emerging. Only a decade later, all adults who have sex with children would become popularly (and at times legally) defined as pædophiles, all pædophiles would be depicted as predatory and 'children' considered naturally vulnerable might be as old as eighteen."[45] Pederasty is not always fully extricable from pedophilia, insofar as it may involve juridical minors and children on the verge of puberty. Moreover, French leftist discourse of the 1970s actually reclaimed *pédophile* as a fresh and radical term lacking the conservative and traditional connotations of *pédéraste* and not yet demonized as the target of a sex panic. This discourse often uses *pédophile* not to refer specifically to sex with prepubescent children, but to signal the potential radicalism of sex between men and adolescent boys.[46] Nevertheless, I think it important to provisionally distinguish these terms, since *pedophile* connotes the abuse of young children and is a product of a neoliberal moment, while the longer history of pederastic practice was centered around either pubescent boys or younger adult men. During a contemporary moment in which pederasty has fallen out of memory, absorbed by the monstrous image of the predatory, sick pedophile, the only sympathetic way to imagine this sexual practice is under the rubric of backwardness and "internalized homophobia." Pederasty is *consigned to the past* and *severed from futurity*—and as a retrograde practice with no bearing on futurity, pederasty's only political purchase is in the negative.

One reason modern pederasty has not received anywhere near the interest, in Queer Studies, that its frequency merits, is that, unlike gender inversion, its historical companion as an organizing principle for same-sex relations, pederasty appears irrelevant to both the present and the future of contemporary queer cultural politics. By contrast, gender inversion connects with a range of contemporary queer issues, including lively feminist debates, during the 1980s and 1990s, on the politics of butch/femme, the politicization of drag culture, and the emergence of a transgender movement during the early 1990s. This is why, unlike age-differentiated sex, gender variance has been central to Queer Studies as well as scholarship on sexuality. While Queer Studies' politicized attunement to the present and the future produces energized scholarship that makes urgent interventions, it also means that the field tends to pass over vast bodies of perverse and arguably "queer" phenomena and broad realms of same-sex historical practice when their relation to the political crises of the present appears either uncertain or counterproductive. Ironically, despite sophisticated work on nonchronological temporalities, Queer Studies, as a field, remains driven by a set of temporal values that orient it, almost triumphally, toward futurity. One of the consequential insights of Lee Edelman's *No Future* was that the political field, as a whole, is futural, the injunction to be political is an injunction to invest in futurity, and the refusal of futurity is seen as a refusal of the political *tout court*.[47] While a series of scholars have responded to *No Future* to argue in favor of alternative political futurities that need not be hetero-reproductive, do not reproduce the terms of the present, and invent utopian potentialities for queer and queer of color lives, few, aside from Heather Love, have taken up the challenge of imagining a Queer Studies *not* oriented toward futurity.[48] Modern pederasty is the detritus of Queer Studies' orientation toward political futurity.

It is instructive that, historically speaking, in dismissing modern pederasty, Queer Studies is assenting to a judgment that was originally that of gay liberalism. Toward the late 1970s, the gay and lesbian movements in both France and the United States respond to the invitation extended to "good" homosexuals to become full citizens by assimilating within the terms of the liberal state by severing homosexuality for the first time from its long-standing association, and in France, its near-identification with pederasty.[49] In France, pederasty was strongly identified with homosexuality and resistant to being cast out of its orbit. However, the campaign to equalize the homosexual and heterosexual ages of consent during the late 1970s and early 1980s, thus removing the last remaining form of positive legal discrimination against homosexuals, proved a strong incentive to gradually sever the long-standing indistinction between homosexuality and pederasty.[50] In the United States, according to Regina Kunzel, "the transformation of a movement for sexual liberation into a movement for civil rights, requiring in turn a respectable homosexual subject deserving of such rights, ultimately led to an effort to remove the 'pedophile' from the category homosexual."[51] Even more consequentially, it led to the removal of age differences more generally from the definitional center of homosexuality.

We might contrast, once again, the relative inattention to pederasty in Queer and Sexuality Studies with the uptake of that other controversially inegalitarian form of sex, BDSM, when both were under attack in the United States during the 1980s and 1990s. In the moments when BDSM needed to be defended, whether by practitioners or by scholars, it was by affirming a set of what Eve Sedgwick calls "hygienic dislinkages" between sadomasochistic play and real social power.[52] BDSM is often portrayed as a contractual, consensual, and safe relation between autonomous adults who agree to perform, for their own enjoyment, roles associated with despotic power.[53] Both practitioners and queer theorists know better: the appeal of BDSM as well as its charge of radical marginality is due to the potentially volatile ways in which it brings social power and power in the scene of play into electric conjunction.[54] Regardless, both the recuparability of BDSM and its promise as an object of study lie in its perceived capacity to frame an exploration of sexual power in terms consonant with both political liberalism and what Gert Hekma terms *erotic egalitarianism*.[55]

Pederasty cannot be absorbed into such a liberal and egalitarian framework, given its long-standing association with illiberal relations of dependency, its lack of remove from the scene of social power, and its involvement of minors juridically incapable of either autonomy or consent. Gay assimilation within the terms of the liberal state requires sexual orientation to be positioned as an invisible and "private" sexual difference coherent with the liberal regimes of private property, family, and alliance. Pederasty's inassimilability to this regime, given its threat to parental and state jurisdiction over minors and to the fantasy of childhood sexual innocence, was resolved by the production of a sex panic around pedophilia that has effectively shut down the possibility of imagining the alternative modes of social organization and sexual companionship that pederasty might foster. Irreconcilable with the kinds of claims it is possible to make according to liberal rights-based strategies, pederasty was precipitously *made retrograde* between the 1970s and 1990s, its potential horizons blotted out as incompatible with the shape of the future to be ushered in by gay liberalism.

But to argue that queer theory's neglect of pederasty is premised on liberal values is paradoxical, to say the least. Queer theoretical work has featured a multipronged critique of liberalism—psychoanalytically, it has critiqued the sovereign independence and rational self-interest of the liberal subject; politically, it has critiqued the privatization of sexuality that founds rights claims within liberalism; and historically, it has critiqued the racialized violences that found and haunt liberal social orders.[56] Queer of color critics such as Cathy Cohen, Sharon Holland, and Jasbir Puar have unmasked the ways in which the ideal of liberal autonomy is entrenched in some queer theoretical celebrations of a heroic, muscular antinormativity. This antinormative autonomy, they point out, has historically been the province of privileged white men capable of "choosing" to jettison social dependencies.[57] Despite its multipronged critique of liberalism and interrogation of the autonomous liberal subjects on which egalitarianism is premised, queer scholarship has had a difficult time envisioning *alternatives to egalitarianism*, because to do so risks leaving existing social inequities unchallenged. Interestingly, recent work by Joseph Fischel and Michael Gill that decenters same-sex sexuality to reorient queer scholarship around the figures of the sex offender and the intellectually disabled person, respectively, is where the most promising theorizations of a nonegalitarian sexual ethics are currently taking place.[58] Similarly, I am suggesting that in its cultivation and eroticization of male dependencies—based on actually existing social inequalities of age, race, and class—modern pederasty might provide a rich site for theorizing the centrality of inegalitarianism and male interdependencies to Western modernity.

Queer scholarship often finds itself leaning on ready-to-hand values of political progress, sexual egalitarianism, and muscular and volitional resistance to norms that are all indebted to liberal theories of the political subject. Pederasty, with its inegalitarianism and political "backwardness," rubs against and therefore alerts us to affective traces of gay liberalism within Queer Studies. I want to propose that, if gay liberalism can inhabit and orient Queer Studies, it is in part because it infuses homosexuality with political agency. Gay liberalism holds that a politicized homosexuality can bring about social transformation and a better, more just (because more egalitarian) future—a belief that is practically axiomatic within a post-gay liberation moment. I belabor this point to foreground how prior understandings of same-sex sexuality that do not relate it, in any obvious or causal way, to social transformation, political futurity, or more egalitarian social relations become "uninteresting," according to the affective field norms of Queer Studies, and fall out of theoretical view. Pederasty reveals the ways in which, despite the field's vociferous critiques of liberalism, liberalism's historical imaginaries—which deem pederasty *passé* and apolitical while attaching nonpederastic homosexuality to a more just political future, however narrowly imagined—continue to resonate within Queer Studies.

Gay liberalism and erotic egalitarianism are part of a contemporary common sense so prevalent and so affectively ingrained that it is difficult to stand apart from and objectify it. This is a great loss for scholarship, as it prevents us from conceiving how richly meaningful and constitutive of the very possibility of same-sex sexuality age differences once were, and in some cases, still are. As Alan Sinfield points out, we lack a critical and theoretical vocabulary for thinking the multiple ways in which sexual relations based in age differences are at once inseparable from social power and at the same time potentially rewarding, not exclusively oppressive, and open to both reversals of power and modes of asymmetrical reciprocity. His book *Sexuality and Power* is an important starting point for thinking the complex relations between age-differentiated male same-sex sexuality and social power.

Modern pederasty challenges queer scholarship to contend with its historical inheritances by theorizing the collaboration between Western modernity and real-life erotic inegalitarianism rather than condemning it, displacing it onto an eroticized Orient, elevating it into contractual BDSM, or hurling it deep into the historical past. I will develop the conceptual promise of pederastic modernity at the end of this chapter. Before doing so, it is first necessary to situate modern pederasty within the broader history of sexuality.

MODERN PEDERASTY IN THE HISTORY OF SEXUALITY

In *How to Do the History of Male Homosexuality*, Halperin defines pederasty as "the male sexual penetration of a subordinate male—subordinate in terms of age, social class, gender style, and/or sexual role."[59] He emphasizes, "This is sex as hierarchy, not mutuality, sex as something done to someone by someone else, not a common search for shared pleasure,"[60] and goes on to describe each partner's distinct role: the younger partner is attractive, the elder experiences desire, and the junior's reward is in some currency other than pleasure, including money and gifts. Halperin's description hits the nerve center of pederasty's offense to contemporary values: this is sex not only as the (mis)use of young people, but as, at its core, *a nonegalitarian, nonreciprocal sexualization of social hierarchy*, an exercise of phallic prowess by a dominant over a subordinate partner. This version of sex is offensive and nauseating to an era defined by its subscription to the ideal (if not always the practice) of erotic egalitarianism.

Pederasty is particularly threatening to the recent valorization of gay and lesbian sex and relationships as especially egalitarian and reciprocal. In their study of British families of choice during the 1990s, Weeks, Heaphy, and Donovan conclude that "the dominant belief in the nonhetero world is that same sex partnerships offer unique possibilities for the construction of egalitarian relationships. A democratized, flexible model of couple relationships has become the ideal."[61] This egalitarian ideal borrows its legitimacy and luster from the greater heterosexual culture. Their respondents claim, however, that it is *more* likely to be realized within same-sex relationships, newly conceivable as defined by gender *symmetry*. Historically, the authors locate the ideal of the "democratic, egalitarian partnership model" as present in gay and lesbian culture during the 1970s and as gradually overtaking a range of other less egalitarian models since then.[62] Halperin would understand this transformation as consonant with the emergence of the "modern" notion of homosexuality itself. He paints, in broad strokes, a massive shift: "Homosexual relations cease to be compulsorily structured by a polarization of identities and roles (active/passive, insertive/receptive, masculine/feminine, or man/boy). Exclusive, lifelong, companionate, romantic, and mutual homosexual love becomes possible for both partners."[63] This is homosexuality as we think we know it today. The problem is that, as properly loving, reciprocal, democratic, companionate, and potentially long-term homosexuality has increasingly gained legitimacy, consonant as it is with the dominant ideal of erotic egalitarianism as well as with the marriage form, older forms—such as pederasty and sex based on "trade" economies—have become *less* legitimate and *more* policed from within and outside the gay and lesbian "community" alike.

It may be that today, power to discipline sexuality and categorize sexual types as normal or deviant operates less through the ideal of heteronormativity than through that of erotic egalitarianism. Insofar as erotic egalitarianism is now the ideal, if not the reality, of heterosexual and homosexual relationships alike, those couples that too ostentatiously broadcast their structuration by age, race, and class polarities appear far more aberrant, suspicious, and threatening than do comparatively innocuous age-, race-, and class-"appropriate" homosexual couplings.[64] Today's queer is less the homosexual than all those perverts who, at the limits of the law, engage in sex across loaded power differentials.[65] These queers, though assuredly nonnormative, do not sit easily with the ethical and political values of Queer Studies. They are, nevertheless, contemporary avatars of the history of sex-same sexuality prior to the recent, though incomplete, emergence of the ideal of homosexuality as erotic symmetry.

Though his aim is to offer a genealogical account of pederasty as a transhistorical practice that stretches even to the present day, Halperin's definition of pederasty as a nonreciprocal practice of sexual subordination is elaborated from his scholarship on Ancient Greece.[66] Moreover, his exclusive focus on Europe excises the centrality of colonialism and race, particularly within the modern period of imperial expansion and racial "science," from the history of sexuality. We must turn to scholarship on the nineteenth and twentieth centuries, as well as to scholarship on sexuality and colonialism to understand the specifics of *modern*, in contradistinction to Ancient Greek pederasty.

For the first obstacle to thinking modern pederasty is that, when commentators remark on it, they tend to instantly read it through the example of Ancient Greece.[67] Pederasty may be the *only* sexual practice to be so persistently associated with a historically distant time and place, despite its continued contemporary practice and its great popularity (as far as same-sex practices go) as recently as the mid-twentieth century. This conflation of pederasty with Ancient Greece fosters a neglect of the concrete specificities of age-differentiated same-sex sexuality in the particular social, historical, and institutional context in question by positioning pederasty as a *historical anachronism*, bizarrely out of place in the modern world and floating free of any contemporaneous system of meaning. To counteract this tendency, historicist work might think *pederasty in the plural*, attending to how intergenerational male same-sex sexual practices are shaped by their class, institutional (prison, schools, military), historical, and geopolitical locations and therefore *differ from one another*, as well as from the archetype of Ancient Greek pederasty, at least as much as they resemble one another.

Presuming that modern pederasty conforms to the master code of Ancient Greek pederasty leads to the assumption that all modern pederasty occurs between an active adult man and a passive adolescent boy. Throughout this book, by contrast, I use "pederasty" in a broader sense to reference *any male same-sex relation*—whether between two adult men, a man and a boy, or two boys of different ages—*built around an eroticized differential of age or generation*. I concede that two people of notably different ages may be drawn to each *despite*, rather than because of this age difference. Since chronological age need not reflect developmental age, an age gap can also be bridged by similar levels of maturity and development. What defines modern pederasty is not, therefore, the mere existence of an age difference. It is the fact that this age difference, whether great or small, *is eroticized* and *structures* the relationship. I define pederasty in this way because in the twentieth-century examples I study—in the boys' penal colonies, men's prison cultures, and in Genet's relationships with younger adolescent *or* adult men—the adult/adolescent boundary has not seemed to be the most important way to define the age difference that, nonetheless, organizes these relationships. William Peniston finds that, in the late nineteenth-century Parisian subculture of men who had sex with men, the traditional pederastic pattern of adult men with adolescents was common, particularly among male prostitutes, who were mostly adolescents, and their clients. The subculture as a whole, however, reflected a shift to age-differentiated relations between older and younger adult men, and, less commonly, to sex between adult men of roughly the same age. Peniston proposes that both the possibility of same-age relationships and the shift from adult/adolescent to *either* adult/adolescent *or* older adult/younger adult relationships reflected a more egalitarian model of male same-sex relations that emerged during the eighteenth century.[68] Although nineteenth- and twentieth-century European pederasty might still be modeled on the ideal relation between a man and an adolescent, that adolescent might also grow into a man within a pederastic relationship; an older pederast might enter into a relationship with a younger man in his twenties or even thirties; and smaller age differences between boys might assume a great erotic significance.

A focus on modern European pederasty troubles the strict epochal and area divides whereby pederasty, assimilated to premodernity or to the Arab-Islamic world, is considered the prototype of sexual acts that do not confer identity, in contradistinction to the "modern" understanding of sexual desire as the determinant of sexual identity. When pederasty is treated as a fixed and known form inherited unchanged from Ancient Greece[69] and immune to the different forms of sexual and social organization that obtain in, for example, twentieth-century prisons, the Arab-Islamic world, and Renaissance Italy, it functions not as an object of historical analysis but as a vector of temporal differentiation whose function is to demarcate, through the trope of sexual backwardness, the absolute difference of an epoch, disciplinary institution, or entire region of the world.[70]

During the early twentieth century, European photographic studios produced ethnopornographic photographs and postcards with exoticized Arab themes for a European clientele. We might read the frequency with which "Arab" male youths and children (who were often Southern European models in Arab costume) were eroticized in such images as attesting both to the existence of a European clientele hungry for pederastic imagery and to the commodification of the Near East as a setting for Europeans' pederastic fantasies.[71] The example of the colonial postcards illustrates that pederasty cannot simply be considered an Arab-Islamic custom that remained unchanged since premodernity while Europeans uniformly adopted a "modern" notion of homosexual identity based on sexual object choice rather than age. To the contrary, European purveyors of pederastic "Arab"-themed postcards were actively participating in this construction of the fantasy of the Arab-Islamic world as a premodern pederastic paradise. Rather than sharply demarcating European from Arab-Islamic histories of sexuality, pederasty might be reconceptualized as *a charged commercial and colonial site of their interrelation*.

Taken together, we might read historical scholarship by Jeffrey Weeks, George Chauncey, Regina Kunzel, William Peniston, and Colin Johnson as positioning pederastic relationships as central to Western modernity. When these relationships occurred across class, they usually involved an exchange of money and gifts from the wealthier to the less wealthy partner. Weeks demonstrates that in late nineteenth- to early twentieth-century England, such exchanges often defined the relationship as one of prostitution. This could be an ambiguous distinction, however, since, at other times, gifts were interpreted as a sign of affection that cemented a same-sex cross-class relationship rather than defining it as only prostitution.[72] Chauncey, Kunzel, and Johnson demonstrate that, in the twentieth-century United States, age-differentiated male same-sex relationships were not exclusively cross-class. They were endemic to poverty and working-class hobo, prison, itinerant laborer, and sailor cultures in the form of wolf/punk relationships in which "*punk* generally denoted a physically slighter youth who let himself be used sexually by an older and more powerful man, the wolf, in exchange for money, protection, or other forms of support."[73] Within the working classes, neither the wolf nor the punk in such a relationship would necessarily have been considered sexually "queer." In the middle classes, however, which were more influenced by new developments in sexology and psychiatry, the notion that same-sex desire could in and of itself define a homosexual identity took root earlier, near the beginning of the twentieth century.[74]

My working hypothesis is that, rather than becoming passé among the bourgeois and upper classes in twentieth-century Europe as same-sex sexuality began to be understood as conferring an identity, *pederasty became homosexualized*. In other words, rather than an unremarkably masculine man, the elder pederast (and possibly, but not necessarily his younger partner) became a bearer of a sexuality ontologically different from that of normal men, a (homo)sexuality oriented toward youths and younger men.[75] Along with Genet, Wilde and Gide might be considered prominent examples of such a homosexualized pederasty—one which could no longer be understood as simply a "masculine" act of sexual domination not animated by a distinct sexuality, but which was not yet simply a sexual orientation to "men" as a gender category uninflected by age, class, and racial/colonial divisions.[76] Modern pederasty names a genealogical overlap between the seemingly incompatible notions of pederasty as a nonreciprocal act of sexual subordination that does not confer a sexual identity and homosexuality as a sexual identity capable of cementing a long-term reciprocal relationship. It becomes all but illegible once pederasty—in the reproved form of pedophilia—is cast out of the definitional orbit of homosexuality altogether. This curious overlap, and the distinctive temporalities, relationship forms, and politics to which it gave rise, have been all but ignored by queer theory.

THEORIZING PEDERASTIC MODERNITY

Thus far, I have performed the first step of attachment genealogy, moving backward from the rub between modern pederasty and contemporary queer sensibilities to the inheritances of liberalism and erotic egalitarianism that pederasty disturbs. The problem of pederasty is its inegalitarianism—its impolite and impolitic admission that it gets off on power, including but not limited to that most righteously reproved form of power between an adult and a minor. I now perform the final piece of attachment genealogy, tracing forward from the troublesome object of pederasty to the alternative set of scholarly and political priorities around which we might reorient queer scholarship.

What is most generative about pederasty for politicized scholarship is precisely its status as, potentially, *the* form of sexual desire most conspicuously animated by social inequality. When Queer and Sexuality Studies focus on sexuality, these fields risk reifying a rather recent understanding of sexuality as an isolable analytic axis and an independent principle of social organization within their methodological protocols and modes of discerning proper objects of study.[77] To counteract this problem, one imperative of recent queer scholarship, and particularly queer of color critique, has been to intersectionally reinscribe sexuality within a range of modes of power and forms of social organization.[78] Well, pederasty, as nothing less than *the eroticization of social power differentials themselves*, can hardly be analyzed apart from social power in the first place. Along with related practices such as racial fetishism, pederasty offers the indispensable opportunity to *directly theorize the erotics of social structure*.[79]

This is a particularly important project because disavowing the centrality and persistence of structural inequalities of age, race, class, and gender to modern Europe has been crucial to the "civilizing" project of European imperialism. Pederasty, along with erotic inegalitarianism more broadly, has therefore persistently been projected *outside modern Europe*—consigned to the distant past and ascribed to Western modernity's racialized and colonized others. In his pathbreaking work, by contrast, Lim returns pederastic desire to modern Europe. A *"pedophiliac Western modernity* bearing the homoerotics of orientalism," he argues, eroticized native boys and men, along with the geographical entity of Asia more broadly, as brown boys awaiting their rice queen cum civilizing white savior.[80] Lim's insights suggest that Western modernity and its imperialist projects produced at least one entirely novel form of same-sex erotic hierarchy—that of the white colonial man and the brown native boy.

The homoerotic figure of the native boy reveals the West's role in not only perpetuating, but also innovating novel forms of erotically charged hierarchy well into late modernity.

Remarking on the romantic spell of the brown boy/rice queen dyad in performance, Lim conjures a hypothetical scene of a young Balinese boy singing to his lover, a white colonial jailed for sex with minors, to ask whether the "reverse scenario in which a young white boy is singing a love song to an old Balinese man jailed in Germany or the United States for 'playing' with him" could be "conceivably romantic."[81] Lim's query might prompt us to inquire into the dearth of queer scholarship on eroticized *white*, as opposed to brown boys. Might erotic Orientalism render the native boy a figure of romance and nostalgia in his position of sexual love for the white man, while, drained of any "tropic spell," the figure of the white boy who submits sexually to an older man can only appear starkly nauseating? Horror at white boyhood perverted, white masculine autonomy called into question, and white innocence stolen propels the differential cultural visibility, legibility, and discomfort of the native boy/white man versus the white boy/white or brown man pairings.[82]

The analytic of *pederastic modernity* builds on Lim's work by positioning twentieth-century pederasty as both a symptom and a diagnostic of the relation between (post)colonial racial difference and a range of potentially less spectacular erotic inequalities—such as adult and minor, masculine and feminine, master and pupil, upper-class and working-class, boss and employee—endemic to Western modernity. The idealization of Western modernity as egalitarian and democratic relies on a contrast with historically distant, racialized, and prison cultures cast as backward and despotic. Similarly, the figment of an egalitarian and mutual "modern homosexuality" figures premodern and often racialized forms of same-sex sexuality as hierarchical and exploitative. The analytic of pederastic modernity undoes both of these binaries. The presence of pederastic sexual relations within the modern West deidealizes Western egalitarianism and foregrounds the reproduction of social inequalities in and through the erotic. Pederastic modernity reveals reputedly egalitarian and forward-looking Western modernity to be, in fact, normatively hierarchical and not fully distinguishable from the carceral and racialized cultures of sexual domination it positions as both anterior to and in need of reformation by it.

Though the critical dimension of the concept of pederastic modernity is perhaps the most portable, I do not wield it only or even primarily as a critique of modern power. Instead, I understand pederastic modernity as the overarching condition of an erotic landscape riven with power within which intimate relationships, queer worlds, and politicized coalitions are made and unmade. We would be remiss to overlook this in order to idealize either the equality and mutuality of modern homosexuality or the democratic potential of male "stranger intimacies" to traverse fraught social differences.[83] We would be equally remiss, however, to understand modern same-sex sexuality's inevitable animation by social power as disqualifying it from queer inquiry as insufficiently antinormative, alternative, or just. For, burdening same-sex sexuality with such expectations of queer exceptionality wishfully positions sexuality as autonomous from social power. Pederastic modernity, on the other hand, requires conceptualizing sexuality as at once *an analytic* and as a not-fully-overdetermined *negotiator* of social power. Pederasty is well suited to engender such an analytic because, unlike homosexuality, it remains constitutively and ostentatiously bound, to this day, to power. As an erotics, it is sparked by differentials of social power; as a reproved practice, it is the object of disciplinary, pathologizing, and stigmatizing power. Pederasty might therefore constitute a surprising, if difficult, object for a politicized scholarship eager to think disability, a critique of the prison industrial complex, commercial sex, and sexual justice together.[84]

As Sinfield points out, pederasty is a curiously reversible form. Though older men tend to control more wealth and institutional power, "notoriously, an older man can make a fool of himself over a young man, or a young woman," and the beautiful and desired young man or woman may come to wield considerable power over the infatuated elder partner.[85] Such relationships may not be egalitarian or mutual, but they also are not necessarily as much of a one-way street as the social positions of each partner would suggest. On a broader scale, pederastic modernity may harbor a similar reversibility. On the one hand, pederastic modernity is a diagnostic of Western modernity's own persistent production and exacerbation of eroticized structural inequalities. But pederasty may also, at times, signal an alternate modernity, undercutting the autonomous, independent, masculine subject of (neo)liberalism in order to carve out a space for relations of interdependence, nurturance, and alternative pedagogy between men and boys who occupy differently marginalized social categories. These two functions, moreover, are not always easily distinguished from one another. The project of thinking pederastic modernity is therefore less a matter of parsing properly queer from uninterestingly normative or starkly oppressive forms of pederasty than of patiently charting the intertwined perils and potentials of pederasty's marginalized erotics of social power.

chapter 2

**LIGHT OF A DEAD STAR:
THE NOSTALGIC MODERNITY
OF PRISON PEDERASTY**

Eric Stanley and Chris Vargas's 2012 film *Criminal Queers* connects the contemporary radical queer politic of prison abolition to the historical memory of queer criminalization and resistance through visual citations of *A Song of Love* (*Un chant d'amour*), Genet's 1950 erotic film set in prison. The climax of the film occurs when, after water-balloon bombing a gay marriage celebration and robbing a Human Rights Campaign store, the film's "criminal queers" liberate the entire population of a prison. With a series of shots of prisoners in orange running free to a punk soundtrack, shepherded by the eponymous queer protagonists, *Criminal Queers* euphorically asks viewers to envision a world in which radical dreams of prison abolition might be actualized. Near the beginning of the film, while Lucy, the black transgender heroine, is in prison, two reenactments of iconic scenes from *A Song of Love* flash before viewers. In one, a fake bouquet of pink flowers tied to a string swings repeatedly from the bars of a cell. In another, Lucy puffs on a coffee straw inserted in a chink in the wall of a prison. Those familiar with *A Song of Love* would recognize these scenes as eroticized efforts at communication between prisoners separated from one another by the architecture of prison cells—in Genet's film, the straw both invokes fellatio and transports cigarette smoke, and the bouquet is eventually caught by the prisoner in the adjoining cell. Such visual citations position *A*

Song of Love's creative search for a means of eroticized connection between prisoners as a prelude to the realized community of prison abolitionists *Criminal Queers* envisions. *Criminal Queers* thereby offers Genet a place in its transhistorical community of radical intellectuals against prison—which also includes Angela Davis, James Baldwin, Frantz Fanon, and Malcolm X—as well as an imagined future without prisons.

Though Genet's late activism led him to develop a strong critique of penal institutions, his writings of the 1940s—that is, precisely those texts written either in prison or in close temporal proximity to imprisonment—clash with both the abolitionist imaginary and the utopian futurity of *Criminal Queers*. In Genet's 1946 memoir-novel, *Miracle of the Rose* (*Miracle de la rose*)—which was partially written in the Santé prison—the imprisoned narrator, Jean, at one point believes that he has found in a young prisoner, Bulkaen, the realization of an impossible dream, that of "a youngster who would love robbery enough to cherish thieves, contemptuous enough of women to love a hoodlum, and also honest enough to remember that *Mettray was a paradise*."[1] Jean's longing, here and throughout *Miracle*, is for a prison love faithful to the pederastic norms—built on status differentials between elder and younger boys—of the boys' penal colony of Mettray. Since Mettray, in which Genet had been incarcerated as an adolescent, was shut down in 1939 after a series of damaging press campaigns, such a prison love would perform the last rites of a social world no longer in existence while honoring the memory of Jean's incarcerated youth. What seems most impossible, within Jean's description of his impossible dream, is the ardent affirmation that *love* should be the sentiment that binds the longed-for adolescent to crime and to criminal men, a love that swells elsewhere in the novel to encompass the entire boys' penal colony of Mettray as well as imprisonment itself. A misogynistic disdain for women, on the other hand, indexes both the ideal adolescent's disposition to pederasty and the violent masculinism of *Miracle*'s carceral cultures. In its embrace of sexist prison cultures, nostalgia for an abolished boys' penal colony, and affirmation of incarceration as *enabling*, rather than repressing, queer sexuality, *Miracle* refuses the contemporary politic of queer prison abolition and its utopian orientation toward a future without prisons.[2]

Genet's profession that "Mettray was a paradise" is nothing short of scandalous in 1946, just after decades of virulent press campaigns exposing the abuses and corruption that ran rampant in the correction houses for minors—informally called "children's penal colonies" to emphasize their repressive dimension—led to their abolition in 1945. Jean seethes, "Idiotic vandals—

Danan, Helsey, Londres, and others—have written that the penal colonies for children should be destroyed."[3] Genet pits *Miracle* against the almost universally popular 1945 abolition of the French children's correction houses. He does so, however, not in favor of the politically conservative belief that harsher forms of punishment make better deterrents to crime, but in the name of the very nonnormative culture of pederasty and crime that reformers used to rhetorically condemn the boys' penal colonies. Genet turns his back on politically "progressive" penal abolition in a bid to preserve the queer by-products of repressive institutions.

In its critical reception, the disposition toward stasis, regression, backwardness, and the past in Genet's literary work has largely been eclipsed by his imaginatively fertile transformations of shit into gold and of abjection into sanctity, as well as by his modernist orientation toward transgression, novelty, and revolution. In addition, the celebration, since the 1980s, of Genet's late activism and political writings has so enshrined him as a radical activist, invested in total political and cultural revolution and unreservedly supportive of anticolonial and antiracist struggle, that it has become all too easy to pass over the backward orientation of some of his early work. As a corrective, this chapter bypasses the magical transfiguration of the death's row convict, Harcamone, to focus instead on *Miracle*'s less spectacular obsession with the past. When critics have engaged Genet's dispositions toward the past, it has usually been to find fault with them. Critics from Jean-Paul Sartre to, more recently, Ivan Jablonka have had difficulty in understanding *Miracle*'s faithfulness to the "obsolete" sexual form of status-differentiated pederasty as anything other than politically retrograde and ethically corrupt.[4] In so doing, they reflect the broader ways in which aesthetic, political, and ethical evaluation remain oriented by a modernist progress narrative—one which puts value in the new, the forward-looking, and the futural and tends to regard turns backward with suspicion or disinterest.

Queer theory has not been exempt from the political and intellectual primacy accorded to futurity. To the contrary, one dominant trend within the field associates the *queer* with whatever, in scrambling the calcified categories of the present, forecasts an open horizon of future possibility not yet written over by power.[5] However energizing, the queer theoretical orientation toward futurity risks being no less presentist, no less inattentive to the imaginaries of the queer past than is the much-critiqued teleologism that understands the past as but a step on the linear trajectory toward the present.[6] It remains critical for queer scholarship on the past to develop methods that offer alternatives to the common moves of either understanding the past as progressing toward the present or selecting from history those imaginaries that help us envision queerer futures. I follow Heather Love in using *backwardness* as a heuristic that incites us to pause at those turns away from the concerns of the present and aspirations for the future that are so often reflexively straightened back into ideals of progress and futurity.[7]

Miracle plumbs a backward feeling unintelligible within the future-oriented narratives of penal reform, homosexual emancipation, and queer prison abolition alike—Genet's perverse nostalgia for the commingled queer pleasures and traumas of imprisonment. This at once nostalgically idealizing and achingly deidealizing "structure of feeling"[8] reminds us that, in the early twentieth century, queer sex and gender were more likely to be associated with arrested development, devolution, and retrograde politics than with "a forward-dawning futurity."[9] *Miracle* therefore gives us access to an alternative affective history of queerness, one that attaches less to progress, futurity, and political transformation than to regress, the past, and political stasis. Though most easily read as a *refusal* of history, I argue that this orientation should instead be understood as itself *a historical disposition*—one reflective not only of the history of queer gender and sexuality as a form of devolution or stalled development, but also of the range of imaginaries of sex and belonging that would be obscured, rather than fulfilled, by the ascendance of both modern gay and lesbian and contemporary queer and transgender politics and community.[10]

Prison pederasty's association with backwardness in *Miracle* should not be taken at face value, as an admission of its alienness to modernity. This chapter explores a key temporal paradox: though quintessentially modern, twentieth-century pederasty is often depicted as properly belonging to premodernity and to those racialized cultures colonized by Europe. The first section of this chapter examines reform-oriented narratives of the boys' penal colonies published during the 1920s–50s. In this body of work, pederasty is less a sexual identity than a figure for those despotic masculine hierarchies that threaten to corrupt youthful white French masculinity. *Miracle*, on the other hand, shocks, and indeed, appears untrue in its effort to articulate the silenced pleasures of Mettray's pederastic inmate culture—the sweetness of submission, the intimacy of masculine dependency, and the pleasures of sexual receptivity in an institutional context of domination, violence, and preadulthood in which no sex act could be fully consensual. The remainder of the chapter unpacks the queer disposition toward the past of *Miracle*'s haunted prison pederasts.

A BARBARIC CULTURE OF SEXUAL HIERARCHY

If Genet's description of Mettray as a paradise proved hard to swallow, this was largely because it scandalously upended established popular tropes about the boys' penal colonies. *Miracle* came on the heels of two influential press campaigns, by Louis Roubaud in *Le Quotidien* during the 1920s and Alexis Danan in *Paris Soir* during the 1930s, that spurred public fascination and outrage with the children's penal colonies and led to their 1945 abolition.[11] These press campaigns set the stage for a series of popular narratives hovering ambiguously between memoir and novel about life in the boys' penal colonies. The texts I study in this section include these two press campaigns, along with the body of narratives of the boys' penal colonies—published during the 1920s–50s and either written by or from the fictive perspective of former prisoners—to which these press campaigns gave rise.

These reform-oriented writings seek to delegitimize the boys' penal colonies by denouncing their abusive and punitive conditions and portraying minors as corrupted, rather than rehabilitated, by the carceral *mœurs* that reigned within them.[12] It is worth keeping in mind that the French term *mœurs* has a series of connotations absent from its English equivalent, *mores*. If the most neutral definition listed in the *Trésor de la langue française* is simply "The ensemble of ways of living that are habitual to a human group or to an individual. Synonym customs," the first definition given is the more loaded "Ensemble of behaviors proper to a human group or an individual *considered in relation to a collective morality.*" In practice, this "collective morality" is most often a sexual morality: a vice squad in French is a *police des mœurs*. The *Trésor* thus specifies, "In partic. A sexual behavior in compliance or not with social norms," and lists another possible meaning as simply "homosexuality."[13] Writings on the colonies regularly employ this slippage between the two meanings of *mœurs*, on the one hand, as morally questionable customs and behaviors and, on the other, as homosexuality. In many writings on the colonies, homosexuality functions simultaneously as the most extreme and shocking example of the corrupt *mœurs* of the children's penal colonies and as a synecdoche that stands in for all other imaginable depravities. The usage of *mœurs* as a polite way of saying homosexuality, as in, "Quite singular *mœurs* that the outside world cannot suspect exist in these houses, either between pupils or even between pupils and guards," thus threatens to lend its sexual connotation to *all* references to the suspect customs of the boys' penal colonies.[14]

This is particularly true in the case of *caïdisme*, the practice of serving and obeying a respected and powerful leader, or *caïd*, in return for his protection. In writings on the boys' penal colonies, the hierarchies, rivalries, and revolts that result from *caïdisme* are regularly singled out as motivations for inmate violence. References to *caïdisme*, moreover, are just as sexually suggestive as references to *mœurs*. Within the context of this highly sexualized discourse on the children's penal colonies, an inmate's proposition to a newcomer—"Who are you going with? I'll introduce you to a *caïd* tomorrow. You have to take a *caïd*, or else you'll be unhappy"—gestures toward the trope of the pederastic *caïd*.[15] While many authors explicitly link pederasty and *caïdisme*, the frequent play on the implicit sexual connotations of both *mœurs* and *caïdisme* points to the existence of a commonplace that the reading public could instantly grasp without too much explanation—that of boys' carceral cultures that intertwine violent hierarchies with sexual domination and submission. As a word that, in its original sense, refers to a North African tribal leader, *caïd* evokes the figure of the Oriental despot against whose illegitimate authority and perverse sexual power France's civilizing mission was rhetorically deployed. Rhetorically, *caïdisme* functioned in reformist discourse to mark the boys' penal colonies as aberrant and un-French institutions implicitly calling for civilizing uplift into the national values of liberty, equality, and fraternity.

Descriptions of the sexual culture of the boys' penal colonies have much in common with the paradigm of wolves (also known as jockers) and punks (also known as kids) within U.S. writings on prison and hobo culture during the early twentieth century. According to Regina Kunzel, "Wolves, sometimes also referred to as 'jockers,' were typically represented as conventionally, often aggressively masculine men who preserved (and according to some accounts, enhanced) that status by assuming the 'active,' penetrative role in sex with other men."[16] Those familiar with prison cultures credited wolves with initiating sex, often predatorily, as their name suggested, bribing, coercing, or physically forcing other men to have sex with them. Hence, neither wolves nor punks were understood to be "homosexual," in the sense of innately and exclusively attracted to men; wolves were protected from such suspicions by their aggressive and dominating masculinity, and "punks were understood to be 'normal' men, vulnerable to sexual coercion by other inmates because of some combination of small physical stature, youth, boyish attractiveness, and lack of institutional savvy."[17] In Kunzel's sources, punks are depicted as the victims of older, stronger, and more savvy men and never engage in sex wholly willingly.

Reform-oriented writings on the French boys' penal colonies understand carceral pederasty according to wolf/punk pairings associated with sexual violence and coercion, rather than presuming an innate homosexual desire or identity. However, although many authors portray prison punks as unwilling victims, others suggest that punks may be seduced into pederasty due to their moral weakness and susceptibility to vice, and that they may even come to enjoy it. Tellingly, although there are a series of French slang terms for the "punk" in such a pairing, I have not come across a term for a wolf in my sources that would distinguish him from other tough, masculine prison boys or men. Though some terms, such as *caïd*, can be used to imply illegitimate sexual domination, these terms can also be used in a neutral, or even positive sense, as a slang term for a leader among prisoners, with no implication of pederasty. The lack of a distinct term for the wolf suggests that it was not considered unmanly or unusual for one man or boy to sexually dominate another in prison. In what follows, although I sometimes refer to the older, more masculine, and more dominant man or boy in a prison relationship as a "wolf" in order to economically signal his adherence to this role, readers should keep in mind that there is no equivalent term in my French sources. I use *pederasty* rather than homosexuality as an overarching term for such prison relationships in order to flag the centrality of hierarchy and age difference, and the lack of purchase of a notion of homosexual identity within them.

"The 'Punk'" ("Le 'giron'"), penned by journalist Louis Roubaud in 1925, conforms to the early twentieth-century understanding of the wolf/punk pairing Kunzel outlines, depicting pederasty as rape and sexual coercion *tout court*. The eponymous "punk" is Raoul, a boy from a "good," presumably bourgeois family, who is incarcerated at Mettray, then transferred to the boys' penal colony of Belle-Île. Raoul is only able to escape constant sexual violation and coercion by the other boys by propositioning another prisoner, Coutanzeau, who responds by kindly pretending to be Raoul's wolf so that the other boys will leave him alone. Significantly, the way for Raoul to escape sexual servitude is *not* to leave the wolf/punk sexual economy—from which there is, in this article, no escape—but to find a faux wolf willing to protect him without demanding sex in return. The inescapability of wolf/punk culture, in "The 'Punk,'" serves reformist aims by demonstrating the colonies' total permeation by a culture of sexual violence and subjugation.[18]

In a letter signed "A former inmate of Mettray, currently at the penal colony, Liberated 1/4 identification number 16738. Renault, Henri," and published by Danan in 1936, however, pederasty is portrayed less as violence and victimization than, simply, as vice. Renault explains as follows why boys give in to this "vice": "Most fall because of cowardliness or self-interest, to avoid blows or want, and to feel that they are under the protection of someone stronger than them."[19] In line with a durable nineteenth-century understanding of pederasty as an evil habit associated with criminal cultures, Renault explains carceral pederasty as a vice to which—in a logical, though ignoble response to a pervasive culture of violence and deprivation—boys lacking in bravery or motivated by self-interest are likely to succumb.[20]

On the surface, Auguste Le Breton's popular novel, *The High Walls* (*Les hauts murs*), published in 1954 and widely read as a memoir of his incarceration at Mettray, differs from these earlier representations in depicting characters that could be understood according to the modern hetero/homosexual binary.[21] In this reading, the plucky principal character, Tréguier, would be "an ordinary heterosexual boy" fighting to dispel any impression of weakness or submission that might lead the predatory homosexual *caïd*, Molina, to try to make him his punk.[22] *The High Walls* is simultaneously available to another reading, however, in which Tréguier's heroic struggle is against not only pederasty, but also the broader carceral culture of dominance and submission it symptomatizes. In this reading, Tréguier would be less a heterosexual than that rarity, an upstanding inmate who resists pederasty as a vice to which any boy might succumb, whether because he is cowardly and weak or seduced by the perverse lure of despotic power and base submission. This memoir-novel hovers ambiguously between the wolf/punk regime and that of the heterosexual and homosexual. Reading the novel according to the heterosexual/homosexual regime alone, however, cannot account for the fact that its characters, including Molina, participate in pederasty less because it is their sexual nature than due to character flaws that draw them to masculine hierarchies and dependencies depicted as constitutively perverse.

Published the same year as *Miracle of the Rose*, Vincent Lapie's 1946 novel *Saint-Florent-Life* (*Saint-Florent-la-Vie*) boldly addresses the subject-forming effects of carceral pederasty without assimilating it to homosexual identity. As its principal character, Michel, explains:

> The "lamb" [*le "fadeur"*], is the "wife" [*la "femme"*], the "chick" [*la "gonzesse"*], the little guy who serves you, whom you help out and protect, but who indulges you [*qui vous a des complaisances*] . . . from behind. I was initiated at the dormitory at Palacé! I resisted at first . . . But afterward, I let them have their way [*je me suis laissé faire*]. I even ended up finding it normal.
>
> To the point that I too want to have a "lamb."[23]

The "initiation" Michel mentions is, in fact, a rape by another inmate, followed by an attempted molestation by the director at Palacé, the outside farm to which Michel is assigned before being sent to the strict boys' penal colony of Saint-Florent.[24] Michel's total corruption into pederasty precedes his no less dramatic rehabilitation through participation in a Boy Scout troop for inmates. This is an interested description, as Vincent Lapie was the pen name of Henri Joubrel, a prominent post–World War II advocate for the reform of juvenile delinquents through the Boy Scouts. *Saint-Florent-Life* suggests both that, if abandoned to a pederastic penal culture, otherwise normal boys may go from victims of rape, to acquiescent lambs, to enthusiastic wolves, and that, if given the benefit of Boy Scout culture, these same boys may successfully sublimate their pederastic attachments into healthy, platonic scouting hierarchies.

Michel's astonishing transformation from amoral pederast into model Boy Scout is possible, in the increasingly pop-scientific world of this text, because his capacity for pederastic affections can easily be rechanneled into Boy Scout hierarchies, themselves modeled on the normative hierarchies of the patriarchal nation. The hook for Michel's rehabilitation is a crush on the handsome adult Chief Paul. After lecturing the boys on the importance of sexual continence as a means of conserving their life force and that of their offspring, Chief Paul asks to speak to Michel in private. As Michel reports, "He didn't reproach my friendship with Bernard," Michel's lamb, for such tender hierarchies are the very bedrock of scouting, "but he asked me to render it more manly [*virile*]."[25] The transition from pederastic couple to couple of manly friends proves remarkably smooth for Michel. Transferred to Saint-Florent, Michel takes the initiative of forming his own Boy Scout troop. Elected captain, he chooses Bernard as his second, and this new scouting hierarchy effectively replaces that of their prior pederastic relationship. Pederasty appears to have been definitively subsumed by the noble hierarchies of scouting. For if, in *Saint-Florent*, pederasty is bad for the vitality of the race, it nevertheless carries within it a crucial positive value, that of an affective attachment to male hierarchies, presented as the structural basis not only of scouting, but also of healthy male homosociality within the modern nation.

While discourses on the boys' penal colonies do depict carceral pederasty according to the bifurcated roles of the wolf and the punk, unlike in Kunzel's U.S. case studies, they do not exclusively portray the punk as an unwilling or coerced participant. Running beside the narrative of rape and victimization is the intimation that participants in carceral pederasty do so because of moral weakness, attraction to vice, or a perverse attachment to hierarchies of dominance and submission. While, ideally, an upstanding and properly masculine boy would be capable of resisting pederasty, these narratives flirt with the possibility that even ordinary boys might succumb when pederasty is the aberrant norm. These writings are ultimately less interested in explaining the cultural logic of the wolf/punk pairing than in depicting the seductive dangers of pederasty as the synecdoche for the depraved *mœurs* of the boys' penal colonies as a whole. As such, they allow for moments in which some boys, usually described in the third person, give in, sometimes with pleasure, to their role as a punk. *The High Walls*, for instance, offers this glimpse of the abject awe of a punk before the sweaty physique of Molina, the pederastic *caïd*: "Pressed against him, a newly arrived blondie gaped with admiration at the strength of his male."[26] The role of boys drawn to pederasty is usually to serve as foil to the almost impossibly heroic ideal of a boy who fights to prove and win his masculine autonomy *despite* a pervasive culture of perverse male hierarchies and dependencies. Nevertheless, eager and willing punks hauntingly figure the infectiousness, as well as the potential seduction, of pederasty in the boys' penal colonies.

Such descriptions participate in a broader national discourse of patriarchal French Republicanism, which holds that it is despotism for a man to submit to another man, but egalitarianism for him, as a properly autonomous masculine head of household, to rule over a wife and children. Placing the discourses of the boys' penal colonies in the context of patriarchal egalitarianism reveals that it is less a matter of rejecting hierarchy in favor of autonomy than of defining *which* hierarchies may be naturalized as healthy and egalitarian (the patriarchal family, the Boy Scouts) and which are legible only as violence, vice, and racialized barbarism. Indeed, the quote above is prefaced by a description of Molina as "bronzed like an Indian, sweat on his brow," and the contrast between the dark-skinned "Indian" *caïd*, Molina, and the blond newcomer pressed against him illustrates the perversion of French boys by a carceral culture depicted as racialized and savage.[27]

EDUCATING PEDERASTIC ATTACHMENT

The hierarchical and pederastic inmate culture of Mettray decried within reformist discourses might be reframed as the paradoxical by-product of one of this institution's most celebrated technologies. At the time of its founding in 1840, Mettray was acclaimed for its innovative attempt to educate the feelings of its wayward youth and thereby ensure their proper moral development through the creation of family-like all-male institutional hierarchies. One of the primary evils attributed to industrialization was the disintegration of the family and of the values associated with it. Hence, the reconstitution of family life was one of Mettray's guiding principles. Organizationally, the colony was divided into "families," that is, groups of about forty to fifty boys living in the same pavilion under the parental authority of a "head of the household [*chef de famille*]" and his second, as well as two "older brothers [*frères aînés*]," chosen from among the inmates. According to Mettray's principal founder, Frédéric-Auguste Demetz, the purpose of this organization was to "*produce familial sentiments* founded on the obedience to paternal authority, role models [*le bon exemple*], the sense of honor, the emulation of what is right, household habits, and the sense of property."²⁸ Demetz conceived of Mettray's familial organization as a means of *educating the feelings* of orphans and delinquents forcibly removed from their "corrupting" working-class family milieus by producing, in them, attachments to "traditional" French values. In 1850, Dr. Ferrus theorized as follows Mettray's innovative principle of what he termed "affective hooking [*l'accrochage affectif*]": "Most of the young inmates being orphans who, not having known the family, scorning its comforts, and, in a manner of speaking, not believing in them, the founders of this colony have tried, first of all, *to create affections in them.*"²⁹ For this doctor, the education and indeed, production of emotion is Mettray's first priority, surpassing intellectual and religious education alike: "Intellectual education is weak; religious education is secondary. What they work to develop are the sentiments of virtue, love of family, the affections, or to use [the Viennese doctor] Gall's word, affectuosity."³⁰ Doctors and psychiatrists raved about Mettray because they saw it as disciplining, training, and stimulating not only inmates' bodies and minds, but, more importantly for the purpose of rehabilitation, their feelings.³¹

Reformist discourses usually imply a shocking contradiction between institutional aims of normalization and perverse inmate cultures, obscuring a tight continuity between the two. It was an institutional initiative to structure inmates' relationships with guards and with one another along the model of the hierarchical and authoritarian patriarchal family and to invest these hierarchies with emotion so as to inspire, in inmates, a love for and willing submission to authority. Rather than producing familial attachments to normative French moral values, however, Mettray may have inadvertently educated boys' *pederastic* attachments—producing, stimulating, and intensifying affective and erotic attachments to male hierarchy and encouraging inmates to find, in such hierarchical social forms, intimacies that could take the place of family life. If this was possible, however, it was because of the structural similarities between the properly patriarchal homosocial hierarchies on which the modern French nation was founded and the sexual and often coercive hierarchies of carceral pederasty.

"The fury of the love which the colonists bore each other, the love which bore them, which threw them into each other's arms, was perhaps heightened by the despair of being deprived of all other tenderness, of family affection."[32] The structure of feeling Genet so beautifully describes as fusing the Mettray boys together in a love tinged with loss was precisely the sentiment produced by Mettray's institutional attempts to train the boys' familial feelings on one another. Rather than a sort of regression, under duress, to savage "Indian" or barbaric "Oriental" hierarchies, sexualized inmate social structures such as *caïdisme* may be better understood as inmate rearticulations of institutionally produced attachments to hierarchy originally promoted as quintessentially French. The reformist project, didactically illustrated in *Saint-Florent-Life*, of converting pederastic sexual hierarchies into platonic Boy Scout hierarchies demonstrates the extent to which, during the 1940s as during the 1840s, male hierarchies cathected with feeling were envisioned as the training ground of healthy French masculinities and, thus, as a choice means of rehabilitating delinquent boys. Rhetorically presented as the symptom of a racialized regression into a barbaric state of domination, prison pederasty might instead be taken as a measure of the centrality of male hierarchies and dependencies to European modernity. Such hierarchies give the lie to the ideal of democratic egalitarianism, signaling the parallels between normative French male homosociality and carceral and racialized cultures thought to be shot through with despotic domination.

When, in the interests of reform, Lapie describes, in *Saint-Florent*, the startling symmetry between pederastic prison hierarchies and the homosocial male hierarchies that are the building blocks of the Boy Scouts and the masculinist nation alike, he inadvertently exposes European modernity as *pederastic*. European modernity is built on mass, same-sex institutions—armies, prisons, and schools—that solicit and implant affective attachments to masculine hierarchies. These attachments would, with some regularity, be eroticized and even sexualized. European modernity is therefore pederastic—that is, structured by the masculinist inegalitarianism of normalized hierarchies between men, men and boys, and between boys, hierarchies that are never far from overt sexualization. To note such "correspondences and similarities between the most sanctioned forms of male-homosocial bonding, and the most reprobated expressions of male homosexual sociality" in the context of the boys' penal colonies is to refuse the separation between "situational," coercive prison sex and normative male friendship and sexuality.[33] It is also to contest racialized distinctions between barbaric prison domination and the egalitarian French social order.

The pederastic foundation of European modernity must be disavowed if Europe is to lay claim to an imperialist civilizing mission. Hence, reform-oriented writings on the boys' penal colonies labor to definitively separate pederasty from normative friendship, the gendered social structure, and Frenchness itself. In these writings, pederasty indexes alluring erotic hierarchies to which, nevertheless, good French boys should not submit, lest, in so doing, they become simultaneously corrupted and racialized as nonwhite, uncivilized, and un-French. Whether depicted as a racialized descent into barbarism or as a deviant attachment that reformers might rearticulate, pederasty is the figure for those unacceptable masculine hierarchies and dependencies incoherent with the French social contract.[34] Its pervasiveness in the penal colonies illustrates the cataclysmically corrupting effects of these institutions on youthful white French masculinity. Reformist discourses figure penal institutions as exceptional pederastic spaces in order to at once champion their reform and maintain the fiction of French masculinity as normatively egalitarian. By focusing on the temptations pederasty is thought to afford otherwise ordinary boys and the structural parallels between descriptions of pederasty and of normative male friendship in the boys' penal colonies, we might instead access pederastic modernity.

MIRACLE OF THE ROSE: THE PULL OF THE PAST

> At present, I need only evoke my childhood loves to redescend to the depths of time, in its darkest dwellings, in a lonely region, where I find only the Colony, formidable and alone. She draws me to her with all her sinewy limbs, with the gesture of sailors who pull a rope out of the water, placing one hand in front of the other while the rope piles up on deck, and I regress, with the Divers of old at my side, to a nauseating childhood which is magnified by horror and which I would never have wanted to leave.
> —Jean Genet, *Miracle of the Rose*[35]

Miracle theorizes the paradoxical requirements of the form of criminal-pederastic development inadvertently fostered by Mettray's culture of male hierarchies invested with feeling. Unlike other narratives of the boys' penal colonies, however, it does so *from the inside*—from the position of the unrepentant adult pederast and incarcerated criminal who seeks to remember and honor the guilty pleasures of the Mettray punk. In the process, *Miracle* develops a striking theory of pederastic subject formation as a mode of being wounded by the past. First, however, Genet sets the reader up, with great fanfare, for a *false* narrative—a kind of pederastic spin on the coming-of-age tale—which begins to fail even before its premises are set forth. In offering a narrative designed to fail, Genet is not only toying with the reader; he is, above all, articulating an understanding of carceral pederasty less as an identity or a sexuality than as a form of development whose nostalgia constitutively condemns it to failure.

Miracle opens with Jean's boastful announcement that he has become, rather belatedly, a real man. Jean's announcement of his gender transformation doubles as a declaration of *Miracle*'s departure from the narrative style of Genet's previous novel, *Our Lady of the Flowers* (*Notre-Dame-des-Fleurs*). While the narrative of *Our Lady of the Flowers* is woven from the imprisoned narrator Jean's masturbatory fantasies of handsome and virile criminals, *Miracle* announces Jean's accession to manhood, his loss of the capacity to idealize criminals, and his transition, heavy with narrative consequences, from a gaze steeped in "wonder" to an "exact vision" of his world. The passage in which Jean weaves these mutual transformations together into what amounts to a fascinating theory of gender and narrative is worth quoting at length:

> The exact vision that made a man of me, that is, a creature living solely on earth, corresponded with the fact that my femininity, or the ambiguity and haziness of my male desires, seemed to have ended. If my sense of wonder [*le merveilleux*], the joy that suspended me from branches of pure air, sprang chiefly from my identifying myself with the handsome thugs who haunted the prison, as soon as I achieved total virility—or, to be more exact, as soon as I became a male—the thugs lost their glamour... I no longer yearned to resemble the hoodlums. I felt I had achieved self-fulfillment.[36]

In this passage, femininity, glossed as "the ambiguity and haziness" of Jean's "male desires," is an erotic desire for resemblance that bestows glamour and seductive power on its objects, the handsome thugs. Femininity is thus the source of wonder (*le merveilleux*), a feat of idealizing and eroticizing poetic perception which, in *Our Lady*, lends itself to escapist fantasy. Femininity, however, also signals the danger of an absolute dependence on and enthrallment by the prestigious model that one seeks to resemble. By becoming "male,"

Jean accedes to a state of autonomy in which he is no longer enthralled by the tyrannical prestige of eroticized criminals. A foreshadowing of gender failure, however, is already embedded in this passage's announcement of Jean's gender transformation. *"Perhaps I feel it less today, after the adventures I am describing, but I felt strong, not dependent, free, unbound. Glamorous models ceased to present themselves."*[37] We are alerted to the fact that the novel before us will be not the narrative of Jean's manly exploits, but the adventure of his failed masculine maturation.[38]

Having lost his feminine faculty to imagine himself in the place of another, Jean writes, "It was now extremely difficult for me to re-immerse myself in my dream-stories, stories fabricated by the disheartening play of solitude, but I found—and still find, despite my new plunge—more well-being in the true memories of my former life."[39] The memoir-novel we find before us is therefore presented as a gendered text, the product of a mature adult masculinity that has outgrown fantasizing and dreaming to focus its clear gaze on the true memories of childhood. When Jean meets the pretty adolescent burglar and former Mettray prisoner, Bulkaen, he therefore embraces the opportunity to not only test his newfound pederastic virility by dominating a younger man, but also to share with another his memories of Mettray. Bulkaen appears to be the realization of Jean's secret desire "to find in someone other than myself the memory of Mettray, as much perhaps in order to relive Mettray as to continue it in my adult life by loving in accordance with the ways [*les mœurs*] of the past."[40] By reliving the *mœurs* of Mettray, this time as the elder and more dominant partner in a pederastic couple, Jean hopes, in line with the carceral norms of pederastic development, to grasp his newfound virility as the mature accomplishment of his past at Mettray.

Jean's plans to fulfill his masculine projects through Bulkaen, however, are textually presented to us *after* the description of their failure. In a textual moment prior to *all* of the above citations, Jean writes that, after first seeing Bulkaen, "I went back to my cell, and the abandoned habit of my abandoned childhood took hold of me: the rest of the day and all night long I built an imaginary life of which Bulkaen was the centre, and I always gave that life, which was begun over and over and was transformed a dozen times, a violent end: murder, hanging or beheading."[41] Rather than aiding him in his project of placidly contemplating his true memories of childhood from the distant perspective of adult maturity, Bulkaen plunges Jean into his childhood habits of fantasizing about great criminals and idolizing their exploits, this time with Bulkaen in the starring role. By alluding to the failure of Jean's virile maturation before this maturation is even on the table, Genet presents manly autonomy as a corrupted ideal, bound to failure, and possibly incompatible with authorship, but no less compelling for that.

Later, as Jean attempts to demonstrate his manliness by attracting the younger man's admiration and desire, he finds that he cannot hold the pederastic power dynamic in place. While acting the conqueror, he feels like a conquered territory, and while affecting impenetrability, his love renders him dangerously permeable. Jean must exert a superhuman self-discipline to keep Bulkaen from abandoning the role of the submissive admirer for the alternate figure of the young tyrant: "I made a final effort to lock myself in behind a door that might have revealed my heart's secret, and enabled Bulkaen to enter me as he would a conquered country, mounted, in boots and spurs, holding a whip, with an insult on his lips, for a youngster [*un gamin*] is never gentle with a man who worships him."[42] Affecting the harshest indifference for fear of appearing vulnerable, engaging in obsessive Proustian speculations about Bulkaen's sexuality and his other possible lovers, both male and female, and abruptly ceding to his desires to express, with inappropriate romantic force, his true feelings, Jean's baroque seduction attempts are a far cry from "the clear simplicity of manliness."[43]

If through burglary, Jean discovered a certain manly independence from the criminals he previously idolized, in love, he falls under their spell once again, caught in the game of masculine imitation. Observing that "transported by his admiration for them, [Bulkaen] chased men," Jean begins looking to masculine models to supplement his own faltering manhood and thereby attract Bulkaen's admiration.[44] Plunged into a recollection of the glorious day in which his first lover, Villeroy, struck the head guard, Guépin, to avenge an affront to Jean's honor, Jean realizes that, in the present, he needs a similar "striking feat" to be worthy of Bulkaen.[45] When Jean therefore provokes another prisoner, Charlot, so that he can fight him in front of Bulkaen, an astonishing metamorphosis takes place:

> Whenever I was about to give in, the memory and soul of Villeroy guarded me . . . I borrowed, I stole the beauty of his stances. A lock of blond hair, taken from God knows where, fell over my eyes. I was quick as lightning. I had to lick Charlot because Villeroy would have licked him. It was with Villeroy's shiny weapons and his failings that I fought. The guards grabbed me, Charlot was carried away.
>
> The guards rushed over to pick up Guépin.[46]

Jean's sudden transformation into blond Villeroy while fighting Charlot evinces the return of Jean's "feminine" habits of imitation at the very moment that he seeks to prove his masculinity. Rather than a spontaneous maturation into an autonomous, nonidealizing manhood that another, younger man might admire, Jean's masculinity is here demonstrated to be a regression to his own idealized memory of his first love. This regression is for Bulkaen's benefit; as Jean must eventually admit, "He was the demon that incited me to greater toughness, greater boldness, greater love: *Bulkaen was my virility*."[47] Far from a feminized love object, Bulkaen is the very source of Jean's masculinity, a masculinity exposed, long before Judith Butler's theory of gender performativity, as both a copy and a performance.[48]

As his manly projects increasingly fail him, Jean begins to yield to the seductions of his memories of Mettray. With intensified lyricism, he evokes Mettray as a veritable paradise of reciprocal love and not-so-reciprocal sex in which, as Villeroy's punk (*giron*), he was able to indulge in the now forbidden pleasures of femininity and sexual receptivity: "Our loves at Mettray! The child couples, the males of which were sixteen! I was sixteen, the age of young ladies. Fifteen is thin and seventeen too hard. But sixteen has the ring of delicate femininity. I loved Villeroy, who loved me. Because he was a child himself (he was eighteen), he was closer to me than anyone . . . ever was."[49] As his past opens to reveal pleasures now denied him, Jean finds in his memories a sweet refuge from the trials of pederastic virility. But if doubts about Bulkaen's love for him oblige Jean "to seek refuge in [his] old loves," to do so is to betray his masculinity and his new role as a tough in favor of more pleasurable memories of being a punk.[50] Masculine memory increasingly resembles feminine fantasy, providing an escape from the present by opening a door to forbidden pleasures and allowing Jean to rediscover the idealized delinquents of his adolescence. In the process, childhood begins to exert its own seductive backward drag, pulling the adult pederast back to a "stage" of development he may never have truly wanted to leave in the first place.

PEDERASTIC EDUCATION

Jean's fall into memory becomes the occasion for a description of the distinctive methods of a pederastic education to whose failure Jean's own faltering adult masculinity nonetheless seems to testify. Like other narratives of the boys' penal colonies, *Miracle* describes Jean's masculine development at Mettray. *Miracle* is the only first-person account of the boys' penal colonies, however, to describe the requirements of the social position of the *vautour* (sometimes used interchangeably with *giron*), a sort of respectable punk within carceral hierarchies. For, contrary to what is often implied in discourses of the boys' penal colonies, sexual bottoms were not necessarily situated at the metaphorical "bottom" of carceral hierarchies, nor were they always fully feminized. When, pleased by the beauty of Jean's voice, Villeroy, the "elder brother" of Jean's "family," chooses Jean as his *vautour* (henceforth translated as "kid"), Jean has the honor of having a powerful protector, an honor which saves him from being forced to sexually service the older boys. Being Villeroy's kid does not spare Jean the rites of passage that define masculinity in other narratives of the boys' penal colonies. During Jean's first night at Mettray, Rio, an older inmate, deliberately knocks Jean's belongings onto the ground. Horrified at the prospect of being relegated to the bottom of Mettray's social hierarchies, Jean masters his fear and fights. However, whereas in other first-person accounts of the colonies, passing the test of masculinity temporarily banishes the menace of pederasty, in this case, the test guarantees Jean entry into pederastic coupledom by proving him a worthy kid for Villeroy. For to be a respectable kid (and here Mettray's masculinism is striking) is to not be fully feminized and, indeed, to offer periodic proofs of one's nascent manhood. As Jean explains, Villeroy "would not have put up—as no big shot [*marle*] did—with having a kid who was a fairy [*une lope*]. He made me fight."[51] In Mettray's world, neither a big shot nor his kid are considered to be in any way queer. The queers are those fairies so fully feminized that they are excluded from masculinity and thus, from a pederastic education altogether. As Villeroy's kid, Jean receives a virile education. He is required to sustain Villeroy's honor by performing masculinity, fighting, and, eventually, taking his own kid. Rather than fixing static and tyrannical hierarchies of dominance and submission, the "noble" form of pederasty between big shots and kids functions as a veritable method for producing, propagating, and schooling prison masculinity.

Mettray's spin on a "sentimental education" depends on a form of love that compels an imitation and even a transformation into the elder partner.[52] As an adolescent, Jean recalls propping up the softness and changeability of his character with his love for "a man of stone with sharp angles," stating, "I was not completely at ease unless I could completely take his place, take on his qualities, his virtues. When I imagined I was he, making his gestures, uttering his words: when I *was* he."[53] This account of pederastic subject formation through identification reconciles *Miracle*'s prior opposition between feminine imitation and virile autonomy, as pederastic education employs the "feminine" capacities of imitating, taking the place of, and even becoming someone else in the service of schooling masculinity. Far from being independent from idealized models, the masculinity formed through a pederastic education is constructed from the adoring theft of another's attributes—his gestures, his words, and even his character.

Since Villeroy is Jean's institutionally assigned "older brother," Jean's attachment to and adoring emulation of him is precisely the method Mettray's founders prescribed to ensure his normative development. Pederastic hierarchies are revealed to be eroticizations of institutional ones, and pederastic development proceeds by overtly sexualizing the loving emulation that was the cornerstone of Mettray's affective education. As is suggested by the revelation that Villeroy is himself kid to a lover incarcerated in the adult prison of Fontevrault, pederastic elders are not "good" role models for French national values; they are delinquents and hoodlums who model the aberrant futures of crime, adult pederasty, and continuing imprisonment. If narratives of the boys' penal colonies use the abject figure of the punk seduced by a culture of male hierarchies, vice, and crime as a foil for nobler characters, *Miracle* seeks to fully develop the almost unintelligible possibility that pederastic cultures might produce crime and adult imprisonment as *themselves* queer objects of admiration and aspiration.

It is not only punks and kids, however, who are susceptible to the perverse lessons of a pederastic education. In one remarkable passage, Genet suggests that the impermeable masculinity of the heterosexual pimp is produced through the *same* loving imitation that characterizes pederastic education:[54] "The little delinquents go to [the insolent pimps] by instinct. They surround them, they listen to them open-mouthed. The pimp impregnates them. And if you shrug your shoulders at what seems a ridiculous ideal, you are wrong, for they obey the amorous impulse which makes them resemble the person they love: a tough [*un dur*], until the time they have finally become that person."[55] Genet dignifies the "ridiculous ideal" of naive young delinquents idolizing and imitating hardened criminals by reworking it as an origin myth about the production of the impermeable masculinity of the *dur*—the tough or, literally, the "hard." In a homoerotic form of reproduction, the tough pimp impregnates or fertilizes (*féconde*) the open-mouthed young delinquents, while the delinquents, in turn, follow "the amorous impulse which makes them resemble the one they love." This impulse acts as a principle of maturation, and the delinquents' march toward their ideal therefore ends when they at last become what they once loved. Becoming "commonplace pimps," however, is presented as at once the apex and a fall:

> They then lose, in hardening, the thrilling tenderness that was imparted by the movement of marching to their goal, the inconsistent flow—which is only a transition—of yearning youth to maturity. Everything within them then forgets that amorous march. They have become commonplace pimps who no longer remember the adventure they had to pursue in order to be these pimps. They, in turn, will be a pole of attraction to other minors, for this is the means, perhaps an impure one, that God uses to fabricate the impassive men of the prisons.[56]

The adventure of "yearning youth" is that of ephemerality, a fleeting passage destined to come to an end once they reach maturity, defined as the freezing of desiring movement and the forgetting of adolescent transit. Genet's fable suggests that heterosexual delinquents and pederastic kids alike are propelled by the principle of adoring emulation that was the cornerstone of Mettray's affective education, and that, alike, they divert it to criminal ends. However, the pimp's "tough" masculinity, unlike that of the pederasts, is founded on the absolute abandonment and forgetting of the homoerotic yearning that compelled him to become masculine in the first place. Audible within Genet's fable is a sigh of regret for the passage of yearning youth that is lost and forgotten once they become "banal pimps" and attain the unremembering, nondesiring stasis that goes by the name of maturity.

THE BRUISE OF METTRAY

In failing to forget his pederastic adolescent loves, Jean fails to transition smoothly from emulating the models he adores to attaining a static, nonimitative masculinity. As is suggested by his abrupt transformation into his boyhood lover Villeroy while fighting Charlot, Jean remains haunted by past loves, vulnerable to their possession of him even as he attempts to prove his manhood. Compared to the hard impermeability of the true tough, Jean is a leaking vessel, full of cracks. As he admits halfway through the text, "There is something within me that knows very well that it would be vain to take pains to appear strong and master of myself, for my flamboyant nature will always appear through a thousand fissures."[57] The French phrase that I have rendered as "my flamboyant nature" and that appears in Bernard Frechtman's translation as "my wild nature [*ma folle nature*]," means both "my crazy nature" and "my nature as a queen" and suggests here a category crisis: is Jean a virile prison wolf, as he has been trying to claim, or is his masculinity, and therefore his status as a wolf, merely a fragile outer shell, inevitably fissured by the pressure of Jean's essential "nature" as a queen? Whereas, in its description of Mettray's inmate hierarchies, *Miracle* quite clearly separates fairies excluded from masculinity from big shots and kids in no way understood to be queer, here, the categories begin to merge.

Medical experts of the time would have understood queens and fairies alike as unambiguous congenital inverts, whose desire for men was a consequence of their inner feminine nature, expressed outwardly in a recognizable feminine style. They might have understood the wolf, however, in one of two ways. Either he was the menacing virile pederast who haunted the imagination of the interwar period, a pervert by "choice" who aggressively propositioned and sometimes successfully recruited other "normal" men,[58] or he was, in a new understanding, *simply a homosexual*, different in gendered style, but not in kind from the prison queen. This latter understanding of the prison wolf, which Kunzel argues was new in the United States during the mid-twentieth century, represents the gradual usurpation of prior understandings of inversion as, at its root, a *gendered* form of deviance (and therefore, of the masculine man who is sexually aggressive toward a younger, weaker, or more feminine man as not, himself, an invert) by a modern notion of homosexual identity, which understands homosexual acts as expressions of homosexual personhood, regardless of gender style.[59] But Genet's pederast is still "early," to use Peter Coviello's term, in relation to modern homosexual identity. For Coviello, "earliness" describes the moments before the consequential coordination of a number of vectors—gender style, erotic desire, deep psychology, personal eccentricity—into the new explanatory rubric of *sexuality*, understood as a private possession of the self. Jean suspects that he is *a queen* rather than a homosexual, *not* because he desires men, but because of his "feminine" failure *to be* a properly masculine, autonomous man. It is only through a careful attention to the language of *Miracle* that we might access the peculiar "earliness" of the prison pederast during this transitional moment in the history of sexuality. *Miracle*'s prison pederast is not yet a homosexual, yet no longer "just" a sexually aggressive, if immoral, man, and is defined as much by his relation to *time* as by the nature of his gendered selfhood or sexual desire.

Far from afflicting Jean alone, the figure of the crack or the fissure soon multiplies throughout the text to fracture even the toughest masculinities. Jean's above confession is, in fact, foreshadowed by a rather cryptic commentary on Jean's former Mettray "husband" Divers. Jean recalls being struck, as an adolescent at Mettray, by Divers's features, darkened as if by a veil of mourning. While Jean is impelled to liken Divers to an angel carved into a glass window, he is forced to acknowledge that this carving has a crack. As he mysteriously comments, "I later discovered the meaning of the crack [*cette fêlure*], which was a second sign of mourning, and of the even more theatrical one that furrows Bulkaen, that furrows all the big shots, from Botchako to Charlot."[60] What is the meaning of these strangely theatrical cracks, signs of mourning borne by all of the Mettray toughs now incarcerated at Fontevrault?

In reminiscing about his youth, Jean unearths an alternative, less triumphal history of masculine hardness. One day, when Jean mistakenly imagines that Villeroy is cheating on him, he undergoes a telling transformation, becoming "what any punk [*giron*] is without his big shot: a temple of anguish."[61] Jean, who at this moment is still soft of character and without a settled identity, suddenly becomes a ceremonial structure in memory of his lost lover, a temple whose hardness exists only to be inhabited by Villeroy's spirit. Although this transformation, born of a misperception, is only temporary, Jean's momentary accession to the state of "any punk without his big shot" foreshadows the transformation that every punk who receives a virile education must undergo—for the first condition of becoming a big shot is to give up one's big shot. When Villeroy definitively leaves Mettray, Jean's pride at his inclusion among the big shots is shadowed by a pervasive sense of loss: "The sadness of his leaving soon lost its primitive meaning and became a kind of chronic melancholy, like a misty autumn, and that autumn is the foundational season [*la saison de base*] of my life, for it often sets in even now."[62] The transition from punk to big shot is founded on loss, a loss which it endures by toughening into a masculine hardness rather than by forgetting it, as do the heterosexual pimps. Reflecting, "I imagine how tough [*dur*] I can seem to others, for Bulkaen's toughness [*dureté*] was likewise composed of his profound desolation at finding himself abandoned," Jean suggests that this history of loss is not his alone; it has shaped Bulkaen as well and might, therefore, characterize all of the tough masculinities forged from carceral pederasty.[63]

Throughout *Miracle*, seduced by memory and perpetually vulnerable to the invasion of desires past, Jean, as a temple hospitably open to Villeroy's living memory, cedes to the pull of Mettray. Jean's chronic state of openness to possession and haunting by the past is figured as a series of tiny openings—fissures and cracks—in the hardness of his masculinity. These fissures suggest a state of being wounded and even broken by the past, and therefore also perpetually receptive to it. When Bulkaen asks Jean to write a poem about two "friends" in the Guiana penal colony, Jean concludes, "Mettray had dealt him a telling blow. He was mortally wounded, despite his laughter and health."[64] By requesting a homoerotic poem about a male couple in a penal colony, Bulkaen displays his wound to Jean. The gash Bulkaen bears is at once the sign that he might be inclined to pederasty and the scar of his injury at Mettray's harshness. Although Bulkaen's gash is described as an indication of secret flaws, Jean loves him all the more after discovering it, for it suggests that, wounded just as Jean is, Bulkaen might be open to carceral loves. Similarly, of Mettray's former prisoners, Jean speculates, "They will have women, but I dare not think that these kids [*ces gosses*] who for so long were courtesans, or males who adored them, could possibly not keep, in their hearts, in their souls, and in their muscles, *the bruise of Mettray*."[65] The "bruise of Mettray," like Bulkaen's wound or the cracks on the surface of the prison big shots, marks the swollen and wounded hardness of pederastic toughs in perpetual mourning for the past pleasures of adolescent imprisonment, youthful femininity, and sexual receptivity.

This is far from the conventional understanding of prison wolves as merely virile and sexually aggressive men. Genet theorizes carceral pederasty as having subject-forming effects, but the subject pederasty forms is not *the homosexual*, a being defined by his sexuality. Instead, the adult pederast is someone queered, whether or not he pursues women, by his wounded—and eroticized—attachment to a carceral youth. The pederastic prison wolf, in *Miracle*, is less a sexual identity than an apparent gendered "toughness" paradoxically defined by its fissured openness to the haunting of past pleasures and desires. He is, in other words, less the bearer of a sexual or gender identity than a state of *having been wounded by the past*. As such, the subjectivity of the prison pederast *requires* the partial failure of its own ideals of virile development, precisely that failure dramatized in the narrative of *Miracle*. By contrast, the masculinity of the "commonplace pimps" requires *both* that, during adolescence, they lovingly imitate adult pimps, *and* that later, they stop, forgetting in the process the queer yearnings of their youth. For if they did not forget, they would, like *Miracle*'s haunted pederasts, be perpetually vulnerable to the past and, therefore, inclined to adult pederasty. Denying their history of homosocial loves rather than invoking memories, the pimps attain a perfect hardness through the disavowal of their adolescent passions. *Miracle* cultivates a queer sensibility that eroticizes the failure, wounding, and corruption of masculine ideals. If I claim this aesthetics of failure as queer, however, it is not because it provides an alternative to hegemonic sexism.⁶⁶ What is queer about *Miracle* is its cultivation of deidealization as a form of *attachment* rather than a renunciation, its eroticization of the very oscillation between idealization and deidealization, and its intimate perversion of, rather than opposition to, normative gendered ideals.

THE PLEASURES OF LOSS

Though Genet's literary work is steeped in loss, none of Genet's texts on loss, including *Miracle*, are legible as works of either mourning or melancholia in the strict psychoanalytic sense of the terms, for they neither put corpses to rest in order to "move on" to new loves nor swallow these corpses whole in melancholic silence.⁶⁷ Rather, Genet's texts counter the hegemonic silencing of queer loss that so often produces melancholia by opening themselves to "libidinal invasion" by a past that *cannot* be allowed to rest, because if the dominant culture were to mourn it at all, it would certainly never be for the queer pleasures it contained.⁶⁸ What is unique about Genet's queer melancholy is that he simultaneously acknowledges the power of trauma, desolation, and loss *and* sings past moments of excessive queer pleasure, pre-gay liberation sites of pederastic love, and historically obsolete queer "paradises," such as the abolished penal colony of Mettray. In novels such as *Miracle of the Rose*, *Funeral Rites*, and *Our Lady of the Flowers*, Genet perversely finds erotic pleasure *within* loss. He cums while writing about the dead, reliving the queer sex acts they performed and the orgasms they experienced (or that he experienced with them) rather than piously memorializing their character and good (or more often, bad) deeds. Genet reminds us that the ache of mourning is a sign that we once experienced some bliss, even if only fleeting or fantasized, whose loss now pains us. Elizabeth Freeman has proposed that "we might imagine ourselves haunted by bliss and not just by trauma; residues of positive affect (idylls, utopias, memories of touch) might be available for queer counter- (or para-) historiographies."⁶⁹ *Miracle*'s carceral pederasts are hurt by a past they do not merely want to forget, for it also contains unintelligible pleasures. Genet's writing might be considered a practice of what Freeman terms *erotohistoriography*, an embodied relation to history, guided by the corporeal sensation, that welcomes the invasion of the present by "pleasures past."⁷⁰ Genet's, however, is an erotohistoriography that does not shy away from the suffusion of past bliss with pain.

Freeman develops her concept of erotohistoriography from a reading of

Maria Torok's 1968 essay "The Illness of Mourning and the Fantasy of the Exquisite Corpse," in which Torok seeks to explain the fact that "a measure of libidinal increase upon the object's death seems to be a widespread, if not universal phenomenon."[71] Picking up on Karl Abraham's suggestion, in a letter to Freud, that mania might be only one of the forms of libidinal increase that often accompany melancholia, Torok boldly proposes, contra Freud: "The illness of mourning does not result, as might appear, from the affliction caused by the objectal loss itself, but rather from the feeling of an irreparable crime: the crime of having been overcome with desire, of having been surprised by an overflow of libido at the least appropriate moment, when it would behoove us to be grieved in despair."[72] The account of erotohistoriography that Freeman develops from Torok, however, is an exceedingly sanguine one that de-emphasizes the inseparability, for Torok, of bliss, pain, and shame in order to affirmatively highlight, instead, the potential convertibility of trauma into pleasure.[73] Freeman takes from Torok the notion of an "inappropriate" erotic response through which a past pleasure is preserved while passing over the fact that, in Torok's account, sexual prohibitions remake this pleasure as pain while repressing the memory of both the erotic response and the blissful moment itself. For Torok, melancholia's negative affect is the result of a censured erotic effusion remade as sexual guilt and shame, while the lost pleasure, in its link to the traumatic erotic effusion, is banished from memory. What Torok calls "the illness of mourning" is less a historical method, less a bodily means of sensing past bliss, than it is a means of encrypting and forgetting it. Tellingly, most of Abraham and Torok's case studies of the illness of mourning have to do with the sexual trauma of incest, in which case it is easy to see why any erotic response would be banished from conscious memory and remade as trauma.[74] On the whole, the illness of mourning seems an unlikely foundation for a practice of erotohistoriography, since it is based on sexual prohibition and trauma, the repression of erotic memory, and the conversion of pleasure into pain.

As a canny writer of queer fables, however, Genet might provide us with just the tale we need to conceptualize a melancholy that memorializes pleasure in and through loss. Just as, in *Funeral Rites*, Jean literalizes Freudian melancholia by fantasizing that he is cannibalizing his lover Jean's corpse, *Miracle* one-ups Torok, envisioning the shamefully inappropriate overflow of libido when one should be mourning in the horrific form of literal necrophilia. During one of Family B's rare summer outings to the river, Deloffre's kid, Toscano, tragically drowns. As Deloffre attempts to revive him by performing the rhythmic motions of cardiopulmonary resuscitation on Toscano's body, "Deloffre's penis grazed his dead kid's buttocks, which were outlined by the wet trunks . . . Finally, there was a moment when he was completely shaken with little shudders: it was neither the wind drying the water on his shoulders, nor fear, nor shame, but pleasure [*la volupté*]. At the same time, he collapsed on the dead body."[75] When Genet later encounters Deloffre at Fontevrault, Deloffre confesses that he is still haunted by Toscano; not by Toscano's ghost per se, but by the shame and horror of having sexually profaned Toscano's corpse:

> One evening he spoke to me again about the latter's [Toscano's] death and told me how horrible it was to be haunted by the kid [*le gosse*]. I asked whether he believed in ghosts. It wasn't a question of that but of the semblance of love he had made on the corpse. That outlandish ceremony on a catafalque of flesh appeared to him to be what it must have been to everyone: a profanation. He lived in the shame, in the horror, of having screwed a corpse and above all of having taken pleasure in the act.[76]

Deloffre's spasm of erotic bliss over his kid's corpse has still not loosened its grip on him; it continues to haunt him, but in the form of horror and shame rather than pleasure. In addition to being haunted by negative affect, Deloffre is haunted by Toscano himself—not by Toscano's ghost, as one might expect, but by his body, which Deloffre fantasizes he inhabits. He confesses to Jean, "I have the feeling I was present at my birth, that I came out of him right after his death. My skull is his, my hair, my teeth, my eyes are his. I feel I'm living in the dead body of my little sweetypuss!"[77] Condemned to wander the earth in his dead kid's body, Deloffre expiates the crime of his orgasm by becoming a living corporeal memorial to Toscano. This passage emphasizes the corporeal dimensions of queer loss. As a sensuous, embodied, and fleshy set of pleasures, touches, and sensations culminating in a prohibited orgasm, Toscano's death, for Deloffre, is experienced, encoded, and memorialized in and through the body. The passage's most significant departure from psychoanalytic doctrine, however, is that whereas both melancholic incorporation and an inappropriate sexual response at the object's loss are banished to the unconscious, Deloffre is able to both remember and recount his orgasm, his shame, and his fantasized inhabitation of Toscano's body, if only to Jean, a fellow former Mettray inmate and pederast.

Deloffre's tale informs us, first of all, that there can be no haunting, whether by bliss or by loss, without some element of interdiction and shame. If he were not overcome with shame at having cum on his kid's corpse, breaking the taboo on sex with the dead, Deloffre would not still be haunted by that fleeting moment of taboo pleasure. Second, Deloffre's tale underlines that the queer bliss that haunts us can only be remembered through a veil of pain, as the traumas of both the lost pleasure and the social interdiction on experiencing and speaking that form of pleasure infuse the lost erotic moment with negative affect. Pleasure and pain must therefore be undecidably conjoined, experienced in and through one another. Third, both Deloffre's orgasm of mourning and inhabitation of Toscano's body strikingly figure the corporeal dimensions of queer loss and queer memory. Finally and most significantly, Deloffre's ability to remember and recount both the fact of having cum on Toscano's corpse and his strong sense of having taken on his dead kid's physical features indicates a mode of being haunted by pleasures past that does not respond to sexual interdiction with the strict repression and forgetting of the libidinal effusion and the loss that elicited it. While Deloffre's haunted embodiment of the lost object is clearly symptomatic of the psychic effects of sexual interdiction, this interdiction has not yet forced Deloffre to bury erotic memory itself in the unconscious. Deloffre's evasion of repression even as he remains haunted by a blissful and traumatizing past delineates a queer melancholy that hovers *between* mourning and melancholia and that might be legible as a means of keeping alive a relation to the traumatizing losses of queer history's ambivalent paradises.

José Muñoz has argued that, for those burdened by historical trauma, there is an everydayness to loss that has made it necessary to learn to *live with* melancholia, not as an abnormal pathology, but as a mode of both individual and communal survival.[78] Muñoz and other scholars of race, colonialism, and psychoanalysis remind us that significant social determinants, such as those of race, class, and sexuality, modulate our relation to the sexual interdictions and social norms that canonical psychoanalysis tends to universalize.[79] Prison wolves such as Jean and Deloffre have already broken a number of social interdictions and weathered a range of shaming nominations—criminal, delinquent, pederast. As a result, they, like the other Mettray boys practicing pederasty, quite simply *could not* have had the same relation to sexual shame and social interdiction as the bourgeois clients through which canonical psychoanalytic theory was elaborated. Genet suggests that carceral pederasts innovated a relation to the losses of queer history that, rather than repressing those losses or locking them away in an unconscious crypt, allows them to haunt the present with the traumatic bliss of lost, forbidden, or silenced pleasures.

The losses that wound carceral pederasts include not only individual lovers (like Villeroy or Toscano) or moments of erotic bliss, but also periods of one's life, and even, *Miracle* insists, obsolete penal institutions in which queer life once flourished. "Someone had carved on the wall: Just as I'm guarded by a prison-door, so my heart guards your memory... 'I shall not let my childhood escape.'"[80] In this piece of convict poetry, tattooed onto a prison wall, prison is represented as a sheltering and preserving enclosure, likened to a heart faithfully guarding its memories. Reading this poem, Jean vows to imprison and preserve his memories of a penal childhood; for there are no scrapbooks, no family photo albums, no carefully preserved mementos to register the significance of Jean's carceral youth. Worse still, Mettray itself—with its institutional "families," pederastic forms of education, and rich social culture—no longer exists. Shut down thanks to the efforts of reporters like Alexis Danan and vilified in the writings of former inmates, Mettray, and with it, Jean's adolescence, is both literally and figuratively in ruins. In one of the most melancholy passages of *Miracle*, upon revisiting Mettray after its closure, Jean writes, "After glancing at these ruins, the sadness of my soul will never be cured. I advanced slowly and all I heard was the cry of a few birds. I found only a corpse. I know that my youth is dead. Nothing remains of the passage of so many hoodlums."[81] Mettray is a cadaver, murdered and forgotten without a burial, and Jean's sadness at its death can never be healed; for there is no way to hold an intelligible discourse about Mettray's forms of queer belonging, no history of its erotic pleasures, and no socially recognizable way to mourn its carceral culture as something of value, as a true loss that can be recognized and communicated as such. The public discourse that figures the boys' penal colonies as barbarous institutions and pederasty as the sign of their moral corruption relegates the pleasures, the pedagogies, and the social forms of the boys' penal colonies to the status of abandoned cadavers and unmourned phantoms. Haunted by his pain at Mettray's passing, Jean is simultaneously haunted by the ghosts of pleasures past, ghosts that prove so seductive that Jean is unable to continue marching forward on the path of pederastic development. Wearing the pleasurably aching wound of his love for Mettray on his sleeve, Jean displays himself as injured by the past, as open to the hauntings of memory, and therefore (within the imaginary of *Miracle*) as queer.

LIGHT OF A DEAD STAR

Miracle's carceral pederasts force us to contemplate the "impossibility" of a pederastic paradise before gay liberation, not within some ahistorical utopian refuge, but at the very heart of modernity's disciplinary and rehabilitative institutions. This is not a denial of pederasty's modernity, but the rendition of a historical structure of feeling that soldered queerness to bittersweet nostalgia by binding it to losses rendered unintelligible within available public discourses. Wounded by a past that also pleasured them, *Miracle*'s haunted pederasts model a queer disposition to history that allows for the pained delight of *commingled affects*. Commingled affects are bodily intensities that have not been granted social meaning or assigned particular narratives as emotions. The difficulty in describing their fusion of pleasure and trauma as well as their unintelligibility within available discursive forms leads me to term them *affects* rather than emotions.[82] The queer "paradise" of Mettray pains through the trauma of pleasures—such as the sweetness of submission, the solace of dependency, the forbidden joys of adolescent femininity, and the bittersweet taste of togetherness in exile and suffering—legible only as corruption, abuse, and pathology within available public discourses. The pleasures of queer history, *Miracle* shows us, come suffused with pain—the pain of their vilification within the public discourses of their own time, of their absence from the empirical historical record, and of the compromised and even coerced positions they had to occupy in order to flourish. We can learn from *Miracle* a queer disposition toward history that neither turns away in horror from the traumas of the queer past nor seeks to recuperate them through a progress narrative of sexual emancipation or a leap into queer futurity. Instead, a queer historical disposition must remain alive to the commingled affects—such as the intensity of a pain indistinguishable from pleasure, the pangs of a lost and "impossible" bliss, and the ambivalent togetherness of abjection—that may have been the conditions of past modes of queer life.

Miracle's description of the abusive, sexist, and sexually coercive institution of Mettray as a queer "paradise" disturbs the progressive and egalitarian ideals that inhabit *queer* today; its focus on an obsolete institution and a nostalgic mode of sexual personhood troubles queer theory's contemporary love affair with the open horizon of future possibility; and its theorization of queer sexuality as a perverse product of modern carceral institutions, rather than as something repressed and victimized by them, unsettles *queer*'s connotation of political opposition. In rubbing against these contemporary orientations, *Miracle* is inhabited by another attachment history of *queer*, one characterized by commingled affect, perverse inhabitation, and nostalgia.

In *Foundlings*, Christopher Nealon, inspired by James Baldwin's *Go Tell It on the Mountain*, imagines the mid-twentieth-century queer text as a "message in a bottle" destined to "some historical 'other' place from which the unspeakability of... love can gain audition."[83] The future anterior of "to have been saved" names the optimism of Nealon's foundling texts, which he here reads as reaching toward a "hermeneutic friend" in some longed-for historical moment of queer possibility who would be capable of receiving their message. In her sympathetic critique, Love argues that the contemporary gay and lesbian historical imaginary that sees itself as throwing a lifeline to lonely figures drowning in the "bad" queer past does more to reassure the present than to actually attend to the experience of that past.[84] Her book, *Feeling Backward*, therefore focuses on queer modernist texts that turn away from a future that might somehow want to claim them. While *Miracle* clearly turns away from the future in which we, its readers, live and toward its own diegetic past, we also know that this memoir-novel is somehow addressed to us, written to receive audition within some posterior historical moment. What are we to make of this temporal paradox? Certainly, *Miracle* does not appear to want to have been saved within a future of queer possibility, since it perversely affirms the destroyed "paradise" of Mettray as the historical site of queer flourishing while appearing more interested in prison pederasts on the verge of being cast as obsolete during the dawning era of modern homosexual identity than in the creatures of this era itself. *Miracle*'s aim, rather, is to project and amplify, far into a future in which it remains ultimately disinterested, the ghostly vibrations of pleasures past.

The stairwell at Fontevrault, Jean recounts, "still vibrates with the first kiss that Pierrot [Bulkaen's first name] gave me there, and with his flight, which was swift and slightly stiff, like that of a chamois."[85] *Miracle* never ceases to affirm that, though the institutions and social forms of the past might disappear, fleeting moments of erotic bliss will vibrate forever. Speaking of his time at Mettray, Jean explains, "I mean—and as far back as I can remember—that it is a *precise span of time*, but that it irradiates, that this *present past* radiates a dark vapour, composed chiefly, I think, of our suffering."[86] History itself is not collapsed here, for Jean is careful to point out that Mettray belongs to a precise moment in time. This is a past, however, that remains present, a *present past* that he imagines as emotively radiating from its historical location into ours. Vibrating, radiating, resonating—historical feelings, located in a particular time, extend themselves beyond it, touching off chords of light, sound, and emotion in the future. On the final page, in what we can take as *Miracle*'s last word on its relation to the future, Jean envisions the reception of this text: "Who, it will be asked, were Bulkaen, Harcamone, Divers, who was Pilorge, who was Guy? And their names will disquiet [*troublera*] like the light disquiets us [*nous trouble*] that arrives from a star a thousand years dead."[87] Frechtman's translation of the French verb *troubler* as "to awe" rather than "to trouble or disquiet" suggests that future readers will be impressed by the grandeur of these imprisoned heroes from the dark days of the queer past. As the verb *troubler* makes clear, however, *Miracle* is written neither to be redeemed by sympathetic readers in a future of queer possibility, nor to be honored as the story of brave queer ancestors, but to trouble our present certainties, including those that attach to the term *queer* itself. Emanating from a defunct historical moment, but still vibrating—like the light of a star long since dead—the queer past retains its agency in the present when it unsettles and disturbs rather than being the object of rescue or worship. Living with the unsettling, arousing, painful, and discomfiting vibrations of the queer past—this is the task Genet assigns those of us who would aspire to a queer historical disposition.

chapter 3

RACIAL FETISHISM, GAY LIBERATION, AND THE TEMPORALITIES OF THE EROTIC

It is a common rhetorical move for contemporary queer activists and theorists alike to hark back to the late 1960s and 1970s as a time in which gay and lesbian politics sought *liberation* rather than rights or assimilation, drew active links between the struggles of sexual minorities and those of other oppressed groups, and understood homophobia and heterosexism to be inseparable from broader structures of capitalist imperialist patriarchal oppression. Gay liberation functions as a significant historical resource for Queer Studies' utopian imaginary of political coalition and as a radical alternative to identitarian and assimilationist gay and lesbian politics in the present.[1] Despite this admiration for gay liberation's coalitional politics and utopian revolutionary imaginary, Queer Studies as a field has tended to avoid analyzing its own relationship to the gay liberation moment or studying either gay liberation's political theories or its on-the-ground practices.[2]

I open, then, with a quote from a French gay liberation text that poses a series of problems for Queer Studies in the present. The text is from the April 23, 1971, special issue of *Tout!*, the leftist journal edited by Jean-Paul Sartre, which served as a platform for the recently formed Front homosexuel d'action révolutionnaire (Homosexual Front of Revolutionary Action, henceforth referred to as FHAR) to publicly declare, to a largely homophobic French left, that homosexuality could be central to class struggle and indeed, revolutionary. The *Tout!* special issue would be banned, ten thousand copies seized, and Sartre charged with an "outrage to public decency" as the journal's editor. The FHAR appears, at first glance, to be a textbook example of the radical, coalitional politics ascribed to the gay liberation movement. Inspired by intellectual Freudo-Marxism, the U.S. gay liberation movement, Third World decolonization movements, and even the African American civil rights and Black Power movements, the FHAR promoted a notion of revolutionary homosexuality in solidarity with radical struggle everywhere. More uncomfortable, for the queer present, is the FHAR's tendency to position *sex* as the basis of solidarity and coalition alike. A centerpiece of the *Tout!* special issue is the following quote, attributed to "Jean Gênet [sic]": "Perhaps if I had never gone to bed with Algerians, I could never have approved of the FLN [Front de Libération Nationale]. I probably would have been on their side anyway, but it's homosexuality that made me realize that Algerians are no different than other men."[3] This quote serves as exergue for the following manifesto:

> WE ARE MORE THAN 343 SLUTS.
> We've been butt-fucked [*nous nous sommes faites enculer*] by Arabs.
>
> WE'RE PROUD OF IT AND WILL DO IT AGAIN.
> SIGN AND circulate THIS PETITION
> WILL THE *NOUVEL OBSERVATEUR* PUBLISH IT???
> AND DISCUSS WITH ARAB PALS.[4]

Modeled after the famous "Manifesto of the 343" ("Manifeste des 343"), which was signed by 343 women who had had abortions, published in the French national periodical *Le Nouvel Observateur* in April 5 of that same year, and known derisively by its detractors as the "Manifesto of the 343 Sluts" ("Manifeste des 343 salopes"), the FHAR version campily publicizes something judged perhaps equally shameful—being butt-fucked by Arabs—to a far more dubious political end. The authors contrast the political effects of white French men being fucked by decolonizing Arabs to those of old-style colonialist pederasty:

> First of all, everyone is obsessed with the cliché of the old European pederast who fucks young Arabs. Aside from the fact that it's never that simple, we want to emphasize that in France, it's our Arab friends who fuck us and never the other way around. Impossible not to understand this as a revenge, to which we consent, against the colonizing Occident. Do you imagine that it's possible for us to have the same relation to Arabs as everyone else or

as the typical French man when we commit with them what bourgeois morality makes out to be the most shameful of acts?

Yes we feel a very strong solidarity of the oppressed with Arabs.[5]

This defense appears to be in bad faith, first, because it flies in the face of the position, propounded by some FHAR members, that rigid active/passive sexual dichotomies are a version of internalized patriarchal oppression,[6] and second, because the Genet quote it uses to exemplify its politics may actually illustrate precisely the old-style pederasty the FHAR paints as politically retrograde.[7] In all its ambivalence, however, this text, along with the Genet quotation that introduces it, is certain of one thing: *homosexual oppression + postcolonial interracial sex = coalitional solidarity.*[8]

To be clear, I am not arguing that this formula, which I will henceforth refer to as *erotic coalition*, was either Genet's or the FHAR's sole coalitional practice. It is worth mentioning that, long alienated from France, Genet felt at home in the Arab world, where he lived on and off throughout his adult life, forming deep and close relationships, both sexual and nonsexual, with Arab men and women. In their accounts of their relationships with Genet, Mohammad Choukri, Leila Shahid, and Edward Said all comment upon the authenticity of Genet's manner of living among and associating with Arabs and keen interest and engagement in the politics of the Arab world.[9] If I focus on erotic coalition, it is less to cast doubt on Genet's ability to relate to both Arabs and black Americans in a way that many appreciated and enjoyed than to reflect on the aspects of his attraction to the Panthers and the Palestinians that are all too frequently denied, left out, or explained away out of an admiration for his political *and* personal relationships with Arabs and black Americans.

There is a split at the heart of Queer Studies' relation to gay liberation: it seeks to forward the gay liberationist imaginary of revolutionary coalition into a queer futurity while at the same time brushing off the naive Freudo-Marxist theory of desire on which liberationists relied.[10] The gay liberationist ideal of erotic coalition, however, makes such a divided reception, on the part of Queer Studies, of "naive" liberationist erotics versus "radical" liberationist coalition untenable. This chapter performs an attachment genealogy of liberationism to argue that psychoanalytic queer negativity, with its celebration of the self-shattering and socially corrosive effects of sexuality, owes a debt to the understudied tradition, exemplified by Guy Hocquenghem, that I term *liberationist negativity*. If a more familiar utopian liberationism celebrates the liberatory and culture-building aspects of homosexual desire, liberationist negativity remains trained on the corrosive effects of queer sexuality on identity and the social order. Contrary to their intent, both liberationist and psychoanalytic negativity, I argue, ultimately idealize desire and jouissance as the privileged sites through which the social order and the identities that compose it can be shattered. Deidealization, on the other hand, means learning to live with rather than redeem or critique the imperfect and messy relations, created by juxtaposition and propinquity rather than causality, between queer eros and the political; it means examining the ways in which gay liberation, rather than being either a naive theory of desire that queer scholarship has blithely superseded or a radical charge from the past that we might reanimate, lives, with all its incoherencies and unresolved problems, within Queer Studies today. This chapter deidealizes both liberationist and psychoanalytic negativity by examining writings by Genet and the FHAR that position the black or Arab sexual penetrator as the fetishized instrument through which the white bottom may enjoy his temporary release from the burdens of identity via self-shattering.

Avowing the living trace of gay liberation within Queer Studies helps make explicit the historical reasons for the divergent approaches to the erotic within dominant strains of queer theory, on the one hand, and scholarship on race and ethnicity, on the other—divergences which scholars of race *and* sexuality, ethnicity *and* desire must constantly negotiate. First, as Sharon Holland has argued, whereas queer theory privileges more autonomous and antinormative modalities of desire, a theory of the vicissitudes of racialized desire within racist social orders must enlist "the erotic as a possible harbinger *of the established order*."[11] Second, prominent psychoanalytic accounts of the erotic within queer theory that do not center race tend to also have little to say about the relationship between the erotic and history, including racial histories of slavery, colonization, decolonization, and civil rights.[12] This failure to think the historicity of the erotic produces a break with critical race theory, which understands race to be *the* preeminent sociohistorical formation, nothing less than a proposal, as Tavia Nyong'o puts it, to "telescope history into biological destiny."[13] By not engaging the historicity of the erotic, queer theoretical accounts of erotic life deprive themselves of the analytic foundation they would need to find common ground with scholarship on race. Although the recent turn to temporality in queer theory has opened new possibilities for considering the time of queer desire as well as the desire for queer history, it has produced a third incommensurability. As I will discuss in more detail later, whereas theorists of queer time have tended to celebrate queer desiring relations between present and past as well as exuberantly nonchronological modes of temporality, critical race theory and postcolonial theory have had to wrestle with a form of temporality that continually brings the trauma, injustice, and injury of a colonial and violently racist past into the present, constraining efforts to move into a different future. The latter version of time is, assuredly, nonchronological and disruptive of progress narratives, but in ways more predictable and burdensome than inventive and world making. Each divergence of queer scholarship on the erotic from key concerns of scholars of race and racialization bears the trace of queer theory's liberationist heritage.

This chapter probes the above impasses between queer and critical race theory by using the liberationist ideal of erotic coalition as an entrée into the problem, both theoretical and political, of racial fetishism. Racial fetishism is the paradigmatic bad relation; it threatens to disqualify otherwise exemplary political coalitions, and it shadows coalition as a utopian ideal of relationality within Queer Studies. I begin by examining how efforts to address the issue of racial fetishism in Genet criticism, Todd Shepard's historical analysis of FHAR discourse, and Tim Dean's queer theory of fetishism stumble upon a problem we have inherited from gay liberation—that of the mutual animation *yet noncoincidence* of the political and the erotic, and more specifically, their divergent *temporalities*. Because we lack a strong account of the relationship between erotic life, temporality, and history, we are unable to contend with the ways in which racialized desire eroticizes the historicity of race, but in ways that fail to align with the teleological temporality of political change. I propose that while erotic attraction may put one into proximity with political movements, political change may feed erotic fantasy, and sexual preferences may be animated *at their origins* by politicized forms of social organization, erotic, psychic, and affective life nonetheless *obeys a different temporality* than do the political movements that seek to transform social orders. Thus, efforts to render fantasy, psychic life, and the erotic coherent with political action and belief, as critics repeatedly have with Genet, must inevitably fudge something.

THE DETRITUS OF CANONIZATION

In a 1975 interview, after giving the properly political reasons for his activism with the Black Panthers and the Palestinian Liberation Organization, Genet reflects,

> What is more difficult to admit is that the Panthers are Black Americans, the Palestinians are Arabs. It would be difficult for me to explain why things are

like this, but these two groups of people have a very intense erotic charge. I wonder whether I could have adhered to other revolutionary movements that are equally as just—I find these movements very just, the Panthers and the Palestinians—but isn't this adherence, this sympathy, also driven by the erotic charge that the whole Arab world or the Black American world represents for me, for my own sexuality?[14]

Genet here confesses what seems "difficult to admit"—that the glue that cemented his celebrated activism with the Black Panthers and the Palestinians may have been a racialized attraction to black and Arab men. Genet's confession here, along with the passages in his posthumously published memoir *Prisoner of Love* that linger over the erotics of the Black Panther Party and the exuberantly unapologetic racial fetishism of his novels of the 1940s, have been sidelined within criticism. When Genet's racialized eroticism *is* addressed in criticism, it is often in order to redeem it via a temporal progress narrative that poses it as *leading to* principled political coalition.

To give a sense of the tone of some of Genet's praise, we can turn to none other than the great critic of European Orientalism, Edward Said, who writes, "Genet made the step, crossed the legal borders, that very few white men or women even attempted. He traversed the space from the metropolitan center to the colony; his unquestioned solidarity was with the very same oppressed identified and so passionately analyzed by Fanon."[15] Before making this redemptive claim, Said acknowledges that "Genet did allow his love for Arabs to be his approach to them" and parenthetically alludes to the fact that Genet's first contact with the Arab world was when he fell in love with a local barber while stationed in Syria as a French colonial soldier. He reassuringly goes on, however, to describe Genet's relationship to Arabs as ideally and extraordinarily free of any Orientalism. Said at once invokes and casts aside the question of colonial erotics or Orientalist exoticism by implying that, while these problematic sentiments may have animated Genet's "initial contacts" with the Arab world "half a century ago" when he was a mere boy of eighteen, they evaporated without a trace into his principled, adult solidarity with Arab revolutionaries.[16]

Said's approach to Genet has long been the rule. Genet is the token white man who is said to be able to cross over and to comprehend fully, for Kate Millett and Hélène Cixous, the oppression of women, for Edward Said, of the colonized, and, for Kobena Mercer, to so skillfully expose the erotic ambivalences of postcolonial cross-racial political commitment that he and Robert

Mapplethorpe are, together, deemed "niggas with attitude."[17] Mercer is by far the most willing to engage with the ambivalent and nonrationalized coexistence, in Genet's writing, of undeniable racial fetishism with politicized critique and political commitment. But in most cases, what animates critical attempts to celebrate Genet's solidarity and belonging with groups that would seem to exclude him is that, for politicized cultural criticism, Genet occupies the place of exceptionality and thus, of hope. He is the exceptional white man who, perhaps thanks to his own social marginalization, is deemed successful in crossing over and sustaining an ethical political solidarity with both women and the racialized oppressed. As such, he stands in for the possibility—even if slim and difficult to achieve—of white antiracist coalitional activism. While such an example may be rhetorically useful, it has led to a telling silence, within criticism, about his uncritical manipulation of racist commonplaces in his early novels. It is as if the shining example of Genet's impassioned political engagement with the Black Panthers and the Palestinians, combined with his own position as a queer outlaw and ex-convict turned fellow-traveler of global decolonizing struggle, were simply too rare and valuable to risk tarnishing with a critique of his colonial erotics and imaginaries.

Like Said, who evokes, in parentheses, Genet's youthful love for a Syrian barber as a mere conduit to a principled solidarity with the Arab world, those critics who do raise the issue of Genet's racialized erotics most often do so only in order to resolve it via a progressive temporal narrative or a vertical architectural metaphor. Genet is the exceptional example of a white man whose attraction to brown and black male bodies *led to* or *was the foundation of* solidarity and political commitment rather than dehumanizing fetishization. Jerôme Neutres's book-length study *Genet sur les routes du Sud*—which, it must be noted, is untroubled by racial fetishism and racialized desire—positions Genet's masterpiece, the politicized memoir *Prisoner of Love* (*Un captif amoureux*), as the culmination of his lifelong infatuation with the men of the global South. In a section titled "Genet's Cross-Racial Desire as Political Solidarity," critic Jarrod Hayes first acknowledges that Genet was a sexual tourist in North Africa before approvingly concluding that, unlike other Orientalists, he "was seduced not by texts, but by political militants of color, and this seduction *led* not only to an oppositional reading but also to a solidarity with revolutionary activities, a solidarity he expressed through engaged writing."[18] Toward the end of their groundbreaking study of French homonormativity, which coins the term *postcolonial pornography* to describe the contemporary incitement of a French gay male lust for Arab and African bodies in structured scenarios of post/colonial inequality, Maxime Cervulle and Nick Rees-Roberts use the metaphor of racialized desire as "the *foundation* of a contestatory political engagement." Leaning on Genet's example, they conclude that the gay eroticization of racialized people "potentially opens the way to a political investment that exceeds the normative frame of the hegemonic gay and lesbian agenda."[19] These critics all make the important move of acknowledging, rather than silencing, the animating role of racialized desire in Genet's political commitments and engaged writing. By taking political outcome as the ultimate measure of racialized erotics, however, they invoke a linear temporal narrative or an architectural metaphor (foundation/superstructure) as a handy shortcut that enables them to positively judge the ethics and the value of potentially problematic racialized desire.

What the various approaches of Genet critics to his racialized sexuality lay bare is the *evaluative dilemma of the erotic*. How do we discern between the desired goal of political solidarity and a suspect identification with and appropriation of the identities and experiences of subordinate groups, between the holy grail of a coalition between the differently oppressed and a form of analogization that levels significant historical and experiential differences, between a praiseworthy attraction to difference and a vilified racial fetishism? How do we do so specifically for the white person attracted to racialized others? Robert Reid-Pharr observes approvingly that "nearly two decades of writing and film making by people of color, and in particular the work of black gay men, has spoken to the experience of sex with whites, painting it at once as liberatory and repressive," only to puzzle over the fact, striking, given such a tradition, that "so few white artists, critics, intellectuals of all stripes, male or female, lesbian or gay, have found it necessary to cover themselves in the mantle of dinge queen, rice queen, or what have you. The desire for black, brown, and yellow flesh remains largely unspoken within either academia, or even within popular publishing," despite the extensive mass marketing of such desires in pornography.[20] While recent scholarship by Darieck Scott, Jennifer Nash, Juana María Rodríguez, and Nguyen Tan Hoang has reclaimed the practice of self-racialization within highly stereotyped racial scenarios as a survival strategy, a vocabulary of desire, and means of accessing ecstasy for people of color intimately shaped by a racially stratified social order,[21] white desires for racialized others tend to be addressed only in order to be critiqued.[22] Critics respond to the ongoing realities of racism and settler colonialism by celebrating the queer potentials of identificatory mobility and perversely racialized desire in one direction only. What is needed is a more nuanced method for parsing desires, identifications, and attachments that go the "wrong" way, from white to racialized subjects. This is, to be clear, not because white desire is more valuable or important, but because scrutinizing it forces us to ask different and uncomfortable questions. When Genet is invoked in left criticism, rather than developing and honing such a critical mode, scholars gesture toward Genet's iconic and exceptional status in order to invoke the imaginary of political coalition across difference and inequality, despite all the dangers they know are attendant on such difficult crossings. For to do the labor of analyzing the complex relationship between Genet's racialized erotics and his antiracist politics would necessarily risk sullying one of the very few concrete representatives of the ideal of an interracial coalition of the oppressed. In failing to embark on an in-depth study of Genet's racialized erotics, however, we continue to neglect the crucial questions that such a study would force us to ask.

In what follows, I respond to the limitations of the frameworks through which scholars have evaluated Genet's racial politics in two ways. First, I use deidealization to circumvent a politics of purity. Genet has been so canonized by left critics as a committed champion of the racialized and colonized oppressed that the potential racism of some of his statements and sentiments seems unthinkable. If it seems incoherent to add the claim that he was *simultaneously* an antiracist author and activist, then this has much to say about the purity that we require from someone's racial politics. I resist this idealizing demand for purity by deploying a logic of accumulation and simultaneity that says, "Yes, and . . ." This is the logic best suited to affect and psychic life, which allows for the ambivalent and simultaneous existence of contradictory realities. Second, I attend to the *asynchronous* temporalities of affect, sexuality, and psychic life. Rather than imagining an exemplary revolutionary Genet heroically capable of casting aside his own colonial formation in order to fight for the Palestinians and the Panthers without a trace of racism or Orientalism, I ask what happens when a Third Republic colonial formation comes into untimely and volatile contact with a historical moment of sexual revolution and revolutionary decolonization. This means exercising an analytic approach that remains attuned to backwardness; for, whereas narratives of revolutionary political action are resolutely futural, calling on the imaginary of a "break" with the past and an opening into a brave new world of radical and novel possibility, psychic and erotic life may prove stubbornly recalcitrant to injunctions to political futurity.

THE FHAR'S ARABS, OR THE EROTICS OF DISCOURSE

The FHAR's elevation of being butt-fucked by Arabs to a declaration of revolutionary homosexual solidarity in the manifesto with which I opened this chapter may appear unredeemable in its racial fetishism as well as its bad faith. After all, in declaring getting butt-fucked by Arabs to be a political act in and of itself, the FHAR need not envision Arabs to be either cosigners of their manifesto or potential homosexual revolutionaries themselves, but only eroticized instruments through which the French gay man might enjoy his punishment for French colonialism. In Maxime Cervulle's incisive analysis, the FHAR's manifesto commodifies the Arab body, first through the "porno-trope of the non-white hypersexual stud embedded within French colonial (and postcolonial) culture" and second, as "a 'necessary' sign of value for so-called revolutionary politics."[23] Indeed, though the text that follows the manifesto gestures toward a union of Arab fuckers and French fuckees in a solidarity of the oppressed, the remainder of the *Tout!* special issue fails to address any of the urgent political issues—such as the housing crisis, Islamophobia, and criminalization—facing France's postcolonial subjects.

Nevertheless, historian Todd Shepard reads the FHAR manifesto positively, as an act of Debordian *détournement* that seeks to parodically resignify the long discursive history of the figure of "Arab men" in French political rhetoric. In "'Something Notably Erotic': Politics, 'Arab Men,' and Sexual Revolution in Post-Decolonization France, 1962–1974," Shepard reconstitutes the discursive context of the FHAR's surprising politicization of sex with Arabs by tracking how the figure of "Arab men" becomes inflamed with political and sexual meaning for journalists and activists on both the extreme right and the radical left during and after the Algerian War of Independence. From the Orientalist "idea that some combination of barbarity, climate, Islam, immorality, and primitive psychology made Arab men, sexually, adepts of sodomy and accepting of man/boy pederasty, as well as, socially, either overly virile brutes or decadent effetes"; to the anti-imperialist rehabilitation of revolutionary Algerian men as the embodiment of healthy, virile masculinity; to the postcolonial development, by xenophobic far right journalists, of a discursive link between the "Arab invasion" of France and rape, sexual "perversion," and homosexuality; to the right-wing caricature of the student protesters of May '68, who were in solidarity with North African immigrants, as just wanting to sleep with Arab men, Shepard maps how the sexualized figure of "Arab men" was deployed and redeployed to give shape to a range of political hopes and anxieties.[24] On its inception, the FHAR therefore entered into a discursive terrain in which leftism, Arabs, and French solidarity with Algerian immigrants had all been (homo)sexualized and Arab men deemed a sexual danger to white French masculinity and femininity alike. In Shepard's analysis, "Rather than deny the stereotypes, the FHAR's emblematic tactic (a form of Debordian *détournement*) was to embrace and reinterpret them: 'Arabs' and homosexuals did do what folklore and pontificating experts said they did."[25] In short, if the far right feared that student leftists wanted nothing better than to surrender their masculinity to be butt-fucked by the "Arab invader," then FHAR militants would write up a manifesto shockingly and defiantly declaring just that.

However valuable and enlightening Shepard's reconstitution of the travels of the figure of "Arab men" in French political discourse during this time period, something is lost when the FHAR's deployment of this figure is considered only a tactical maneuver within an existing discursive field. This is where Shepard comes up against the limits of historical discursive analysis, a method that requires him to remind us that the FHAR's "arguments tell us relatively little about the accuracy of either their promises or the lived experiences and lessons drawn that they evoked."[26] Lived experience, feeling, and erotics are considered empirically unverifiable on the evidentiary basis of political discourse alone. In what follows, I attend to both genre and emotion so as to methodologically expand Shepard's important analysis to provide an account of the relationship between discourse and erotic life.

The second major publication to which FHAR members contributed, a lengthy 1973 special issue of the journal *Recherches* edited by Félix Guattari and titled *Three Billion Perverts* (*Trois milliards de pervers*), is clearly far more than an act of political rhetoric. This collectively authored heterogeneous "semiotic revolt," whose tone is by turns ribald, whimsical, learned, intimate, and incendiary, is composed of a combination of erotic photos and drawings, homosexual *détournements* of comics and illustrations from French Boy Scout novels, masturbatory autobiographic narratives, and transcribed conversations, along with more recognizably political declarations and analyses.[27] As its title underlines, the special issue prioritizes the frank exploration of heterogeneous sexual imaginaries and practices above properly "political" analysis and argumentation. This erotic and, indeed, pornographic frankness is likely why Guattari was found guilty, as the editor, of affronting public decency: his apartment was searched, and the existing journal issues were confiscated. It also enables us to read the special issue as an invaluable historical documentation of the French liberationist erotic imaginary.

Three Billion Perverts leaves no doubt as to the centrality of Arab men to the sexual imaginary of liberationism. It opens with a mammoth chapter—fifty-eight pages long, or one-third of the entire publication—titled "Arabs and Fags" ("Arabes et Pédés") that focuses less on politics per se than on the pleasures and travails of postcolonial sex with Arab men. The anonymous author of "'Arab' Sex" ("Le sexe 'arabe'") signals his quasi-ethnographic intent immediately by explaining that he will place "Arab" in scare quotes throughout so as to remind his readers that most of the so-called "Arab" citizens of the French Maghrebian postcolonies are actually Berbers. He matter-of-factly informs his readers, "It is very easy for a Westerner, young or old, to have homosexual relations with 'Arabs'—that's a fundamental fact. It is easier to hit on an 'Arab' in Paris or in the provinces, in Bruxelles, in Amsterdam, than to hit on a European. Almost all young Arabs are ready to sleep with men."[28] He goes on to generalize that, unlike Europeans, these young "Arabs" do not see same-sex relations as pathological or guilt-inducing and regard the resulting relationship more as a manly friendship than as something based on romantic love. Texts such as "'Arab' Sex" retain Orientalist generalizations and tidy East-West oppositions while reversing their habitual connotations—in light of the celebrated Arab-Islamic propensity for friendly buggery, Judeo-Christian civilization is characterized as both excessively sentimental and damagingly moralistic. These texts imply that homosexual revolution, for the white French man, might take place through the rejection of the Judeo-Christian romance of the couple and repression of same-sex sexuality in favor of the embrace, through easily available sex with Arabs, of what is imagined to be a permissive Arab-Islamic cultural practice of sex between men.[29]

In other contributions, however, the Orientalist commonplace that understood "active sodomy ('buggery') as emblematic of the excessive virility of 'Arab' and Muslim societies—an uncontrolled, uncivilized, and crude exercise of male power that used sexual penetration to dominate women and boys and even to degrade other men" returns with a vengeance.[30] If one refrain in the "Arabs and Fags" chapter is a celebration of Arab men's uncomplicated attitude about sex with men, another is a complaint about their "phallocratic" understanding of sexual penetration and sexist attachment to what one contributor calls the "Islamic 'code of love' with its one-way combinations, its distribution of roles fucker/fucked [*enkuleur/enkulé*]."[31] In the transcribed discussions, "The Arabs and Us" and "Rue des Vertus," the white French discussants protest that their Arab sexual partners treat them like wives, servants, and sex holes. They express frustrated desires to have more intimate relationships with them, to be permitted to penetrate them, and to have them stimulate their penises during sex. Throughout the "Arabs and Fags" chapter, white French contributors understand Arab men's commitment to "phallocracy" to be consonant with the ever-present threat of sexual violence. They describe experiencing domestic violence, sexually charged encounters that turn violent, rape at knifepoint, and unwantedly painful and aggressive sex.[32] Despite this chorus of critiques, when Arab sexual partners defy Orientalist stereotypes, they are most often met with surprise and disinterest: some contributors relate their astonishment when Arab partners actually desire to be penetrated or distaste when they want to have a more intimate relationship, and one recounts becoming disinterested in his Arab sexual partner, a student, after he becomes "Europeanized" and begins to wonder if he is homosexual.[33] Such frequent, if not universal, reactions of surprise, distaste, and disinterest demonstrate the extent to which white French gay men who sought out sex with Arabs at this time were well versed in a particular set of ideas about what pleasures and problems could be expected from a participation in a sexual economy thought to be distinctively Arab-Islamic.

To name some of the genres through which such racialized ideas are conveyed, "Arabs and Fags" provides white gay French men with: a how-to manual for sex with Arab men, a quasi-ethnographic explanation for why sex with Arab men is so easy to come by and a set of contrasts between Arab-Islamic and Judeo-Christian attitudes about sex between men,[34] a range of masturbatory erotic narratives narrated by white French men who desire Arab sex partners, a sexual travelogue to Morocco[35] and to the immigrant neighborhood of Belleville in Paris,[36] a guide to a series of Parisian public sex sites where Arab partners might be found,[37] a forum for a discussion of the challenges and drawbacks of sex with Arab men,[38] an incitement to debate and critique the potential racism of "Arabophilia,"[39] and an opportunity to hone gay liberationist political stances on sexual positions, gender roles, and romantic couples in relation to Arab-Islamic buggery. Though the chapter clearly does, as Shepard argues, both repeat and resignify the sexualized discursive figure of "Arab men," it does so in ways that clearly go beyond the tactical and the ideological. In the sheer excitement of erotic writing, the narratives of the "Arabs and Fags" chapter exuberantly exceed or even neglect to reference the political frameworks—of erotic coalition, solidarity between the marginalized, and sexual liberation—within which sex with Arabs could be made to yield political value. That is to say that, though the FHAR did seek to instrumentalize the ideological utility, potential for *détournement*, and sheer shock value of sex with "Arab men," many of its members were also evidently *turned on* by this discursive figure's erotic charge. This should not surprise us; as Sara Ahmed has proposed, a discursive sign may become "sticky" with emotion by virtue of a history of repeated circulation and use:

> Signs become sticky through repetition; if a word is used in a certain way, again and again, then the "use" *becomes* intrinsic; it becomes a form of signing. It is hard then to hear words like "Pakis" without hearing that word as insulting. The resistance to the word acquiring new meaning is not about the referent; rather the resistance is an effect of these histories of repetition of the word "Paki." This repetition has a binding effect; the word works to generate others as "Paki"; it has particular effects on others who recognize themselves as the object of the address. The "binding" effect of the word is also a "blockage": it stops the word moving or acquiring new value. The sign is a "sticky sign" as an effect of a history of articulation, which allows the sign to accumulate value.[40]

Following Ahmed's methodological insight, we might reread Shepard's article as providing an account of the history—of circulation, use, repetition, and redeployment—by which the discursive figure of "Arab men" in French political discourse became charged with eroticism. This is to propose that *historicity can carry an erotic charge*. That is, if particular discursive figures are repeatedly articulated in association with eroticism, particularly over a long historical period, then the eroticism discursively ascribed to this figure, like the insult attached to the word *Paki, becomes* intrinsic. Such historically eroticized figures *generate effects*: they electrify erotic imaginaries, impel some people to seek out, or to scrupulously avoid, particular kinds of sexual encounters, and compel others to painfully, or perhaps pleasurably, recognize themselves in the figure's distorting mirror. FHAR members were sufficiently moved by the historically accumulated erotic charge of the discursive figure of "Arab men" to roam the streets of Paris in search of interracial sex and to retranslate the resulting fantasies and actual sexual encounters into discourse, recirculating them in the form of the narratives and transcriptions printed in the "Arabs and Fags" chapter. Whether FHAR members describe "Arab men" as wondrously free of sexual repression or as disappointingly phallocratic, whether they imagine sex with Arabs as a political act or narrate the pleasures and travails of sex with Arab men *without* direct reference to politics, they are intensifying, redirecting, and responding to this discursive figure's accumulated erotic charge. In so doing, they are engaging in the social and cultural practice of racial fetishism.[41]

THE TEMPORALITIES OF RACIAL FETISHISM

In describing racial fetishism's erotic charge as ignited by a history of social and cultural practices, both embodied and discursive, I seek to shift the discourse on fetishism from the rhetoric of the demystification of false value and pathological desire to an analytic of the temporal operations by which fetishes are produced and sustained. When the discourse of fetishism is taken up in scholarly writing, it has often been in order to condemn, pathologize, critique, or unveil the ways in which value or desire is invested in anything from a commodity (Marx's dancing table), to a sexualized inanimate object (Freud's erotic fetish), to a category of the human (Homi Bhabha's racial stereotype).[42] Such critical analyses tend to sideline the colonial history of the discourse of fetishism's rhetoric of demystification. As William Pietz has elaborated in an important series of articles, the discourse of the fetish, from the late medieval Portuguese *feitiço* and the sixteenth-century pidgin *fetisso*, was coined by Europeans in the intercultural contact zone of the West African coast to adjudicate between European merchants' and West Africans' incompatible ways of assigning value to material objects. Thus, Pietz reminds us, "the discourse of the fetish has always been a critical discourse about the false objective values of a culture from which the speaker is personally distanced."[43] Postcolonial and critical race theorists have tended to ignore this long colonial history in order to capitalize on the critical potential of the Freudian characterization of the fetish as both a disavowal of difference and a form of split belief.[44] For instance, the Freudian framework enables Bhabha to critique the anxious "disavowal of difference" of "skin/race/culture" at work in racial stereotyping and David Eng to explain the white fetishist's refusal to see the Asian penis when it is clearly there.[45] I remain wary, nevertheless, of the ways in which the discourse of the fetish, with its telling colonial heritage, both shores up the critic's position of nonfetishistic critical superiority and all-too-comfortingly suggests that we can cordon off "deluded" and "perverted" investments of value and desire from "objective" and "normal" ones.

In what follows, I develop a non-Freudian account of racial fetishism that responds to recent interrogations of the political efficacy of critique by doing something other than critiquing, condemning, and unveiling.[46] Instead, I take Sharon Holland's dictum that "there is no raceless course of desire"—that is, that within racist cultures, racialized eroticism is, for better or worse, normalized rather than the property of the perverse, racist few—as an invitation to account for the process by which race becomes eroticized.[47] Since race is *the* preeminent historical production, the "raw matter" of this eroticizing process is history itself. By developing a theory of the complex connections *and* disconnections between the temporalities of the erotic and those of politics and history, I think through the problem of the relationship between erotics and politics that gay liberation has bequeathed, unresolved, to queer theory.

Dean's *Unlimited Intimacy: Reflections on the Subculture of Barebacking* depathologizes fetishism in order to revalue the expansive and varied eroticization of everything from piss to "the bug" of HIV itself in contemporary gay male barebacking subcultures. Contra canonical psychoanalytic accounts of fetishism as a psychic defense against the traumatic knowledge of women's "castrated" state, Dean proposes an understanding of fetishism as the extraordinarily creative "fantasmatic transformation of objects that have no preordained psychic value" for the purpose of sexual pleasure.[48] Reminding us that a certain psychic labor must take place before even ordinary genitals can be rendered erotic, he contends that, rather than being a minoritarian practice, fetishism—that is, the erotic investment of something not inherently erotic—is, in fact, the condition of *all* erotic desire.[49] Heteronormative cultural scripts stigmatize some forms of fetishism as perverse, disgusting, and "fetishistic," while naturalizing others, such as the male desire for female tits and ass, effacing, in the process, the psychic history of investments that rendered them erotic in the first place.

Dean's investment in depathologizing fetishism leads him to be wary of queer critiques of racial fetishism which, he warns, "tacitly repathologize fetishism" in ways that he finds troubling.[50] Taking on Dwight McBride's protest, in "The Gay Marketplace of Desire," against the dehumanization of a racial fetishism that would reduce him to the stereotypical bearer of a big black cock, Dean, striking the note of a nonjudgmental libertarianism of desire that is also sounded in French gay liberation texts, warns against the "Orwellian" connotations of any effort to submit fantasy to political dictates, even antiracist ones.[51] Dean takes issue with both McBride's humanism and his alleged moralism. He argues that *all* desire "impersonalizes" its objects by fragmenting them into infraindividual partial objects: "Under the sway of the unconscious, erotic desire fragments and partializes those totalized forms that consciously we recognize as persons. It is not whole persons whom we find sexually arousing but partial objects; we find an individual to be arousing by discerning in him or her the lineaments of a partial object."[52] Far from distressing queers, this should be cause for celebration, since desire's depersonalization and partialization of its object dissolves precisely those static, hierarchical identities that Dean, in harmony with much queer psychoanalytic criticism, takes to be the disciplinary basis of social oppression. Desire, for Dean, is necessarily fetishistic, and fetishism fragments the static identities of heteronormativity and racism alike. What McBride should be protesting, Dean implies, is not racial fetishism, but racial stereotyping: "Stereotypes concern identity, not desire; by contrast, fetishism is a form of desire largely independent of identity."[53] Dean's implication is that, as a form of desire that functions independently of identity, fetishism *cannot be racist*, since racism works by reifying identity in the stereotype. He offers a handy method of distinguishing the two operations: "Stereotyping works synecdochically by taking the part for the whole (African American male sexuality is reduced to the big black dick), whereas fetishism works with parts that, strictly speaking, do not form part of a larger whole."[54] Fetishism is saved, as it involves partial objects whose referent is not ever a "whole," and stereotyping alone must be to fault for racist modes of desire. But "racist modes of desire" are precisely what cannot be accounted for here. By insisting that desire and identity are mutually exclusive and that "stereotypes concern identity, not desire," Dean leads us to counterfactually conclude that neither identities nor stereotypes, including racial stereotypes, are capable of inciting desire. Hence, according to his own logic, there can be no racist desire—no desire that is animated by racist stereotypes rather than innocently and, one must suppose, arbitrarily racialized part-objects.

While Dean proposes *the part for a whole* versus *the part for itself* as a handy formula to distinguish the synecdochal stereotype from the self-referential fetish, *both* what he terms a stereotype *and* what he terms a fetish are more aptly characterized by the *metonymic* formula, *a part for a series of other parts*.[55] I will work through this claim through a reading of Dean's own primary example of the eroticization of "the bug" of HIV. If "the bug" became a fetish in gay barebacking cultures, it is because, during the decades of the AIDS virus's deadliest career among gay men, HIV became a figure for a metonymic chain of contagious social abjections as well as for the peculiar riskiness, filth, and appetite for destruction of gay male sex itself.[56] What Dean underlines is the fact that, in fetishizing the bug, gay men not only took on and eroticized, but also transfigured this historically specific series of phobic narratives, so that the HIV *also* came to signify the desire for "unlimited intimacy," free of condoms and *inside* the body, as well as a kind of biological kinship with the one who infected you and the chain of those who, together, infected him. Dean's study of the fetishization of the bug of HIV does not, in fact, conform to his formula—*the part for itself*—since the desire of barebackers is not for

HIV *in itself* as a sexy partial object, but for the incoherent series of narrative fragments—operative both in homophobic culture and in gay male cultural elaborations of it—responsible for infusing "the bug" with erotic power. The fetish here indexes neither deluded social value nor perverse desire, but a creative and erotically efficacious telescoping of *multiple* histories within one erotic figure. It is *both* HIV's historical complex of associations around death, risk, filth, and gay abjection *and* their subcultural elaboration into versions of kinship and intimacy that we might understand as constituting the invisible history that, condensed into this particular fetish, renders it, for some, so powerfully erotic.

Racialized sexuality operates less through the fixed and oversimplified identity Dean associates with the stereotype than through the powerfully erotic condensation of a series of incoherent partial narratives, historical in origin, described above as the workings of fetishism. Granted, in the case of racial fetishism, these narrative fragments are associated with personages in a way that nonhuman fetishes like the bug are not. Such erotic/phobic personages should nevertheless be held apart from the coherence and reductive simplification associated with the stereotype.[57] What I want to term instead the *erotic/phobic assemblage* is incoherent and contradictory rather than schematic and oversimplifying.[58] As a fetish, its erotic power condenses that of a series of historical narrative fragments. What we are dealing with, then, is not a part for a whole—the big black cock for the big black buck—but rather a part for a heterogeneous metonymic chain of other parts, each of which may have its own history. Dean poses identity and the stereotype as contrary to the fragmentation of the self that is the always queering and indeed, implicitly utopian function of desire. By contrast, the erotic/phobic assemblage might help us to deidealize the value of self-shattering in much psychoanalytic queer theory, since such an assemblage is capable of at once inciting racist desire *and* propelling sexual self-annihilation. To illustrate what I mean by this, I will analyze examples of racial fetishism from the FHAR's *Three Billion Perverts* and Genet's *Thief's Journal* (*Journal du voleur*) and *Our Lady of the Flowers* (*Notre-Dame-des-Fleurs*).

In a transcribed discussion between self-identified Arabophiles from *Three Billion Perverts* published under the telling title "The Arabs and Us" ("Les Arabes et nous"), certain discussants describe, as a central aspect of the erotics of passive anal sex with Arab men, an experience of self-dissolution much like that which a certain psychoanalytically influenced tradition of queer theory has enshrined as exemplifying the shattering of social identities in sex. M. at one point declares, "I want there to be no more persons, no more egos. What I want: is a functioning that produces pleasure, which is incompatible with the encounter of two persons who stand face to face [*s'affrontent*]. I don't want to be a person."[59] M.'s highly articulate understanding of sexual pleasure as having nothing to do and, in fact, being *incompatible* with selves, egos, and identities uncannily predicts Bersani's and Dean's accounts of the erotic.[60] His language more immediately evokes French gay liberation activist, theorist, and FHAR member, Guy Hocquenghem, who was himself influenced by Deleuze and Guattari's *Anti-Oedipus* (1972). In his 1972 classic, *Homosexual Desire* (*Le désir homosexuel*), Hocquenghem theorizes the cruising and public sex culture of men who have sex with men as exemplifying the ontology of desire as an impersonal, uninterrupted flux. The flux of desire continually produces machinic sexual assemblages whose sole characteristic is to *function*, that is, to be erotically efficacious, destroying, in the process, gendered desiring subjects and objects. For Hocquenghem, the tendency of sex toward machinic, antihumanist connections undoes social identities and disintegrates subject/object, self/other, active/passive, male/female, and oppressor/oppressed binaries.

Unlike utopian Freudo-Marxists, Hocquenghem does not necessarily see sex as the foundation of better social order or gay liberation as a movement to bring about a better world. He writes, "The gay movement is a wildcat movement because it is not the signifier of what might become a new form of 'social organization,' a new stage of civilized humanity, but a crack in what Fourier calls 'the system of the falsity of civilised loves.'"[61] In his insistence on the disintegrating, disorganizing, corrosive power of sex, Hocquenghem, more than other gay liberationists, anticipates the queer theoretical orientation some have named *queer negativity*. Nevertheless, in his faith in the politically resistant, and indeed, revolutionary potential of sexual practice, as well as his certainty that, in its queer essence, *sex is itself anti-identitarian*, he is very much of the Freudo-Marxist liberationist moment. Hocquenghem reveals that the shared foundation of French homosexual revolutionaries was less a faith in the utopian social potential of "liberating" "repressed" sexuality than the more general conviction that sexuality, in its essence, is a force uniquely suited to overturn the hierarchies and challenge the identitarian divisions on which the (capitalist, imperialist, patriarchal) social order rests.

If Hocquenghem, Deleuze and Guattari, and other anti-Oedipal thinkers credited sex and/or sexual desire with the utopian capacity to overthrow the Oedipal coding of the symbolic order, and therefore, society itself, it was because a "structuralist social contract"—influenced by Jacques Lacan and

Claude Lévi-Strauss and with far-reaching ramifications in family and immigration policy—had previously located the bedrock of the Symbolic order, the social, and the nation alike in, precisely, Oedipal kinship. In Camille Robcis's analysis, this structuralist social contract, in fullest force from 1945 to 1970 in France, reified an idealist version of kinship and "sexual difference" at some distance from empirical and historical transformations in family structure and gender roles.[62] In mandating free and frequent sexual exploration, particularly across categories of age and race, as a politically transformative good, homosexual revolutionaries displayed a more empirical and praxis-oriented view of sex and gender. Their sexual practice, nevertheless, reveals the idealism of the premise, inherited from structuralism, that liberating sex would dissolve French civilization and the identities that composed it. Not only did the practice of revolutionary sex *not* immediately dissolve the French social order; it also proved detrimental to the FHAR's ideal of coalition—between gay men, pederasts, lesbians, and feminists, as well as between homosexuals and Arabs. The major political weakness of their sexual ideology—as is suggested by FHAR lesbians' protests at the FHAR's centering, in theory as in practice, of a gay male culture of cruising and public sex, advocacy of pederasty and pedophilia, and dismissive attitudes toward rape and other modes of sexual domination and coercion—was that it failed to address all the ways in which sex in a not-yet-utopian society routinely fails to overturn power hierarchies and social identities and, indeed, often seems to be disquietingly animated by them.[63]

Hocquenghem might therefore be profitably reevaluated as a precursor to Bersani-influenced psychoanalytic queer negativity.[64] This is a disturbing genealogy, since Bersani himself critiques all those involved in "the redemptive reinvention of sex" as echoing the rhetoric of sexual liberationism, which he presumably eschews.[65] Hocquenghem, however, and after him Bersani, outline an alternative gay liberationist affective orientation, one that I term *liberationist negativity*. Rather than celebrating the positive ethical and political value of queer erotics, liberationist negativity remains trained on the corrosive effects of queer sexuality on identity and the social order.[66] Psychoanalytic queer theory, exemplified by Bersani's "Is the Rectum a Grave?" and *Homos*, Lee Edelman's *No Future*, and Dean's *Unlimited Intimacy*, encodes liberationist negativity's affective history in its positioning of jouissance and/or sexual desire as the privileged site(s) through which the social order and its identities can be shattered.[67] Taking as a given the inescapability of power throughout the social, identitarian, and political field, this lineage credits sex and/or jouissance with the unique capacity to destroy something otherwise pernicious and intractable about how social power works. We have seen how, for Dean, the magnetization of erotic desire by partial objects rather than wholes empowers it to fragment the disciplinary social identities of race, gender, and sexuality. For another example, we need only return to Bersani's "Is the Rectum a Grave?" After deflating any illusions that white gay men or lesbians are any less racist, sexist, or politically conservative than other U.S. citizens and emphatically assenting to Catherine MacKinnon's and Andrea Dworkin's theses on the inescapable isomorphism between penetrative sex and social power, Bersani nevertheless locates a certain utopian redemption in sexual self-shattering. If, as he writes, "the self which the sexual shatters provides the basis on which sexuality is associated with power," then jouissance destroys the fundamental unit of politics and power in its ecstatic shattering of the self.[68] Such an investment, however negative, of some aspect of sexual practice with the possibility of destroying, if only during the momentary yet repetitive instant of jouissance, that which anchors the social order inherits the utopianism of liberationist negativity. This is less the familiar queer utopianism of sex positivity than the no less utopian investment of sex with the unique power to shatter the foundation of the political order itself.

Having situated psychoanalytic queer negativity as the heritor of liberationist negativity's acidic utopianism, let us return to M.'s *racialization* of self-shattering. Presenting himself as the most articulate theorist of the group, M. analyzes sex with Arabs as the ideal means of attaining the dissolution of his ego that he understands to be the apex of sexual enjoyment. The devil is in the details here, and M. makes it clear that in order to achieve the desired annihilation of his personhood, he pursues exclusively passive sex with an interchangeable series of Arab men who do not, or who are not permitted to, pursue any relation beyond the anonymous fuck. What he seeks, in other words, is precisely the highly eroticized figure of the aggressively phallocratic Arab-Islamic bugger that French gay men at the time were teaching one another to anticipate and to desire as well as to criticize and to fear. For M., the pleasure of such an encounter is that "you feel negated, killed, by this Arab who butt-fucks you [*qui t'encule*]. And it's awesome."[69] At this point, G. and P. have already articulated various components, which they sometimes problematize, of their desire for passive anal sex with Arabs, such as an indiscriminate search for "erect cocks," "the desire to feel like a hole," a means of "consuming virility," and a mode of desire in which "you think of sticking them in your ass, and that's all. And it stops there."[70] M. goes on to analyze the workings of racial fantasy that sustain such fetishistic desires in a locution that shifts from "me," detailing his own fantasy, to "he," contrasting it with the Arab's lack of any fantasy life, to "we," joining his subjectivity to that of the other white French men in the group: *"Me,* I get off [*jouis*] intellectually on the idea of abandoning myself to him. *He* fucks, but he doesn't have that intellectual distance. *We* remain intellectuals playing at abandoning ourselves to savagery, to the beast."[71] Crucial to the pleasure of white self-annihilation is a highly scripted fantasy scenario, in which the white man, who fancies himself as an intellectual with a highly developed ego and psychic life, abandons himself to "the Arab beast," himself brutely unthinking and devoid of any fantasy life, who proceeds to execute the white man and annihilate his highly developed subjectivity with his giant cock, while releasing "the beast that sleeps within"—the "beast" of subjectivity-destroying jouissance inside of the "civilized" white man.[72] What M. desires is neither the part for itself—Arab cock—nor the part for a whole—Arab cock for the tyrannical Arab bugger—but rather a scripted fantasy scenario whose positions are enabled by the mutual interanimation of a series of racist historical fragments—the bestial and uncivilized native, colonialist hierarchies of intelligence and psychic complexity, despotic Orientalist Arab hypervirility, anticolonial Arab masculine potency, the sexual threat of a postcolonial "Arab invasion," gay liberationist Arab phallocracy, and so on . . . The erotic/phobic narrative fragments thus assembled are historically and logically incoherent—the uncivilized native beast occupies an entirely different position within European-authored evolutionary, civilizational, and historical hierarchies of being than the Oriental despot. This assemblage is called up, not because it makes sense, obeys historical progression, or corresponds to intellectual and political beliefs, but because it is *efficacious*—it impels the ecstatic self-annihilation that, for M. and psychoanalytic queer theory, constitutes the apex of sexual intensity. Within this scenario, the erotic/phobic assemblage—what Dean would assimilate to the stereotype—at once *incites desire* and achieves the depersonalizing shattering of self, ego, and identity more efficaciously, one is led to believe, than would sex with mere (white) human beings. Fetish *versus* stereotype, stereotype *versus* desire, racist dehumanization *versus* universal depersonalization . . . the boundaries simply will not hold.

M.'s account is of crucial interest in its underlining of the *temporal* aspect of self-shattering. His narrative delineates a mode of sexual ecstasy ignited by the explosive incompatibility of the temporalities inhabited by the white man and racialized other. The complimentary play of echoes between the "Arab beast" and the "beast" released within the white man indicate that jouissance is fantasized simultaneously as the release of the (racialized) inhuman within the (white) human and as a devolution to an archaic stage in species evolution. In other words, M. is fantasizing a *shattering-into-archaic-beastliness* impelled by the encounter of civilized white time with the prehistoric time of the racialized other. Here, the specificities of the history of Arab racialization are lost in *the fantasy of the prehistoric*—itself a historical product of colonial racial "science"—which might well be evoked, with equivalent efficacy, by an interchangeable series of nonwhite ethnicities. The use of the trope of prehistoric beastliness to render distinct nonwhite ethnicities ahistorically equivalent is apparent also in the illustrations that accompany "The Arabs and Us." These illustrations reprise the popular French comic starring the white French boy, Bibi Fricotin, and, beginning in 1947, his African friend, Razibus, and depict them having oral and anal sex. Razibus was drawn, at the time, using extremely simianized racial iconography, such that he appears more monkey than boy. When contextualized in relation to the text, the result is that the African as monkey signifies the Arab, and that this conjoined figure of simianized racialization is the object of Arabophilic desire. Simianization is key here, since it is a figural rendition of the European scientific racist fantasy that nonwhite peoples were further down the evolutionary scale, and closer to man's evolutionary past as ape, than white men. The white sexual fantasy of being shattered, by passive anal sex with nonwhite men, into prehistoric time, relies on a slippage from the specific histories of black and/or Arab racialization to the fantasy of race as a figure for the prehistoric inhuman itself.

Genet himself proves adept at manipulating both fragments of racialized history and fantasies of temporal incommensurability in the service of erotic self-shattering. In a passage from Genet's 1949 *Thief's Journal*, the narrator, Jean, who has spent the novel playing assistant and would-be sexual submissive to more masculine outlaws, temporarily enters into a reciprocal and tender relationship with the young Lucien. He cannot help but be nostalgic, however, for his ideal lover, the brute Criminal. To stay his nostalgia, he evokes the following erotic fantasy of being fucked by the black thief, Sek Gorgui, in prison:

> The big black [*le grand nègre*] will stretch out gently on my back. The black, vaster than night, will cover me. Gently, but with sure precision, his tool will enter me. It will not tremble. It will not jerk hastily like mine. That presence within me will so fill me that I shall forget to come. All his muscles will be conscious, however, of being the tributaries of a virility converging

at that hard and violently charged point, his whole body quivering for its good and its happiness. We shall be motionless. He will drive deeper. A kind of sleep will lay the black down on my shoulders; I shall be crushed by his darkness, which will gradually dilute me. With my mouth open, I shall know he is in a torpor, held in that dark axis by his steel pivot. I shall be giddy. I shall have no further responsibility. I shall gaze over the world with the clear gaze that the eagle imparted to Ganymede.[73]

It is surely no accident that, at the very moment when the narrator seeks to call up the fantasy of the perfect brute male, his body a mere tributary of his penis, capable of crushing the narrator in the darkness of his unadulterated physicality, it is a *black* thief that he evokes. For Jean's fantasy is fundamentally about being relieved of the burden of thinking subjectivity, and that relief is racialized as *darkness*. The passage above therefore metonymically connects a range of darknesses—of black skin, of pure corporeality without mind, and of the superlative savagery and hypervirility of black criminality. Just as in M.'s theorization of racialized desire, the choice of this assemblage is in its efficacy in disintegrating the white self—Jean envisions being crushed and dissolved in the unthinking, massive, embodied darkness of the black penetrator. As in M.'s description of sex with Arab men, Jean's fantasy is also implicitly about being freed from temporality. The black thief is imagined as inhabiting a dark night at once liberated from and "prior" to the diurnal rhythms of work, culture, and social participation. Jean's ecstatic release from his embodied white selfhood is therefore of a piece with his dissolution into the atemporality of the black's vast prehistoric "night." By the end, Jean emerges renewed, light and unburdened, with a fresh clarity of vision described as being drawn from classical, rather than African sources. He has stolen this renewal from the black thief, who lies torpid and asleep over him, fixing Jean's body in place and relieving him of worldly responsibilities while allowing his poetic vision to sail. By embodying the soporific darkness of unadulterated corporeality, the black top allows the white bottom to become pure vision without subjectivity, freed from the material body the black penetrator has occupied, the self he has dissolved, and the diurnal temporality he cloaks in night.[74]

So compelling is the fetish of black African difference that when Jean endeavors to recall a moment when he saw his cellmate Clement Village sobbing, he can think only of his mythical black penis—"He was weeping. His lovely eyes were swollen with tears that ran down to his mouth. 'Oh! Oh!' But I, here, all alone, remember only the elastic muscle he dug into me without using his hand. I remember that living member to which I would like to raise a temple."[75] Just as the gay liberationist Arabophiles' desire for the erotic/phobic assemblage of the Arab bugger may render a *political* relationship with their Arab sex partners antierotic, Jean's myopic focus on Clement's all-powerful phallus keeps him from wondering at the possible reasons for an incarcerated black man's sorrow. Far from an innocent fetish, as Dean suggests could conceivably exist, for a black penis that would represent nothing outside itself, in the passage above, the black penis's potency and animacy (Jean refers to it as "this living member to which I would raise a temple") is borrowed from the historical narrative fragments—of colonial conquest, racial pseudoscience, and racialized Enlightenment oppositions of light and darkness—that are eroticized *through* it. This is what Frantz Fanon theorizes, not as a stereotype but, more precisely, as "a historical-racial schema" that whites have "woven ... out of a thousand details, anecdotes, and stories."[76] Though this historical force proves efficacious in pleasurably disintegrating Jean's self, it may well be as injurious to people of color as it is contrary to our interests and potential desires to become in time. A famous passage from "L'expérience vécue du Noir," or "The Lived Experience of the Negro"—bizarrely and misleadingly translated as "The Fact of Blackness"—from *Black Skin, White Masks* depicts the fragments of history that make up the historical-racial schema as composing, not an inhabitable identity, but a violently alien assemblage. For the person of color, the force of the historical-racial schema, which is congruent with what I have been calling the erotic/phobic assemblage, consists in its capacity to explode one's phenomenologically lived sense of one's embodied capacities and potentials. In Fanon's vivid phrasing, the result is "a hemorrhage that left congealed black blood all over my body."[77] Thinking through this image of bloody injury, we might issue a Fanonian rejoinder to Dean: the historical-racial schema is neither a disciplinary identity nor a stereotype from which we can be liberated by the fragmenting operations of erotic desire and sexual jouissance; it is an incoherent historical assemblage that proves, for people of color, directly and painfully shattering, with or without sex; even as, for white racial fetishists, it functions as the preferred instrument for an enjoyably temporary and much sought-after erotic and ecstatic shattering of the self.[78]

    These readings of racial fetishism should lead us to question the idealization, within psychoanalytic queer theory, of self-shattering jouissance as something *beyond* the political that dissolves the social identities on which political orders allegedly rest. Far from destroying social identities, racialized self-shattering *relies on* incoherent histories of race, which it continually reanimates and reinvests with desire and erotic force.[79] To put it bluntly: *sexual self-shattering is not a utopian escape from the social order, but a method of its maintenance.* Rather than being the Achilles heel of racist social orders, sexuality can operate as their *lifeblood*, reinvigorating and nourishing archaic fragments of racial history that might otherwise fall out of collective memory. In fact, I would argue that the source of sexuality's *negativity* is less its fragmentation of corporeal and psychic integrity than its *uncontrollable historicity*—the ways in which its embodied imaginary is continually hurtling backward to violently oppressive historical and cultural pasts. In this sense, racial fetishism is *always* a form of what Elizabeth Freeman has termed *erotohistoriography*, a method of using bodily pleasure to access residues of the past within the present.[80] However, as I will address more fully at the end of this chapter, whereas Freeman aligns erotohistoriography with an unpredictably nonlinear embodied politics of history, racial fetishism demonstrates that the history into which the erotic throws us is as likely to be predictably oppressive as surprisingly counternormative.

For Fanon, the most critical problem is that the temporality of the historical-racial schema, woven from the anecdotes, images, and historical fragments of a racist and colonialist past, entraps the black in past time.[81] As Kara Keeling explains in her important reading of the neglected role of temporality in Fanon's account of blackness,

> According to Fanon, a colonized and civilized society marks a condition of existence in which the black's being is precluded by his perceptible "blackness" because past images, stories, and the like constantly overwhelm perceptions of his present. Under these circumstances, the black is a cliché; the preponderance of commonly available past colonial images of blacks (tom-toms, cannibalism, etc.) flow easily into any present perception of a black and become indistinguishable from it. The circuit thereby created seems to be closed—there is no possibility of a conception of a future that could be different from the colonial past.[82]

Racial fetishism, in the examples we have examined, relies on and eroticizes a temporal incommensurability between white men and men of color. Contrary to 1970s ideals of erotic coalition, this version of racial fetishism excludes the possibility of political solidarity, given that solidarity would require a conception of the Arab and the black as *existing in time*. It would require imagining an Arab sexual partner that is capable of reevaluating his sexuality in response to his sexual interactions with white gay liberationists and of desiring a different political futurity, and thus, as cohabiting temporality with white coalitionists. As Holland remarks, "We often talk of inequalities that emerge in black/white meeting, but we rarely understand those structural impediments and inequalities in terms of the phenomenological readings of time and space."[83] She continues, "It is precisely because the black subject is mired in space and the white subject represents the full expanse of time that the meeting of the two might be thought of as never actually occurring in the same temporal plane."[84] My readings have shown that the trope of the temporal noncoincidence of white subjects and subjects of color powers racial fetishist fantasy. This mode of racial fetishism stymies the liberationist ideal of erotic coalition insofar as it requires the white man and the man of color to occupy incommensurate temporal planes that can only cross, temporarily, in the white man's timeless instant of sexual self-shattering.

EROTIC TEMPORALITIES IN MOTION

During this time period, however, fantasies of racialized timelessness could not have been more counterfactual, as the 1940s through the 1970s saw racialized people form movements—for decolonization, indigenous sovereignty, civil rights, and Black Power, to name a few—that set in motion profound political and social transformations. Far from consigning people of color to a mythic prehistoric or colonial past, Genet's writings of the 1970s and 1980s bear witness to his keen interest in the revolutionary movements of the Black Panthers and the PLO. If, with the FHAR's Arabophiles, we see the more typical case of a racial fetishism that stymies political coalition, in Genet, we see what some critics have interpreted as the more hopeful example of racial fetishism leading, over time, to political alliance. But according to what understanding of the temporality of the erotic is this possible? Can racialized sexuality "lead to" political coalition in anything like a linear, causal way, leaving fetishism behind as a thing of the past? Or, alternatively, is there such a thing as "progress" in erotic life; that is, did Genet continue to eroticize black and Arab men while replacing problematic, outdated, and backward narratives with the more empowering ones furnished by the political movements of people of color? This set of questions requires a reframing of the temporalities of the erotic as temporalities *in historical motion*.

Linda Williams credits black activists for having forever transformed the stereotype of the black "buck," a scare figure produced to protect the plantation regime of white patrilineage, by transformatively reinhabiting it as a position of resistant and erotic black power. As a result, she suggests that while contemporary pornographic depictions of black men as hypersexual may make the archaic and phobic black "buck" scare-figure distantly vibrate, they are primarily attuned to the novel erotics of black power: "The 'iteration' of the refunctioned stereotype does not deny it, but uses it in historically new ways that are more erotic than phobic."[85] Williams's optimistic understanding of the historical transformation of phobic figures as both progressive and unidirectional allows her to confidently assert that, in porn, the black stud stereotype appears dressed in its historically refurbished and nonphobic attire.

In his posthumously published 1986 memoir of his political activism, *Prisoner of Love* (*Un captif amoureux*), it is often the case that when Genet calls the Panthers to memory, a sexualized imagery comes to mind. At one point, he pauses in the midst of a sexual analogy in order to explain why it is that the Panthers necessarily evoke phallic images of male sexuality:

> At the beginning of 1970 the Party still had both the suppleness and the rigidity of a male sex organ: and it preferred erections to elections.
>
> If sexual images keep cropping up it's because they're unavoidable, and because the sexual or erectile significance of the Party is self-evident. Not so much because it was made up of young men, great screwers who would just as soon shoot their load with their women in the daytime as at night, but rather because their ideas, even if they seemed rather basic, were so many sprightly rapes committed against a very old and dim but tenacious Victorian morality.[86]

Capitalizing on precisely the historical transformation to which Williams referred, that of the bestial black rapist into the politically resistant and sexually potent black man, Genet uses black male hypersexuality, in which he professes to not *literally* believe, as the hermeneutic through which to read Black Panther politics. He understands the Black Panthers' novel political ideas as ideological "rapes" of an outdated white bourgeois morality and visualizes their affective politics of black pride and resistance as a rising and supple penis. We would be right to interrogate the effects of such a masculinized reading of a political movement which, however much it sought to project a mediatized image of black male prowess, also put many *women* into positions of power and concretely enacted a politics of collective nurturance, offering community health care and free breakfast and shoes for schoolchildren.[87] Bracketing this concern, however, we might ask whether this constitutes an example of the historical transformation in the racialized erotic imagination to which Williams refers, one that, in Genet's case, might allow eroticization and politicization to coexist. In *Prisoner*, the erotic lexicon of Black Power, premised on a defiant and heroically virile political subjectivity, seems to supersede the archaic black sexual brute of Genet's novels of the 1940s.

And yet, as the Genet quote above exemplifies, there is no way not to feel the vibration of archaic racist narrative fragments in their historically novel, putatively reclaimed versions, whether they are authored by Genet, the Black Panthers, or contemporary pornographers. The archaic black savage and plantation-era black buck both resonate in the resistant sexualized masculinity of Black Power. It is, in fact, the older iterations, and the affectively dense histories of pain, fear, humiliation, and arousal they evoke, that lend the historically reclaimed version both its power and its redemptive promise. Historical narrative fragments touch off complex conmingled affects that, while seemingly contradictory, have been historically conjoined to one another; humiliation and pride, fear and arousal color one another and call one another up. Hence, it is impossible to say that the newer version is "more erotic than phobic," while implying that the older one was more phobic than erotic, as if the erotic and the phobic components could be surgically separated and measured. The erotic charge of a powerful black masculinity draws from and transfigures the fear and humiliation of the set of historical narrative fragments it reinhabits and transforms. But in erotic and affective life, transformations are never complete, new versions reactivate historical narrative fragments, and transfigurations always risk reverting to an older form.

As Williams herself notes, one intent of the sexualized masculinity of Black Power was precisely to strike fear into white Americans by inhabiting and redeploying the phobic plantation-era figment of the marauding black buck. Genet's telling choice of "rape" as a metaphor to describe the Panthers' challenge to the "Victorian" morality of the U.S. white middle class is indicative of the extent to which he remains attuned to those aspects of Panther rhetoric and self-presentation that reclaim and rework more abject and phobic racialized historical fragments. If this is the case, it is because, as we have seen, Genet had long been erotically responsive to precisely those colonial and slavery-era narrative fragments that the Panthers sought to reinhabit, transform, and put into political and temporal motion. Unlike the assemblage of narrative fragments that had formerly composed blackness, the resistant, powerful masculinity of Black Power was capable of political action and oriented toward futurity. Through it, Genet's long-standing racial fetishism of black men, *without becoming any less fetishistic,* could be reoriented toward an erotics of political potency. If Genet could write, in *Prisoner*, that the armed young Palestinian *fedayeen* appeared to be "not merely a transfiguration but also a materialization of my fantasies,"[88] it is because Genet's erotic life was sensitized to the erotic/phobic scenarios of colonial and decolonial desire—in this case, the incoherent assemblage of historical fragments regarding Arab men that were set vibrating by the mediatized 1970s images, projected throughout the world, of "Palestinian terrorists."[89] By taking colonial-era narrative fragments that deemed blacks and Arabs sexually dangerous and excessive and reinvesting them with a bold and resistant political power, the Panthers and the Palestinians went to work directly on the white racial erotic imaginary. Their innovations engendered a form of racial fetishism that could be *turned on* by political potency, but unstably so, since such an arousal risked reanimating less politically viable fragments of racial history.

I want to emphasize here that the aspects of Genet's activism with the Panthers and the Palestinians explored in chapters 4 and 5 did not supersede Genet's racial fetishism. We might envision this racial fetishism as an undertow pulsing beneath the other erotic, political, and temporal currents of Genet's pull toward these two movements. Racial fetishism does not "lead," strictly speaking, to anything outside itself; it does not "become" something other than itself. It may carry one *into proximity with* certain groups, thereby allowing a different sort of relation to them to develop, but its temporalities, distinct from those of political transformation, ensure that, rather than "intersecting" with the political, racial fetishism, as a separate, multitemporal undercurrent, may only resonate or interfere with it.[90]

CODA: QUEER TIME/RACIALIZED TIME

Contemporary iterations of proud minoritarian identities are not detached from the volatile and not merely unidirectional affective history they redeem and redeploy. Reflecting on a collection of highly personal writings by Gary Fisher, many of which give voice to his desire to enact, with white male tops, historically charged scenarios of interracial domination, violation, and degradation, Robert Reid-Pharr writes:

> Even as we express the most positive articulations of black and gay identity, we are nonetheless referencing the ugly historical and ideological realities out of which those identities have been formed. Fisher thus insists that within the process of creating (Black) identity one necessarily traffics in

the *re*articulation of the very assumptions embedded within Jefferson and Hegel. There is no black subjectivity in the absence of the white master, no articulation in the absence of degradation, no way of saying "black" without hearing "nigger" as its echo.[91]

To be clear, this is not because slavery, pathologization, and colonialism are the static and unchanging originary "truths" of contemporary minoritarian identities—the master code through which to read the present. Race is the effect of a contentious multiplicity of strategically deployed "racial projects."[92] Likewise, the set of meanings that adhere to same-sex sexuality have undergone an astonishing mutation within the last generation. But progressive changes won by activists and culture producers do not erase collective historical memory, particularly that which impels affective and erotic response. For there is no unidirectional "progress" within affective and erotic life; reclaimed figures draw on the entire affective force of the history of investments and transformations that led up to them and run the risk of a wholesale reversal into precisely the degrading histories they were intended to redeem.

If, as Dean argues, all sexuality is fetishistic, then it is also true that all sexuality is profoundly and complexly historical. The part-objects, scenarios, and narrative fragments that we find arousing move us to the rhythm of multiple invisible yet felt histories. If our sexuality sometimes responds to "archaic" beliefs and histories we wish were forgotten, it is because sexuality itself is a complex and multitemporal form of collective memory—one which informs us of our own constitution, as erotic subjects, within social orders that produce terror, pleasure, and power out of various forms of inequality and oppression. Conscious thought may undergo political development, abandoning earlier positions for newer ones understood as more enlightened and just, but the temporalities of the erotic are incoherent—at once archaic and capable of stunning metamorphoses, but never orderly or developmental. Racialized erotic life foils the queer theoretical desire to equate queer sexuality with liberation, political resistance, or a movement beyond the social order altogether by confronting us with the irreducibly historical but never simply progressive temporalities of the erotic.

Does the fact that such erotic temporalities are nonlinear mean that they are thereby "queer"? Holland locates a rift between the nonchronological temporalities of queer theory and those of contemporary racism. Citing Freeman's work on the queer capacity of embodied pleasures to counter the logic of temporal development, Holland writes, "Unlike its erotic counterpart—cast as exceeding the boundaries of duration—racism consistently embeds us in a 'past' that we would rather not remember, where time stretches *back* toward the future, curtailing the revolutionary possibilities of queer transgression." Race, she argues, is where the "capricious nonlinearity" Freeman attributes to queer eroticism becomes "an exacting and disabling recursivity."[93] This chapter bears out Holland's point, extending her critique of queer time by investigating what occurs when the nonchronological time of queer eroticism is *racialized*. The nonlinear but assuredly nonliberatory temporalities of queer racial fetishism, we have seen, often pull insistently *backward*, to violent, degrading, and unjust pasts that we would rather not remember and that prove incommensurable with the time of political transformation and becoming. But why is it that queer time should be associated with a politically enabling freedom from the time lines of normative development in the first place? Although sophisticated queer theory has publicly cast off "naive" 1970s accounts of the revolutionary effects of sexual liberation and the efficacy of sex as a method of political coalition across difference, its field habitus remains infused with the intoxicating sexual utopianism of the 1970s, which envisions queer erotics as unlocking revolutionary social, political, and temporal possibilities or, on the antisocial side, as dissolving otherwise intractable disciplinary social identities. In defining erotohistoriography as "a politics of unpredictable, deeply embodied pleasures that counters the logic of development," Freeman exemplifies the ways in which a liberationist affective history animates queer theoretical practice.[94] In noting this, my purpose is less to critique Freeman's generative work than to acknowledge the ways in which, to a queer theorist, nothing could be more natural than to expect to find a gravitational pull between queer erotics, progressive politics, and counternormative temporality. This "naturalness," I am arguing, is itself the product of an incompletely recognized liberationist inheritance. Encoded less in its theoretical apparatus than in the *expectations* and *methods* by which the affectively dense term *queer* bundles together the politically radical, the futural, and the nonnormative, this liberationist inheritance accounts for the fact that work on queer time has tended to be attuned to capricious mobility and alternative futures, in contrast to scholarship on racialized or postcolonial time, which has sought to tend to the still open, still damaging wounds of the historical past.

It is in this very turn toward a difficult past, however, that Jennifer Nash locates a potential synergy between "black time" and "queer time": "'Black time,' to riff on Judith Halberstam's concept of 'queer time,' upsets linear, positivist narratives of historical progress and exposes the 'seething' presence of the past in everyday life."[95] Here I see Nash as gesturing toward the other affective history that resonates within the term *queer*, that of still-aching hurt, damage, and stigma. Queer scholarship, such as Heather Love's *Feeling Backward*, attentive to this affective history, articulates a version of queer time that is nonlinear, if not always capriciously or unpredictably so. This is a form of queer time that pulls recursively back to dark histories, countering the modernist logic of progress and development, but with politically ambivalent or even regressive effects. In its entanglement in disempowering histories of racism as well as homophobia, such a mode of queer time may well spoil interracial queer coalition. It is crucial, nevertheless, to attend to queer temporalities turned toward the seething, haunting past as well as to the open horizon of the future, to queer erotics that fall into the well-worn and predictable grooves etched by power as well as those that forge exuberantly experimental paths. Whereas much work in Queer Studies gestures evocatively toward potential sites of structural symmetry, intersection, and resonance between queer and racialized experience, the approach I advocate documents and accounts for why what *could* theoretically have led to solidarity often *did not*. This noncoincidence, between queer and racialized shame, between queer and racialized marginality, between queer and racialized time, as well as their occasional moments of synergy is part of what work on the seething past is tasked with investigating. Focusing on the ways in which queer time keeps hurtling back to a shameful past it can neither supersede nor shake off puts work on queer temporality into conversation with scholarship on the dilemma of postcolonial and racialized time: that of the stuck past, of historical change that fails to be completely revolutionary, and of identities and communities built out of the emotional detritus of history. This approach is also the only way to contend with those painful, politically ambivalent, and disturbing aspects of our affective histories that *continue to have effects*, even when ignored or disavowed, and that therefore signal unfinished intellectual and activist labor for the present. Such a project is contingent on Queer Studies confronting its liberationist inheritance in order to, at long last, deidealize the queer erotic.

chapter 4

PEDERASTIC KINSHIP

> Outcasts (whether they are prison inmates, refugees, orphans, or queers) try to find new ways to link up with each other, recreate networks of obligation and affiliation that resemble the family, and thus find a place where they belong. Daddy (and mommy) fantasies are one way to make a new, nonbiological family within the subculture of self-aware pervs.
> —PATRICK CALIFIA, introduction to *Doing It for Daddy*

In the above quote, from his introduction to the 1994 volume of queer Daddy/Boy and Girl erotica, *Doing It for Daddy*, Patrick Califia lends BDSM Daddy play a certain gravitas by likening it to the creation of queer families of choice. While the discourse of chosen family is recent, dating only from the 1980s in North America and Britain, Califia's description here has a deeper historical resonance, invoking the pre-Stonewall emotion Christopher Nealon has termed "foundling" and identified as oscillating between a sense of queer exile and wild longings for reaffiliation.[1] By combining the queer historical emotions of exile and longing with the empowering new ideal of freely elected and creatively constructed families, Califia is able to infuse even the stigmatized practice of BDSM Daddy play with the full force of both queer historical injury and reparative aspiration. I am less interested here in whether or not Califia's description of Daddy play as a form of kinship is empirically accurate than in the redemptive logic of his argument. Why is it that identifying a relational form as "queer kinship" implicitly dignifies it, redeems it, and invests it with pathos? What are the limits of such a redemption? This chapter tests the boundaries of the discourse of queer family by investigating an even more sexually, ethically, and politically dubious kinship form than BDSM Daddy play, namely, modern pederasty.

I develop a reading of pederasty as a potential kinship form from Genet's own relational and erotic practices. From his first sexual experiences in the boys' reformatory of Mettray through his last significant relationship with Mohammed El Katrani, Genet's sexuality could never adequately be described as merely "same-sex"; for it to spark, it also required a meaningfully eroticized difference of age or status. As an adult, Genet was repeatedly attracted to adolescents and young men whom he considered to be sexually "normal" and whose liaisons and marriages with women he actively supported. He seems to have adapted to his pederastic attraction to younger men who were not, or not exclusively, homosexual by taking on the fatherly role of a benefactor (his last lover, El Katrani, even referred to him as *père*, or "father") and "sponsoring," so to speak, their heterosexual lives. Particularly as he grew older, Genet monetarily supported the families of each of his young men, even after they were no longer active lovers, a practice which culminated in his simultaneous financial support of three separate households—that of his deceased German Algerian lover Abdallah Bentaga's circus friend, Ahmed Lahoussine, that of his French protégé Jacky Maglia (himself the stepson of Genet's former younger lover, Lucien Sénémaud), his wife and their children, and that of his Moroccan lover, El Katrani, his wife Amina, and their son, Azzedine. In addition, Genet took an active role in both designing and financing the family houses of both Maglia and El Katrani. Genet's pattern of building houses for his younger lovers and financially sustaining their heterosexual households is particularly striking given that Genet himself lived an itinerant life until the very end, staying in hotels or in a tiny corner of his friends' or lovers' homes and owning little more than a suitcase and some books that he would leave on his friends' bookshelves. This pattern also echoes his lifetime habit of insinuating himself into the homes of heterosexual couples. As his biographer Edmund White writes, "The experience was always the same—Genet the precocious child admitted in the morning to the bedroom of his indulgent parents," to whom he would then read what he had been up all night writing.[2]

In his various intimate relationships to heterosexual households, Genet hovered ambiguously between marginalized queer guest, adopted child, and fatherly benefactor. However, he never fully became a part of any home (even the ones he built and sustained himself), nor ever established his own independent home. At the same time, Genet was not only *not* attracted to other homosexual men; he was also what might be called homophobic, bragging about beating and robbing older queer men as a young prostitute/would-be thug, openly disdaining his gay fans, and keeping a sympathetic distance from the French gay liberation movement, which nevertheless took him up as an icon, during a time when he was otherwise deeply politicized. His pederastic eroticization of "normal" men may have acted as a solvent of any identitarian or communitarian bond based on a shared sexual identity.

How are we to read Genet's repeated pattern of insinuating himself into the intimate domesticity of heterosexual couples, of intentionally financing, for his lovers, heterosexual households in relation to which he would be both guest and benefactor, in short, of intentionally perpetuating the regime of heterosexual kinship, property, and domesticity in order to cultivate a place for himself on the edges of it? In a 1983 interview, in reference to his status as an orphan, a ward of the French state, and a foster child, Genet claims, "by escaping from the family I escaped from the feelings I might have had for the family and from the feeling the family might have had for me. I am therefore completely—and I was from very early on—completely detached from all familial feeling."[3] Clearly, this statement gives voice to a profound sense of rupture. Genet's compulsive repetitions of his own position on the margins of heterosexual family renders it equally clear, however, that his professed lack of familial sentiment is more wish than fact. In his own memoir, White reports realizing that Genet "had a pattern of marrying off his lovers and then building or planning to build houses for the new couple in which there would always be a room for him, though he seldom visited," and speculates, "It was as if the abandoned child were creating parents and a hearth to which he'd never be completely welcome."[4] Genet's life patterns are difficult to conceptualize because they require theorizing pederasty as *a kind of relationship to heterosexual kinship*. This version of pederasty is parasitically dependent on heterosexual kinship, going so far as to actively reproduce it in order to reproduce his place on its eroticized margins.

This chapter tests the boundaries of the highly idealized discourse of queer family by focusing on a version of queer kinship likely to revolt contemporary queers. *Pederastic kinship* draws attention to the kinship function of many modern pederastic relationships and theorizes the complex interrelations between pederasty's kinship forms and those of the heterosexual family. I trace the shape of pederastic kinship within Genet's life practices of affiliation, including his habit of introducing himself into the domesticities of heterosexual couples, his practice of financing the heterosexual households of his younger male lovers, and his fantasy of himself as the adopted foundling of the Black Panther Party. By demonstrating that Genet's passionate attachment to the Black Panther Party was structured by an erotics of pederastic intergenerationality, this chapter reveals, as Angela Davis wrote regarding Genet's posthumously published memoir *Prisoner of Love*, "suppressed moments of the history of sixties nationalism" and of sexual politics alike.[5]

IDEALIZING QUEER KINSHIP

As the exergue to this chapter suggests, we queers have had a tendency to imagine ourselves as what Nealon calls "foundlings," exiled from family and from broader networks of belonging and searching, in the mode of both loss and redemption, for some other, better form of affiliation. Though Nealon develops the concept of foundling from a study of queer U.S. fiction from the first half of the twentieth century, this imaginary continues to resonate throughout the twentieth century and even into the twenty-first, with repercussions for the status of kinship in queer scholarship, culture, and politics.

We might discern the pathos of a queer exile from kinship behind the vehemence of radical gay liberationist critiques of the heterosexual nuclear family. The Front homosexuel d'action révolutionaire, or FHAR's conviction of homosexuality's radical opposition to the Oedipal family, like Guy Hocquenghem's certainty that liberating anal eroticism would destroy the entire "house of cards" of French Oedipal phallocracy,[6] transmutes the dross of homosexuality's *exile* from kinship into the gold of its revolutionary *opposition* to kinship. This signature queer structure of feeling predates gay liberation. In 1897, André Gide's character Ménalque, the implicitly pederastic tempter of youth modeled on Oscar Wilde, famously declares, "Families, I hate you! Closed homes, shut doors, jealous possession of happiness."[7] With Ménalque, Gide influentially figures the adult pederast as the youth's liberator from the enclosure and privatization of the bourgeois family. This queer tradition defiantly embraces the position of exile from kinship while seeking to convert the injury of exclusion into the agential force of opposition and critique.

The pathos of exile from kinship generates a powerful longing for return, a longing that has proven difficult to defuse with radical injunctions to oppose the family. It incites idealization—if not of the family, then of *some* form of belonging that would make good on the family's failings. As evidenced by the emotional testimonies of marriage-seeking lesbians and gays during the recent U.S. battles for marriage equality, idealization and nostalgic longing can inform intense desires for legally ratified marriage. A legally recognized nuclear family form need not, however, be the only terminus of these longings. Jeffrey Weeks, Brian Heaphy, and Catherine Donovan remark that their British respondents thought of gay and lesbian chosen families made up of friends, lovers, exes, and sometimes children "as equivalent to the idealized family (and infinitely preferable to the real one)."[8] In her parallel U.S. ethnography, Kath Weston notes that, while many informants affirmed the excitement of creating families outside of established social models, others understood chosen families as a substitute for blood family ties lost upon coming out: "'There will always be an empty place where the blood family should be,' one man told me. 'But Tim and I fill for each other some of the emptiness of blood family that aren't there.'"[9] Chosen family channels both the longings generated by exile from the heterosexual family and the critical injunction to not repeat its hierarchies and exclusions into the creation of a novel form of kinship. Chosen family might thereby be regarded as a foundling form of queer kinship: in it, the pathos of exile, the longing for return, and a critical animus against the heterosexual family meet in the fantasy of finding a family qualitatively different from and better than one's own. The diverse and intense affective energies it magnetizes ensure that a chosen family remains highly idealized as at once free from the contradictions of conventional kinship and uniquely capable of fulfilling the yearnings for love, care, and belonging that the romance of "family" generates.[10]

Gay/lesbian and queer scholarship has frequently abstracted a queer politics and sociality to come from the specific historical narrative that leads from exile from kinship to the creation of queer chosen families. To cite just one example, John D'Emilio ends his canonical article "Capitalism and Gay Identity" by proposing,

> Already excluded from families as most of us are, we have had to create, for our survival, networks of support that do not depend on the bonds of blood or the license of the state, but that are freely chosen and nurtured. The building of an "affectional community" must be as much a part of our political movement as are campaigns for civil rights. In this way we may prefigure the shape of personal relationships in a society grounded in equality and justice rather than exploitation and oppression, a society where autonomy and security do not preclude each other but coexist.[11]

D'Emilio argues for the creation of a utopian social order based on the chosen family model. In so doing, he exemplifies the way in which the idealizations of the discourse of chosen family are often transferred into invocations of queer kinship, politics, and sociality.

The utopian energy with which queer kinship became invested beginning in the 1980s accounts for the redemptive effects of Califia's invocation of exile and chosen family in relation to BDSM Daddy play in 1994. Is pederasty beyond such redemption and thus, outside the bounds of the discourse of queer kinship? Alan Sinfield's assertion that erotic relations between uncles and nephews are a repeated trope within the contemporary Western literature of age-differentiated male same-sex sexuality raises a series of uncomfortable questions about the relation between pederasty and heterosexual kinship. To what extent have relations of mentorship, dependence, and care between intergenerational kin served as a model for age-differentiated couples? In what sense is the *fantasy of intergenerational incest* itself formative of pederastic relations? Thomas, a self-identified pedophile interviewed for *Fous d'enfance* (*Crazy for Childhood*), a 1979 special issue of the journal *Recherches* on pedophilia, speculates, "If a kid gets attached to an adult, he kind of puts him on a pedestal. He is, at one and the same time, someone he looks up to, the brother he'd like to have, the father he'd like to have, the adult he'd like to be."[12] Using the vocabulary of kinship, Thomas asserts that the boy looks up to the pederast or pedophile as an idealized family member, one who might supplement for the absence or failings of actual family members.[13] His notion of an ideal queer kinship that redeems the failings of heterosexual family eerily resonates with the later discourse of queer chosen family. Contemporary queers are more likely, however, to vehemently silence these echoes than to hear, in them, an alternative modality of queer kinship. In at once resonating and clashing with contemporary imaginaries of queer kinship, pederastic kinship calls for the deidealizing work of attachment genealogy.

If pederastic kinship remains untheorized, the examples above make it clear why. Proponents of gay and lesbian chosen family have celebrated its putative egalitarianism.[14] Pederastic kinship's potentially exploitative erotics of hierarchy and difference debases this ideal. In the case of pederastic kinship, the general reticence to think pederasty I analyzed in chapter 1 is intensified by the horror and trauma of incest, even if only metaphorical. The subcultural valorization and public affirmation of queer kinship are contingent on desexualizing intergenerational kinship and blotting out the historical memory of pederastic kinship, as well as of intergenerational lesbian erotic kinship forms. (We might think here of Simone de Beauvoir's legal adoption of Sylvie Le Bon, who was a seventeen-year-old student when de Beauvoir met her at age sixty, in a relationship Le Bon curiously describes as "carnal but not sexual.")[15] Indeed, the first step of campaigns for gay and lesbian family and adoption rights has been to use expert testimony and statistical analysis to disprove the old stereotype equating gays and lesbians with pedophiles and child molesters.

To be clear, I neither presume that all pederastic kinship relations are predominantly nurturing nor seek to dissociate pederastic kinship from abuse. It is hardly my intention to reclaim, for instance, the version of pederastic kinship that prompted Europeans who settled in colonies to claim native servant boys as at once their proxy child and sexual minion.[16] Indeed, situating pederastic kinship within a genealogy of queer kinship need not be a matter of "reclaiming" it at all. Instead, this move might disturb the tendency, within Queer Studies, to equate naming an object *queer* with claiming, for it, an unequivocally positive political value.[17] What is most conceptually challenging about pederastic kinship is that, as an overarching category, it includes *both* pederasty's most nurturing *and* its most damagingly exploitative dimensions.

THE UNTHOUGHT OF PEDERASTIC KINSHIP

Pederastic kinship is difficult to think within the two major twentieth-century discourses defending or politicizing pederasty—gay liberation and homosexual masculinism. French gay liberationists valued pederasty as a total challenge to the Oedipal family, which they took to be the foundational unit by which sexuality was repressed, patriarchal and "phallocratic" social hierarchies internalized, and capitalism reproduced. For these revolutionaries, pederasty presented itself as the ideal means of contesting parents' proprietary ownership of their children and repression of their children's sexuality, which they theorized as the original model for repression in all its forms.[18] Whereas homosexuality could only secede from the Oedipal family, pederasty offered a means of attacking its very principles.[19] Overlapping with gay liberationist writing on pederasty, but less oriented toward the goal of total political and social revolution was a more diverse leftist body of writing during the 1970s that championed pedophilia as an inevitable step in the progressive liberation of sexual morality. In sociologist Pierre Verdrager's analysis, these authors, who were all men, sought to allot pedophilia a positive political value by focusing on the limit cases of sex with an adolescent boy, rather than with either a prepubescent boy or a girl of any age, positioning pedophiles as the sole adults capable of liberating child sexuality from disciplinary institutions including the family, and describing the pedophile-child relation as less asymmetrical than the parent-child relation.[20] In this leftist discourse, the overarching justification for pederasty/pedophilia is its putative capacity to liberate the sexuality of minors from the disciplinary institutions of family and school and to establish a near-egalitarian harmony between pederasts/pedophiles and minors, in contrast with the relations of hierarchy and capitalist ownership between children and their parents.

Nevertheless, the discursive explosion around pederasty/pedophilia during the 1970s allowed other perspectives to emerge.[21] For instance, in debates and commissions hosted by French gay liberation groups, some individuals expressed reservations about the politics of pederasty in relation to the Oedipal family. The chapter on pedophilia in the 1973 publication *Three Billion Perverts: Encyclopedia of Homosexualities* (*Trois milliards de pervers: Grande encyclopédie des homosexualités*), censored as recently as 2002 in the special issue's online publication,[22] opens with a transcribed dialogue between Max, a forty-year-old pederast who prefers adolescents but occasionally has sex with prepubescent boys, and his former boy beloveds, twenty-five-year-old Truc and nineteen-year-old Albert, both of whom are now heterosexual. While both the FHAR and the regional Gay Liberation Groups (GLHs) that would succeed the FHAR's dissolution in 1974 championed pederasty as a means of liberating the sexuality of minors, Max recounts how, inconveniently enough, one FHAR commission of minors campaigned to liberate youth sexuality *from* pederasts. He paraphrases the youth commission as follows: "We don't want to be hit on by guys, forced to make love, as if minors were the sexual objects of pederasts, a Platonic, pedagogical, really reactionary pederasty, guys like Montherlant, Peyrefitte: they say in fact that those guys are old-style pedagogical pederasts, so liberation from school goes with the liberation from those kinds of pederasts."[23] Albert, who affirms that he enjoyed having sex with Max when he was younger but rebelled against his adult authority at seventeen, says, "That's what sucks. What you call the traditional pederast ... it's that in fact you convey a repressive part of the family ... a perverted family since you add sexuality."[24] Max responds that, given strictures against adult-child sex, he had to present himself as a serious, helpful grown-up before the parents, offering to tutor Albert with his math homework, for instance. Truc postulates that, since pederasty is considered so monstrous, pederasts have to operate under the cover of a respectable (and, in gay liberationist thought, oppressive) pedagogical adult/child relation. In saying this, he seems to imply that, if freed from repressive social strictures, pederasty might liberate itself from pedagogical and familial power relations entirely.

The liberationist politicization of pederasty/pedophilia was founded on an idealized opposition between pederasty and the family. One liberationist responds as follows to the hypocrisy of parents' antipederastic arguments, "'pederasts do not respect children, they influence them, they take possession of them.' *All I'm saying is that this is a fight between owners.*"[25] While Scott Gunther quotes this critique as an example of the liberationist thesis pitting pederasts against parents' ownership of children, read literally, the quote negatively identifies pederasts, *like* parents, as would-be owners of children. As all these examples demonstrate, liberationists stumbled on evidence that pederasty's generational divisions often facilitated asymmetrical relations that some characterized as familial, in their pedagogical function as well as their hierarchies of ownership, influence, and authority over children. While liberationists usually sought to reject the notion that adult/child power differentials meant that children and minors were incapable of consenting to or enjoying sex with adults, they found it harder to dismiss these power differentials when they infused the extrasexual dimensions of the pederastic relation. In a contradiction liberationists proved unable to resolve, the inscription of relations of education, kinship, and adult authority *within* pederasty threatened to contaminate it with the regulatory, repressive functions of the nuclear family that it was pederasty's liberationist role to explode. Tellingly, in the dialogue on "Pedophilia," pedagogical, familial pederasty is labeled "traditional" or "old-style," in implicit contrast to the fresh, new, politicized idea of pederasty/pedophilia as a means of liberation.[26]

If gay liberationists lauded pederasty's challenge to the Oedipal family and social structure, the neoclassical reclamation of pederasty trumpeted its coherence with both the patriarchal family and the homosocial state. In *Inversions*, the first French homophile periodical, two men with such opposed politics as Camille Spiess, a Swiss-born fascist sympathizer, and André Gide, a leftist critic of colonialism, both celebrate pederasty as a virile culture-building and nation-sustaining form of homosociality consonant with patriarchal dominion over women's sexuality and reproduction.[27] *Corydon*, Gide's 1920 defense of pederasty, champions a classically influenced pedagogical pederasty, unlike the "pathology" of gender inversion, as a method of training youthful masculinity and discharging excess male sexual energy so as to protect women's sexuality, preserving women for their role as mothers.[28] In the German context, Andrew Hewitt demonstrates that homosexual masculinists, among whom he includes Hans Blüher, Benedict Friedlaender, John Henry Mackay, Adolf Brand, and Friedrich Radszuweit, theorized bisexual pederasty as the joint between the heterosexual family and the homosocial state. For Friedlaender and Blüher alike, the pederastic patriarch's same-sex desire orients him toward the homosocial bonding with other men that they theorize as the erotic impulse behind culture building and nation building. This culture-building homosexual eros, in turn, guards the pederast from the dangers of a feminized and racialized (as Jewish) overvaluation of the family and concomitant disinvestment in the social, making him a superior Aryan man.[29] Overall, French and German early twentieth-century pederastic masculinists, some of whom were anti-Semitic and sympathetic to fascism, envisioned pederasty as solidifying, rather than challenging or providing alternatives to, a stable social and moral order founded on masculine superiority and the exclusion of women from civil society.

Neoclassical masculinists' and gay liberationists' diametrically opposed accounts of pederasty's relation to the heterosexual family share a certain ideological purity. By figuring pederasty as either the joint between the heterosexual family and the homosocial state or as the privileged revolutionary challenge to the Oedipal family and social order, neither discourse leaves much room for the intermingling of pederasty and kinship that informed Genet's and other pederasts' life practices, and that some gay liberationists remarked with consternation. It is instructive that, even as pedophilia was being claimed as a liberatory and egalitarian cause during the 1970s, marginal thinkers on the far right continued laying claim to pederasty as an erotic instantiation of the conservative social values of authority, pedagogy, and hierarchy.[30] This binary—sexual egalitarianism on the left, sexual hierarchy on the right—is the product of a historical failure to cultivate a queer public discourse that is something other than univocally condemnatory concerning the ethics and politics of the erotic inequalities that once defined male same-sex sexuality and that continue, unacknowledged, to animate it today.

PROVINCIALIZING CHOSEN FAMILY

Genet's late writings and life practices are indicative of a particular relationship between pederasty, kinship, and the social order that neither masculinists nor liberationists were able, given their strongly partisan political stances, to explore. This is what I term *pederastic kinship*—not a championing of pederasty as either gluing or opposing the familial social order, but a means of thinking the age-differentiated pederastic relation as, *in and of itself*, an intergenerational kinship form. If pederastic kinship remains unthought within the major twentieth-century defenses of pederasty, it is perhaps because it troubles the purity of ideologies that would locate pederasty's value in either its challenge to or its tidy coherence with the heterosexual family and national social order. Pederastic kinship is a *constitutively impure form*, less an opposition to or exile from family than a "doing" of family differently, a "perverted family," in former boy-beloved Albert's words, given the admixture of sexuality.[31] In its disturbing sexualization of the family and eroticization of generational, racial, and classed inequalities, pederastic kinship generatively unsettles a series of contemporary assumptions about what counts as queer family.

The two best-known models of queer kinship are the 1980s and 1990s Anglophone model of "chosen family"—a "family" of gay and lesbian lovers, friends, exes, and, in some cases, children—and the more recent model of lesbian or gay nuclear family, with or without the legal rights and privileges heterosexual nuclear families enjoy. Since the lesbian or gay nuclear family stays close to heterosexual family structures, blurring the boundaries between heterosexual and queer families more than it queers kinship itself, the chosen family model would appear to be the queerer form. Chosen family is not, however, *the* paradigm for queer kinship, but *one* historically specific mode. As Weston notes, chosen family emerges from a 1980s reinterpretation of the 1970s ethos of "coming out" as a test of family bonds.[32] This model of queer kinship is therefore contingent on an understanding of homosexuality as a primary identity, rather than a sexual practice. It draws on the "ethnic peoplehood" model of homosexuality as the organizing principle of community formation, and therefore, a mode of likeness and potential kinship.[33] Given the constitutive reliance of gay and lesbian chosen family on the trope of identitarian likeness, it is not surprising that North American chosen families of the 1980s aspired to be nonhierarchical and were usually composed of either gay men or lesbian women within the same age and income bracket.[34]

The term *chosen family* presupposes the currency of a neoliberal discourse of choice that enshrines the freedom of the individual to choose everything from her "lifestyle" to her family members. As Elizabeth Freeman argues, by sacralizing choice, chosen family implicitly denigrates the traditional role of family as a site for interdependence, obligation, and responsibility for another's care. Furthermore, it obfuscates the economic and cultural inability of many queers to freely "choose" to abandon the networks of care offered by their "blood" families in order to create a family with other gays or lesbians based purely on affinity, regardless of needs for housing, medical care, citizenship, and financial support.[35] The idea of coming out as a test of family bonds is most resonant within U.S. context where the notion of the individual pitted against the family enjoys great symbolic currency and provides a meaningful lens through which to read struggles between queer progeny and their straight progenitors.[36] Chosen family, then, is a form of queer kinship historically bound to a neoliberal, post-gay liberation time and place. As such, it resonates with queer attachments to the values of egalitarianism, individual autonomy, and elective affinities.

Both the discourse of chosen family and utopian aspirations of the discourse of queer kinship are rooted in a prior sacralization of the family. Why honor your friendships by renaming them as family, after all, unless you consider family a higher form of intimacy? The fact that there is *no parallel* in France to the discourse or practice of chosen family provincializes the sacralization of family and bid to raise friendship to the status of kinship that were so influential in U.S. and British queer cultures.[37] A provincialism is raised to the status of a universal when the historically contingent U.S./British idealization of chosen family is carried over into the theoretical idealization of queer kinship.

Recent U.S. queer of color scholarship has expanded and repoliticized the notion of queer kinship. Roderick Ferguson has argued for an understanding of African American families, which have been vilified as insufficiently heteropatriarchal and scapegoated for African American economic and social disenfranchisement, as queer social formations.[38] Juana María Rodríguez includes, in her expansive list of nonnormative raced and classed families excluded from proper neoliberal kinship,

> multigenerational extended families who cohabit because of economic need, cultural conventions or their own desires; families whose social and sexual networks extend beyond one couple of one household; "unstable" households that are in a state of flux with people entering and exiting as space, money, and need dictate; or families that are denied the ability to live together due to immigration policies, economic need, or practices of institutionalization.[39]

I build on Rodríguez's double move of exposing the neoliberal propriety of dominant contemporary models of queer kinship and expanding the imaginary of queer kinship beyond both gay and lesbian identity and the sacralization of autonomous "choice" by exploring the relation between kinship and same-sex sexuality *prior to* the solidification of queer kinship around identitarian notions of gay and lesbian identity and community.[40] Pederastic kinship is a pre-gay liberation version of queer kinship based neither on an ideal of likeness nor on a shared sexual identity, but on a series of eroticized differences. Though technically a "chosen" relation, rather than sacralizing choice or autonomy, pederastic kinship takes up the reproductive labor of intergenerational transmission and financial, material, and bodily care. As practiced by Genet, it indexes both a disinterest in the emergent notion of homosexual community as a "family" of likeness and a reaffiliation across difference with younger, and often racialized, heterosexually oriented men.[41]

QUEER HISTORICAL ORPHANAGE AND FOUNDLING REAFFILIATION

Genet's practice of pederastic kinship take a "foundling" form. Nealon's *Foundlings: Lesbian and Gay Historical Emotion before Stonewall* argues that queer U.S. authors during the first half of the twentieth century

> were groping their way toward a notion of homosexuality defined by a particular relationship to the idea of history. This relationship, which I call "foundling," entails imagining, on one hand, an exile from sanctioned experience, most often rendered as the experience of participation in family life and the life of communities and, on the other, a reunion with some "people" or sodality who redeem this exile and surpass the painful limitations of the original "home."[42]

Nealon's figure of "foundling" turns on *kinship*—that most basic, immediate, and intimate unit of belonging—as a resonant metaphor for historical and social belonging more generally. It evokes, within the overall category of kinship, the culturally significant distinction between a biological "blood" family generated by heterosexual reproduction within marriage and a nonbiological, adoptive family, forged through voluntary reaffiliation. Affectively, it draws on the pity and vulnerability evoked by the figure of the foundling, paradigmatically imagined as a babe abandoned by its family and left, exposed to the elements, on the doorstep of those who may or may not choose to welcome and care for it. It also suggests the wild hope of redeeming abandonment by being "found" by a loving and caring family. When applied to early and mid-twentieth-century queers reaching for an imagined sense of belonging, foundling "works" by playing on all of the above meanings to evoke the pathos of loss and abandonment as well as a compensatory hope and yearning. Nevertheless, *Foundlings* seeks to stave off the teleological assumption that what foundling authors were reaching for, without living in a historical moment in which they might know it, was either the community of self-identified lesbians and gays that we enjoy today, or the seamless national belonging that both U.S. gay and lesbian civil rights and French abstract universalism promise. This was a time in which queer longings for affiliation had no obvious terminus; rather, they carried with them a sense of openness and potentiality.

At foundling's kernel is the proposition that *a rupture from belonging is also a rupture from time.* Kinship knits sanctioned belonging to time by virtue of its generational dimension—its linkage of the individual into an intergenerational chain that extends both backward into the time of ancestors and forward into the futurity of descendants, with property inheritance and child rearing as the primary modes of concrete transmission mediating between past and future. The relation between kinship and time has been much explored, of late, within queer theoretical scholarship. Jack Halberstam, for instance, has influentially proposed "queer time" as "a term for those specific models of temporality that emerge within postmodernism once one leaves the temporal frames of bourgeois reproduction and family, longevity, risk/safety, and inheritance," underlining the legitimate family's role in regulating and rhythming temporal extension.[43] As a social institution, one function of the family is to extend the wealth and the laboring and reproductive life forces of a bounded, multigenerational group of people over time. However, as the history of the legislation of interracial marriage and the regulation of the citizenship-conferring capacities of marriage, adoption, and legal and/or biological filiation suggest, modern kinship has always also been a biopolitical device for regulating the racialized reproduction of the nation. Since the nineteenth century in France, legitimate filiation's privileged role in cementing the social order and, therefore, the nation has been explicitly theorized as well as materially reinforced through Europe's earliest and most extensive family policy infrastructure. Camille Robcis terms *French familialism* the long-term coupling of the notion of the legitimate heterosexual family as the nonpolitical and ahistorical foundation of the French state and social order and positive policy measures designed to promote and regulate this family form. As demonstrated by the 1939 establishment of the Haut comité de la population, charged with both promoting births and handling immigration policy, and the 1999 passing of the PACS, which granted gender-neutral civil unions the same rights as marriage, *except*, significantly, filiation and nationality, French legal policy and infrastructure has long affirmatively acknowledged the "fundamental interrelation of kinship and nation."[44]

Foundling's proposition that a rupture from kinship is experienced as a break from collective temporality and broader networks of belonging therefore makes a great deal of sense. I turn now to Genet's shockingly understudied short prose piece, "Fragments..." (1954), to flesh out the experience and the social logic of queer historical orphanage, which ensues when practices of same-sex sexuality break the bonds of both hegemonic belonging and meaningful temporal extension. Written during a singularly difficult period of Genet's life, in which, after completing all five of his novels and his first two plays in a mere three years, he experienced a period of literary sterility, fell into unrequited love with Decimo, a young Roman prostitute sick with tuberculosis, and may have attempted suicide, "Fragments ...," whose projected title was originally "Open Letter to Decimo" ("Lettre ouverte à Decimo"), turns its pitiless and despairing gaze to pederasty, which it locates in absolute rupture with the natural, legal, and social orders, with temporal continuity and extension, and even with signification itself.

"Fragments..." fully assents to each accusation in the arsenal of condemnations of homosexuality. Pederasty's principles, it asserts and repeats, are originary culpability, sterility, and death. "Fragments..." describes pederasty as historically adrift, cut off from convention, and incapable of elaborating its "own" coherent ethical and cultural system. Within the "other" cultural system, however, that of heterosexuality, pederasty *does* have a signification—"the notion of rupture" itself[45]—sterility as a rupture from biological fertility, culpability as a rupture from the legal and moral order, and death as the consequence of the refusal of Woman, essentialized here as the necessarily heterosexual principle of life, fertility, and generational continuity.[46] Consequentially, discontinuity fragments the pederast's every gesture and creation, rendering the very notion of a pederastic "civilization" a contradiction in terms. "Accumulating, as it develops, gestures and considerations perverted by notions of rupture, of limits, of discontinuity, it [pederastic civilization] constructs only apparent tombs."[47] This sense of rupture and meaninglessness is perhaps at its most acute in the pederast's sexuality itself. "Is it possible," the speaker asks in an anguished and unanswered query, "that my erotic frenzies constantly turned on myself or on the granite my lovers are, that these frenzies whose aim is my pleasure alone, accompany an order, a morality, a logic linked to an erotics leading to Love?"[48] In its absolute and consequential rupture from the French familialist social order, this is something like pederasty as liberationists imagined it. However, during the historical lag between a bisexual pederasty that could still be imagined as the joint between family and nation and a liberation movement that would celebrate pederasty's challenge to the family as revolutionary while offering pederasts a reparative solidarity with "three billion perverts," homosexualized pederasty languishes in unlivable rupture.

"Fragments . . ." most often uses the French term *la pédérastie* rather than *la homosexualité* and its cognates. At times, it employs the common French usage of *la pédérastie* as an overarching category for all male same-sex behavior, notably in one passage that refers to *ces folles*, "those queens," as *les pédérastes*—two categories which André Gide, for example, would have kept rigorously separate.[49] Whenever an actual same-sex relationship is described, however, it is clear that "Fragments . . ." is using *la pédérastie* in its more specific sense. Here, the pederast is a sexually queer older man whose object of desire is a younger man or adolescent.[50] I propose, then, that the poem's reflections on the relationship between homosexuality, rupture, and time should be read as elaborated specifically from the age-dissonant pederastic relation. This is significant because, whereas a relationship between two homosexual men of roughly the same age might always aspire to long-term coupled domesticity, the pederastic propulsion toward younger men and boys often excludes pederasty from the self-enclosed form of the long-term couple.[51] The impossibility, referenced in the "Fragments . . ." of basing a coherent social order on pederasty alone is overdetermined by the fact that pederasty is not a self-contained sexual system; the pederast's desire often propels him toward nonpederasts who are interested in women or "trade" who use homosexual sex as a means of financial support. As Genet's practice of financing the heterosexual households of his younger lovers suggests, pederasty most often either had to envelop or operate on the margins of the more foundational unit of the heterosexual couple. Traditionally, if not in Genet's practice, pederasty was defined as a temporally bounded relation—the younger partner was expected to outgrow pederasty in order to pursue women, and the elder to lose interest once the younger began to grow facial hair.[52] Incapable of providing the foundation for a self-enclosed couple, much less a family, and often sustainable only in the short term, homosexualized pederasty meant at once a queer historical orphanage from heterosexual kinship and the network of continuity, belonging, and meaning it cements, and an inability to completely reject or escape it. But if pederasty is a failure, a rupture, and an exile within heteroreproductive national-historical time, it may also provide an untimely conduit for queer transmission, extension, and affiliation. Queer historical orphanage is the *prelude* to the imaginative longings for reaffiliation and alternative belonging Nealon terms *foundling*. But what would an *enacted*, rather than imagined, form of foundling reaffiliation actually look like?

In an important late interview, Genet responds to a question about his perverse admiration of Hitler during the Nazi occupation of France by locating his status as an orphan, along with a chain of disaffiliations and reaffiliations that radiate from it, at the origin of *both* his early admiration of Hitler *and* his late identification and belonging with oppressed people of color:[53]

> I remind you that I have neither a father nor a mother, I was raised by Public Welfare, I found out very early on that I wasn't French and that I didn't belong to the village—I was raised in the Massif Central. I found this out in a very stupid, silly way: the teacher asked us to write a little essay in which each student would describe his house. I described mine; it happened that the teacher thought my description was the prettiest. He read it out, and everyone made fun of me, saying, "That's not his house, he's a foundling [*un enfant trouvé*]!" and then there was such an emptiness, such a degradation. I immediately became such a foreigner [*un étranger*] ... oh! The word isn't too strong, to hate France is nothing, you have to do more than hate, more than vomit France, finally I ... and ... the fact that the French army, the most prestigious thing in the world thirty years ago, that they surrendered to the troops of an Austrian corporal, well, to me, that was absolutely thrilling ... When a nation is so completely subdued by military force, one has to admit that France was humiliated, and I can only adore someone who had wrought the humiliation of France. Afterwards, I could only find myself [*me retrouver*] in oppressed people of color and in the oppressed revolting against the Whites. Perhaps I'm a Black whose color is white or pink, but a Black. I don't know my family.[54]

This passage smacks of a certain self-mythologization and of a rather transparent desire to excuse his erstwhile praise of Hitler by relating it at once to the pitiful story of an abandoned child and to his more admirable political sympathies with the racialized oppressed. However, insofar as the key feelings Genet describes—hatred of France, disidentification with France and with his own white Frenchness, glee at the Nazi humiliation of France, and identification with the political movements of colonized and formerly enslaved people of color—are consistent with what he expresses in his writings from the 1940s through the 1980s, it is worth taking seriously an emotional logic that may, at first, strike us as repugnant. The passage delineates a series of conceptual leaps—between being a foundling and not having a right to the house in which he lives, between being denied a home and not being French, between hating France and being overjoyed at its humiliation by Hitler's troops, and between the overall national estrangement he associates with foundling and his inability to be at home except with oppressed people of color, indeed, his claim to *be* "a Black whose color is white or pink."[55] In closing with "I don't know my family," Genet neatly ties the knot by reemphasizing his abandonment by his birth family as the origin and the cause of this temporally extended train of hatreds and sympathies, disaffiliations and reaffiliations, disidentifications and cross-identifications. This is a disturbing attachment genealogy, to be sure, of the value, idealized within Queer and Critical Race Studies scholarship, of transnational and interracial coalition.

Genet describes this train of associations as having an identifiable origin—his maternal abandonment—and a discrete precipitating event—the schoolchildren's traumatizing mockery. His investment of the stigma of maternal abandonment with such consequential power reproduces and sustains the "gendered mandate demanding that women 'mother' those they birth, and mother them in ways that are legible to normative models of care."[56] However, the ways in which the anecdote ties Genet's legal status as a foster child to a vast web of meaning that stretches to encompass the world-historical events of the Nazi invasion of France, decolonization, and Third World revolutionary movements suggest that the passage traces the affective impact of a social logic rather than explaining a relation of causality. The conceptual leaps in the passage above accurately delineate the bonds that glue imagined communities of racial and national belonging under French familialism, while demarcating those excluded from those communities, however nominally "white" or legally "French" they may be.[57] They prescribe that a foundling—fostered, during a period before children could be legally adopted, in exchange for payment by the state welfare service until age twelve—is not kin, will inherit neither the family patronym nor its property, and, thus, lacks a home, that most basic symbol of belonging.[58] With no home or family that can be said to belong to him, the foundling, who comes from afar, in turn, does not belong to the village.[59] In spelling out to the boy Genet his exclusion from each of the organic unities of family, home, and village, the schoolhouse children are practicing "estrangement," which, as Nayan Shah reminds us, is "an active process of forcible dislocation, removing people from 'an accustomed place or set of associations,' souring the grounds of shared 'membership' by sowing feelings of hostility, distrust, and 'unsympathetic and indifferent' regard."⁶⁰ While Shah is dealing with the estrangement of migrant workers in North America, Genet reminds us that, in Third Republic France, the conceptual connection between nation and lineage was so strong that even a French citizen by birth and ancestry could become estranged from *la patrie* when proper lineage was disfigured by prostitution, illegitimate reproduction, and state-sponsored fostering.⁶¹ Although, in the narration above, estrangement appears to happen all at once and definitively—in one fell swoop that awful day in the classroom—it may be more helpful to understand the classroom story, whether invented or real, as the allegorization of a process of, in Kobena Mercer's words, being "unhomed by nationality and not identifying with France" that must have occurred over a span of years, if not decades, as Genet was made to feel queerly different and gradually acquiesced to, then famously embraced that unbelonging in the form of flight, pederasty, desertion, and crime.⁶² While, notably, pederasty makes no appearance in the passage above, at other points it figures as one of the primary outcomes of Genet's maternal abandonment. The narrator of *The Thief's Journal* (*Journal du voleur*) states, "Abandoned by my family, I already felt it was natural to aggravate this condition with the love of boys, and this love with theft, and theft with crime or a complacent attitude in regard to crime. I thus resolutely rejected a world which had rejected me."⁶³ Like Nealon, Genet deploys foundling's full set of mythic meanings as a ruptured relation to both heterosexual kinship and national historical belonging. He converts his literal status as an orphan into an account of queer historical orphanage by playing on the structural symmetries between ruptured heterosexual lineage, the sense of being abandoned and "unhomed" by the *patrie*, or paternal nation, and a pederastic exile from kinship and nation alike.

The schoolhouse quote invaluably spells out the connection between the two poles of queer historical orphanage and foundling reaffiliation across Genet's entire lifespan of attachments and revulsions. In it, queer historical orphanage leads to a disaffiliation with France so extreme that an admiration for Hitler, who humiliated and defeated France, is its logical consequence. This is less a foundling reaffiliation with the racially purified "community" proposed by National Socialism than a fantasy of vengeance in estrangement. Genet goes on to suggest that his lifelong sense of queer historical orphanage eventually propelled him into a politicized reaffiliation with oppressed people of color. This claim is borne out at other moments when Genet evokes the centrality of the foundling structure of feeling within political movements and coalitions. Genet claims in a late interview, "The Panthers put into play an entire affectivity that we lack, and this affectivity did not come from the fact that they were of African descent, that they're black; it's simply that they're banished, they've been banished and outlawed for four centuries, and they found each other again in the expression 'brothers.'"[64] Genet here attributes the stereotypical emotional expressivity of black Americans neither to biological race nor to cultural "difference," but rather to a political and historical transformation with an intense affective dimension—the movement from being "banished" within a white supremacist society to finding one another in the black idiom of politicized kinship expressed by the terms *brother* and *sister*. Genet describes the "festival" of togetherness that united him with the hunted Palestinians similarly in *Prisoner of Love*: "The days and nights spent in the forests of Ajloun, between Salt and Irbid, on the banks of the Jordan, were a celebration, a fête. A celebration that can be defined as the fire that warmed our cheeks at being together despite the laws that hoped we'd have deserted one another. Or the escape from society into a place where people were ready to fight with us against that society [*s'échapper de la communauté afin de rejoindre un lieu où, contre elle, nous retrouverons des complices*]."[65] Genet is consistent in his repeated returns to this particular structure of feeling—a "festival" or an "affectivity" that unites the oppressed in exclusion—a feeling that seemed to fulfill his foundling longings for reaffiliation out of the condition of queer historical orphanage.

I situated homosexualized pederasty in "Fragments . . ." as languishing in a time lag between bisexual neoclassical pederasty and oppositional gay liberationist pederasty. This should not be taken to mean that Genet's sense of pederasty as lived rupture was waiting to be redeemed by either the revolutionary futurity and expansive imagined community that gay liberation would offer pederasts a couple of decades later or the version of homosexuality cleansed of pederasty and congenial to coupled stability that would solidify during the 1980s. Rather than imagining foundling as a yearning forward toward the historical achievements of today, we may better conceive of it as a "sideways" movement animated by potentialities that have not been fully realized by the political gains of the present and an affective energy that could not be satiated by belonging to either a gay and lesbian community or a national "family," and not only because these promises remain inadequately achieved.[66] Foundling is probably best understood not as a socially named and recognized emotion, but as an affect that had not found its form or a "structure of feeling" that had not yet precipitated into any prescribed narrative.[67] It led Genet to bypass the forms of politicized belonging through sexuality offered by gay liberation in the early 1970s in order to seek an erotic kinship across difference and generation with the Black Panthers and the Palestinians.

PEDERASTIC KINSHIP IN REVERSE

White informs us that sixty-year-old Genet was in love with the twenty-seven-year-old David Hilliard, the Panther Chief of Staff charged with Genet during his two-month-long speaking tour of U.S. colleges in 1970. Such an infatuation should not be understood as merely homosexual and interracial, but specifically as *pederastic*, sparked, as was Genet's sexuality in general, by eroticized differences of age, generation, and race. When Genet details a fantasy concerning Hilliard in *Prisoner*, however, it is not a sexual pederastic fantasy, but an eroticized fantasy of kinship. And rather than imagining himself as the benevolent white father of Hilliard and, by extension, his historically novel and generationally youthful movement, Genet places himself in the position of a child. Voicing one of our central questions here, he asks, "What did it mean, my pink and white presence among them?" and responds, unexpectedly, "This: for two months I was to be David's son. I had a black father thirty years younger than myself. Because of my ignorance of America's problems, perhaps also because I was naïve and not very strong, I had to seek a reference point in David. But he was very careful with me, as if my weakness had somehow made me dear."[68] Voiding the common association of age as synonymous with wisdom and power, Genet here elaborates a generationally reversed and racially improbable kinship from the conditions of his middle-aged white Frenchness—his ignorance of black American politics, his aging body, and his uncertainty in a novel national, racial, and historical context. As a balding, physically fragile, comparatively ignorant white and pink "infant" who barely speaks any English, Genet happily places himself in the care of Hilliard, who in turn, appears to hold him dear (Hilliard and Genet would remain friends for many years, and Hilliard at one point intended to write a book about Genet's involvement with the Black Panther Party).[69] As Kobena Mercer notes, Genet rejects the horizontal political trope of brotherhood or fraternity with the Panthers for the vertical fantasy of being parented.[70] This fantasy of intergenerational kinship is elaborated from a specifically pederastic attraction. It echoes Genet's pattern of assuming the position of "child" in relation to heterosexual households, though he was sometimes the same age or older than the "parents" he created. What are the implications of Genet's *reversal* of the pederastic age differential and interpretation of pederastic erotics in explicit kinship terms?

A passage from *Prisoner of Love* that stages Genet's fantasy of adoption by the Panthers in the mythic register of foundling offers an entry point into these questions:

> Instead of a child, they'd [the Black Panthers] discovered an abandoned old man [*un vieillard abandonné*], and that old man was a White... It was like the fulfillment of a very old childhood dream, in which strangers, foreigners—but more like me deep down than my own compatriots—opened up a new life to me. This childishness, almost innocence, was forced on me by the Panthers' kindness, which it seemed to me they bestowed on me not as a special favour but because it was their very nature. To become an adopted child when one was already an old man was very pleasant: it brought me both real protection and an affectionate education [*une éducation affectueuse*]. The Panthers were well known for their pedagogical qualities.[71]

By whom or by what was this old man abandoned? While it is true that Genet was abandoned by his mother as an infant and never knew his birth family, the expression "an abandoned old man [*un vieillard abandonné*]" suggests either a more temporally recent or a more ongoing form of abandonment. Genet suggests that by taking him in, the Panthers not only allay his ongoing sense of abandonment, but also fulfill "a very old childhood dream," one of foundling reaffiliation with a foreign people more like him than his own countrymen. Both the transnational and collective dimension of Genet's foundling dream and the deep and ongoing sense of abandonment conveyed by the expression "abandoned old man" indicate that he is not simply describing a literal orphan's desire for a new family. Rather, his status as an orphan resonates with and intensifies queer historical orphanage's broader sense of exile from familial and national belonging. Here, queer historical orphanage is, specifically, an orphanage from the French nation that requires, as a counterweight, adoption not merely by a new couple of parents, but *by an entire foreign people*. Finally, in characterizing the Panthers as essentially pedagogical, parental, and kind, particularly in relation to an old pederast, Genet offers us a countermemory of the Panthers that contradicts their dominant image (explored in greater detail in chapter 5) as macho thugs.

Although Genet may have lived his foundling fantasy, it appears to have remained a *fantasy* insofar as Genet was neither *really* kin to the Panthers, nor *actually* Hilliard's son. This would seem to be an example of the common use of kinship as a metaphor to convey a strong subjective sense of identification and belonging. Or is it? Anthropologists have long understood kinship to be a series of social practices that orchestrate small-scale social relations rather than an essentialized relation of biological descendance. Though "kinship" is often used metaphorically to name little more than a sense of identification or an imaginary of belonging, scholars attentive to kinship's social, material, economic, and temporal aspects should be wary of ignoring the *practice* of kinship. Freeman warns specifically against jettisoning "the centrality of bodily dependence and renewal to kinship," reminding us that "as a practice, kinship is resolutely corporeal. Its meanings and functions draw from a repertoire of understandings about the body, from a set of strategies oriented around the body's limitations and possibilities."[72] Such strategies typically include imagining one's patronym or descendants as extensions of oneself in the face of one's own time-bound bodily mortality, caring for physically vulnerable ill, elderly, or young kin, and, in a capitalist society, performing the work of social reproduction in order to physically and emotionally renew one's kin for the labor force. In each of these examples, kin are called on to supplement and fill in for the limitations of one another's bodies. As a series of social practices, kinship acknowledges responsibility toward others' bodily limitations. Genet's relationship to the Panthers, which is structured around the vulnerability of his aging body and which solicits the Panthers' protection and vigilance, might thus be said to enact kinship as a social practice of bodily care.

When Hilliard insists on calling a doctor for Genet's flu, Genet says to him, "You're a mother to me."[73] If Genet's relation to Hilliard can be described as kinship, it is certainly one of kinship's queerer forms. It reverses both the pederastic age differential and, at times, Hilliard's gender while violating the taboo on miscegenation to forge an interracial kinship bond. More significant than its perversions and violations of the heterosexual kinship rules of a static order of generational succession, a single fixed gender position per person, and the idealized exclusion of eroticism from filial bonds, however, are the *ends* of this relation's techniques of renewal. As Freeman points out, heterosexual kinship's extension, supplementation, and renewal of bodily limitations also occurs on the level of duration, responding to the temporal mortality of human bodies by asking the descendant to carry on, extend, or conserve the legacy of the ancestors, typically in a way that reinforces normative social hierarchies and values. If this is the case, then what exactly would queer kinship seek to extend in time? In "Fragments . . ." so absolute is pederasty's rupture from heteroreproductive temporality that Genet cannot imagine pederasty "reproducing" anything other than death itself. As he elaborates in an important footnote, "Signification of pederastic passion: it is the possession of an object that will have no other fate than the fate required by the lover. The loved one becomes an object charged, in this world, with representing death (the lover)."[74] So severed from the heteroreproductive world of renewal, reproduction, and life is pederasty that the pederastic "relationship" can only be described as the pederast's deadly effort to reproduce himself in his young beloved, turning the beloved into an object that reflects only the pederast. In the process, the beloved is twice killed, once as an autonomous individual, and once again, since the pederast he represents is himself, the incarnation of death in a heteroreproductive world dedicated to life. In "Fragments . . ." the temporality of pederasty is so ruptured, so damaged that it can extend nothing, bind no relationship, and elaborate no culture. In a nightmarish version of Edelman's "no future," it can only reproduce its own figuration as death, metaphorically killing the other in the process.[75]

This may be an intriguing view of pederasty for a queer theorist, but it is not one that a pederast can live with. As he emerged from the suicidal depression in which he wrote "Fragments . . ." and acquired new life through politicization, Genet also developed a new understanding of pederasty. His later reflections on pederasty's generative and pedagogical aspects suggest that homosexualized pederasty may, indeed, transmit *something* across time, though this something may not resemble the pedagogies of national belonging and capitalist productivity articulated through proper heterosexual kinship. In a 1964 interview with *Playboy* magazine, Genet describes pederasty's "pedagogical aspect":

> I have of course made love with all the boys I have taken care of. But I wasn't concerned only with making love. I have tried to re-create with them the adventure that I had, an adventure whose symbol is bastardy, betrayal, the refusal of society, and finally, writing, that is the return to society by other means. Is this attitude peculiar to me? Pederasty, because it places the pederast outside the law, obliges him to question social values, so that if he decides to take care of a boy, he won't take care of him in a dull and simplistic way. He will show him the contradictions, both of reason and of the heart, that are imposed by a normal society.[76]

Sinfield has proposed that age-differentiated models offer "a way for lesbians and gay men to reproduce their kind: some girls and boys may pass through, serially, to the woman's or man's position, and so on from generation to generation" and names Genet as "a notable individual who was involved in such a sequence."[77] In the above quote, however, Genet describes pederasty less as a serial reproduction than as a form of queer pedagogy. This pederastic pedagogy *does* seek to transmit or extend something to the younger partner, but this "something" is less a content than a queer orientation—a critical disposition toward a "normal society" and a trajectory that leads from social marginality to "a return to society by other means." In the interview, he goes on to explain that his latest boy, Jacky Maglia, stole cars and that this made it immediately clear to Genet that Maglia should become a race car driver, returning his antisocial energies to society in a noncriminalized and indeed, remunerated mode that still allowed for the charged and foreshortened temporalities of risk and speed. Maglia was the stepson of Genet's former younger lover Lucien Sénémaud, best known for his starring role in Genet's 1950 erotic short film, *Song of Love* (*Un chant d'amour*). Genet had known Maglia since he was eight or nine years old and had always exerted a strong influence on him. Edmund White is careful to point out that Genet's infatuation with Maglia, and thus any potential sexual relation with him, did not begin until Maglia was about twenty-two.[78] Regardless, Genet's long-standing paternal role in Maglia's life all but literalizes pederastic kinship's incestuous combination of filiation and sexuality.

"In every case, with young people," Genet continues, "I have had to invent, to take account of their temperaments, their characters and tastes, each time to do something that resembles a creative act."[79] Genet is noticeably upbeat. Whereas in "Fragments . . ." he required the pederast's annihilation of his object of affection in his meaningless effort to repeat, through him, his own sterility, here, he envisions pederasty as a creative rather than a deadly act, as a mode of nurturance that helps develop something unique about the beloved youth, rather than condemning him to "represent" the elder, and as a queer education in how to live a life more or less *within* the bounds of the law, but for ends the law cannot anticipate. In a letter, Genet tells a high school boy he was trying to influence that there are "an infinite number of ways to escape bourgeois culture, and it's up to you to find the one that suits you best."[80] What draws Genet to these usually heterosexually oriented youths is a certain perverse antisociality he intuits within them, which he seeks to cultivate as the principle of a marginalized art form and thus "a return to society by other means." While this in some ways resembles a parent's efforts to direct their child toward meaningful and socially productive activities, what Genet seeks to nurture is precisely what is queerest, most perverse, and most antisocial in these youths. His hope is that, rather than casting him out of society altogether, the youth's perversity might give rise to a socially recognized form of creativity.

Genet's late pederastic practices thus answer to the aspiration "to have something queer exceed its own time" that Freeman identifies as central to queer kinship.[81] As we saw earlier, however, most of Genet's younger lovers ultimately pursued marriage and heterosexual reproduction, some in houses he helped them to buy. Pederastic kinship is therefore an impure and paradoxical form. On the one hand, its relation to heterosexual kinship is necessarily *parasitic*. As we have seen, the homosexualized pederast's erotic relation to a nonhomosexual means that the pederastic couple can neither constitute its own independent nucleus nor form a stitch in a larger fabric of belonging with other homosexuals. The pederast's fatal attraction to heteronormativity threatens to render him insufficiently queer—his foundling reaffiliation is with heterosexuals living in conventional family units, not with other sexual deviants with whom he might elaborate alternative social and cultural forms. At the same time, however, Genet's pederastic relationships constitute a literal kinship form irreducible to that of the heterosexual family. As long-term small-scale relations of intergenerational affective and material dependency, Genet's relation to his lovers' heterosexual households is more accurately described by the language of kinship than by that, say, of sexual friendship. Insofar as kinship is always also a relationship to time and an effort to extend something in time, Genet's pederastic relations, in their pedagogical dimension, can be said to enact a form of kinship transmission. Genet's pederastic kinship attaches to heteronuclearity in order to attempt to transmit, through it, a stylized deviance that cannot be contained by the identitarian concepts of homosexual or heterosexual. As a response to the experience of queer historical orphanage, pederastic kinship might be thought of as the erotic attempt—with no guarantee of success—to reproduce a *livable* deviance that passes into and through heterosexuality to reattach the pederast, in an untimely beat, to history.

If pederasty can function as a queer education, an effort to repair a temporality damaged by queer historical orphanage, and a queering of kinship, it nevertheless challenges the egalitarian ideal at the heart of recent celebrations of queer kinship. The version of pederastic education Genet describes enacts a relation of power characterized both by the elder partner's liberty to creatively mold the trajectory of the younger and by the conversion of eroticized social differences into kinship dependencies. Pederastic kinship's fusion of social, erotic, and kinship inequalities is elaborated from existing social hierarchies. It risks cultivating an attachment from which, for the socially subordinate partner in particular, *there may be no possibility of autonomy or escape*. Genet's lover, prior to Maglia, was the German Algerian Abdallah Bentaga, who had been working as a stable boy for circus horses when Genet met him. Deciding that he would become a high-wire artist, Genet convinced him to desert the French army, into which he had been conscripted during the Algerian War of Independence (which Genet considered a war against his own people, since Bentaga was Algerian), paid for his training, traveled across Europe as his manager, and designed his acts, which grew more and more dangerous. The measure of Genet's enthusiasm for Bentaga's career may be taken by the 1957 prose poem he dedicated to Bentaga, "The Tightrope Walker," which infuses this socially and artistically marginalized creative form with outsider glory. This enthusiasm, however, was cut short when Bentaga fell during a high-wire act that Genet had designed for him in Kuwait, injuring himself so badly that, no longer capable of his former acrobatic feats, he would be forced to gradually retire from performance. Confined to a Paris apartment financed by Genet during the last years of his life, Bentaga obsessively devoured Genet's books as he quietly watched his lover champion Maglia's career as a race car driver.

As the author of Bentaga's career and of that career's demise, Genet bears responsibility for Bentaga's depression and suicide, committed with sleeping pills Bentaga bought for Genet. Genet's heavy-handed pederastic pedagogy effectively killed Bentaga, who seems to have grown dependent on his white, famous, and comparatively wealthy lover's approval, and who would have been hampered from remaking himself by the literally murderous racial climate that reigned in France during and just after the Algerian War of Independence.[82] The Paris Massacre of 1961, in which police violently repressed a protest by the FLN, killing, by some estimates, hundreds of Algerians and other North Africans and throwing their bodies into the Seine, took place two years after Bentaga's injury and three years before his suicide. The power that Genet exercised over Bentaga as a result of his combined pederastic dominance and cultural, racial, and financial capital ensured that Bentaga *would not recover* from Genet's loss of interest in him. Bentaga's suicide grimly illustrates the very real dangers of pederastic dependency, particularly when intensified, in an interracial relationship, by white privilege. Genet may have understood himself as a marginal figure, a queer "outlaw" who was not "French," a "black" with pink and white skin. Yet the tenacious effects of his French nationality and white skin could not be dislodged by his repeated practices of disidentification and unbelonging.

If Genet's white Frenchness proved stubbornly immobile, his pederastic kinship with the Panthers elaborated a novel relation to racial difference via a flip in generational time. The reversal of generational time that we see in Genet's relationship with the Panthers in general and David Hilliard in particular, however, is not unrelated to the stuck time of white privilege that he inhabited with Bentaga. Mercer has suggested that Genet's late political activism with the Panthers and the Palestinians was a means of mourning Bentaga.[83] I propose that Genet's greatest tribute to Bentaga was not "The Tightrope Walker," but rather the reconfiguration of generational time and of pederastic kinship that he elaborated in his alliance with the Panthers.

When Genet claims that his alliance with the Panthers fulfilled a "very old childhood dream" in which foreigners "opened up a new life to me," we should understand this literally.[84] Genet's trip to the United States in 1970 was a lifeline, lifting him out of the lassitude and depression—marked by his attempt to claim his own life in 1967—in which he had sunk after Bentaga's suicide. Reeducation was an integral part of this sense of renewal. Genet's references to the Panthers' "pedagogical qualities" and to the "affectionate education" they gave him resonate with his own understanding of pederasty's erotics of pedagogy. Panther pedagogy taught the reasons for and methods of counterhegemonic struggle, envisioned socialist alternatives to racial capitalism in the United States, and emphasized black estrangement in order to refigure black Americans as belonging, not to the U.S. nation, but to decolonizing peoples across the globe. Could the Panthers have seemed like "kin" to Genet insofar as their radical pedagogy recalled to him his own journey from criminality to writing, a trajectory which he had already made into the principle of a pederastic form of kinship based on the intergenerational cultivation of something—particular to each person—that exceeded the demands of capitalism and of the nation? In enacting his childhood dream of being a foundling taken in by a foreign people more like him than his own countrymen, Genet reverses his pederastic differential with the Panthers—rather than identifying something antisocial in the Panthers that he seeks to cultivate, Genet becomes like a child to better learn what queer excesses the Panthers seek to cultivate *in him*. In the process, he defuses the potential of existing racial, generational, and cultural hierarchies to overdetermine the meaning of his relationship with the Panthers (the Panthers' very need for a famous white European spokesperson demonstrates the extent to which such hierarchies set the stage for Genet's presence in the United States).

As a movement, the Black Panther Party actively cultivated the kind of identification and kinship to which Genet so eagerly responded. As Amy Ongiri has shown, by figuring themselves as *the* revolutionary vanguard movement within the United States and offering up black American oppression *the* transferrable blueprint of identity-based oppressions, the Panthers—at times inaccurately remembered as an identitarian black nationalist movement—solicited and invited identification and reaffiliation not only from other ethnic nationalist movements, but also from those who might understand themselves as oppressed due to their gender or sexuality.[85] This pedagogy, in which they enlisted Genet, employed transversal modes of identification, affiliation, and, most expansively, belonging in order to propagate the desire for a revolutionary alternative to a racist and exploitative social order. The history of the Black Panther Party's solicitation of transversal modes of identification and affiliation and early efforts to form alliances with the Women's Liberation Movement and the nascent Gay Liberation Movement are perhaps what Angela Davis had in mind when she wrote that "Genet's *Un Captif Amoureux* reveals suppressed moments of the history of sixties nationalism."[86]

In reversing the order of generational succession between Hilliard and himself, Genet eschews the position of the benevolent White Father, ready to transmit a canonical understanding of Marxism to wayward black subproletarian Marxists. By positioning himself as the son of Hilliard and, by extension, of the collectivity of the Panthers, Genet acknowledges his relation of debt to the Panthers, both as the beneficiary of their bodily care and as one transformed by their transmission of a revolutionary alternative to racial capitalism. To be clear, although this temporality is oriented toward the future and suggests a certain degree of critical agency in its reversal of the pederastic differential of age and power, I am not arguing that an individual can choose to intervene in her own erotic structures or sever them from the past for the sake of ethics or politics. To the contrary, the pederastic patterning of Genet's erotic inclinations might itself be understood as evidence of the social structuring of sexuality. As I argued in chapter 2, Genet's pederasty was the by-product of explicit efforts to school the embodied sentiments and sensations of delinquent minors in the boys' penal colony of Mettray by creating affective attachments to "family-like" all-male hierarchies. This version of pederastic practice is constituted as reversible across the course of a lifetime—within the prison subcultures Genet describes, although initiated into sexuality as a younger receptive partner, at a certain age, one must outgrow that position for that of the older, insertive partner, changing at once one's sexual orientation (toward younger, instead of older men) and one's sexual position (from receptive to insertive) so as to avoid being feminized and labeled a prison queen. This sexual "progress" is never complete; it leaves, as its remainder, the tender memory, and even the practice (White argues that Genet never became fully a top), of the pleasures of sexual receptivity, being protected, and receiving an affectionate education. I have argued throughout that there is no "progress" within erotic life, only the superimposition of more recent erotic imaginaries or the resignification of older erotic structures. Ideally reversing once and only once across the course of a lifetime, pederasty retains, in its psychic life, a *virtual* reversibility, whether or not this is ever acted on. This capacity to reverse generational roles may be inherent in the form of modern pederasty practiced by Genet, constituted as it is by the impossible injunction to move definitively from the position of pederastic youth to that of pederastic elder. By drawing on pederasty's potential for reversibility as well as his historically constituted foundling longings for reaffiliation, Genet practiced a reversed form of pederastic kinship with the Panthers that both mourned Bentaga and served as a tribute to him.

CONCLUSION: THE QUEER USES OF PEDERASTY

Insofar as pederastic kinship at once evokes and troublingly eroticizes the privileged patriarchal relation between a father and a son and pedagogical relation between a mentor and a pupil, it begs the question of what exactly is being taught or transmitted within such a practice of kinship. Historically, for many pederasts within privileged economic and institutional positions, what has been transmitted within the pederastic relation is patriarchy and social privilege. As I have argued, however, pederasty is neither historically nor structurally uniform. Genet's pederastic practice, drawn from penal and subproletarian cultural norms, sought to transmit a critical disposition and to cultivate perverse, though not necessarily "gay" excesses and resistances to capitalist productivity and nationalist belonging. The mode of kinship Genet understands as being offered up by the Palestinians and the Panthers is based more on exclusion, estrangement, and disinheritance than on a proprietary identity, and seeks to transmit alternatives and revolutionary wishes more than inheritances and traditions. It actualizes a form of queer kinship based as much on desires to be reparented and reeducated into alternative modes of belonging as on eroticized differences. "Orphaned" from his own nation by the ruptures in affiliation of illegitimate birth, maternal abandonment, and pederasty, Genet's trajectory leaps over gay liberation to reattach, with an untimely beat, to the Panthers' very different history of oppression, estrangement, and struggle, which he allows to "reparent" and reeducate him. This version of pederastic kinship constitutes one of the potentials of the sideways reaffiliative energies of the foundling structure of feeling.

Though pederastic kinship may fulfill some of what queer scholarship desires from relational forms, I do not want to lose sight of all that is troubling about its potentially exploitative inegalitarianism, political multivalence, and parasitical relation to heterosexual kinship. As we have seen, rather than seceding from, opposing, or providing an independent alternative to heterosexual kinship, pederastic kinship remains parasitically dependent on it. This is a version of queerness libidinally drawn to heterosexuality, one whose pedagogies, which must pass through heterosexual kinship, are not guaranteed any degree of success. Whereas some versions of queer theory have tended toward a certain purity, claiming as "queer" negation and antisociality, on the one hand, or utopian alternatives that escape capture by the major social scripts of power, on the other hand, pederastic kinship is nauseating in its constitutive *impurity*. What could be more normative, after all, than the culture of extramarital male sexual license, from which women have been barred, on which pederastic kinship relies? The impurities of pederastic kinship disappoint the historical desire, which animates the discourse of chosen family, for a queer kinship form appreciably distinct from and politically and ethically superior to the heterosexual family. In cleaving to patriarchal structures of social power as often as it deviates from them and incompletely distinguishing itself from heterosexuality, even as it innovates novel relations to kinship, history, and generational/racial/transnational difference, pederastic kinship moves intimately *athwart*, rather than *against* heteronormative kinship.[87] It is this political polyvalence of pederasty, the impossibility of definitively claiming it for any one critical or political function, that renders it such a potentially transformative object for queer scholarship.

But what about pederasty's constitutive inequalities? Was Genet's pederastic pedagogy really a cultivation of something unique within the beloved, or was it instead a narcissistic "creation" of the beloved in the pederast's image? Were his and other pederasts' offers of career assistance, money, and housing less examples of kinship as a form of care than mundane payments for sexual favors, or worse, means of sexually exploiting more economically and socially vulnerable young men? Pederastic kinship is an ambiguous form in which it is difficult to distinguish kinship from domination, coercion from care. What pederasty might reveal, however, is that this holds true for kinship and sexual relationships more generally, in which abuse, coercion, and inequality are the flip side of interdependency, pedagogy, and care. Rodríguez reminds us that "most of the sexual contracts we enter have everything to do with various forms of coercion that are mandated by the social bonds we inhabit. Whether with a partner, date, trick, or wife, sex in all its forms can become a social obligation that is offered in exchange for dinner, domestic harmony, rent, safety, or our own sexual pleasure."[88] Neither "trade" economies nor familial obligations can be definitively shut out from queer kinship and sex. This is not to deny that pederasty's inegalitarianism and attractions across social difference, when combined with sexuality, can reproduce the social vulnerabilities of age, class, national origin, and race in ways more extreme than in the forms of kinship and relationship sanctioned today. However, the impulse to brand pederasty as *essentially* coercive, dominating, and abusive, *in a way that other sexual and kinship relations are not*, makes pederasty the scapegoat for inequalities from which no relationship, and certainly no form of kinship, can be free. Pederastic kinship functions as a productively disturbing attachment genealogy when it restores power and inequality to overly idealized imaginaries of queer kinship.

chapter 5

ENEMIES OF THE STATE: TERRORISM, VIOLENCE, AND THE AFFECTIVE POLITICS OF TRANSNATIONAL COALITION

If there was one question that interviewers would consistently ask Genet after 1970, it was the "why" of his impassioned activism with the Black Panthers and the Palestinians, which compelled him to displace himself to go directly to the aid of these movements. For two months in 1970, Genet traveled underground in the United States with the Panthers, giving speeches on their behalf at a total of fifteen universities. He cut his visit short only when he was summoned by immigration authorities, having been denied a visa due to his sexual deviance and suspected communism. Over the next two years, Genet traveled to the Middle East five times to visit Palestinian refugee and militant *fedayeen* camps, pausing his visits only when, placed under surveillance during a 1972 trip to Jordan, he unwittingly led police to a Palestinian friend who was arrested and beaten immediately thereafter.[1] Having accompanied his close friend Leila Shahid to Beirut while ill with throat cancer in 1982, Genet was among the first witnesses of the aftermath of the massacre of Palestinian refugees at Shatila, a sight which moved him to pen "Four Hours at Shatila" ("Quatre heures à Chatila") and to begin writing his political memoir, *Prisoner of Love* (*Un captif amoureux*), in belated fulfillment of his 1970 promise to Yassir Arafat to write a book about the Palestinian revolution.[2]

Such a close involvement with movements not considered to be one's "own" was rare, even during this highly politicized time. Although interviewers' interrogations were therefore predictable, Genet nevertheless responded to them with a certain impatience. In a 1983 interview, he meets such a question with his own interrogation. He begins by recounting taking a train, in England, that was full of Jewish Brits traveling to Israel, and continues, "I imagine that you wouldn't stop to wonder why the English would go to help Israel when it was in danger. Why are you asking me the reason for going to help a people in danger? There were affinities between the English Jews and Israel. Between the Palestinians, the Panthers, the Red Army Faction, and myself, there are affinities. And it's natural for me to go and help them."[3] Genet's retort denaturalizes taken-for-granted assumptions about the necessary relationship between religious, ethnic, or national identity and engaged activism, assumptions that would deem it "natural" for English Jews to help a beleaguered Israel, but that would find curious the compulsion of a white French pederast, raised Catholic, to fly to join the Palestinians. To be sure, Genet never argues that his activism was simply a principled matter of doing what is just. Here, he claims that a sensed affinity as strong as that between English Jewish Zionists and Israel binds him to the Palestinians, the Black Panthers, and the German Red Army Faction (RAF). This chapter further layers the attractions to these movements explored in chapters 3 and 4 to excavate another source of affinity. What the Black Panther Party, the PLO, and the German RAF all had in common during the 1970s and 1980s was their media portrayal, in Europe and North America, not as political movements, but as illegal criminal and/or terrorist organizations advocating violence and hatred against the political system of sovereign states itself. Jérôme Neutres remarks, "Of the organizations he supported, Genet remembers above all what renders them indefensible in the eyes of Western public opinion: terrorism," a fascination that proved costly to the French reception of *Prisoner of Love* as well as to Genet's own reputation.[4]

During the late 1960s and the 1970s, the U.S. government reacted to the perceived threat of the Black Panther Party's advocacy of armed self-defense and radical critique of U.S. racial capitalism by branding the party an illegal criminal organization and a threat to national security. Vice President Spiro Agnew declared the Black Panther Party a "completely irresponsible anarchistic group of criminals" and FBI director J. Edgar Hoover famously named it "the number one threat to the security of the United States."[5] The nation's very recent transition from legalized white supremacy, with Jim Crow laws reigning in the South, to official liberal antiracism led the FBI to codify its concerted campaign of repression against the party as one against "black nationalist hate groups." Ironically, the FBI coopted the antihate language of the civil rights movement to justify state violence against a movement that sought to empower black communities in the United States and to transform the interlocking systems of capitalism, neo-imperialism, and white supremacy that continued, post–civil rights, to oppress them. This was the public face of COINTELPRO, the FBI program aimed at neutralizing and dismantling the Black Panther Party by spreading false rumors and deepening rivalries both within the party and between it and other black nationalist groups. Meanwhile, local police units provoked and terrorized the Panthers, leading to highly publicized shoot-outs and high-profile arrests. As Charles Jones has argued, police harassment constituted a highly effective form of repression against the Panthers—jailing Panther members, often on drummed-up criminal charges, at once forced the party to spend its energy raising exorbitant bail funds and publicizing the plight of incarcerated Panthers and lent credence to their public image, particularly among whites, as an armed gang of black thugs and common criminals.[6]

Although the image of the party as a gang of thugs and a danger to national security was intensified by police and FBI actions, the origin of this image was within the party itself. In his memoir, Panther chairman Huey Newton claims to have devised the party's first armed actions—armed patrols against the police and an armed protest of a gun control bill at the Sacramento legislature—as a "recruiting device" for black urban youth.[7] While such Panther actions may have looked like armed terror against the state to much of white America, within black urban communities, they were intended to communicate the notion that the "peacekeeping" forces of the state—the police, the courts, the legislature—were, in actuality, forces of violence against a subordinated black people, and that, as such, they might be resisted by an organized counterviolence. This message had a particular currency during an era of decolonization in which black Americans were seeing, in the newspapers and on televisions, colonized people of color rise up globally against their European rulers, and in which race itself was being rescripted as a *global* world-historical dialectic of violent domination and armed revolution. Jeffrey Ogbar has argued that by marching in military formation and wearing uniforms inspired by those of Third World revolutionaries, the Panthers made visually apparent their understanding of black people in the United States as a colonized population in anticolonial resistance rather than American citizens petitioning for equal rights.[8]

If the Black Panther Party was seen an illegal "hate group" of armed thugs in violent opposition to the peacekeeping forces of the U.S. state, the PLO was officially considered a terrorist organization by most Western states during the late 1960s and early 1970s, when the Popular Front for the Liberation of Palestine's (PFLP) campaign of airplane hijackings galvanized international attention.[9] As R. S. Zaharna demonstrates, prior to these hijackings, the Palestinians were not even named as a people in popular Western media outlets like *Time* magazine; rather, they were assimilated to the rest of the Arab world as "Palestine's Arabs."[10] Like the Panthers' highly publicized advocacy of armed self-defense against representatives of the U.S. state, the PFLP's airplane hijackings simultaneously put the Palestinians on the map as a movement and led to their delegitimation as terrorists. Likewise, the Baader Meinhof Group, also known as the German Red Army Faction, which planned kidnappings and bombings within Germany in solidarity with global anti-imperialist and anticapitalist struggle, was popularly described as a "gang" of homegrown European terrorists.

Through interviews and archival research, Neutres has demonstrated that, in addition to supporting, to a greater extent than any other political group, the "terrorist" PLO, Black Panther Party, and German RAF, Genet also entertained *his own* terrorist plots. In 1957, Genet proposed to his friend Francis Jeanson, who coordinated the French support network for the Algerian National Liberation Front, a series of attacks on French industrial targets. Jeanson's group refused terrorist strikes on principle, but Genet was *only* interested in participating in a violent action. Later, as a part of an information group on Morocco in the early 1970s, Genet pushed forward a plot to assassinate King Hassan II, which, once again, went nowhere.[11]

Following Neutres's important work in *Genet sur les routes du Sud*, I understand Genet's failed terrorist plots and his support of "terrorist" organizations to be rooted in his lifelong estrangement from and hatred of the French state, which he held responsible for imprisoning him.[12] In chapter 4, I analyzed a late interview in which Genet directly relates his lifelong hatred of France, which initially made him love Hitler as France's conqueror, to his later sense of belonging with oppressed people of color. Between loving Hitler as France's conqueror and experiencing a sense of passionate belonging with the Panthers and the Palestinians, however, a consequential shift occurred, one which leads Genet, in this same interview, to retrospectively reclassify Hitler's invasion of France as "a conflict within the white world."[13] If, in the 1940s, France looms so large in Genet's imagination that the significance of Nazism is primarily its capacity to humiliate and subjugate the French nation, by the 1970s, Genet had come to understand the enemy to be not France specifically, but the imperialist and neo-imperialist European, U.S., and Israeli states, and, above and beyond them, the very system of sovereign states responsible for leaving derelict and without recourse to legitimate violence entire populations of people without land or statehood. This chapter investigates what was entailed in the transnational shift of the structure of feeling I term *enemies of the state* that would come to cement Genet's coalition with the Panthers and the Palestinians.

If, like his interviewers, we position Genet in relation to the major contemporary identity categories of nationality, religion, and race, then his strong sense of affinity with the Panthers and the Palestinians is befuddling. If, however, we foreground Genet's own strong identification as a delinquent and criminal, and by extension, an outlaw and enemy of the French state, then his relation to the Panthers and the Palestinians, vilified as criminal and terrorist enemies of liberal states, might be rescripted as one of *shared opposition* to state violence rather than one of improbable identification across difference. In another interview, Genet states, offhand, "Obviously, I have been drawn toward people in revolt."[14] Understanding the foundation of Genet's coalition with the Panthers and the Palestinians on their shared revolt against the state means inquiring into the political potentials of the historical constitution of male homosexuality as a form of criminality. It requires, furthermore, mapping the shift in both the geopolitical positioning and "type" of illegality between the homosexual as petty criminal breaking the laws of the French state and the "terrorist" as a non-state-based enemy of liberal states.

Whereas, in his writings of the 1940s, Genet praises notoriously harsh and abusive disciplinary institutions for forming hard pederasts lost to society, in his unpublished 1981–82 film script "The Language of the Wall" ("Le langage de la muraille"), he rails against French disciplinary and penal institutions for their role in French imperial conquest and settlement. Similarly, whereas his novels of the 1940s heroize criminals who break the laws of the French state, his late political writings seek to convey how revolutionaries vilified as "terrorists" challenge liberal states' monopoly on "legitimate" violence.[15] I understand these shifts geopolitically, as an affective turn from *national* enemies of the bourgeois French state to a geographically and racially diverse set of movements represented as threats to a *global* way of life—that of liberal democracy itself. It was important to Genet's sympathies that each of his chosen political causes during the 1970s and 1980s—the German RAF, the Black Panther Party, and the PLO—was popularly represented as *criminal and/or terrorist*;

not as coherent, legitimate political organizations, but as a threat to society, the nation-state system, and modern warfare themselves. In short, Genet the "criminal queer" passionately identifies with radical revolutionaries he understands to be, like him, *enemies of the state*.

This process of identification across difference with those with whom he shares the oppositional affinity of being an enemy of the state, however, is neither seamless nor ego enhancing. As Genet conducts research in the Mettray archives, discovers, during his visit to the United States, the utility of prison in criminalizing blackness, and comes to relativize the importance of the French state in relation to colonial and neoliberal global networks of power, his own status as a queer outlaw is diminished. The shift in Genet's self-understanding from exemplary queer outlaw in the context of Europe to "the colonizer's janissary" in the greater landscape of global colonial, postcolonial, and neoliberal networks of power responds to questions at the heart of contemporary critiques of *homonationalism*.[16] In Jasbir Puar's influential definition, homonationalism names the late twentieth-century redefinition of certain privileged, usually middle-class, white, and coupled LGBT citizens as productive forms of life worthy of protection by police, surveillance, and counterterrorist state violence.[17] Having vacated their historical position of "enemies of the state," gays and lesbians in liberal states now find themselves opportunistically positioned as the avatars of the sexual freedom and gender egalitarianism that it is the state's newfound role to champion and to protect against the hateful abuses of terrorist networks and illiberal rogue states. Critics of *pinkwashing*—the Israeli government campaign to portray Israel as a welcoming and sexy destination for gay and lesbian tourists from the West and a safe haven for Palestinian queers rejected by an Arab-Islamic culture imagined to be necessarily homophobic—have examined Israel/Palestine as a particularly charged site for this new adjudication of homonationalism.[18] The emergent body of work on homonationalism and pinkwashing analytically shifts the scale of the political within which queerness operates, bringing the large-scale technologies of biopolitics, necropolitics, racialization, and global neoliberalism into focus for Queer Studies. In this expanded optic, the gay married U.S. couple who practice BDSM and find men on online dating sites to join them in threesomes and group orgies, though sexually queer, may be at one and the same time representatives of homonationalism through which the United States justifies its military interventions into regimes that represent "hate" and sexual illiberalism on the global scale.

Homonationalist critique therefore renders urgent an attention to the contradictory positioning of distinct modes of queerness within the various *scales of the political*. In keeping with the book's focus on affective politics, this chapter contributes to homonationalist critique an investigation of the conditions under which it is possible not only to understand but also *to feel* an expanded transnational political landscape. Through archival research, I read "The Language of the Wall," Genet's unpublished 1981–82 film manuscript on the imperialist utility of the boys' penal colony of Mettray, and "Violence and Brutality," his almost universally excoriated 1977 newspaper article in support of the German RAF—as windows into a crucial shift between the 1940s, in which Genet imagines himself a pederast and a criminal, and therefore, an enemy of the French state, and the 1970s, in which he identifies passionately with nonnational revolutionary groups that defend the use of political violence against liberal states. The first section argues that "Language" symptomatizes the crisis of Genet's discovery, during his research in the archives of the boys' penal colony of Mettray in which he had been incarcerated as a youth, of Mettray's, and by extension, *his own* complicity in French colonial conquest and settlement. The second section turns to "Violence and Brutality" and other late writings to illuminate Genet's efforts to at once critique the use of the term *terrorism* to designate certain forms of violence as biopolitical threats to be eliminated and to sketch a counterimaginary of vital violence not affiliated with statehood. Ultimately, I argue that both texts contribute to homonationalist critique a window into the affective and intellectual labor required to shift the structures of feeling that animate queer revolt so that they might sensually apprehend the scale of the global.

Unlike the other chapters, this chapter fleshes out Genet's satisfying realization of a contemporary queer ideal—that of an oppositional antinormative coalition. If Genet realizes this ideal, however, he does so without fully delivering on the hopes that animate it. The afterword to this chapter uses the example of Genet's late activism to deidealize the aspirations that animate the utopian imaginary of queer coalitional oppositionality.

THE POLITICAL FUTURES OF QUEER CRIMINALIZATION

It may seem paradoxical to associate pederasty with an antagonistic relationship to the state in the French context, given that France became the first European state to decriminalize consensual sodomy in private between adults after the French Revolution in 1791. A number of historians have demonstrated, however, that nineteenth- and twentieth-century French medical, legal, and criminological experts were *more* adamant than their British or German counterparts about the necessary relation between male homosexuality, or pederasty (*la pédérastie*) as it was more frequently called, and crime.[19] According to William Peniston, "despite the fact that France was the first country in Europe to abolish its laws against sodomy, it was also the first country in Europe to develop a systematic practice of treating same-sex sexuality as crime."[20] Nineteenth-century Parisian police characterized "pederasts" as unethical, immoral men whose deviant desires and furtive, yet public cross-class sexual liaisons rendered them agents of social disorder and dangers to youth.[21] In what follows, I put "pederasts" in scare quotes to reference this usage, which covers *all* male same-sex behavior, not only the age-differentiated kind, but with the specific connotations of criminality, danger to youth, and disorderly public, cross-class sex.[22] During the nineteenth century, men who had sex with men in public were most commonly charged with an "offense to public decency," interpreted as sex acts in public that harmed "innocent" witnesses (who were often aroused voyeurs), though they were also less commonly charged with inciting minors to debauchery (usually interpreted as prostitution). Known or suspected "pederasts," particularly from the working classes, were frequently subject to extralegal surveillance and harassment—they might be followed, arrested, detained, interrogated, and discharged without ever being charged with a crime.[23] This policy of surveillance and harassment was in effect because police "believed that pederasts were prone to criminal behavior and that criminals were prone to pederastic acts."[24] It was therefore not a question of *if* but of *when* a "pederast" would commit a crime, and police made every effort to catch him in the act.

The success of the gay and lesbian rights organization the Comité d'urgence anti-répression homosexuelle, or CUARTH, in severing homosexuality from pederasty during the late 1970s and early 1980s, paving the way to the equalization of the heterosexual and homosexual ages of consent by 1982 and, thus, abolishing the only remaining legal form of positive discrimination against homosexuality, might be seen as ending the strong association of homosexuality and criminality in France. But what is the meaning of this historical transformation? From the vantage point of the present, it is easy to view the historical identification of homosexuality with crime as a homophobic distortion, albeit with material consequences. This common view holds that homosexuality has no relation whatsoever to criminality: gay men and lesbians do not have criminal personalities; gay and lesbian association is not a cause of social disorder; homosexuality is not a vice; homosexuality has no relation to pederasty; and criminal socialities are not disproportionately homosexual. If, at one point, many homosexuals *were* arrested and *did* participate in the criminal underground, this was simply because the assimilation of homosexuality to criminality excluded them from the formal economy and forced them to engage in illegal activities, including prostitution, in order to survive. The depathologization and decriminalization of homosexuality are celebrated as landmark wins of the gay and lesbian movement; and the nonrelation of homosexuality to either psychological disorders or crime is taken as a self-evident truth rather than a product of history.[25] Tainted as it is by histories of shame and oppression, there has, until recently, been little interest in the theoretical and political consequences of the long-standing constitution of homosexuality as a form of criminality. Yet it is inevitable that the realities of prisons and policing would have shaped the self-conceptions, social allegiances, and relations to law, the moral order, and the state of queer and gender-variant people living during the nineteenth century and the early to mid-twentieth century.

It was neither necessary nor self-evident, however, that the formation of a mass gay and lesbian activist movement during the 1970s would lead to the severance of homosexuality's genealogical connection to criminality and to the consolidation of a mainstream gay and lesbian political platform in which prisons, surveillance, and policing do not play a role. In his 1972 classic, *Homosexual Desire* (*Le désir homosexuel*), French gay liberation theorist Guy Hocquenghem is still able to state, point-blank, "Homosexuality is first of all a criminal category."[26] He goes on to ground homosexuality's revolutionary potential in its ontological relation to criminality. In an interview published in 1973, he reflects, "There is a very clear relation, in Genet for example, between homosexuality and criminality" and proposes, "it is this relationship between fags [*pédés*] and delinquents that make homosexuals a group lost to society, a rather astonishing revolutionary movement."[27] Hocquenghem represents the historical memory of a politics not of decriminalization, but of following through to its limits the criminal constitution of homosexuality as, in the words of the 1960 Mirguet amendment, a "social scourge."[28]

With the emergence of engaged scholarship in Critical Prison Studies, the historical criminalization of homosexuality and gender variance is becoming a topic of renewed scholarly interest. Eric Stanley and Nat Smith's landmark 2011 coedited volume, *Captive Genders: Trans Embodiment and the Prison Industrial Complex*, seeks to ground a queer and transgender Critical Prison Studies in the history of the criminalization of sexual and gender variance. It sketches, both in its individual essays and in its structure (the opening section is titled

"Out of Time: From Gay Liberation to Prison Abolition"), a new historical narrative (one which originally emerged within queer and transgender activist organizations) that connects 1960s queer and transgender activism against policing to the contemporary criminalization of transgender and gender-nonconforming people, particularly of color, in order to demonstrate the necessity of a contemporary politic that would place "prison abolition at the center of queer/trans liberation."[29] Stanley's introductory essay opens by invoking the example of the 1969 Stonewall Riots: "In a blast of radical collectivity, trans/gender-nonconforming folks, queers of color, butches, drag queens, hair-fairies, homeless street youth, sex workers, and others *took up arms* and *fought back* against the generations of oppression that they were forced to survive."[30] His language here illustrates the utopian imaginary, which I will argue Genet's own late activism exemplifies, of an anti-identitarian coalition in opposition, here explicitly violent, to representatives of state violence and repression. Heeding both Hocquenghem's forgotten vision of a queer politics that would emerge from, rather than rejecting, criminalization and *Captive Genders'* call for a genealogy of queer antagonism with prisons and policing, this chapter positions Genet's coalitional activism with the Panthers, the Palestinians, and the German RAF as one of the political futures of the historical constitution of homosexuality and "pederasty" as forms of criminality.

"THE CARCERAL ARCHIPELAGO OF EMPIRE"

> Genet's an ex-inmate himself, a rebel and homosexual;
> although I don't understand a word he says—and he claims not
> to know English—I feel we are completely and easily accepted by
> him, that this world-famous writer is a comrade in arms.
> —Hilliard and Cole, *This Side of Glory*

Incarceration was a crucial link between Genet and the Panthers. David Hilliard's intuition, in the epigraph above, that the Panthers could trust Genet and that Genet understood the Panthers despite their differences of nationality, race, and language, as well as a significant generation gap, was founded on his sense that, like so many Panthers, Genet intimately understood what it meant to have the threat of prison and the terror of the police ever looming on the horizon. Hilliard (who would himself be arrested in Genet's presence for reading a statement in court) knew that, unlike many of the idealistic white leftists who attempted to help the Panthers, Genet's experiences of police repression, social opprobrium, and incarceration were more the result of ignominious criminality than of high-minded social protest.[31] In turn, Genet's activism in solidarity with the Panthers would focus on working to liberate imprisoned Panthers and Panther supporters.[32] Genet's Panther and post-Panther-era writings suggest that part of his complex attraction to the Panthers was based on what he saw as their shared formation by criminalized and carceral cultures.[33]

But if criminalization and imprisonment were the common ground between Genet and the Panthers, Panther writings nevertheless map the politics of prison differently than had Genet up to this point. Panther writings stress both the U.S. prison system's direct postslavery inheritance of the task of repressing and exploiting black populations in the United States and the similarities between the police repression of black "internal colonies" within the borders of the United States and the global policing, led by the United States, of decolonizing peoples abroad.[34] Genet's novels of the 1940s, on the other hand, demonstrate little awareness of the role of French disciplinary and reformatory institutions in imperialist projects and no analysis of the position of the black men that occasionally figure, primarily as sexual and racial fetishes, within them.

Despite his lack of reflection on this in his novels, Genet's personal history of foster care, imprisonment, and colonial military service outlines one common institutional trajectory within the French "carceral archipelago of Empire."[35] Genet was subject to an interconnected series of state and private institutions whose objective was to both neutralize and utilize the most disorderly of French lower-class urban youth as colonialists abroad. Born an urban orphan, he was marked as a potential problem subject to be tracked and placed by state institutions throughout his life. In line with Third Republic–era concerns about industrialization, the loss of "traditional" rural French values, and the criminality of the deracinated working classes of the industrial city, the French Public Welfare Service "rented" Genet out to foster parents in the French countryside for pay.[36] Like many Public Welfare wards, Genet failed to conform to the humble station in life for which he was being groomed. As a result, he underwent, and resisted, a series of placements before being acquitted for acting "without discernment" in order to be sentenced, as a delinquent minor, to the private boys' penal colony of Mettray at the age of sixteen.[37] Officially known as a "correction house [*maison de correction*]" and classified as a private, "philanthropic" institution, Mettray was a cross between a prison, military school, and agricultural colony. It was situated on hundreds of acres of farmland, which its inmates were forced to work. At the same time,

Genet recounts that Mettray's inmates slept like sailors in hammocks and practiced naval drills on a landlocked ship in the courtyard. As he succinctly puts it, "Mettray was used to train sailors."[38] Nor was this military preparation provided in vain. The presence of a recruitment office on site won the army its position as the second major employer of former Mettray inmates, and a series of incentives funneled the majority of enlistees to the French colonial territories.[39] Genet took full advantage of these incentives when he enlisted in the army at Mettray's recruitment office in 1929. As a ward of the state volunteering to serve in Syria, he was able to leave Mettray *two years* before the end of his sentence and to collect an additional supplement of twenty francs per month.[40] Reflecting on this situation in *Prisoner of Love*, Genet refers to himself as "the colonizer's janissary," suggesting that, like the Christian janissaries under the Ottoman Empire, he was a member of an alien insurgent class simultaneously pacified and granted power by being given a stake in military conquest and rule.[41] Genet would, however, resist this offer of relative power and respectability. He later portrayed himself as a bad colonial soldier, sneaking away to play cards with Syrians at night, taking a Syrian barber as his lover, and building a military tower that would collapse during its inauguration ceremony.[42] Neither Genet's poor soldiering nor his eventual desertion of the army for a life of tramping and petty crime, however, could free him from institutional surveillance and control. Genet would only desert the army to come under the auspices of the adult prison.

In *Discipline and Punish* (*Surveiller et punir*), Foucault refers to Mettray as "the most famous of a whole series of institutions which, well beyond the frontiers of criminal law, constituted what one might call the carceral archipelago."[43] The term *carceral archipelago* names the system of detentions, "pedagogic" and reformatory institutions, and military and work camps that, while outside the penal system proper, constitute, with it, a strategically interconnected institutional network of discipline and surveillance. As Ann Laura Stoler has pointed out, however, Foucault's exclusive focus on the French mainland limits the reach of the carceral archipelago, obscuring its concrete extension to the French overseas territories. Stoler's term, "carceral archipelago *of empire*," on the other hand, underlines the significance of imperial rule and settlement to the ontology of European disciplinary institutions. Stoler demonstrates that institutions for the "education" and reform of poor Europeans, poor and mixed-race colonial settlers, and colonized natives were often modeled on one another, and that the boys' reformatory of Mettray served as an influential prototype. A surfeit of both realized projects and utopian schemes sought simultaneously to reform orphans, petty delinquents, and the urban poor, and to solve the problems of colonial settlement and pacification by deporting potential mainland insurgents abroad as colonial soldiers and settlers.

Absent from Genet's early novels is any critique of the imperial valences of French carceral institutions. In 1981, however, a solid decade after his engagement with the Panthers, Genet abruptly returns to the topic of Mettray, albeit with startling changes in genre, tone, and affect. If, previously, Genet resisted the urge to condemn the abusive conditions at Mettray, nostalgically invoking the pederastic cultures that once flourished there, in his 1981–82 film manuscript, "The Language of the Wall," he accusatively and obsessively documents the institution's complicity, over almost a century and under a series of monarchs, emperors, and Republican leaders, with the joint objectives of social pacification, economic profit, and colonial conquest and exploitation. This film script marks the first time that Genet not only acknowledges, but actually *prosecutes* Mettray's role within the carceral archipelago of empire.

GENEALOGICAL PASSIONS: "THE LANGUAGE OF THE WALL"

"The Language of the Wall" is a strange and unwieldly text whose cinematic missteps signal Genet's excessive attachment to the project. Genet signed a contract in 1981 only to draw back in 1982, just after the shooting schedule had been set, making "Language" his third and last film script to be left unrealized. "Language" is, moreover, far less cinematic than Genet's other unrealized film scripts, "Nightfall" ("La nuit venue") and "The Penal Colony" ("Le bagne"). This may be because "Language" was Genet's only film script to be based on his original historical research at the Mettray archives in Tours.[44] The 452-page manuscript's subtitle "A Hundred Years, Day after Day" ("Cent ans, jour après jour"), announces its project of presenting the tedium of institutional time across a long historical expanse. Generically uncategorizable, "Language" is at once a historical fiction, staging the intrigues of the powerful, a historical documentary, dramatizing archival documents, and a biting political satire along the lines of Genet's plays, intercut with glimpses of the lyrical carceral dramas typical of Genet's early novels. The dearth of blocking, heavy reliance on dialogue rather than images or actions, and inclusion of generic markers of nonfiction scholarly writing, such as footnotes, render the manuscript anything but cinematic. Its content is, at times, ploddingly documentary. It begins, for instance, with Mettray's opening ceremony, during which its founder, Frédéric Auguste Demetz, reads Mettray's *twenty-three* formal rules and regulations in their tedious entirety. As in Foucault's "The Lives of Infamous Men," Genet here opts for the direct transmission of an archival document, in all its unabridged and unadorned "dryness," responsible for ruling the lives of insignificant and forgotten inmates.[45]

The majority of the manuscript is dedicated to the exposure of what Genet refers to as Mettray's "secret purpose":

> The secret purpose, which I discovered in documents of which you shall have all the photocopies, was the cultivation of six hundred hectares of land by an unpaid workforce; the transformation of somewhat unruly youth into troops broken in to discipline, already prepared for military authority and for brilliant military strikes in the colonies (in Algeria first of all), and throughout the world, whether as sailors, as soldiers, or as farmers.[46]

Genet goes on in this letter to claim that Mettray inmates provided the human fuel for European colonial projects, recruited as farmers for Algeria and as soldiers for the conquest of Mexico. At the same time, he notes that the multiplication of independence movements in the colonies was paralleled by a surge in prisoners' riots and strikes within France. Mettray followed the "the decline of France," which lost control of its subjects and saw the hypocrisy of its paternalistic ideals of education and uplift exposed at one and the same time in its mainland carceral institutions and in its overseas colonial territories.[47] Genet here implies that carceral spaces within the nation and colonized territories abroad, similarly exploited by the large-scale economic interests that powered French imperialism, might be similarly linked in revolt.

The manuscript didactically and repetitively hammers home the theses outlined in Genet's letter. "Language"'s first point is that, under every political regime over the century of Mettray's existence, regardless of whether a monarch, an emperor, or a republican was in power, the demand for the effective socioeconomic population management that Mettray offered remained constant. It shows how Mettray's promise to turn orphans, vagabonds, and potentially anarchic young delinquents into productive farmers and disposable soldiers through the institution of moralizing labor met with approval and with generous financial support from heads of state and wealthy entrepreneurs until Mettray's decline after Demetz's death in 1905. Second, "Language" explores the tangle of semantic and political resonances and dissonances between the colonizer, the colonized, the colonialist, and the inmate of a penal "colony." In French, the latter two terms have the same name, *colon*; and "Language" shows that Mettray's *colons* (inmates) all too often become *colons* (colonialists) if not *colonisateurs* (colonizers) once freed. One passage suggests that Mettray and the Algerian colonial regiments served the same strategic purpose, that of rendering productive the anarchic energy of insurgent youth. According to Captain Richard, the script's principal ex-inmate turned colonizer, the youngest agitators of the revolutionary July Days are sent to Mettray, and the rest become soldiers in the colonial regiments of Algeria. Captain Richard's own presence in Algeria, however, demonstrates that this is not an either/or situation, and that the young insurgents who are sent to Mettray may also "graduate" to serve in the colonial armed forces in Algeria or another territory.

Insofar as they are made to perform forced labor for almost no pay while confined on something called a "colony," however, the situation of Mettray's inmates is closer to that of the *colonisé* (colonized) than to that of the *colon*. This rapprochement is sharply exposed in the scene immediately following Mettray's opening ceremony, which cuts between a series of departing carriages in which the invited ambassadors and philanthropists are discussing Mettray. In one carriage, Alphonse de Lamartine enthusiastically lauds, in the language of high liberal humanism, Mettray's noble aims of paternalistic reform. The ambassador of Great Britain responds, blasé, "We have the same colonies in Great Britain and in South Africa," and calculates, "but they bring in less than our blacks!"[48] The penal "colony," whether in the mainland or in the colonies proper, serves the same economic purpose as colonialism—albeit, as the Ambassador suggests, somewhat less profitably—the exploitation of a subject people. Further blurring the line between *colon* and *colonisé*, "Language" suggests that from an administrative perspective, the *colon* (colonialist) settling Algeria, like the *colon* (inmate) at Mettray, is only a commodified body to be managed and rendered productive. One particularly dramatic scene depicts a colonel's search for *colons* to work as farmers in Algeria through the iconography of the slave market. Thirty of Mettray's *colons* are made to strip before the colonel so that he can test their muscles, open their mouths to inspect their teeth, and scrutinize their genitals for signs of venereal disease. Through its use of such charged iconography, this scene suggests that both Mettray's *colons* and the colonial farmers in Algeria that many of them will become are little more than human chattel: a series of bodies to be inspected, selected, placed, and put to work, ambivalently aligned with enslaved labor at the very moment that they are being vetted as potential settler colonialists.[49]

Blanchard and Leroy, two ex-Mettray prisoners who serve in the French army during the conquest of Hanoi, exemplify the fundamentally contradictory position of Mettray's *colons/colonisateurs/colonisés*. One scene shows them discussing the merits of their position as soldiers in Indochina, which, they agree, is superior to being at Mettray. As colonial soldiers, they can get away with ignoring their superiors while also having Annamite servants polish their shoes and wash their shirts. The very act of comparison, however, implies that the boys' penal colony and the French colonial army are commensurate institutions. In the end, the military training Blanchard and Leroy received at Mettray, the slightly greater freedom they are able to enjoy in the colonial army, and the gratifying bonus of a racialized people's servitude achieve their intended effects: despite their occasional indiscipline, the two ex-inmates become model colonial soldiers. In the next scene, their captain sends a congratulatory telegram to the director of Mettray, reporting that he is nominating both ex-inmates for the prestigious Médaille Coloniale. The next day, the same captain, "unmoved" upon receiving word that Blanchard and Leroy have been discovered decapitated, sends a telegram of condolences to the director of Mettray, who orders their names inscribed on the Tableau d'Honneur for their heroic deaths in military service.[50] The hapless prisoners cum colonial soldiers are revealed to be little more than disposable weapons, exchanging their lives for an inscription on a penal colony's tablet of honor.

SHIFTING THE AFFECTIVE "LANDSCAPE" OF QUEER REVOLT

Reading the long, overburdened, and didactic manuscript of "The Language of the Wall," one has the impression that Genet wanted to put everything that he discovered in his research—every moralizing discourse, every debate on penology and profitability, every one of the colony's financial contributors, every negotiation with a head of state, every colonial war, and every historical event that occurred during Mettray's existence—into his film. The result is a script that seems intent on proving the same points over and over again, "day after day," as its subtitle indicates, and in excruciating detail. As a result, "Language" has little of the affective or narrative power of Genet's other works. If it does not succeed in moving its readers, however, it does give the impression of being, *in itself*, the record of a passion. Every scene is infused with a newfound zeal for meticulous research, maniacal documentation, and indignant denunciation. Through this strange document, itself sheltered in an archive, one glimpses Genet, possessed by the archive, producing an unwieldy and uncinematic dramatization of that archive. The denunciatory passion of "Language" certainly was not the product of any tardy discovery that the penal colonies were inhumanitarian, a discourse against which Genet pitted his early novels (see chapter 2). Rather, it was born of Genet's discovery of how Mettray fit into a vast governmental-colonial-military-economic network of administration and exploitation. In his research at the Mettray archives, Genet discovered, not the *abuse* of Mettray's inmates, which he had trained himself to love, but their *use*, which he could not pardon.

The denunciative and expository passion encoded in "Language" seems driven by a newfound animus—absent from Genet's early works—*against* prison, the penal colonies, and the broader system of imperial, economic, and governmental interests in which they play a role. It registers a profound shift— from intimacy and love to outrage and denunciation—in Genet's feelings regarding prison, carceral cultures, and, especially, his beloved penal colony of Mettray. If Genet had long regarded himself as a creature of prison—someone whose sexuality was formed in incarceration, whose most profound sympathies were with the imprisoned, and whose cherished sense of being an abject outlaw required prisons and police to set him apart as such—then the animus of "Language" is, significantly, directed against all that had so far constituted him as a queer outlaw. Obsessively tracing the complicities of former Mettray prisoners with the project of French colonial exploitation and rule results in a demystification of the position of the outlaw—Genet's own position—whose perversity and amorality his early novels so often celebrate. What drives "Language" is thus the energy of a certain *self*-denunciation resulting from Genet's discovery of Mettray's—and therefore his own—complicity in a series of nationalist, imperialist, and capitalist projects. Genet's discovery, while in the United States, of the U.S. prison system's stunning enforcement of racial domination and terror may have impelled him to scrutinize the institution that he had always considered, if not his birthplace, then at least the site of his founding myth. Whereas previously, Genet had been able to see himself as the quintessential outlaw and menace to society, after having witnessed several racist incidents in the United States in which black people near him were harassed, searched, and arrested, he was forced to conclude, "They didn't bother me because I'm white and as such I present no danger to American society."[51] Such transparent utilizations of the U.S. criminal justice system to perpetuate deeply rooted racialized inequalities, when reinforced by the Panthers' analyses of prison's connection to both slavery and imperialism, must have pushed Genet to interrogate Mettray's role in the French projects of social management and imperial exploitation. It is the combination of the burden of "proving" such underground connections, over a long historical period and across several continents, with Genet's "archive fever" that resulted in such an overburdened and uncinematic abandoned film script.[52]

While "Language" may not make for a "good" film, it does register the extended repercussion of Genet's involvement with the Panthers, suggesting that his identification with them through shared experiences of imprisonment eventually required a transformation not only of his political analyses, but also of his very feelings regarding prison. Specifically, Genet's engagement with the Panthers helped him shift his optic from the level of the prisoner's experience to that of the penal colony's function within a series of interconnected strategies of population management, economic exploitation, and colonial expansion. We might understand this as a shift in Genet's *landscape of queer revolt*. Victoria Hesford coins the term *landscape of female revolt* to account for the divergences behind two strikingly similar 1970s images of female revolt—Valerie Solanas's knife-wielding white street hustler and Patricia Haden, Donna Middleton, and Patricia Robinson's poor, urban black woman with a razor cupped in her hand. These parallel images offer "a glimpse of something not effectively realized during the moment of women's liberation's arising: the possibility of an alignment between black and white women based on corresponding if not equivalent social exclusions."[53] How to build a politics on this potential alignment is another question, however, for despite their affinities, these two figures of revolt emerge from vastly different *landscapes* that necessitate different strategies of activist transformation. For Solanas, the "landscape of female revolt" was that of white bourgeois sexism, particularly among New Left men, whereas for Haden, Middleton, and Robinson, it was the much vaster scene of global capitalism spearheaded by the United States.

Similarly, Genet's figure of the queer outlaw and the Panthers' figure of the gangster-turned-black-militant activated affinities that both Genet and the Panthers found compelling. At the same time, however, the *landscapes* of their forms of carceral revolt differed significantly. For Genet's queer outlaw of the 1940s, the object of anger and revolt was the French state as the protector of French bourgeois moral superiority; for the Panthers, it was the vast target of transnational (neo)imperial racial capitalism. For coalitional affinities between similar emotions of revolt and analogous forms of subjection to be effectively realized, there must also be a broader grasp of the "landscape" within which each revolt is situated. For Genet, this meant embarking on a project of archival research that would position Mettray—the mythical womb of the queer outlaws and enemies of France he so adores—within the broader landscape of transnational (neo)imperial racial capitalism that the Panthers had helped him to glimpse.

This was more than an intellectual exercise in leaping from the micro to the macro level in order to understand the interrelations and contradictions between large-scale economic, governmental, and geopolitical forces. It required Genet to embark on his own project of *attachment genealogy* in order to relentlessly scrutinize his own foundling myth. "Language" is the document of this project of genealogy: an inquiry that unsettles contemporary categories, such as that of the queer outlaw, that are naturalized as the very foundation of identity and action. This is a form of historical inquiry with *affective* repercussions— the loss of the position of exemplary social abjection and uniquely resistant criminality, an affective shift from love of prison to rage against it, and, most importantly, the ability to not only understand but also *sense oneself* within an empirically vast transnational landscape of revolt. "Landscape" is a particularly useful metaphor here. Just as appreciating a vista as a landscape requires a prior aesthetic sensitization, sensing a *landscape of revolt* requires a habituated "affective mapping,"[54] for instance, of how an emotion like anger distinguishes objects, subjects, and avenues for action within a subjective scene. What one identifies as the *object* of anger, as of love, is determined by the learned ability to *sense* one's anger (or love) as putting into relation elements within a particular landscape. A shift in the scale of the landscape of one's revolt therefore modifies both how this revolt *feels* and to what (violent, activist, coalitional, denunciatory) actions it can be imagined to lead. The transnational expansion of Genet's landscape of queer revolt therefore modified his feelings about prison, transporting them from ambivalent love to indignant anger, while disaggregating imprisonment as the stable ground of his own position of queer revolt.

The notion of affective landscapes of revolt might reorient contemporary queer work on homonationalism. Instead of identifying more and less resistant, more and less complicit versions of queerness within the vast scene of global bio- and geopolitics, scholarship on homonationalism might attend sympathetically to the diverse *scales* on which revolt, marginalization, and resistance operate and to the labor it takes to retrain oneself to affectively sense an enlarged landscape. I want to emphasize that the expanded transnational landscape within which Genet learned to affectively apprehend both prison and the figure of the European queer outlaw *was not more true* than the narrower one that had nurtured his prior feelings of love for prison, hatred for France, and queer revolt. It need not be a matter of grading landscapes of revolt, but of understanding what they enable as well as what enables them to change. Genet's discovery of the complicity of the European queer outlaw as colonial stooge impelled him to affectively apprehend his revolt on a vaster scale, correspondingly shifting both the target of his anger and hatred and the site of his alliances. The rest of the chapter explores how the transnationalization of Genet's landscape of queer revolt enabled him to retheorize the question of violence on the global stage.

"VIOLENCE AND BRUTALITY": ENEMIES OF THE *LIBERAL* STATE

"Violence and Brutality" ("Violence et brutalité"), Ulrike Genet's preface to *Texts of the Prisoners of the "Red Army Faction" and Last Letters of Ulrike Meinhof* (*Textes des prisonniers de la "Fraction Armée Rouge" et dernières lettres d'Ulrike Meinhof*), published as an opinion piece on the first page of *Le Monde* on September 2, 1977, was his most controversial piece of political writing. Every French newspaper published a flood of indignant letters denouncing Genet's article. This extremely negative response, which might be expected of a defense of urban European terrorism on the front page of the major national French daily newspaper, was exacerbated by bad political timing. Genet penned the article, at the request of Klaus Croissant, the lawyer of the Baader Meinhof group, at a time when its three leaders, condemned to life in prison, had been in isolation for months, were exhausted by hunger strikes, and were all but forgotten by public opinion. Three days after its publication, however, in a kidnapping that claimed three casualties, Hanns-Martin Schleyer, the president of the Federation of German Industries, was held hostage by members of the Red Army Faction demanding the release of fourteen imprisoned RAF members. Genet's article, which appeared in German translation in *Der Spiegel* on September 12, gave the impression of having been written after, and in defense of, Schleyer's kidnapping. In October, in rapid succession, an airplane was hijacked and the pilot executed, the group's three imprisoned leaders died in an alleged collective suicide, and Schleyer was assassinated by his kidnappers. Genet's defense of the RAF's terrorist methods could not have come at a worse time.

In addition to the article's bad timing and controversial defense of European urban terrorism, letter writers responded to what they saw as Genet's unfounded and irrational distinction between "bad" bourgeois brutality and "good" violence.[55] Genet seeks to communicate the justness of political violence through a strikingly uncharacteristic nexus of metaphors. Writing, "The kernel of wheat that germinates and breaks through the frozen earth, the chick's beak that cracks open the eggshell, the impregnation of a woman, the birth of a child can all be considered violent," he seeks to forge a relation between violence and vital life processes.[56] As we saw in chapter 4, the historical imaginary that binds pederasty, national estrangement, and crime excludes birth and reproduction, which are instead associated with familial and national belonging, as its antitheses. Genet's uncharacteristic foray into an alien set of metaphors around processes of birth and the reproduction of life is in the service of an act of radical resignification. If, within liberal rationality, terrorism is horrifying because associated with the indiscriminate, irrational, and hate-driven will to death, then in this article, Genet reverses that rationality, placing terrorist violence against the state on the side of life, and the liberal state itself on the side of "brutality" and death. "Violence and Brutality" is legible an early attempt, on Genet's part, to use the "transparent violence" of terrorism to reveal the masked violence of power.[57]

Though letters to the editor denounced this article as an apology for terrorist violence, it is worth noting that it makes no reference to any of the specific terrorist acts of the RAF and only mentions the word *terrorism* twice, in a parenthetical aside enclosed by a clause referring to the political arguments of the RAF: "Their political arguments, smothered, it's true, by a violent action here called 'terrorism' (parenthesis: another word, 'terrorism,' that should be applied as much and more to the brutalities of bourgeois society)."[58] This parenthetical aside seeks to do the massive work of shifting the illegitimate and monstrous violence associated with terrorism onto a bourgeois society of normalization, wealth accumulation, and private property protected by the liberal state itself. But what exactly are these "brutalities of a bourgeois society"? In an earlier passage, Genet's denunciation of manifestations of the "organized brutality" of the bourgeois state includes "the architecture of public housing projects; bureaucracy; the substitution of a word—proper or familiar—by a number; the priority, in traffic, given to speed over the slow rhythm of the pedestrian; the authority of the machine over the man who serves it; the codification of laws that override custom; the numerical progression of prison sentences. . ."[59] Many of the items listed exemplify what Foucault has termed *governmentality* (*la gouvernementalité*), that is, the range of strategies—disciplinary, statistical, bureaucratic, legal, and biopolitical—used to render populations both self-governing and governable.[60] Governmentality requires biopolitics—the politics of life itself—as at once its primary *strategy* and one of the most compelling *rationalities* through which it can be explained and defended. Since a biopolitical state (and Foucault argued that the modern liberal, Nazi, and communist states were all biopolitical states) is one that derives its legitimacy from its promise to enhance the lives of its citizens, governmental methods are invariably rationalized as a means of enhancing the life of the population, protecting citizens from irrational and unpredictable acts of violence, and defending them against external threats. The architecture of public housing projects, the replacement of words, including proper names, by numbers, the codification of laws, and the conversion of crimes into quantities of duration in prison are all forms of rationalization that allow for the surveillance, administration, discipline, and control of populations. They do so, however, via methods whose very uniformity, standardization, and rationality are supposed to guarantee the neutral and equivalent application of justice. In this way, state technologies of rationalization are associated with the peaceful governance and administration of violent and lawless elements within the population. Arbitrary violence, not to mention the possibility of arbitrariness itself, is documented, controlled, and disciplined through methods that do not themselves appear violent.[61] Gone are the dramatic public executions and the gruesome spectacles of torture of the "despotic" premodern state; the liberal modern state protects its population and demonstrates the value it attaches to life by *administering arbitrariness*, not punishing violence with counterviolence.

Genet seeks to oppose the biopolitical rationality that poses the liberal state as the keeper of peace against the irrational violence of crime and terrorism by denouncing the apparently peaceful methods of the state as brutality in disguise. The choice of the term *brutality* here, rather than simply something like "state violence," is significant. The connotations of "brutality"—from the term *brute*, defined as "one of the lower animals as distinguished from humans" and, by extension, "the animal nature in humans"—encompass both "inhumanity" and "savage cruelty."[62] *Brutality* thus counters with precision the liberal state's definition of itself as civilized, humane, and nonviolent. In its apparent ill-suitedness, *brutality* functions as a performative term, one that works to materialize the disavowed violence of the liberal state and to tarnish its veneer of civilized rationality. Genet has good reason to use it in this article. The "civilized" and "nonviolent" methods of punishment employed against the imprisoned RAF leaders—life imprisonment, solitary confinement, and sensory deprivation, as opposed to the death penalty, physical torture, or hard labor under harsh conditions—are *negative* rather than positive forms of punishment in which different forms of deprivation and absence, rather than overt violence, accomplish the brutal work of gradually destroying the prisoner's body and mind.

Rather than focusing his article narrowly on a critique of the inhumane conditions in which the RAF prisoners were held—a critique which would inscribe itself within a liberal governmental rationality—Genet seeks to make the "brutality" of the RAF leaders' conditions of detention coterminous with the legal foundations of the liberal state itself. Whereas the codification of laws, within liberal states, is supposed to guarantee the peaceful, egalitarian, and transparent reign of law and order over warlike conditions of internal violence, Genet writes, "a trial against violence [that is, against the RAF's terrorist methods] is brutality itself."[63] This is a fundamental challenge both to the central tenet of the liberal state—its duty to protect its citizens against brutal conditions of violence—and to the principle that the legal system is an inherently peaceful mode of governance. Genet gestures here toward a genealogy of the liberal, law-based state not as the historical triumph of order and peace over relations of arbitrariness and violence, but as an inscription of inherently violent relations of domination within state institutions.[64] Rather than a peaceful legal apparatus confronting a violent terrorist group, Genet would have us see a battle between two distinct forms of violence—one, "brutality," that is able to hide its exercise of domination by speaking within the logic of a liberal biopolitical rationality, and another, vilified as "terrorism," that both unmasks this relation of domination and opposes to it a counterviolence that Genet finds just.

Whereas, until the recent War on Terror, terrorism had been considered a problem of *criminal* violence to be addressed by the police, Genet defends the RAF's tactics as the *political* violence of revolutionary warfare against a "brutal" state. The RAF is particularly just, in Genet's eyes, because it seeks, through terrorist methods, to bring decolonizing struggle into the metropole. The article's epigraph is a paraphrased quotation from Karl Marx's article "The Future Results of British Rule in India," which Andreas Baader cited in a section of the book that was edited out of the final, published version:[65] "The deep hypocrisy and the barbarity of the bourgeoisie are displayed with impunity before our very eyes, whether we look at the metropole where its domination has taken on respectable, civilized forms, or at the colonies where it is simply brutal."[66] Understanding imperialism and neo-imperialism, with the violence, domination, and superexploitation they require, as integral parts of the functioning of "peaceful," "civilized" states is perhaps *the* most efficient way of exposing the brutality of the liberal state and challenging its monopoly on legitimate violence. Genet therefore opposes the official interpretation of the "Baader-Meinhof Gang" as a "gang" of anarchists and terrorists by emphasizing their self-inscription within a genealogy of revolutionary, anticapitalist, liberatory violence. The revolutionary terrorist groups of the late 1960s and early 1970s—including the German RAF, the Weather Underground, the Black Panther Party, and the PLO—challenge the liberal state's portrayal of itself as peaceful and just and legitimate the use of political violence against it. "Violence and Brutality" relays an important effort to address the political construction and, therefore, the potential resignification of terms such as "illegitimate violence," "legitimate violence," and "peace." If it failed to convince its European readership, it is because its rescripting of violence too fundamentally challenged the very tenets of liberal rationality, coterminous with "common sense" itself. To transnationalize the coalitional structure of feeling, enemies of the state, to enemies of *liberal* states, Genet had to envision an alternative to the biopolitical rationality that identified liberal states as inherently peaceful and challenges to them as monstrously violent.

"TERRORISM" AS A POLITICAL PERFORMATIVE

It is noteworthy that "Violence and Brutality"'s inflammatory argument that the liberal state is, by definition, a brutal entity deserving of life-giving terrorist counterviolence is not carried over into *Prisoner of Love*'s later meditations on the Palestinians. Doubtless, Genet would not have wanted to bring the kind of virulently negative reception that "Violence and Brutality" elicited upon the Palestinians, particularly given the extent to which the PLO had already been delegitimized as a terrorist organization. In the place of "Violence and Brutality"'s incendiary rhetoric, the overwhelming majority of *Prisoner*'s passages on the Palestinians consist of thoughtful meditations on the politics, history, and everyday life of the Palestinian people. For example, after engaging in a political and theological discussion with Palestinians, Genet playfully comments,

> The gathering was no doubt enchanted by the nocturnal presence of young drinkers of tea and orange juice listening to and teaching an old Frenchman, an outsider suddenly set down under the trees in a winter that had begun with Black September, in the midst of terrorists laughing without cynicism, verbally inventive mockers, a bit wild, but as proper as seventeen-year-old seminarists, terrorists whose very names made newspaper pages tremble like leaves. Their exploits on land and in the air were reported with fear and disgust, a disgust well imitated on faces and in words.[67]

This passage is typical of Genet's approach in *Prisoner*, which, rather than dwelling on the terrifying image of Palestinian terrorism, seeks to deflate this image by juxtaposing it with the anodyne and even pastoral everyday life of "these gentle terrorists."[68]

At other times, Genet explores pointedly both the complex of terror and disgust generated by Palestinian terrorism and the political utility of the accusation of terrorism. An anonymous speaker in *Prisoner* reflects that "the word terrorist has metal teeth and the red jaws and face of a monster." Why is the terrorist not only terrifying, as its linguistic root indicates, but actually monstrous and disgusting? The same speaker continues: "Hunting Israel makes one neither an adversary nor an enemy, but a terrorist. Terrorism is supposed to deal death indiscriminately, and must be destroyed wherever it appears."[69] The implication is clear: monstrosity is not inherent in terrorist violence; rather, the attribution of monstrosity to terrorism serves a political purpose—it removes the terrorist from the theater of modern politics altogether.[70] Since the Palestinians oppose Israel without having a recognized sovereign state of their own, they are neither adversaries nor enemies—that is, political opponents—but "terrorists," where to be a "terrorist" means being given over to a death-driven indiscriminate destruction of life, and hence, being worthy of death by any means necessary. Talal Asad has argued that the "terrorist" is not only someone whose exercise of violence does not abide by the Geneva Conventions. It is someone for whom this violence in violation of international treaties is interpreted as an irrational, apolitical, and, particularly after 9/11, hate or religion-driven threat to civilization itself. This apolitical threat authorizes liberal states to exercise a disproportionate counterviolence that may, itself, violate the Geneva Conventions in order to protect liberalism and, therefore, peace. Hence, although Genet writes that an alleged act of Israeli terrorism involving two Israeli soldiers who masquerade as homosexuals in order to kill three Palestinian officers was a kind of "heroism," he also is careful to note that "Newspapers all over the world described the assassination, but none of them called it terrorism on another country's sovereign territory. No, it was considered as one of the Fine Arts."[71] Rather than being seen as a monstrous, irrational, and hateful exercise of illegitimate violence, this alleged act of Israeli terrorism is admired for its stagecraft and implicitly deemed a necessary response to Palestinian terrorism. Again, Genet zeroes in on the political performativity of the term *terrorism*, a term that appears increasingly contentless.

Both the PLO's "terrorist" status and the official classification of the Black

Panther Party as an anarchic hate group are the consequence of what Neutres suggests is one of Genet's principal points of identification with these two groups: their lack of land.[72] As Genet writes, "Both the Blacks and the Palestinians are without land. Their two situations are not completely identical, but they are alike in that neither group has any territory of its own."[73] As organizations without a sovereign territory, their acts of political violence and self-defense are liable to be delegitimized and rendered monstrous as criminal acts or terrorist strikes. A Palestinian soldier who serves as Genet's interpreter at one point savvily plays on the family resemblance between the French words *terre* (land / the Earth) and *se terrer* (to hide; literally, to hide in a hole or against the ground, like an animal), on the one hand, and *terreur* (terror) and *terroristes* (terrorists) on the other, in order to deconstruct the foundation of legitimate violence on sovereign territory: "If all of Earth [*la terre entière*] is a kingdom of terror [*de la terreur*] we know whom to thank. But you distribute terror [*la terreur*] while hiding yourselves [*en vous terrant*]. At least the terrorists [*les terrorists*] I'm talking about voluntarily expose their bodies. That's the difference."[74] In this formulation, global terror is the work not of mobile, transnational terrorist networks, but of sovereign states themselves—states which, as the untranslatable term *se terrant* suggests, hide themselves away in their sovereign territories as they terrorize others at a distance. The ascendance of the principle of state sovereignty and division of the globe into sovereign states and their overseas territories are therefore the methods, not of peace, as liberalism dictates, but of terror. They create a new global underclass of people without states and of movements without nations whose political violence can only be understood as terrorism. If, as Genet writes, refugee camps are "the refuse of 'settled' nations," then stateless people's "terrorist" violence is the refuse of landed states' right to military sovereignty.[75] Landed sovereign states' greater access to the technological products of military industry and license to use them ensure that violence, by these states, is mediated through machines and technology and may occur at a distance—paradigmatically now, through drone warfare—while protecting the bodies and lives of soldiers. It is their lack of access to the high-tech arsenals of wealthy states that leads terrorists to use their bodies as weapons. They "voluntarily expose their bodies," and since "legitimate violence is fundamentally mediated violence," this unmediated corporeal exposure to violence elicits horror, appearing gruesomely barbaric in an era of increasingly "civilized" long-distance warfare.[76] Asad has exposed the tautological rationalization by which the greater corporeal risks that militarily and implicitly ethnically inferior people must assume demonstrates the lack of value they accord human life, which makes it "proper" for them to die in much larger numbers.[77]

"Terrorism" is illegitimate violence; but racialized international relations of power are all that distinguish legitimate from illegitimate violence. It is not the nature of an act of violence that determines whether or not it may be considered terrorism; rather, the international standing of the organization responsible for that act determines its acceptability. If the organization is a sovereign liberal state, such as Israel, the act will not be considered terrorist regardless of its method or the number of civilian lives it claims; if it is either an organization without a sovereign territory, such as the PLO or Hamas, or an illiberal state, its violent methods are exponentially more likely to be considered terrorist. Asad concludes, "it is not cruelty that matters in the distinction between terrorists and armies at war, still less the threat each poses to entire ways of life, but their civilizational status," which continues to be understood in explicitly racialized terms.[78] As Edward Said has convincingly demonstrated, nineteenth-century Zionists' ability to win the support of Europe and the United States early on for their project for a Jewish national home in Palestine was largely based on their use of colonialist tropes (such as the duty to render productive the empty land or the land left fallow by the natives) that enjoyed widespread legitimacy at the time, and, relatedly, their positioning of Israel as a beleaguered extension of "European civilization" within the backward and barbaric Arab world.[79] The continued life of the colonial thesis of a racialized civilizational disparity between Israelis and Palestinians accounts, to a large extent, for the damning attribution of "terrorism" to the Palestinians and not to the Israelis, regardless of the exponentially higher civilian casualties the Palestinians have suffered. Hence, political counterperformatives such as President Evo Morales of Bolivia's declaration, in July 2014, that Israel is a "terrorist state" and request that the UN High Commissioner prosecute Israel for "crimes against humanity" remain important as a means of unmasking the racist biopolitical rationality that undergirds the distinction between "terrorist" and "legitimate" forms of violence.

FEELING BIOPOLITICAL GENEALOGIES

As a political performative, the term *terrorism* introduces a cleavage within the realm of biopolitical life: it demarcates those who are defined as a threat to life and to entire ways of life and who are therefore legitimate targets of state violence. In *"Society Must Be Defended,"* Foucault argues that the corollary of the biopolitical state's responsibility to protect and enhance life is "state racism," that is, the production of a division between *lives worth defending* and *threats to that life from which society must be defended*. The biopolitical threat is not the same as the adversary or the enemy, for this would endow what should be seen as a threat to life itself with a human political rationality. In this sense, the political performative of terrorism fulfills the objectives of state racism: to turn what could be conceived as humans and political adversaries into contentless and inhuman threats to life itself, and thus, to legitimize eliminating them. As Leerom Medovoi argues:

> *Terrorism* does not name a substantive critique of any social order, nor an alternative conception for social order . . . Terrorism becomes, like murder or rape, the naming of a deviant type against which society must be defended. This is the sense in which the external racial enemy has been folded back into a biopolitical project of the traditionally domestic sort: the surveillance, policing, and punishing of a race of "abnormals" who exist in advance of their criminal acts, and who thus should be detected, identified, and neutralized preemptively, before they actualize the potential social threat that they pose.[80]

The Palestinians and the Black Panthers sketch the contours of an earlier moment in the genealogy of global terrorism, one prior to that defined by 9/11, the war on terror, and the rise of ISIS, in which we live in today. Medovoi here proposes that the genealogy of terrorism stretches back further still. As a politically contentless and biopolitically threatening incarnation of pure deviance, terrorism is rooted in nineteenth- and early twentieth-century medicalized conceptions of criminality, homosexuality, and other abnormal "types."[81] This genealogy of global terrorism has the potential to correct the bifurcated reception of Foucault Puar has critiqued, whereby queer scholars engage his work on sexuality and scholars of race and postcoloniality grapple with his writings on state racism, but only rarely are both valences of the biopolitical thought together.[82]

This insight leads us to a provocative question: if terrorists are the newest incarnation within the genealogy of "abnormals" within which Genet himself—as a child delinquent, homosexual, and criminal bearing the psychiatric diagnosis of "moral madness [*folie morale*]"[83]—was also located, then could Genet's identification and sense of affinity with the Panthers and the Palestinians have been as much a recognition of *biopolitical kinship* as it was an attraction across difference? At issue is how it becomes possible to *feel* genealogical connections that span not only great expanses of time, but also changing geopolitical landscapes of governmentality. After all, the existence of a genealogical link between contemporary terrorists and nineteenth- and early twentieth-century "abnormals" does not mean that, in practice, most queers, neuroatypical people, or convicts feel a sense of belonging either with one another or with terrorists as their biopolitical "kin"; nor does it imply that such a sense of belonging, were it to be activated, would necessarily be politically desirable. I want to speculatively suggest that *enemies of the state* names a structure of feeling that opposes European criminal-queers constituted as deviant to the biopolitical states that had constituted them as such. This structure of feeling disposed Genet, initially, to love all of France's enemies, including Hitler and his SS troops, and, later, those violent "terrorist" threats to all liberal, sovereign states. Loving the latter groups, however, required a seismic shift in the landscape of revolt within which *enemies of the state* operated. For, in order to love the violence of the RAF or of the Palestinian *fedayeen*, Genet had to contend with the forces that would delegitimize them as apolitical death-driven threats to peace and life themselves and thereby mark them out for death, neutralization, and imprisonment. In short, *global biopolitics, as enforced by liberal states*, came into view as the broader landscape within which the struggles of the Panthers, the Palestinians, and the German RAF were staged. The intellectual labor, in Genet's late writing, of working out and contesting the liberal rationality that undergirds the delegitimation of particular forms of violence as "terrorism" is legible as an attempt to understand the global landscape of revolt into which his biopolitical affinities with the Panthers and the Palestinians had thrown him.

THE AFFECTIVE AND INTELLECTUAL LABOR OF COALITION

As Genet writes early on in *Miracle of the Rose*, "I do not love the oppressed. I love those whom I love, who are always handsome and sometimes oppressed but who stand up and rebel."[84] As a structure of feeling[85] within a landscape of revolt, *enemies of the state*—particularly handsome and masculine young black and brown enemies—powerfully animated Genet's sense of attraction to and belonging with the Palestinians and the Black Panthers. Bypassing the nationalist aims of these movements, Genet cultivates an anti-identitarian affinity based on the hatred of liberal states that he attributes to them. Asked, in a 1970 interview, why the Panthers' cause became his own, he responds,

> If I'm sincere, I have to say that what touched me at first was not their concern to re-create the world. Of course, that will come, and I'm not insensitive to it. But what made me feel immediately close to them was their hatred for the white world, their concern to destroy a society, to smash it. A concern that I had when I was very young, but I couldn't change the world all alone. I could only pervert it, corrupt it a little.[86]

What made Genet feel immediately close to the Panthers was precisely the media, U.S. government, and police-driven image of them as a hateful group of violent black thugs.[87] Genet was similarly drawn to "the enchanting spectacle" of Palestinian terror promoted by Zionist media.[88] Writing, in *Prisoner*, that the Palestinian soldiers, "adorned" with guns, were, like the Panthers, "not merely a transfiguration but also a materialization of my fantasies," Genet shows himself to be erotically attuned to what Gil Hochberg identifies as "the colonial fantasy of the sexy terrorist."[89] Though, as Genet knew, "hatred" was a delegitimizing and insufficient explanation of the complex reasons for the movements of the Panthers and the Palestinians, what made him feel intuitively close to them, nevertheless, were the ways in which they appeared to share Genet's previously solitary hatred of society and desire to destroy it. We might speculate that Genet's sense that there were "affinities" between the Panthers, the Palestinians, and him and that it was "natural" that he should go help them was an intuition of their biopolitical kinship within a long genealogy of state racism ... even as this attraction was simultaneously energized by racist discourses linking race, virility, and violence (see chapter 3).

However, just as biopolitics had to go global in order to confront the terrorist (or required the figure of the terrorist in order to extend itself globally), Genet's affective landscapes of queer revolt had to become transnationalized in order for his attachment to the Panthers and the Palestinians to become something other than merely fetishistic. This required him to embark on an attachment genealogy of Mettray, and thus of the previously gratifying figure of the queer outlaw, that situated both within the complicitous landscape of imperialism and transnational racial capitalism. It also required a theorization of violence—one of the originary points of Genet's attraction to the Panthers, the Palestinians, and the RAF—both as it operates within the liberal rationality that marks these groups as criminal and terrorist threats to be eliminated and as it might be reimagined within a counterimaginary of vital revolt. Genet at once senses a biopolitical connection that subtends the identity categories of race and nationality and performs the affective and intellectual labor of shifting his landscape of revolt in line with that, more expansively transnational, within which the movements of the Panthers and the Palestinians were staged. In so doing, Genet demonstrates the ways in which the political potential of *queer* as a positional term of anti-identitarian coalition between groups analogously marginalized requires, if it is to be effective, the labor of bringing dissimilar affective landscapes of revolt into alignment. Queer coalition, particularly when interracial and transnational, demands an interrogation of one's own identity that may lead to a disaggregation of the self and a set of affective reorientations that are as likely to be excruciating, frustrating, and disconcerting as ecstatically pleasurable. It is through such affective and intellectual labor that we render coalition *effective*, making a historical structure of feeling such as "queer revolt" both mean and *feel* differently than it did before.[90]

However, Genet did not labor to shift his affective landscape of queer revolt out of political commitment and high-minded solidarity. This affective labor offered him a sizable payoff. By identifying with the Panthers and the Palestinians, he was able to recuperate the charge of radical oppositionality that the complicitous figure of the European queer outlaw, once situated within a transnational frame, could no longer deliver. Coalition was, among other things, a means of identifying the most resistant and threatening movements through which Genet could route his oppositional wish.[91] The following afterword deidealizes the imaginary of queer coalitional oppositionality that Genet's late activism exemplifies.

AFTERWORD: DEIDEALIZING OPPOSITIONAL QUEER COALITION

During the late 1990s, *an antinormative coalition across difference* was offered up as the radical promise of Queer Studies' often corrosive critiques of identity. In 1997, Cathy Cohen influentially echoed David Halperin's definition of *queer* as an "oppositional relation to the norm," reiterating that the radical potential of queerness was in its "ability to create a space *in opposition to dominant norms*, a space where transformational political work can begin."[92] The consequential *difference* is Cohen's bid to shift *queer*'s field of reference to center racialized sexualities: "I envision a politics where one's relation to power, and not some homogenized identity, is privileged in determining one's political comrades. I'm talking about a politics where the *nonnormative* and *marginal* position of punks, bulldaggers, and welfare queens, for example, is the basis for progressive transformative coalition work."[93] As her subtitle memorably both queries and proposes, might a nonidentitarian coalition of "Punks, Bulldaggers, and

Welfare Queens" be our best hope for "The Radical Potential of Queer Politics," and, we might add, of Queer Studies itself? This proposition found itself at the center of an emergent queer of color critique in 2004 with the publication of Roderick Ferguson's *Aberrations in Black*, which concludes that "in this historic moment, probably more than any other, oppositional coalitions have to be grounded in nonnormative racial difference."[94] An oppositional coalition of the sexually and racially deviant has been positioned as the answer to the question of Queer Studies' political value as well as the utopian relational imaginary in which the field's aspirations for social transformation are perhaps most intensely invested.

If nonnormative coalition is a potent queer ideal, it is because it promises to reconcile three aspirations that animate contemporary work in Queer Studies: to be *against the norm*,[95] to be *politically radical*, and to open the way to *world making*. Coalitional collectivities based not on fixed identities but on a shared position of distance in relation to norms suggest the potential for radical political activism outside the strictures and complicities of identity politics. The very collective assembly of nonnormative figures held apart by contemporary categories of identity—punks, bulldaggers, and welfare queens; or, in Genet's case, criminal queers and anticolonial militants—invokes, as its horizon of possibility, an alternative social world to come in which such a collective would have a rightful place. Oppositional queer coalitions therefore promise, satisfyingly, to make good on some of the key critical, political, and utopian aspirations that animate queer scholarship. However, to make such collectivities *the object of analysis* rather than invoking them as the glimpse of a utopian futurity to come requires an interrogation of the aspirations that animate them.[96] In particular, we would have to acknowledge that the aspiration that queer scholarship and its objects be *antinormative, politically radical*, and *world making*—which functions as if each term is a sufficient guarantee of the other (i.e., to be antinormative is to be political is to engage in world making; to engage in world making is to be political and antinormative . . .)—is, in actuality, *a dissimilar and contradictory set of injunctions*. Genet's attachment to the Panthers and the Palestinians, which does not fully deliver on the hopes that animate desires for oppositional queer coalition, illustrates both the internal contradictions between the aspirations that animate this ideal and the risks inherent in its foundation on negative affect.

First of all, Genet foregrounds the fact that the ideal of oppositional queer coalition is *unstably based on negativity*. In much queer scholarship, what binds coalition is *negatively* defined—it is a shared *abjection*, an *exclusion* from normativity, a common *marginalization* as deviant, a *disidentification* with hegemonic ideals, or a stance of *opposition* in relation to state power.[97] This means that queer coalition is a form of attachment founded on the unstable energy of negative emotions, such as shame, aggression, anger, and hatred. If Genet was drawn to the popular representation of the Panthers and the Palestinians as violent enemies of liberal states, and what initially made him feel close to the Panthers was "their hatred for the white world," then to what extent are we willing to acknowledge not only much touted shame, but also *hatred* and *violence*, with their destructive and uncontrollable effects, as the affective basis for oppositional coalitions?[98] The negativity that animates much activism may mobilize negative emotions, such as hatred, whose political consequences are difficult to control or to predict in ways that we do not always acknowledge. For instance, Deborah Gould argues that the normative emotional idiom of anger within ACT-UP, which so powerfully energized its direct action activism, eventually made it difficult to recover from the accusatory infighting and to address the racialized political tensions that began tearing the movement apart during the early 1990s.[99] What I am advocating is deidealizing, *without abandoning*, the imaginary of oppositional queer coalition by avowing the volatility and instability of the negative emotions and affects that drive it. Genet's hatreds—of France and the French bourgeoisie, of liberal states and of "the white world"—at once exemplify the potent politics that *can and do* emerge from oppositionality and negative affect and foreground the risks and limitations of such a politics.

We might turn to Sara Ahmed for an understanding of hatred as at once a mode of attachment and "a form of intimacy." "Hatred," she writes, "is ambivalent; it is an investment in an object (of hate) whereby the object becomes a part of the life of the subject even though (or perhaps because) its threat is perceived as coming from outside."[100] Genet's hatreds are attachments that rely on and, indeed, that *affectively sustain* the power of that which he revolts against. In a 1975 interview, Genet responds to the question "Can you say what your political revolution would be like?" with a qualified "No," since "a revolution would probably not allow me to revolt, that is, to revolt individually." In an important formulation, he elaborates, "My point of view is very egotistic. I would like for the world—now pay attention to the way I say this—*I would like for the world not to change so that I can be against the world.*"[101] As Jonathan Dollimore astutely remarks, "Genet presupposes what he would challenge."[102] Genet's statement illustrates Janet Jakobsen's caution that "Opposition to the norm ... can present the problem of being definitionally determined by what we would resist."[103] In frankly avowing the egoism of his stance of opposition, Genet suggests that there can be a kind of *pleasure* in always being against something. He thereby gives us insight into the satisfactions of a kind of selfhood—one that Queer Studies as a field also cultivates—that knows itself through perpetual critical oppositionality.

Finally, Genet's attachment to the Panthers and the Palestinians elides the fact that these groups were not only *against*; they were also *for*. Whereas Genet was most interested in the festive ferment of the revolutionary moment, in which residual structures of feeling were transformed and custom thrown to the winds, and in the queer satisfactions of a violent oppositionality, the Panthers and the Palestinians are also seeking to imagine and to bring about another mode of social, political, and economic organization.[104] More than revolting or opposing, these movements are about world making, that is, about working to imagine and to bring a future into being, a future they do not hesitate to name. The Palestinians, for instance, have named statehood, land, and national sovereignty among their desired political goals. There is thus a fundamental contradiction in Genet's attachment to the Palestinians: whereas he is electrified by their position as enemies of liberal states, what they seek is, precisely, statehood. If the usual principle of coalitional solidarity might be summarized as "different identities, same goals," then what does it mean to be in coalition with the Palestinians *without* supporting their goals of statehood and sovereignty? In a 1983 interview, Genet declares: "Listen: the day the Palestinians are institutionalized, I will no longer be on their side. The day the Palestinians become a nation like other nations, I won't be there anymore." To his interviewer's question about whether the Palestinians know and accept this, he responds, "I think that's where I'm going to betray them. They don't know it."[105] In one respect, this betrayal exemplifies the purity of Genet's queer stance: Genet follows through to its logical conclusion the principle of *queer* as an opposition to norms by categorically opposing the nation-state system as the linchpin of international biopower. Given this rigorous commitment to queer opposition, Genet can only be with the Palestinians while they are in the process of revolt, vilified as terrorists, exiled from landed sovereignty and from the legitimizing form of the nation-state. Had they achieved the political future for which they were struggling, there would have ended his solidarity with them. If, as Lee Edelman has provocatively argued, every political claim on behalf of a future affirms the heteroreproductive social order, Genet finds a way of being radically political that evades this quandary by being contingent on the movement's desired political futurity *not coming about*.[106]

My point is neither to criticize Genet by arguing that true coalition would have required that he take seriously the Palestinian bid for sovereignty nor to praise him for his commitment to oppositional radicalism, even when it required betraying his Palestinian comrades.[107] Rather, I am interested in what Genet's contingent and antifutural queer alliance with the Palestinians reveals about the aspirations of Queer Studies and the ideal of oppositional coalition in particular. Genet's late coalitional activism demonstrates the incoherence of the joint aspirations, in Queer Studies, to be *against the norm, politically radical,* and *world making*. Genet is resolutely against the biopolitical norms that mark the Palestinians for death; however, his againstness is also a form of intimacy that freely admits its desire that norms be sustained so that his opposition to them, and the satisfactions therein, might continue unabated. His position is at once unquestionably radical, in its advocacy of violence and categorical opposition to the nation-state system, and yet curiously apolitical, in its avowed desire that the world *not* change so that he might continue to be *against* it. Were Genet still living, would his continued attachment to the Palestinians have required the tragic prolongation of the Israeli/Palestinian conflict such that, at the time of this writing, Palestinians *still* lack a recognized nation-state and sovereign territory and are *still* fighting in an armed struggle that is *still* viewed as a terrorist disregard for the value of life by the mainstream Euro-American-Israeli media? Whether politically radical or apolitical, it is clear that Genet's oppositional coalition with the Palestinians is *neither future oriented nor world making*. In this respect, it is fully coherent with the purity of a queer stance of opposition to norms, which must renounce alternative futures, the emergence of new worlds, and minoritarian cultures alike insofar as *no alternative, no future, and no culture can be free of the creation of new norms*.

To admit this is to *deidealize* oppositional coalition. The ideal of oppositional coalition is animated by risky and volatile affective attachments. It is constitutively unable to fully deliver on the competing aspirations—for antinormative oppositionality, political radicalism, and world making—that animate it. If Queer Studies is to examine in situated detail, as I am arguing it ought, the practice of coalition and the life-worlds of deviant socialities, it must first deidealize its various political and historical imaginaries and disaggregate their assumed relation to one another. For an attention to the variegated textures of *queer*, as it exits the realm of high theory to be assumed, embodied, and enacted within particular social contexts, requires us to deidealize the queer imaginaries we treasure the most, abandoning the purity of queer negativity, utopianism, and oppositionality alike to embrace and theorize a range of queer *im*purities. I see this as a means of *living with* our queer attachments; for deidealization is another word for love.[108]

epilogue

HAUNTED BY THE 1990S:
QUEER THEORY'S AFFECTIVE HISTORIES

Instead of avoiding the failure of Queer Studies' field imaginaries, *Disturbing Attachments* has instead sought to pursue the insights to which failure might lead. This has required a certain respect for my object. Not "respect" in the sense of celebrating Genet, excusing him, or remaining convinced of his essential goodness, but in the far different sense of being willing to pursue his wily and sometimes contradictory affective motivations, the most apparently irredeemable aspects of his relations, and the disappointments inherent in even his most oppositional political coalitions. *Disturbing Attachments* has demonstrated that politically "bad" relations and modes of attachment, such as pederasty and racial fetishism, may generate surprising theoretical and historical insights, though these cannot be counted on to reinforce Queer Studies' field imaginaries. It has demonstrated that politically "good" queer objects, such as political coalition and uninstitutionalized relations, merit a rich historicization and careful analysis that will, in turn, inevitably disturb the utopian aspirations Queer Studies brings to them. Since one way of redeeming what we find disturbing or problematic is through a developmental progress narrative (which, perhaps not incidentally, is the canonical temporality of the single-author study), I have sought to theorize the multiple and polyphonic temporalities of the erotic and of political activism. While I have argued that Genet's "queerness" *did* magnetize his attraction to the Palestinians and the Black Panthers, I have sought to exactingly render the multiple determinants—pederastic, carceral, and colonial—of this queerness, its range of relations to activism, and its divergent political and ethical effects. Attending to these multiplicities—outside any progress narrative or singular evaluative judgment—has been one means of attending to complex personhood.

What writing this book ultimately taught me is that if Genet did not consistently do the things I *felt* he ought to do, the *feelings* that I—as a Queer Studies practitioner—brought to the project had their own history, a history *Disturbing Attachments* centers and interrogates. Throughout the book, I have examined how a set of disavowed and undertheorized historical imaginaries—of gay liberationist utopianism and negativity, of liberal autonomy and egalitarianism, of idealized Anglophone "chosen family," and of 1960s and post-1960s social movements that have persistently linked gay and lesbian sexuality to political futurity—inhabit and orient the field habitus of contemporary Queer Studies, influencing what aspects of the queer past are made available for queer theorization. Up to this point, however, there has been a glaring hole in the book's historical attachment genealogies—that of the U.S. early 1990s—a period just beyond the chronological scope of the book's case studies (Genet died in 1986), yet foundational to its primary theoretical interlocutor, queer theory. The epilogue proposes that the future of the field of Queer Studies—as well as its relevance for scholarship on prior historical periods, racialized populations, and areas outside the United States—requires a reckoning with the field's affective haunting by the inaugural moment of the U.S. 1990s. I conclude by considering how this book's method of attachment genealogy and heuristic of deidealization might open the way toward an interdisciplinary future, grounded in the specificities of *multiple* racial, geographical, and historical contexts, for the field of Queer Studies.

QUEER AND NOW

Before elaborating on the significance of the 1990s, I want to begin with a text that marks an important moment in Queer Studies scholarship, the introduction to the 2005 special issue of *Social Text* edited by David Eng, J. Jack Halberstam, and José Esteban Muñoz and titled "What's Queer about Queer Studies Now?" Published as a field intervention that markedly highlighted the work of "a younger generation of scholars," this special issue, as described in its Introduction, sought to foreground the question of "the political utility of queer" in its assessment of "what's queer" about contemporary Queer Studies scholarship.[1] The antennae of political utility, in turn, orient the editors to identify the target of queer critical intervention as a series of "late twentieth-century global crises" which they describe, quoting Walter Benjamin, as "historical emergencies."[2] Their list of the "emergencies" to which this special issue responds includes

> the triumph of neoliberalism and the collapse of the welfare state; the Bush administration's infinite "war on terrorism" and the acute militarization of state violence; the escalation of U.S. empire building and the clash of religious fundamentalisms, nationalisms, and patriotisms; the devolution of civil society and the erosion of civil rights; the pathologizing of immigrant communities as "terrorist" and racialized populations as "criminal"; the shifting forms of citizenship and migration in a putatively "postidentity" and "postracial" age; the politics of intimacy and the liberal recoding of freedom as secularization, domesticity, and marriage; and the return to "moral values" and "family values" as a prophylactic against political debate, economic redistribution, and cultural dissent.[3]

The editors' list is significant in several ways: it unambiguously affirms *queer* as a term capable of intervening in a social and political field conceived more broadly, for Queer Studies, than in the past; it centers within the field large-scale processes—such as militarization, racialized criminalization, and shifting forms of migration—whose link to the humble object of "queer sexuality" is, though not insignificant, at least not immediately foregrounded; and it therefore attenuates *queer*'s reference to sexuality. This list is also indicative of the special issue's important and generative role as both a platform and a mission statement for the centering of issues of race and global geopolitics in the field. While this expansion of the field of queer scholarship is undoubtedly energizing, readers may well wonder what makes it cohere. What makes *queer* gravitate to these points of intervention and not others? Why not, in fact, *everything*?[4] For the editors of this special issue, what coheres in this field of intervention is, on the one hand, a concern with the exigencies of the "now," and, on the other, an understanding of *queer* as "a political metaphor without a fixed referent."[5] The latter, much quoted, formulation is important, for the "fixed referent" which the authors affirm *queer* to be lacking is clearly the referent of sexuality, or, even more narrowly, gays and lesbians. Freed of its historical debt to same-sex sexuality, *queer* is defined as *that which flies wherever the demands of political urgency might call it*. Above all, this is a powerful statement for the cutting-edge relevancy of the field.

Queer theory has long celebrated *queer* as an almost infinitely mobile and mutable theoretical term that, unlike *gay and lesbian* or *feminist* need not remain bound to any particular identity, historical context, politic, or object of study, and that, for that very reason, promises a cutting-edge political intervention. Hence, while what they designate as the scope of queer scholarship may be new, Eng, Halberstam, and Muñoz's proposal that *queer* not be constrained to its historical reference to same-sex sexualities, cultures, and movements and their understanding of *queer* as definitionally oriented toward urgent political interventions is not. This is, in fact, something that the editors acknowledge in their citations of Judith Butler's "Critically Queer" and Michael Warner's introduction to *Fear of a Queer Planet*, two foundational texts in early 1990s queer theory. In "Critically Queer," published in the first volume of GLQ in 1993, Judith Butler argues, in what has become a field-defining statement:

> If the term "queer" is to be a site of collective contestation, the point of departure for a set of historical reflections and futural imaginings, it will have to remain that which is, in the present, never fully owned, but always and only redeployed, twisted, queered from a prior usage and in the direction of urgent and expanding political purposes and perhaps also yielded in favor of terms that do that political work more effectively.[6]

Somewhat tautologically, perhaps, the relevance of *queer*, as a term, is described as contingent on its constant *queering*. We see here, already, the proposition that *queer* can never be *queer enough*; that is, that the future of queer scholarship depends on always queer*ing* and being *queerer than* what came before.[7] Here, also, we find the claims, which Eng, Halberstam, and Muñoz echo and sharpen, that *queer* must always be "queered from a prior usage," never allowing its meaning or field of reference to settle, and that what guides this constant queering movement is none other than "urgent and expanding political purposes." *Wherever political urgency calls*, queer *must follow*. While this may sound like a declaration of *queer*'s infinite adaptability and limitless futurity, Butler ends on a less sanguine note, evoking the possibility of *queer*'s eventual demise, its potential need to be "yielded in favor of terms that do that political work more effectively." This sentence clause, tacked on almost as an afterthought, is in fact an important recognition of the temporality, the timeliness of *queer*, as well as the possibility that we may have to abandon it. In the 1993 foreword she pairs with her 1991 essay "Queer and Now," Eve Sedgwick muses, "I suppose this must be called the moment of Queer," which seems immediately to evoke the worry that "in the short-shelf-life American marketplace of images, maybe the queer moment, if it's here today, will for that very reason be gone tomorrow." This worry proves fleeting, however, and Sedgwick steps back from the abyss to issue the reassuring and redeeming claim "that something about *queer* is inextinguishable."[8] Butler, by contrast, seems to recognize that the political charge of *queer* is a product of historical conditions; and that, under different circumstances, *queer* might become a term unsuited for the aspirations with which history, in the U.S. moment of the early 1990s, had freighted it.

Insofar as early 1990s queer theory was, in part, a bid to bring some of the energy, in-your-face defiance, political urgency, and transgressiveness of on-the-ground queer activism into the academy, its early appeal was inseparable from its affective connection to a range of events outside the academy.[9] If *queer* offered itself up, at this time, as a name for a set of theoretical interventions around the relations between sexuality, normativity, and the political, it was because of the current and recent cultural contests it invoked: the genocidal Reagan administration's nonresponse to the AIDS crisis; the associated resurgence of violent homophobia; a newly performative, in-your-face, and media-savvy form of activism in groups like ACT-UP, the Lesbian Avengers, and Queer Nation; highly publicized battles over the state funding of queer artists like Robert Mapplethorpe and David Wojnarowicz; and the ongoing legacy of the "sex wars" that roiled feminists and birthed a vocal feminist sex radicalism during the 1980s.[10] *Queer* was not only a term explicitly mobilized within a series of highly charged political and cultural conflicts; it was a term that seemed *to carry within it* the loaded transgression and charged sense of struggle around sex and sexual cultures that was cropping up, seemingly everywhere, and taking a multitude of inventive cultural forms during the 1980s and 1990s.[11] This was the sense in which *queer* was of the "now," and the early 1990s was, indeed, "the moment of Queer."[12] Born of a desire to fuck up the "normal business in the academy" by carrying into scholarship the political charge and current urgency of sexual politics, queer theory was, as Heather Love reminds us, *never intended to age.*[13]

That was then, this is now. The introduction to "What's Queer about Queer Studies Now?" is a field statement about how Queer Studies can have a future that *stays true to* its originary charge of political urgency and "nowness" in a much-changed landscape for sexual politics and cultures. The sentence that ends with the call for an understanding of *queer* as "a political metaphor without a fixed referent" begins by invoking "the contemporary mainstreaming of gay and lesbian identity—as a mass-mediated consumer lifestyle and embattled legal category," staking the issue of the renewal of Queer Studies on the crisis of gay and lesbian culture's loss of its transgressive political charge.[14] In 2005, gay marriage was the civil rights issue of the day, and in the mainstream mass cultural arena, *queer* was more likely to invoke consumer culture-centric popular television shows such as *Queer Eye for the Straight Guy* and *Queer as Folk* than images of mass protest, the shock of transgression, or a sense of life-or-death urgency. At the same time, racialized homophobia and transphobia continued to have a deadly and enervating, though highly uneven, impact across populations and geographies. What future for Queer Studies when *queer* is no longer the term of *the now* and when its historical link to same-sex sexuality is no longer sufficient to guarantee its politicality? Eng, Halberstam, and Muñoz respond by definitionally centering *queer*'s meaning on its *charge of political urgency*, which was an affective product of the moment of the 1990s, rather than its historic reference to same-sex sexuality. At a moment when "gay and lesbian" no longer describes a radical and transgressive political constituency, however, this taxes Queer Studies with pushing itself to remain continually *on the move*, forever in search of that object, diagnosis, or scene of intervention that will make good on the political promise that inaugurated this field-that-was-not-meant-to-be-a-field. Robyn Wiegman has argued that fields founded on aspirations for social justice must "perform inexhaustibility continuously."[15] Given its central anti-identitarianism claim, that is, the much reiterated definition of *queer* as, paradoxically, *undefined*, but as emphatically *not* synonymous with same-sex sexuality, Queer Studies is perhaps unique in having been founded on the "durational strategy" and "aspirational horizon" of being always *elsewhere* than where it was before.[16]

Queer anti-identitarianism and indefinition, however, produce their own problems. The use of *queer* as a false umbrella term that, in practice, most often refers to gay white men has often been exposed and critiqued. For Hiram Pérez, the transparent subject of much queer theorizing problematically replicates the "race-neutral objectivity" of "the university's ideal bourgeois subject," and for Jasbir Puar, his ideal state of "freedom from norms" draws on the values of autonomy, individualism, and choice enshrined within liberalism.[17] In a linguistic analysis of the term *queer*, Mel Chen critiques the ways in which anti-identitarian field statements by David Halperin and Michael Warner tend to mystify *queer*'s indefinition and idealize its mobility.[18] Biddy

Martin has analyzed the ways in which the value accorded to queer mobility implicitly denigrates a static "feminine" domain of enmeshment in kinship and reproduction.[19] These critics and others have amply demonstrated that it is both dangerous and disingenuous to obfuscate the subject of queer anti-identitarianism and to idealize *queer*'s definitional openness. Less discussed is the worrisome harmony between *queer*'s much trumpeted mobility, flexibility, adaptability, and portability and the demands for accelerated obsolescence and flexible and mobile labor that characterize late capitalism.[20] Might Queer Studies resist the demand that it constantly sell a new product that satisfyingly reproduces the cutting-edge cachet of its founding moment, as well as the implication that to fail to do so is to be, simply, dead? "What's queer about Queer Studies *now*?" we hear ... and *now*? ... and *now*?

I want to propose that queer mobility and indefinition function within Queer Studies as both *a disciplinary norm* and *a front*. A disciplinary norm because Queer Studies has become a field paradoxically defined by its lack of a defined object of study and its quasi-infinite mobility of reference. A front because, whereas field statements affirming *queer*'s inexhaustible definitional mobility claim to open up queer theory as an antidisciplinary mode of inquiry that is open to radical transformations and becomings, they actually work to secure it as a field that need not be accountable to its own history (which now spans, in its named institutional form, more than two decades) because it is already beyond it. A front, moreover, because little queer scholarship actually uses *queer* in an entirely dereferentialized manner. To avow, however, the tacit consensus that queer scholarship does in fact reference sex, gender, and sexuality would be to pin the field down, exposing it as defined not by whatever is most radical, urgent, and cutting-edge, but by the ordinary vicissitudes of the politics of gender, sex, and sexuality in social context. If this is the case, then how can we get out of the bind produced by the requirement that *queer* retain its originary charge of transgression, avant-garde novelty, and political potency by always meaning something new without, for that matter, restricting the imaginative and politicized expansion of queer inquiry that is the most valuable legacy of Eng, Halberstam, and Muñoz's special issue?

QUEER'S AFFECTIVE HISTORIES

We might begin by zeroing in on, rather than running away from the current problem of *queer*'s affective deflation. In an astute analysis, Chen ascribes *queer*'s deanimation both to its loss of affectivity, as the term has been partially reclaimed from its status as an insult, and to its stultifying fixation into a noun and identity category. According to Chen, *queer* "has been both re-animated and de-animated. While it continually reanimates in new formations—thanks particularly to queer of color, transnational, disability, and trans scholarship— it has also achieved nominal frame as an identity; but it has simultaneously coalesced, gotten sticky, inertial, lost its animation and its drive in the context of the United States."[21] In concluding by arguing that *queer*'s future is contingent on its capacity to overcome its current inertia and stickiness by being modified by something else, Chen ultimately seeks to reanimate *queer* by giving it a future that diverges from its past. However, at the same time, Chen offers a linguistic history of *queer* that precedes the 1990s, including Gloria Anzaldúa's theorization of *mestiza queer* during the 1980s—a "first" that is not usually taken up as a foundation for queer theory—and E. Patrick Johnson's account of the African American vernacular term *quare*, seeming to imply that reanimation could proceed through an excavation of the alternative historicities that swarm within and beside *queer*, rather than only by the term's future movements. Indeed, Chen relates the term's loss of both animacy and affectivity to its *loss of historicity*, analyzing how *queer* as "a nominal category can seem to 'forget' its history."[22] Could *queer* be rendered lively, then, by an engagement with its *multiple* pasts, by a reanimation of its dense affective historicity, rather than only by a future of continual modification by something else?

I want to propose that, rather than continuing to celebrate queer mobility and indefinition, we ground *queer* in its various contexts, histories, genealogies, and inheritances. For these contexts are the source of *affective histories* that influence, without it being acknowledged, what meanings adhere to *queer*, how this term is deployed, and what happens when it takes on life in new contexts. Rather than regarding queer's *stickiness* as *a problem* to be overcome by ever more mobility, I propose that we account for *how* the associations *queer* has accrued in its travels—within mostly U.S. and Anglophone political and academic discourses—assure that *only certain* forms of nonnormativity, *only particular* sex acts seem to attach to it.[23] We need to understand what coagulation of historical affects gives body to *queer* and to attend to what becomes of these affective histories when *queer* travels to novel historical, geopolitical, conceptual, and demographic locations.

Avowing the affective histories of *queer*—which often display themselves less though explicit claims than in affective dispositions toward and away from certain terms—would require our willingness to admit that *queer* is not endlessly open-ended, polyvalent, and reattachable. Instead, it is a term sticky with history, that bears the impression, in its characteristic gestures, dispositions, and orientations, of its travels in time and space. For Sara Ahmed, "stickiness" describes the ways in which terms accumulate affectivity through histories of use: "Signs become sticky through repetition; if a word is used in a certain way, again and again, then the 'use' *becomes* intrinsic; it becomes a form of signing."[24] Ahmed's understanding of how emotions and historicity are intimately conjoined might usefully be brought to bear on scholarship on the affectivity of the term *queer*. In *The Cultural Politics of Emotion*, she demonstrates that figures and key terms that seem inherently laden with emotion often conceal the history—of circulation, repetition, and association with other terms—that has resulted in their accumulation of affective value. In other words, historicity makes figures and terms "sticky"—particular emotions, particular proximate terms become bound to them, while others become blocked, sliding inconsequentially past. This is how terms can get "stuck," becoming difficult to resignify, redeploy in novel circumstances, or project into new constellations of association. The discipline of Queer Studies has worked hard to keep *queer* slick rather than sticky, unbound, detachable, and able to reattach itself to an endless array of new objects and methods.[25] Nevertheless, I would argue that the very polyvalent richness of *queer*—the fact that it remains a highly charged term that can evoke, simultaneously and contradictorily, injury, negativity, utopianism, transgression, defiance, righteousness, superiority, radicalism, hipness, and rage, but most often some combination, some metonymic attraction between a series of those terms—indicates that *queer* is *not* slick but rather the stickiest of terms. It has been *made* sticky not only by its career, its course within mostly U.S.-centered academic conversations, but also by its historical emergence in precisely the U.S. scene of the 1990s that contemporary Queer Studies often seems so eager to forget and to move beyond.[26] Forgetting this history is useful to the field, precisely because it permits us to refuse to define or to historicize *queer*, to say we are holding it open to indefinite becomings, all the while making implicit and explicit arguments that draw both their conviction and their appeal from *queer*'s affective charge, that is, from its disavowed historicity.

To investigate and contend with the historicity of *queer* would mean both remembering the contexts of *queer*'s academic emergence during the 1990s and excavating the alternative historical imaginaries that teem within *queer*. The task of unpacking the legacy of the 1990s, however, seems particularly urgent. For I suspect that however far contemporary Queer Studies travels in topic, methodology, and scope from the concerns of early 1990s queer theory, it *remains haunted* by the electric 1990s convergence, under the banner of *queer*, of same-sex sexuality, political urgency, and radical transgression.[27] This accounts for certain contradictions of queer inquiry during a contemporary juncture in which neither the political urgency nor the transgressive effects of *queer* can be taken for granted.

THE AGENCIES OF HISTORICITY

This is not to say, however, that *queer* has become detached from political radicalism. I would argue, to the contrary, that it remains haunted by the political and transgressive charge of the early 1990s moment, and that this haunting orients it toward particular political and intellectual projects in the present. One symptom of this haunting is the fact that, as I write this, *queer* is likely to carry a *nostalgic* charge. For many self-identified queer subjects as well as queer scholars, *queer* signals a disidentification with the contemporary mainstreaming and assimilationism of gay and lesbian politics and culture and, as Lucas Hilderbrand has written regarding the significance of the gay AIDS crisis for those of us who came of age after it, a "nostalgia for a previously radical queer community."[28] In a significant shift, *queer* has gone from being *of the "now"* to being *a rejection of the "now."* Indeed, if Muñoz's *Cruising Utopia: The Then and There of Queer Futurity* (2009) is such a visionary and timely book, it is because it theorizes contemporary queers' disaffection with the present and yearning for a more radical time and place. Declaring, "The present is not enough," Muñoz boldly identifies queerness with the utopian longing for a different futurity that does not proceed, in an inevitably linear fashion, from the fallen state of the present.[29] As he repeatedly specifies, the present that is not enough is that "of neoliberal ideology and the degradation of politics brought about by representations of queerness in contemporary popular culture": it is contemporary queer normalization within the folds of neoliberalism that has ruined the present.[30] But the "Then" of the book's subtitle is not only the future. *Cruising Utopia* seeks to reactivate the past through a "queer utopian memory" that is ultimately oriented toward helping us glimpse a more expansive futurity.[31] Finding the radical political charge of the queer early 1990s flagging in the present, scholarship that we might characterize as *radically nostalgic* seeks to reanimate and indeed to intensify this charge by characterizing, as queer, a *utopian longing* that draws hope for the future out of the radical aspects of various pasts. *Queer's* affective historicity is reanimated and transformed through multiple temporal torsions, imbuing *queer* with an intensified utopianism that draws its energy from the pangs of nostalgia and loss.

By contrast, most scholarship on homonormativity and homonationalism—in its trenchant critiques of the incorporation of homosexuality into neoliberal governmentality and a defanged multicultural diversity that consolidates familiar gender, racial, and geopolitical hierarchies—is far from utopian. Nevertheless, I am interested in how, in the sheer *energy* of its critique, scholarship on homonationalism and homonormativity seems still to be animated by the now-injured aspiration that queer sexuality *ought to* attach to radical politics and to an antiassimilationist stance toward the institutions of the state. That is, it seems to me that what drives the prominence of critiques of homonormativity and homonationalism in contemporary Queer Studies is a historical disappointment—of those political and antiassimilationist energies that continue to reverberate in *queer*, even as some versions of queer sexuality have become absorbable into a neoliberal politics of lifestyle choice and anodyne diversity.

The energy of queer work on homonormativity and homonationalism, as well as the readiness with which it disidentifies with normalized gay and lesbian subjects, betrays its continuing animation by the *queer*'s affective histories and, as a result, its unwillingness to give *queer* up to its deanimated and defanged contemporary uses. On a linguistic level, we see this desire to preserve and redirect the politically potent affective histories of *queer* in a bifurcation in the term's meaning and uses. In much scholarship on homonormativity and homonationalism, terms such as *queer liberalism* or the *disciplinary queer* position *queer* as an affectively neutral and deradicalized descriptor for privileged gay and lesbian subjects absorbed into techniques of neoliberal global governance.[32] At the same time, another *queer* is often preserved as the carrier of *queer*'s affective histories and of the political aspirations of the field of Queer Studies. This *queer* refers either to authentically oppressed and truly resistant queer political subjects, or, in a dereferentialized form, to those processes or forces *uncapturable* within any of the systems of governance or power being diagnosed and critiqued. Jasbir Puar's *Terrorist Assemblages* (2007) is exemplary in its refusal to allow *queer* to wishfully and ahistorically signify antinormativity or anti-identitarianism at this contemporary juncture. Indeed, the book's conclusion forwards a notion of queer*ness* as a complex and shifting assemblage that cannot be pressed into the binaries of normative/antinormative or resistant/complicit. By the end, however, it is this very evasion of simplistic analytic binaries that allows queerness to be celebrated as uncapturable by power: "a queer praxis of assemblage allows for a scrambling of sides that is illegible to state practices of surveillance, control, banishment, and extermination."[33] Redefined as a "scrambling" of affective and bodily practices, queerness rebecomes something of political value, for it promises a futurity in excess of the technologies and rationalities of power in the present. But, we might ask, what is it about *queer* that allows it to be the name for *that which exceeds power*, even as it simultaneously designates those gay and lesbian subjects who are the contemporary *agents* of state power? Through this bifurcation in the meaning of *queer*, *queer*'s affective histories may be preserved against the failure of contemporary gay and lesbian politics to make good on them.

MULTIPLYING *QUEER*'S AFFECTIVE HISTORIES

I am interested in how much work in contemporary Queer Studies responds to *queer*'s present failure of the past aspirations that continue to inhabit it with a renewed utopianism that relocates the affective energies of *queer* onto objects and analytics—from transnationalism to affect to assemblages—deemed more politically and theoretically promising than mere same-sex sexuality. Despite *queer*'s disappointments, we cannot seem to allow it to fail, for that would not only threaten the future of the field of inquiry that bears its name, but also the possibility of using Queer Studies as a resource for the renewal of contemporary queer political imaginaries. As a result, queer scholars deploy *queer*'s lush connotations, bifurcating from the denotative use of *queer* as an umbrella for LGBT to exploit instead some connotative sense of *queer* that appears better suited to forward the transgression and political potency with which the term became laden around the early 1990s. My hypothesis, then, is that what Queer Studies has institutionalized, above an object of study or method, is a set of historical emotions generated within U.S. queer culture and politics around the early 1990s, and indeed, that these historical emotions propel the inchoate method that animates what objects may be claimed as *queer*.

This may be unwelcome news for scholars whose entry points to *queer* are elsewhere than the U.S. 1990s and who seek to make queer scholarship relevant outside this narrow context of institutional emergence—I am thinking particularly of queer scholarship on non-U.S. areas, prior historical periods, and racialized populations. My argument, to be clear, is not that Queer Studies needs to confine itself either to the historical time and place of *queer* or to the "object" of same-sex sexuality. To the contrary, I am arguing that any redeployment of *queer* outside its narrow context of emergence that keeps *queer*'s affective histories intact—seeking, for instance, to preserve the convergence of same-sex sexuality, political urgency, and radical transgression—is unwittingly reinscribing its 1990s U.S. origin story. For one reason why queer scholarship on Asia, Africa, and Latin America, as well as on earlier historical periods, tends to be marginalized within the field as a whole is because it examines sites in which *queer* operates in markedly different ways from what has been canonized within Queer Studies. In their introduction to a 2016 special issue of GLQ on Queer Studies and area studies, Anjali Arondekar and Geeta Patel incisively critique the tendency of queer scholarship to mine the global South for examples rather than epistemologies, failing to attend to how such key "concepts as loss, margin, normative, and nonnormative" emerge from a U.S. political context.[34] Recent U.S. politics and histories inform not only the conceptual apparatus of Queer Studies, but also the very affective method by which new subjects, politics, practices, and concepts are claimed as queer in the first place. Finding a "match" between a historical or area studies example and one of *queer*'s affective connotations—such as shame, camp irony, or radical opposition—can offer a gateway from Sexuality Studies to Queer Studies scholarship, a wider audience, and a certain theoretical cachet, but at the cost of reinscribing *queer*'s U.S. affective histories at the center of work on new contexts. In order to make good on the expansion of the terrain of queer scholarship since the "What's Queer about Queer Studies Now?" special issue, we might instead rework *queer*'s affective historicity so that *queer* can do new kinds of work with different objects and archives in a range of historical, cultural, and geographic contexts. This may mean allowing *queer* to come not only *to mean* but also *to feel* differently than it does now.

Disturbing Attachments has proposed *attachment genealogy* as a method that focuses on analytically queer forms of nonnormativity that clash with *queer*'s current affective and political connotations in order to excavate the historical attachments that inform *queer*'s aversion to these particular objects. The ambition of such a method is to at once bring into view and to multiply the historical and social conditions that shape what is possible, imaginable, and sensible under the sign of *queer*. In this way, rather than being mined for case studies that are legitimated as queer by virtue of their coherence with the conceptual apparatus and feeling states of queer scholarship, history, geography, and race might be valued for the divergent queer epistemologies and affective histories they generate. The method of attachment genealogy systematizes the attentiveness to the emergence of theory and feeling alike from specific contexts and histories that is exemplified in the richest and most thoughtful new queer scholarship.

When we use Queer Studies to think more historically distant times, racialized populations, and non-U.S. geographies, we are not using *queer* as a mobile and reattachable theoretical term without a history. The transformative and intellectually generative effects that may come from recontextualizing queer are not the sign that *queer* has yet again elastically adapted itself to a new object; rather, they are the product of *queer*'s dense affective histories undergoing chemical reactions with new contexts. Avowing its affective histories would allow Queer Studies to begin the work of recontextualizing itself within new racialized and geopolitical landscapes. The outcome of such a process could not be predicted in advance. It might, however, generate a mutation in the field habitus of Queer Studies that could retrain its felt relations to its objects, aims, and methods of study. This process could be seen as a condition of possibility rather than as a burden or a drag. Because if *queer* is to have life, if it is to be driven to do new things and grapple with new problems, it is through the force and the course of its ongoing affective history. This is how, in Ahmed's terms, emotions, as the flesh of time, may also "open up futures."[35]

In excavating queer attachments that clash with the affective histories of queer theory, *Disturbing Attachments* models such a form of inquiry. I have followed Genet's trajectory in order to reground *queer* in socialities—including early twentieth-century French prison cultures, pederastic kinship, liberationist "erotic coalition," and revolutionary decolonization movements—that precede *queer*'s 1990s articulation as a politics and a theory. My approach has been to use historicized queer socialities to deidealize queer theoretical aspirations. For example: the queer theoretical orientation toward *futurity* marginalizes and dismisses a whole body of work on the past, or else it requires work on the past to prove its value in relation to queer futurity; psychoanalytic queer *negativity* inherits the unsustainable utopianism of a gay liberationist faith in the *exceptionality* of sex—its unique capacity to destroy the Symbolic order and the identities that perpetuate it; the status of *coalition* as the political payoff of anti-identitarian critique depends on a disavowal of the fact that *actual coalitions* are fraught, riven by multiple interests and complex hierarchies; likewise, *alternative socialities* not only suffer the psychic traumas and material costs of unintelligibility and nonrecognition, but also are only "alternative" in relation to some oversimplified hegemony, for *all alternative relations generate their own norms*. It may, in fact, be impossible to do situated and grounded work on *any* queer object—from alternative relations, to coalition, to sex, to time—without running afoul of the aspirations that animated one's choice of object in the first place.

Disturbing Attachments has responded to this dilemma by zeroing in on the alternative affective histories that emerge in the moment of a queer ideal's deflation. By theorizing nostalgia for the commingled affects of pleasure and trauma in incarceration, the animation of erotic life by racial histories, the oscillation between queer historical orphanage and foundling reaffiliation, and the biopolitical feeling that joins pederasts and terrorists as "enemies of the state," it has mapped the emergence of queer affective, erotic, and relational modes from their historical and geographic conditions. I see excavating such alternate affective histories as a crucial means of expanding the epistemologies and feeling states of queer inquiry and, thus, rendering it more responsive to historical, racial, and geopolitical difference. Through its method of attachment genealogy and heuristic of deidealization, *Disturbing Attachments* has sought to materialize a new range of objects and a more varied "archive of feelings" for Queer Studies.[36]

notes

INTRODUCTION

1 I thank Jade Brooks for the latter anecdote.
2 For a reading of Genet's afterlife as an "authentic queer French 'archetype,'" see Provencher, *Queer French*, 55.
3 On homonationalism, see Puar, *Terrorist Assemblages*.
4 Stewart and McGregor, "Jean Genet's Psychiatric Examination in 1943," 798.
5 White, *Genet*, 337.
6 See, in order, Genet, *Pompes funèbres*, 303–4; Genet, *Funeral Rites*, 253; Genet, *L'ennemi déclaré*, 311–13; Genet, *The Declared Enemy*, 269–70; White, *Genet*, 316–17.
7 Bersani, *Homos*, 161.
8 Genet, *The Maids and Deathwatch*, 63. "Ce couple éternel, du criminel et de la sainte" (Genet, "Les bonnes," 156).
9 See Mao and Walkowitz, *Bad Modernisms*.
10 Durham, "Editor's Preface," 1.
11 Genet, *The Declared Enemy*, 261. "Un imposteur qui n'a jamais écrit de livre" (Genet, *L'ennemi déclaré*, 302). My translation of "D'utiliser la merde et de vous la faire bouffer" (Genet, *Pompes funèbres*, 190).
12 I draw on Deborah Gould's understanding of *queer* less as an identity or a theory than as a *sensibility*, which she historicizes as emerging from 1990s ACT-UP activism. Gould, *Moving Politics*, 256.
13 See Caserio et al., "The Antisocial Thesis in Queer Theory."
14 For examples of Genet critics who applaud him for his identification with other forms of social marginality, see Malgorn, *Jean Genet*; and Eribon, *Une morale du minoritaire*, 323.
15 See Warner, *The Trouble with Normal*; Cohen, "Punks, Bulldaggers, and Welfare Queens"; Ferguson, *Aberrations in Black*.
16 Gordon, *Ghostly Matters*, 4.
17 For an argument in favor of recognizing the "ordinariness" of queer cultures, that is, their intelligibility and enmeshment in the social world, see Love, "Doing Being

Deviant." See also Martin, "Extraordinary Homosexuals and the Fear of Being Ordinary."

18 On the contradictions of queer antinomianism, see Warner, "Normal and Normaller," 134–36.

19 For an early and still relevant critique of the "redemptive reinvention of sex" into democratic and ethical queer socialities, see Bersani, "Is the Rectum a Grave?" Deidealizing scholarship in Queer Studies includes Holland, *The Erotic Life of Racism*; Love, *Feeling Backward*; Viego, *Dead Subjects*; Scott, *Extravagant Abjection*. Important works affiliated with queer negativity include Bersani, *Homos*; Edelman, *No Future*; Halberstam, *The Queer Art of Failure*.

20 See, for example, Halberstam, *Female Masculinity*, 15; Hale, "Leatherdyke Boys and Their Daddies," 223.

21 Weiss, "The Epistemology of Ethnography"; Wiegman, *Object Lessons*, 316.

22 Genet, *Our Lady of the Flowers*, 110. "Nos ménages, la loi de nos Maisons, ne ressemblent pas à vos Maisons"; "On s'aime sans amour" (Genet, *Notre-Dame-des-Fleurs*, 93).

23 Warner, "Normal and Normaller," 123–24.

24 The search for critical and alternative queer epistemologies drawn from the history and culture of people of color is foundational to the enterprise of queer of color critique. For a sharp critique, from an area studies perspective, of the failure of queer theory to take up epistemologies from the global South, see Arondekar and Patel, "Area Impossible."

25 Shah, *Contagious Divides*.

26 Exciting forthcoming scholarship by Nayan Shah, Sima Shakhsari, and Christina Hanhardt centers undocumented immigrants, refugees, and drug addicts within queer scholarship. I do not mean to suggest that they idealize these figures. In some cases, a careful focus on the particulars of their marginalized positions is leading scholars to reach beyond the binaries of celebration versus critique as well as the queer habit of idealization.

27 Butler, "Afterword," 227.

28 See Foucault, *The History of Sexuality*, 92–102.

29 My term *field habitus* draws on Robyn Wiegman's understanding of the often untheorized aspirations, values, and moral judgments that organize field imaginaries, while emphasizing both the affective and the habituated dimensions of the fluency practitioners acquire. Wiegman, *Object Lessons*, especially 15–16.

30 Holland, *The Erotic Life of Racism*; Love, *Feeling Backward*; Viego, *Dead Subjects*; Scott, *Extravagant Abjection*.

31 See Klein, *Love, Guilt, and Reparation*; Sedgwick, "Paranoid Reading and Reparative Reading." For a reading of reparation as inevitably inflicting some harm, see Elizabeth Wilson, *Gut Feminism*, 177–78. My thinking on deidealization is inspired by Love's reminder that a dimension of damage is inherent in the reparative position, as in Sedgwick's late work: "Recognizing that it is not only reparation but damage at work in Sedgwick's late essays will let us begin the hard work of deidealization. And that's love too." Love, "Truth and Consequences," 240.

32 For accounts of how Queer Studies has absorbed older traditions of empirical his-

torical and Sexuality Studies scholarship while denying them citation, see Duggan, "The Discipline Problem"; Rubin, "Geologies of Queer Studies"; Love, "Doing Being Deviant."

33 Edmund White writes, "Genet considered the whole subject of robbing homosexuals a huge joke and claimed that he had taught several other young thieves how to do it. His sense of solidarity with other thieves was certainly stronger than his links with other homosexuals, especially at a time when homosexuality was still experienced either as a source of shame or an object of ridicule. Given that Genet was not attracted to other homosexuals and regarded rich men as particularly alien, his sympathies and antipathies are easy to understand if not to respect" (White, *Genet*, 316–17).

34 Sedgwick, *Tendencies*, xii.

35 Valentine, *Imagining Transgender*, 63. See also Ferguson, *The Reorder of Things*, 217.

36 Berlant, *Cruel Optimism*, 113.

37 My critique of queer exceptionality is inspired by Amber Jamilla Musser's analysis of how queer thinkers as different from one another as Michel Foucault, Leo Bersani, and Lee Edelman position masochism and self-annihilation the exceptional outside of liberal modernity and its technologies of identity and power. Musser, *Sensational Flesh*, 12–21.

38 Scott, *Extravagant Abjection*.

39 Dinshaw herself cautions, "the condition of heterogeneous temporalities can be exploited for destruction as well as expansion: Ernst Bloch recounts chillingly the Nazis' deployment of temporal asynchrony in recruiting Germans who felt backward in the face of an alien modernity," and a number of other participants in this roundtable discussion issue caveats along similar lines. Dinshaw et al., "Theorizing Queer Temporalities," 178. Important exceptions from this general tendency include Love, *Feeling Backward*, and Rohy, *Anachronism and Its Others*.

40 Davis, "Black Nationalism," 292.

CHAPTER 1: ATTACHMENT GENEALOGIES OF PEDERASTIC MODERNITY

1 For instance, David Halperin argues that when Foucault enjoins his readers "to *become* homosexual" in "Friendship as a Way of Life," "his remarks make sense only if he understood his term 'homosexual' according to my definition of 'queer'—as an identity without an essence, not a given condition but a horizon of possibility, an opportunity for self-transformation, a queer potential." Halperin's vision of *queer* not as a sexuality, but as a potential, not as an identity, but as a mode of self-transformation, not as something achieved, but as a futural horizon draws Foucault's more utopian ruminations, inspired by North American gay male cultures of the 1970s and 1980s, into the center of queer theory. Halperin, *Saint Foucault*, 79.

2 Foucault, "Friendship as a Way of Life," 136. "Qu'est-ce que c'est que ça, être entre hommes, 'à nu' hors de relations institutionnelles, de famille, de profession, de camaraderie obligée? C'est un désir, une inquiétude, un désir-inquiétude qui existe chez beaucoup de gens" (Foucault, "De l'amitié comme mode de vie," 983).

3 Love, *Feeling Backward*, 79.
4 Foucault, "Friendship as a Way of Life," 136. "Est-ce qu'on peut dire que le rapport au désir et au plaisir, et à la relation qu'on peut avoir, soit dépendant de son âge?" "Oui, très profondément. Entre un homme et une femme plus jeune, l'institution facilite les differences d'âge; elle l'accepte et la fait fonctionner. Deux hommes d'âge notablement différént, quel code auront-ils pour communiquer? Ils sont l'un en face de l'autre sans arme, sans mots convenus, sans rien qui les rassure sur le sens du movement qui les porte l'un vers l'autre. Ils ont à inventer de A à Z une relation encore sans forme, et qui est l'amitié: c'est-à-dire la somme de toutes les choses à travers lesquelles, l'un a l'autre, on peut se faire plaisir" (Foucault, "De l'amitié comme mode de vie," 983).
5 Early on in the interview, Foucault announces that the problem is to know "what can be done in relation to the quasi identification between homosexuality and love between young people" (Foucault, "Friendship as a Way of Life," 135, translation modified). "Ce qu'on peut fair par rapport à la quasi-identification de l'homosexualité et de l'amour entre jeunes." Foucault, "De l'amitié comme mode de vie," 982.
6 Foucault, "Friendship as a Way of Life," 136. "Deux jeunes garçons se rencontrant dans la rue, se séduisant d'un regard, se mettant la main aux fesses et s'envoyant en l'air dans le quart d'heure. On a là une espèce d'image proprette de l'homosexualité, qui perd toute virtualité d'inquiétude" (Foucault, "De l'amitié comme mode de vie," 983).
7 Of the marked change in imagery in gay magazines and periodicals of the 1970s and 1980s, Scott Gunther writes, "In the new gay imagery of the 1980s, glossy pictures of handsome men began to appear with greater frequency. Unlike the images of waiflike adolescents that dominated the revues of the early 1970s, with their pederastic implications, the prevailing images of the 1980s were quite clearly of adults—men with fully formed, strong bodies and abundant facial hair. This provoked one anonymous contributor to *Gai pied hebdo* to ask whether the appreciation of 'clean, adult, and healthy homosexuals did not lead at the same time to a reinforcement of the repression of pedophiles'" (Gunther, *The Elastic Closet*, 78). Foucault's interview takes place in *Gay pied*, which will be replaced in 1982 by the more mainstream, commercial magazine *Gay pied hebdo*. "Conspicuously absent from this second incarnation," Gunther writes, "were articles and images related to pedophilia, pederasty, transsexuals and transvestites, sadomasochism, and public sex—subjects which had appeared frequently in the press of the early '70s, but also in the first incarnation of *Gai pied* under Le Bitoux's direction" (Gunther, *The Elastic Closet*, 76). This claim may need to be nuanced, since Pierre Verdrager notes that the magazine *Gai pied hebdo* (1982–92) *did* publish articles defending pederasty and pedophilia throughout its existence, even as this defense became less and less tenable in French culture at large (Verdrager, *L'enfant interdit*, 133–34).
8 In Gunther's analysis, the tactic of the gay rights–oriented organization, CUARTH, was to publicly distance homosexuality from pederasty and pedophilia by presenting moderate, assimilationist public demands, such as the equalization of the ages of homosexual and heterosexual consent, while confining more radical voices

advocating pederasty and the abolition of the age of consent to the group's internal debates, forums, and publications.

9 Foucault signed a 1977 petition, along with Althusser, Derrida, Hocquenghem, and other public intellectuals, demanding that the French penal code eliminate all reference to the age of sexual majority. In his April 4, 1978, France-Culture radio discussion with Guy Hocquenghem, Jean Danet, and P. Hahn, first published as "La loi de la pudeur" in *Recherches* in April 1979, Foucault proposes that, rather than fixing a specific age above which consent is presumed and below which it is thought impossible, minors should be credited with being able to explain whether or not they were subject to sexual violence and coercion. Foucault, "La loi de la pudeur"; translated as Foucault, "Sexual Morality and the Law."

10 Rubin, "The Leather Menace," 112.

11 This is not to say that the history of pedophilia in relation to homosexuality was symmetrical in the United States and in France. In the United States, the "Save Our Children" campaign's spokesperson Anita Bryant's characterization of gay men as monstrous pedophiles led, within a few years, to the gay movement's abandonment of boy-lovers, represented by the NAMBLA. By contrast, French activists responded to Anita Bryant's campaign with an organized affirmation rather than a rejection of pedophilia. They organized the first mass Parisian gay demonstration in 1977 in response to the demonization of gay men and pedophiles alike across the Atlantic. They also programmed pederasty-themed events. For instance, the Groupe de Libération Homosexuelle Politique et Quotidien (GLH-PQ) held a "homosexual week" with one day dedicated to "Pederasty" and the "Sexuality of Children."

12 Foucault, "Friendship as a Way of Life," 136. "Annule tout ce qu'il peut y avoir d'inquiétant dans l'affection, la tendresse, l'amitié, la fidélité, la camaraderie, la compagnonnage, auxquels une société un peu ratissée ne peut pas donner de place sans craindre que ne se forment des alliances, que ne se nouent des lignes de force imprévues" (Foucault, "De l'amitié comme mode de vie," 983).

13 Foucault, "Friendship as a Way of Life," 138. "Mode de vie peut se partager entre des individus *d'âge, de statut, d'activité sociale différents*" (Foucault, "De l'amitié comme mode de vie," 984).

14 Foucault, "Friendship as a Way of Life," 138.

15 Sedgwick, *Tendencies*, xii.

16 Halperin, *Saint Foucault*, 80–91.

17 Rubin disputes the characterization of "Thinking Sex" as founding any field by referencing the work of scholars who came before her in Rubin, "Blood under the Bridge."

18 Rubin, "Thinking Sex," 385.

19 In a notable exception, Gillian Harkins argues that Rubin's ability to imagine in 1984 that boy-love, much like homosexuality, was on the verge of being recognized as a legitimate sexual orientation is the result of her inability to predict the ways in which neoliberal governance would seize on the figure of the monstrous pedophile as a useful incitement toward ever-expanding extralegal forms of surveillance and control (Harkins, "Foucault, the Family and the Cold Monster of Neoliberalism").

20 Quoted in Gunther, *The Elastic Closet*, 54.
21 See the FHAR publications, *Tout!* and *Trois milliards de pervers*.
22 See Schérer and Hocquenghem, "Co-ire"; "Fous d'enfance." For a thorough sociological study of the arguments used the condone pedophilia during the 1970s and the reasons why these arguments no longer functioned, and indeed, appeared incomprehensible by the 1990s, see Verdrager, *L'enfant interdit*.
23 On the demise of the pro-pedophilia cause in France by the late 1980s, see Verdrager, *L'enfant interdit*; Ambroise-Rendu, *Histoire de la pédophilie*.
24 Verdrager, *L'enfant interdit*, 151–74. On the U.S. context, see Harkins, "Foucault, the Family and the Cold Monster of Neoliberalism." On the uses and harmful effects of sex panics around pedophilia, see Levine, *Harmful to Minors*; Rubin, "Thinking Sex."
25 Cauchy, Lacombe, and Lamien, "Qui a peur des pédophiles?" Though the topic of this series of articles is pedophilia, all of the examples given are of sexual contact between men and adolescent boys.
26 Historical scholarship that examines twentieth-century age-differentiated male same-sex sexuality includes Kunzel, *Criminal Intimacy*; Chauncey, *Gay New York*; Gunther, *The Elastic Closet*; Johnson, *Just Queer Folks*; Revenin, *Une histoire des garçons et des filles*. For a summary of anthropological scholarship on age-differentiated male same-sex sexuality, see Adam, "Age, Structure, and Sexuality."
27 In Wilde's words, the "love that dare not speak its name" was "such a great affection of an elder for a younger man as there was between David and Jonathan, such as Plato made the very basis of his philosophy, and such as you find in the sonnets of Michaelangelo and Shakespeare. It is that deep, spiritual affection that is as pure as it is perfect. It dictates and pervades great works of art like those of Shakespeare and Michaelangelo . . . It is beautiful, it is fine, it is the noblest form of affection. There is nothing unnatural about it. It is intellectual and it repeatedly exists between an elder and a younger man, when the elder man has intellect, and the younger man has all the joy, hope, and glamour of life before him." Quoted in Wood, "Creating the Sensual Child," 164.
28 For works that do think through the significance of intergenerational or age-differentiated relationships in the nineteenth- and twentieth-century "gay" literary canon, see Wood, "Creating the Sensual Child"; Sinfield, *On Sexuality and Power*; Eribon, *Réflexions sur la question gay*. For a reading of the significance of interracial and often intergenerational sex between French men and Arab boys within French and Francophone colonial and postcolonial literature, see Mack, "Untranslatable Desire."
29 Lim, *Brown Boys and Rice Queens*, 8.
30 Sinfield, *On Sexuality and Power*.
31 Cvetkovich, *An Archive of Feelings*, 112–15; Sedgwick, "Afterword," 283.
32 C. Jacob Hale writes, "Playing as a boy does not necessitate age-play; status as a boy may simply indicate a masculine bottom status—submissive or masochistic or both—different from that of a slave. However, in my experience age-play is more common in leatherdyke boy-daddy settings than it is in gay male ones. When boy-daddy age-play occurs, play ages may bear no relation to the legal ages of the

players; daddy may be younger than her boy, according to their birth certificates" (Hale, "Leatherdyke Boys and Their Daddies," 224).

33 Rodríguez, *Sexual Futures, Queer Gestures, and Other Latina Longings*, 59.

34 Referring specifically to the possibility of consensual sex between adults and minors, Guy Hocquenghem remarks in 1979 that the problem with the notion of consent is that "nobody signs a contract before making love." He proposes that, legally, what sexual consent really means is the absence of violence or coercion (Foucault, "Sexual Morality and the Law," 285). Rodríguez proposes that the "futural register of consent," which is always a consent to "something as yet unexperienced and therefore unknown" means that consent must operate as a promise to respect the possible withdrawal of consent (Rodríguez, *Sexual Futures, Queer Gestures, and Other Latina Longings*, 61). Joseph Fischel argues that the legal framework of consent is a clumsy instrument with which to address sexual harm (Fischel, *Sex and Harm in the Age of Consent*).

35 Juana María Rodríguez observes that Daddy play, far from being specific to queer-identified people, has become ubiquitous. She writes, "It bears emphasizing that most linguistic uses of Daddy in sexual play have very little to do with incest play or BDSM, and function instead as convenient and portable narratives to describe gendered relations of care, attesting to the ways that kinship itself functions as a perverse package of delineated social relations. This resignification becomes an opportunity to account for the domestic sphere as a site where erotic and affective imprints, always already inflected by the textures and gestures of familial culture, are established" (Rodríguez, *Sexual Futures, Queer Gestures, and Other Latina Longings*, 58).

36 In his empirical study of Canadian men who have sex with men, Barry Adam notes that the minority who prefer older or younger men seem to lack a shared language—whether drawn from mainstream or from gay culture—for articulating this preference. Their discourse, he proposes, is characterized by a "creative bricolage of meanings" (Adam, "Age Preferences among Gay and Bisexual Men," 419). Given the historical loss of a common language with which to conceive and describe the contemporary practice of age-differentiated male homosexual sex, the S/M vernacular of Daddy/Boy and the gay vernacular of twink might be called upon to body forth contemporary pederastic desires.

37 Daddy play emerged into prominence in gay leather cultures during the 1980s, as is suggested by the holding of the first San Francisco Leather Daddy contest in 1983. I thank Margot Weiss for bringing the latter detail to my attention.

38 Nealon, *Foundlings*, 14.

39 Foucault, "Nietzsche, Genealogy, History," 94, 82. "La dissociation systématique de notre identité"; "tout au contraire: elle inquiète ce qu'on percevait immobile, elle fragmente ce qu'on pensait uni; elle montre l'hétérogénéité de ce qu'on imaginait conforme à soi-même" (Foucault, "Nietzsche, la généalogie, l'histoire," 154, 142).

40 Halperin, *How to Do the History of Homosexuality*, 107.

41 Foucault, "Nietzsche, Genealogy, History," 88. "L'histoire sera 'effective' dans la mesure où elle introduira le discontinue dans notre être même. Elle divisera nos

sentiments; elle dramatisera nos instincts; elle multipliera notre corps et l'opposera à lui-même" (Foucault, "Nietzsche, la généalogie, l'histoire," 147).

42 Foucault, "Nietzsche, Genealogy, History," 88. "Le jeu consolant des reconnaissances" (Foucault, "Nietzsche, la généalogie, l'histoire," 147). For different readings of the role of affect and emotion in Foucauldian historical methodology, see Dinshaw, *Getting Medieval*, 136–42; and Love, *Feeling Backward*, 46–52.

43 Muñoz, *Cruising Utopia*, 1.

44 Manalansan, *Global Divas*.

45 Harkins, "Foucault, the Family and the Cold Monster of Neoliberalism," 103. This is to say not that adult-child sex did not exist before this historical moment, but that it was not organized around the figure of the pedophile, as an abnormal type of person defined by a nearly uncontrollable sexual attraction to children that, without intervention, would inevitably result in violation and harm. On adult-child sex in France before the conceptual invention of pedophilia, see Ambroise-Rendu, *Histoire de la pédophilie*. On the legal fiction of the pedophile, see Fischel, *Sex and Harm in the Age of Consent*.

46 On the brief leftist reclamation of pedophilia in France, see Verdrager, *L'enfant interdit*. For a linguistic history of the word *pédérastie*, see Féray, *Grecques, les moeurs du hanneton?* The latter book espouses an essentialist understanding of pederasty as a noble, pedagogical practice inherited, unchanged, from Ancient Greece and divorced from anal sex, which colors the linguistic history it offers.

47 Edelman, *No Future*.

48 For works that argue in favor of queer and queer of color futurities that cannot be encompassed by Edelman's positioning of futurity as necessarily heteroreproductive, see Muñoz, "Cruising the Toilet"; Muñoz, *Cruising Utopia*; Rodríguez, "Queer Sociality and Other Sexual Fantasies"; and Freeman, *Time Binds*. For an exemplary reading of backward queer modernist dispositions turned away from both the present and the future that seeks neither to redeem nor to critique them, see Love, *Feeling Backward*.

49 For a history of this process in France, see Gunther, *The Elastic Closet*. For a sociological account of the arguments that, first, brought pedophilia and pederasty in line with homosexuality and sexual liberation in France then, definitively severed this connection, see Verdrager, *L'enfant interdit*.

50 Gunther argues, "In exchange for successful assimilation, the less palatable elements of the early 1970s movements—particularly the pedophilic, pederastic, sadomasochistic, transsexual, transvestite, promiscuous, and public-sex elements—had to be excluded or at least ignored by those occupying the new gay spaces of the '80s. Thus, by the mid-1980s, through a process of exclusion within the gay community itself, the more radical demands of the early 1970s were effectively silenced, if not left behind" (Gunther, *The Elastic Closet*, 68).

51 Kunzel, *Criminal Intimacy*, 216. Fischel argues that the "sex offender," whose paradigmatic and most extreme form is the pedophile, "has been juridically codified as the exhaustive figure of sexual amorality and dangerousness, a position vacated by the once homophobic but now more dignified juridical construction of the homosexual" (Fischel, *Sex and Harm in the Age of Consent*, 170).

52 Sedgwick, "Afterword," 282.
53 As Hart and Dale demonstrate, the much-touted emphasis on consent, negotiation, and the teaching and learning of different techniques in gay BDSM subculture is of historically recent vintage, dating from the 1970s and 1980s, when BDSM practitioners sought recognition within the wider gay movement. Around this time, in a change lamented by some practitioners, "total domination by an all-knowing master of a willing slave whose trust runs beyond the need for verbal communication is less a part of the s/m scene than before." The former version of BDSM practice, emphasizing total domination without verbal negotiation, has not been explored or reclaimed by queer theorists. Hart and Dale, "Sadomasochism," 345–46.
54 For queer scholarship that acknowledges that BDSM's erotic charge is drawn from its continuities with the scene of social power, see Sedgwick, "Afterword"; Rodríguez, *Sexual Futures, Queer Gestures, and Other Latina Longings*; Musser, *Sensational Flesh*.
55 Hekma, "The Drive for Sexual Equality."
56 The queer critique of liberalism is too vast to adequately document here. See Bersani, *Homos*; Warner and Berlant, "Sex in Public"; and Reddy, *Freedom with Violence* for prominent examples within each of the aforementioned categories.
57 Cohen, "Punks, Bulldaggers, and Welfare Queens"; Holland, *The Erotic Life of Racism*, 9; Puar, *Terrorist Assemblages*, 22.
58 Fischel, *Sex and Harm in the Age of Consent*; Gill, *Already Doing It*.
59 Halperin, *How to Do the History of Homosexuality*, 113.
60 Halperin, *How to Do the History of Homosexuality*, 115.
61 Weeks, Heaphy, and Donovan, *Same Sex Intimacies*, 109.
62 Weeks, Heaphy, and Donovan, *Same Sex Intimacies*, 106.
63 Halperin, *How to Do the History of Homosexuality*, 133–34.
64 Sinfield explores how, in contemporary gay male culture, sex across differences of gender expression, age, race, and class is increasingly regarded with suspicion (Sinfield, *On Sexuality and Power*).
65 I am making a similar argument here to legal scholar Joseph Fischel, who provocatively defines consent as the new paradigm differentiating good from bad sex in order to ask, "Are sex offenders the new queers?" (Fischel, *Sex and Harm in the Age of Consent*, 7). By centering erotic egalitarianism rather than consent, I move beyond the legal framework to scrutinize a cultural ideal that situates sexual subjects differentially, whether as sex offenders (sex with minors, with the disabled, for hire) or merely as suspiciously into power (sex across class, across race, across generation but between adults).
66 For his work on male same-sex practices in Ancient Greece, see Halperin, *One Hundred Years of Homosexuality*.
67 For a critique of the tendency to consider prison sexuality, particularly between men of different ages, timeless and to liken it to practices in Ancient Greece and Rome, see Kunzel, *Criminal Intimacy*, 3. It is also common for Genet critics to describe the sexual system of his novels with reference to Ancient Greece. In reference to a moment in *The Thief's Journal* when Armand no longer wants to fuck

Jean after Jean has proven himself a peer by beating and robbing homosexuals, Genet critic Gier Uvslokk writes that Armand "now seems to behave according to the customs of Ancient Greece: the narrator is henceforth part of the world of toughs, and Armand, like all self-respecting *erastes*, only sleeps with *eromenoi*." "Semble maintenant opérer selon les coutumes de la Grèce antique: le narrateur fait désormais partie du monde des durs, et Armand, comme tous les *érastes* qui se respectent, ne couche qu'avec des *éromènes*" (Uvslokk, *Jean Genet*, 118).

68 See Peniston, *Pederasts and Others*, 9, 111–19.

69 As Heaney notes, "Both because of its association with anal sex and the undemocratic power differential between partners that it symbolized, the prevalence of the pederasty model in Greek male sexual relations complicated the sexological embrasure of the Hellenic." She analyzes how John Addington Symonds sought to resolve this problem by claiming that anal sex was imported into Greek pederastic practice from the Near East. Heaney, "The New Woman," 10.

70 See El-Rouayheb, *Before Homosexuality in the Arab-Islamic World*; Al-Kassim, "Epilogue," 200–202; Boone, *The Homoerotics of Orientalism*, 67–68.

71 See Boone, *The Homoerotics of Orientalism*, 279. On European postcards eroticizing "Arab" women, see Alloula, *The Colonial Harem*. Boone's study of André Gide's journals highlights the fact that Gide profited from a sexual tourism industry in colonial French North Africa that made local boys available to European pederasts in return for money or gifts.

72 Weeks, "Inverts, Perverts, and Mary Annes."

73 Chauncey, *Gay New York*, 88.

74 Chauncey finds that, in the United States, middle-class men who identified as different on the basis of their same-sex sexuality began to call themselves "queer" during the 1910s and 1920s. He does not position the widespread emergence of a homosexual/heterosexual binary, however, until midcentury, partly in response to Cold War homophobia (Chauncey, *Gay New York*, 101, 13).

75 Indeed, the version of transactional homosexuality Weeks maps in late nineteenth- and early twentieth-century London already conforms to this model, in which the elder partner is homosexualized, whereas the younger partner might be sexually normal and motivated only by gain (Weeks, "Inverts, Perverts, and Mary Annes").

76 Wilde and Gide both famously consorted with younger, lower-class, and colonized men and boys. They exemplify a form of pederasty in which the erotics of age differences were often intensified by differences of class, race, and colonial status, and in which sex was often transactional.

77 For accounts of how sexuality emerged as an independent axis of social difference separable from gender, race, class, and nation, see Valentine, *Imagining Transgender*, 63; Ferguson, *The Reorder of Things*, 217.

78 See, for example, Ferguson, *Aberrations in Black*; Holland, *The Erotic Life of Racism*; Pérez, *A Taste for Brown Bodies*.

79 Sinfield opens the way to using polarized erotics as a diagnostic of the sexual life of social power in Sinfield, *On Sexuality and Power*.

80 Lim, *Brown Boys and Rice Queens*, 4, my emphasis.

81 Lim, *Brown Boys and Rice Queens*, 64.
82 Sodomy prosecutions in the early twentieth-century U.S. disproportionately involved men and boys or male youth. Nayan Shah demonstrates that, in the North American West, sodomy prosecutions targeted transients and Asian and Mexican foreigners, interpreting American boys and youth as needing protection from the "dangerous" classes (Shah, *Stranger Intimacy*, 129–52).
83 For work on male stranger intimacies across social differences, see Delany, *Times Square Red, Times Square Blue*; Tim Dean, *Unlimited Intimacy*; Shah, *Stranger Intimacy*.
84 For an example of such work, see Fischel, "Against Nature, against Consent."
85 Sinfield, *On Sexuality and Power*, 115.

CHAPTER 2: LIGHT OF A DEAD STAR

1 Genet, *Miracle of the Rose*, 48–49, my emphasis. "Un adolescent qui aimerait assez le vol pour chérir les voleurs, méprisant assez les femmes pour aimer un voyou, enfin assez honnête pour se souvenir que Mettray était un paradis" (Genet, *Miracle de la rose*, 65–66).
2 On the utopian queer futurity of prison abolition, see Ben-Moshe et al., "Critical Theory, Queer Resistance, and the Ends of Capture," 277–78.
3 Genet, *Miracle of the Rose*, 170, translation modified. "D'imbéciles vandales, Danan, Helsey, Londres, d'autres, ont écrit qu'il fallait détruire les bagnes d'enfants" (Genet, *Miracle de la rose*, 222).
4 See Sartre, *Saint Genet, comédien et martyr*, especially 135; Jablonka, *Les vérités inavouables de Jean Genet*.
5 José Muñoz's *Cruising Utopia* has most prominently argued for using the queer past to glimpse utopian futurities.
6 A body of work on nonlinear, queer temporalities has prominently critiqued teleological progress narratives. See especially Halberstam, *In a Queer Time and Place*; Freeman, *Time Binds*.
7 See Love, *Feeling Backward*.
8 Throughout this book, I use "structure of feeling" to refer to collective affective states that emerge from specific sociohistorical conditions. Structures of feeling are indicative of a minoritarian or emergent social experience that is not officially recognized within public discourses of what constitutes appropriate emotional response. As Raymond Williams writes, "Structures of feeling can be defined as social experiences *in solution*, as distinct from other social semantic formations which have been *precipitated* and are more evidently and more immediately available" (Raymond Williams, *Marxism and Literature*, 133–34).
9 Muñoz, *Cruising Utopia*, 1.
10 Love, *Feeling Backward*, 7.
11 Roubaud's articles were published in book form as *Les enfants de Caïn*. Danan followed suit by publishing a selection of his letters from former inmates of the boys' penal colonies in the volume *Maisons de supplices*. Given that Roubaud's articles

tend more toward sensationalism and less toward denunciation, it is likely that Danan's accusatory and focused press campaign had greater influence on the abolition of the children's correction houses.

12 The trope of the corruption and abuse of otherwise innocent orphans and victims of bad parenting was particularly effective given that, legally, many inmates had not been found guilty of any crime. They were, to the contrary, acquitted for having acted without understanding the criminal nature of their actions. Those from working-class, "broken," or foster families were sentenced to "supervised liberty" in one of the children's correction houses, many of which were, like Mettray, officially classified as private, philanthropic, and "paternal," rather than punitive institutions. See Gaillac, *Les maisons de correction 1830–1945*; and Fishman, *The Battle for Children*.

13 "Ensemble des façons de vivre habituelles à un groupe humain ou à un individu. Synon. coutumes"; "Ensemble de comportements propres à un groupe humain ou à un individu et *considérés dans leurs rapports avec une morale collective*"; "En partic. Comportement sexuel conforme ou non aux normes sociales"; s.v. "Homosexualité," *Trésor de la langue française informatisé (version simplifiée)*, "moeurs," accessed May 12, 2007, http://atilf.atilf.fr/dendien/scripts/tlfiv5/advanced.exe?8;s=3593040525; my emphasis, my translation.

14 "Il existe dans ces maisons des mœurs tout à fait spéciales, que le monde extérieur ne peut soupçonner, soit entre pupilles, soit même entre pupilles et surveillants" (Danan, *Maisons de supplices*, 96). This and all further translations of narratives of the boys' penal colonies are my own.

15 "Avec qui te mets-tu? Je te présenterai demain un caïd. Il faut que tu prennes un caïd, sans ça tu seras malheureux" (Larique, "Mettray-Eysses, ligne directe I").

16 Kunzel, *Criminal Intimacy*, 64.

17 Kunzel, *Criminal Intimacy*, 65.

18 Roubaud, *Les enfants de Caïn*, 124–33.

19 "Un ancien colon de Mettray, actuellement au bagne, Libéré 4/1 matricule 16738. Renault, Henri"; "La plupart tombent par veulerie, ou par intérêt, pour éviter les coups, la misère, et pour se sentir sous la défense d'un plus fort que soi" (Danan, *Maisons de supplices*, 147, 146).

20 On the nineteenth- and early twentieth-century constitution of *la pédérastie* as a vice associated with criminality and criminal cultures, see Peniston, *Pederasts and Others*.

21 The book is described on its back cover as an "autobiographical narrative resounding with truth [*récit autobiographique criant de vérité*]." *Les hauts murs* has proven a narrative of lasting popularity. It has gone through several publications, and, in 2008, was adapted by Christian Faure into a film by the same name.

22 White, *Genet*, 69.

23 "Le 'fadeur,' c'est la 'femme,' la 'gonzesse,' le petit qui rend des services, qu'on aide, qu'on protège, mais qui vous a des complaisances . . . par derrière. J'ai été initié, moi, au dortoir de Palacé! J'avais résisté au début . . . Mais après, je me suis laissé faire. J'ai même fini par trouver ça normal. Au point que j'ai envie d'avoir mon 'fadeur,' mois aussi" (Lapie, *Saint-Florent-la-Vie*, 83, my translation).

24 Saint-Florent appears to be a rather transparent disguise for the boys' penal colony of Saint-Hilaire.
25 "Il ne m'a pas reproché mon amitié avec Bernard"; "mais il m'a demandé de la rendre plus virile" (Lapie, *Saint-Florent-la-Vie*, 144).
26 "Tout contre lui, un blondinet nouvellement arrivé, béait d'admiration devant la force de son mâle" (Le Breton, *Les hauts murs*, 156–57).
27 "Molina, cuivré comme un Indien, la sueur au front" (Le Breton, *Les hauts murs*, 156).
28 "*Produire des sentiments familiaux* fondés sur l'obéissance à une autorité paternelle, le bon exemple, le sens de l'honneur, l'émulation au bien, l'habitude de la maison, le sens de la propriété" (quoted in Léger, "Souvenirs d'un colon," 119, my emphasis).
29 "La plupart des jeunes détenus étant des enfants trouvés qui, n'ayant pas connu la famille, en méprisaient les douceurs et pour ainsi dire n'y croyaient pas, les fondateurs de cette colonie ont essayé tout d'abord de *leur créer des affections*" (quoted in Gaillac, *Les maisons de correction 1830–1945*, 84, my emphasis, my translation).
30 "L'enseignement intellectuel y est faible; l'enseignement religieux secondaire. Ce qu'on s'applique à développer, ce sont les sentiments du juste, l'amour de la famille, les affections, ou, pour me servir d'un mot [du docteur viennois] Gall, l'affectuosité" (Gaillac, *Les maisons de correction 1830–1945*, 84, my emphasis, my translation).
31 Michel Foucault argues that the mid-nineteenth century was a historical moment in which *affective abnormality*, particularly in relation to family feeling, was being pathologized as *the* major indicator of an abnormal personality (Foucault, *Abnormal*, 147–52).
32 Genet, *Miracle of the Rose*, 103. "De l'amour que se portaient les colons, l'amour qui les portait, qui les jetait l'un contre l'autre, la furie était peut-être augmentée par le désespoir d'être privé de toute autre tendresse, de l'affection d'une famille" (Genet, *Miracle de la rose*, 135).
33 Sedgwick, *Between Men*, 89.
34 In her study of homosexuality in France between the two world wars, Carolyn Dean outlines an enduring imaginary that associates pederasty with secrecy, egotism, and antidemocratic social formations: "Homosexuality, blinded finally by its 'egotism' and intractability, is incompatible with the social contract on which civilization is based. Homosexuality was thus an abuse of power in an ideally democratic regime predicated on the transparency of all of its male citizens" (Dean, *The Frail Social Body*, 141).
35 Genet, *Miracle of the Rose*, 110. "Il me suffit aujourd'hui d'évoquer mes amours d'enfant pour que je redescende au fond du temps dans ses plus ténébreuses demeures, dans une région solitaire, où je ne retrouve plus que la Colonie, formidable et seule. Elle me tire à elle de tous ses membres musclés, avec ce geste des matelots qui lèvent de l'eau un filin, une main se portant devant l'autre au fur et à mesure que la corde s'entasse sur le pont et je retrouve, auprès du Divers regagné, une enfance nauséeuse et magnifiée par l'horreur, que je n'eusse jamais voulu quitter" (Genet, *Miracle de la rose*, 144).
36 Genet, *Miracle of the Rose*, 25–26. "L'exacte vision qui faisait de moi un homme,

c'est-à-dire un être vivant uniquement sur terre, correspondait avec ceci que semblait cesser ma féminité ou l'ambiguïté et le flou de mes désirs mâles. En effet, si le merveilleux, cette allégresse qui me suspendait à des rinceaux d'air pur, en prison naissait surtout de ce que je m'identifiais avec les beaux voyous qui la hantent, dès que j'acquis une virilité totale—ou, pour être plus exact, dès que je devins mâle—les voyous perdirent leur prestige... Je ne désirais plus ressembler aux voyous. J'avais le sentiment d'avoir réalisé la plénitude de moi-même" (Genet, *Miracle de la rose*, 36).

37 Genet, *Miracle of the Rose*, 25–26, my emphasis. "*Peut-être moins qu'aujourd'hui, après l'aventure que j'écris*, mais je me suis senti fort, sans dépendance, libre, délié. Aucun modèle prestigieux ne se présentait plus à moi" (Genet, *Miracle de la rose*, 36, my emphasis).

38 Genet, *Miracle of the Rose*, 26. Genet, *Miracle de la rose*, 36.

39 Genet, *Miracle of the Rose*, 30. "Grande fut la difficulté à me replonger dans mes histoires rêvées, fabriquées par ce jeu désolant de la solitude, mais je trouvai—et je trouve encore malgré ma plongée nouvelle—davantage de bien-être dans les souvenirs vrais de mon ancienne vie" (Genet, *Miracle de la rose*, 42).

40 Genet, *Miracle of the Rose*, 48. "Retrouver en un autre qu'en moi le souvenir de Mettray, autant peut-être pour rejoindre Mettray que pour le continuer dans ma vie d'homme en aimant selon les mœurs d'alors" (Genet, *Miracle de la rose*, 65).

41 Genet, *Miracle of the Rose*, 24. "Je remontai dans ma cellule et l'habitude abandonnée, de mon enfance abandonnée, me reprit: tout le reste de la journée et toute la nuit, je bâtis une vie imaginaire, dont Bulkaen était le centre, et je donnai toujours à cette vie, vingt fois reprise et transformée, malgré moi, par le jeu des événements inventés, une fin violente: assassinat, pendaison ou décollation" (Genet, *Miracle de la rose*, 34).

42 Genet, *Miracle of the Rose*, 63. "Je tentai un dernier effort pour refermer sur moi une porte qui montrerait le secret de mon cœur, et qui risquait de laisser Bulkaen entrer en moi comme en pays conquis, monté, botté, éperonné, cravaché et l'insulte à la bouche, car il n'est jamais tendre le sentiment que porte un gamin à un homme qui l'adore" (Genet, *Miracle de la rose*, 84).

43 Genet, *Miracle of the Rose*, 27. "La claire simplicité de la virilité" (Genet, *Miracle de la rose*, 37).

44 Genet, *Miracle of the Rose*, 184, translation modified. "Transporté par son admiration pour eux, [Bulkaen] courait vers les hommes" (Genet, *Miracle de la rose*, 240).

45 Genet, *Miracle of the Rose*, 120. "Un acte d'éclat" (Genet, *Miracle de la rose*, 157).

46 Genet, *Miracle of the Rose*, 121–22. "Aux instants que j'allais flancher, le souvenir et l'âme de Villeroy me gardèrent... J'empruntais, je volais la beauté de ses attitudes. Prise on ne sait où, une mèche de cheveux blonds tombait jusqu'à mes yeux. J'étais d'une vitesse folle. Je devais vaincre Charlot car Villeroy l'eût vaincu, c'est avec ses armes luisantes et ses défauts que je combattais. Les gâfes m'arrachèrent, on emporta Charlot. Les surveillants accoururent pour relever Guépin" (Genet, *Miracle de la rose*, 159).

47 Genet, *Miracle of the Rose*, 240, my emphasis. "Il était le démon qui m'incitait

à plus de dureté, à plus d'audace, à plus d'amour: . . . *Bulkaen était ma virilité*" (Genet, *Miracle de la rose*, 311, my emphasis).

48 Genet's description of pederastic virility as a compelled performance predicts Judith Butler's famous theory of gender performativity. However, whereas Butler is concerned with the compelled performance of normative male masculinity and female femininity within a "heterosexual matrix" of same-gender imitation and opposite-gender attraction, Genet locates the compelled performance of virility within a pederastic economy of same-sex attraction polarized along the axes of age, power, and sexual position. This pederastic economy of desire reverses over time, from the position of sexually receptive punk to that of sexually aggressive wolf. See Butler, *Gender Trouble*.

49 Genet, *Miracle of the Rose*, 118, translation modified. "Nos amours de Mettray! Les couples d'enfants où le mâle avait seize ans. J'avais seize ans, l'âge des jeunes filles. Quinze ans sont grêles et dix-sept ans trop durs. Mais seize ans a un son d'une délicate féminité. J'aimais Villeroy qui m'aimait. Parce qu'enfant lui-même (il avait dix-huit ans) il était plus près de moi que personne . . . ne le fut jamais" (Genet, *Miracle de la rose*, 154).

50 Genet, *Miracle of the Rose*, 106. "À chercher refuge dans [ses] vieilles amours" (Genet, *Miracle de la rose*, 139).

51 Genet, *Miracle of the Rose*, 202, translation modified. "N'aurait pas accepté—comme aucun marle ne l'acceptait—que son vautour fût une lope. Il m'obligeait à me battre" (Genet, *Miracle de la rose*, 262–63).

52 Flaubert, *A Sentimental Education*.

53 Genet, *Miracle of the Rose*, 26. "Un homme de pierre aux angles nets"; "je n'avais tout à fait le repos que si je pouvais tout à fait prendre sa place, prendre ses qualités, ses vertus; lorsque je m'imaginais être lui, que je faisais ses gestes, prononçais ses mots: lorsque j'étais lui" (Genet, *Miracle de la rose*, 37).

54 At other points, Genet makes it clear that within criminal subcultures, the pimp, with his knowledge of and control over women, is considered the epitome of virile heterosexuality, whereas the burglar, who lacks control over women and who works either alone or with other men, is always a potential pederast. Since the inmates of Mettray are too old to learn to control female sexual commerce when they are released, Genet writes that they become burglars or sailors (that is, potential pederasts) rather than pimps.

55 Genet, *Miracle of the Rose*, 165. "Les petits voyous vont d'instinct vers [les macs insolents], ils les entourent, ils les écoutent, la bouche entrouverte. Le mac les féconde. Et si l'on hausse les épaules à propos d'un idéal qui paraît ridicule, on aura tort car ils obéissent à l'impulsion amoureuse qui les oblige à ressembler à celui qu'ils aiment: un dur, jusqu'au jour où, enfin, ils sont devenus celui qu'ils aimaient" (Genet, *Miracle de la rose*, 215).

56 Genet, *Miracle of the Rose*, 165. "Ils perdent alors, en durcissant, l'émouvante tendresse que leur donnait le mouvement de marche vers leur but, l'inconsistant écoulement de jeunesse désirante à maturité et qui n'est que passage. Alors tout en eux oublie cette marche amoureuse. Ils sont devenus un mac banal, sans davantage se souvenir de l'aventure qu'il leur fallut parcourir pour être ce mac. Ils serviront à

leur tour de pôle attractif à d'autres minos, car c'est de ce moyen, peut-être impur, que Dieu se sert pour fabriquer les hommes impassibles des prisons" (Genet, *Miracle de la rose*, 215–16).

57 Genet, *Miracle of the Rose*, 126, translation modified. "C'est quelque chose en moi qui sait très bien qu'il serait vain de me donner du mal pour paraître fort et maître de moi, car ma folle nature apparaîtra toujours par mille fissures" (Genet, *Miracle de la rose*, 165).

58 See Carolyn Dean, *The Frail Social Body*, 130–72.

59 See Kunzel, *Criminal Intimacy*, 79–80.

60 Genet, *Miracle of the Rose*, 85. "Je découvris plus tard le sens de cette fêlure, deuxième signe de deuil, et de celle, plus théâtrale encore, qui sillonne Bulkaen, qui sillonne tous les marles, de Botchako à Charlot" (Genet, *Miracle de la rose*, 112–13).

61 Genet, *Miracle of the Rose*, 137, translation modified. "Ce qu'est n'importe quel giron sans son marle: un temple de détresse" (Genet, *Miracle de la rose*, 179).

62 Genet, *Miracle of the Rose*, 126, translation modified. "La tristesse de son départ perdit bien vite son sens primitif pour devenir une espèce de mélancolie chronique, pareille à un automne embrumé, et cet automne est la saison de base de ma vie car il réapparaît souvent, maintenant encore" (Genet, *Miracle de la rose*, 164).

63 Genet, *Miracle of the Rose*, 215. "Je devine ce qu'aux yeux des autres, je puis paraître dur, car la dureté de Bulkaen était faite aussi de sa profonde désolation de se voir abandonné" (Genet, *Miracle de la rose*, 279).

64 Genet, *Miracle of the Rose*, 208. "Mettray l'avait talé au bon endroit. Il était touché à mort malgré son rire et sa santé" (Genet, *Miracle de la rose*, 270).

65 Genet, *Miracle of the Rose*, 151, translation modified, my emphasis. "Ils auront des femmes, mais je n'ose croire que ces gosses qui furent si longtemps courtisanes, ou mâles les adorant, puissant ne pas garder au cœur, à l'âme et dans les muscles *la meurtrissure de Mettray*" (Genet, *Miracle de la rose*, 198).

66 See Halberstam, *The Queer Art of Failure*.

67 Sigmund Freud understands normal mourning as allowing for the gradual decathexis of the lost object and the reinvestment of libido in new objects. He understands pathological melancholia, on the other hand, as occurring when, for some reason, a loss is withdrawn from consciousness, resulting in an inability to mourn the lost object. Instead, in a regression to the oral phase of development, the ego cannibalistically incorporates the object into itself (Freud, "Mourning and Melancholia").

68 Torok, "The Illness of Mourning and the Fantasy of the Exquisite Corpse," 110.

69 Freeman, *Time Binds*, 120.

70 Freeman, *Time Binds*, 119.

71 Torok, "The Illness of Mourning and the Fantasy of the Exquisite Corpse," 110.

72 Torok, "The Illness of Mourning and the Fantasy of the Exquisite Corpse," 110.

73 See Freeman, *Time Binds*, 119.

74 See Abraham and Torok, "Mourning *or* Melancholia."

75 Genet, *Miracle of the Rose*, 255–56, translation modified. "Le sexe de Deloffre frôlait les fesses de son vautour mort, dessinées par le caleçon mouillé... Enfin, il eut

un moment tout secoué de petits frissons: ce n'était ni le vent séchant l'eau sur ses épaules, ni la peur, ni la honte, mais la volupté. En même temps il s'abattait tout à fait contre le corps du petit mort" (Genet, *Miracle de la rose*, 331).

76 Genet, *Miracle of the Rose*, 261–62. "Un soir, il me reparla de sa mort et me dit toute son horreur d'être hanté par le gosse. Je demandai s'il croyait aux revenants. Il ne s'agissait pas de cela, mais le simulacre d'amour qu'il avait fait sur son cadavre, cette insolite cérémonie sur un catafalque de chair lui apparaissait ce qu'elle devait être à tous les yeux: une profanation. Il vivait dans la honte—dans l'horreur d'avoir baisé un mort et, surtout, d'y avoir pris du plaisir" (Genet, *Miracle de la rose*, 338).

77 Genet, *Miracle of the Rose*, 262. "J'ai l'impression que j'ai assisté à ma naissance, que je suis sorti de lui aussitôt après sa mort. Mon crâne, c'est le sien; mes tifs, mes dents, mes châsses, c'est les siens! J'ai l'impression que j'habite le corps mort de ma petite gueule d'amour!" (Genet, *Miracle de la rose*, 338).

78 Muñoz, *Disidentifications*, 74.

79 Some examples of work that seeks to reground the insights of psychoanalysis in specific social locations, see Muñoz, *Disidentifications*; Fanon, *Black Skin, White Masks*; Khanna, *Dark Continents*.

80 Genet, *Miracle of the Rose*, 30. "'Comme une porte de prison me garde, mon cœur garde ton souvenir . . .' Je ne laisserai pas mon enfance s'échapper" (Genet, *Miracle de la rose*, 42).

81 Genet, *Miracle of the Rose*, 236–37, translation modified. "D'avoir jeté un coup d'œil sur ces ruines, jamais ne guérira la tristesse de mon âme . . . Je n'ai trouvé qu'un cadavre. Je sais que ma jeunesse est morte. Il ne reste plus rien du passage de tant de voyous" (Genet, *Miracle de la rose*, 306).

82 See the distinction between affect and emotion in Massumi, *Parables for the Virtual*.

83 Nealon, *Foundlings*, 182.

84 Love, *Feeling Backward*, 31–52.

85 Genet, *Miracle of the Rose*, 149. "Vibre encore du premier baiser que Pierrot m'y donna, et de sa fuite rapide et un peu raide comme celle d'un chamois" (Genet, *Miracle de la rose*, 194).

86 Genet, *Miracle of the Rose*, 114, translation modified, emphasis in the original. "J'entends—et du plus loin de ma mémoire, qu'elle est un *espace précis du temps* mais qu'elle irradie—que ce *passé présent* rayonne une buée sombre, faite surtout, je le crois, de notre souffrance" (Genet, *Miracle de la rose*, 150).

87 Genet, *Miracle of the Rose*, 291, translation modified. "'Qui étaient Bulkaen, Harcamone, Divers, qui était Pilorge, qui était Guy?' demandera-t-on. Et leur nom troublera comme la lumière nous trouble qui arrive d'une étoile morte il y a mille ans" (Genet, *Miracle de la rose*, 376).

CHAPTER 3: RACIAL FETISHISM, GAY LIBERATION, AND THE TEMPORALITIES OF THE EROTIC

1 See, for example, Muñoz, *Cruising Utopia*, 19–20; Ferguson, *The Reorder of Things*, 216–17; Abelove, "New York City Gay Liberation and the Queer Commuters," 88.

2 One notable exception is Regina Kunzel's study of radical gay liberationists' activism in prisons. Kunzel, *Criminal Intimacy*, 191–224.

3 "Peut-être que si je n'étais jamais allé au lit avec des algériens, je n'aurais jamais pu approuver le F.L.N. J'aurais probablement été de leurs bord, de toute façon, mais c'est l'homosexualité qui m'a fait réaliser que les algériens n'étaient pas différents des autres hommes," *Tout!*, 7. The FHAR is quoting Genet's response, in a 1964 interview for *Playboy* magazine, to a question about his *pédérastie*. The original publication, however, was in translated English and refers to "homosexuality" rather than "pederasty." In the original French oral transcript of the interview, which was not available to the FHAR, Genet claims that he regards pederasty as "une bénédiction" and speculates, "Peut-être que si je n'avais pas fait l'amour avec des Algériens, je n'aurais pas été en faveur du F.L.N. Mais non, je l'aurais été sans doute de toute façon. Mais c'est peut-être la pédérastie qui m'a fait comprendre que les Algériens étaient des hommes comme les autres" (Genet, *L'ennemi déclaré*, 24).

4 "NOUS SOMMES PLUS DE 343 SALOPES. / *Nous nous sommes faits enculer par des arabes.* / NOUS EN SOMMES FIERS ET NOUS RECOMMENCERONS / SIGNEZ ET FAITES SIGNER AUTOUR DE VOUS / LE NOUVEL OBSERVATEUR LE PUBLIERA-T-IL ??? / ET DISCUTONS EN AVEC LES CAMARADES ARABES" (*Tout!*, 7).

5 "D'abord, tout le monde vit sur l'image du vieux pédé européen qui se tape des petits arabes. Outre que ça n'est jamais si simple, signalons qu'en France se sont nos amis arabes qui nous baisent et jamais l'inverse. Comment ne pas y voir une revanche consentie par nous sur l'occident colonisateur? Croyez-vous qu'on puisse avoir les mêmes rapports que tout le monde ou que le français moyen avec les arabes quand on commet avec eux l'acte que la morale bourgeoise rend le plus honteux? Oui, nous nous sentons une solidarité d'opprimés très forte avec les arabes" (*Tout!*, 7).

6 The rejection of active/passive sexual roles was not universal within the FHAR. Indeed, according to Marie-Jo Bonnet, the embrace of sexual roles by FHAR men as well as the embrace of femininity by queens in the Gazolines caused tension with lesbians who eventually split from the FHAR. Bonnet, "De l'émancipation amoureuse des femmes dans la cité," 94.

7 This is to say that Genet's relationship with his Arab lovers, who were usually younger men rather than adolescents, was pederastic. See chapter 4 for more details.

8 Guy Hocquenghem champions such a notion of erotic coalition by arguing that the gay movement might respond to debates about the politics of postcolonial sex with Arabs by insisting "not on a kind of solidarity of principle but on a desiring relation" (Hocquenghem, *Homosexual Desire*, 141). "Une intervention qui n'est pas fondée sur une solidarité de principe mais sur un rapport de désir" (Hocquenghem, *Le désir homosexuel*, 166).

9 Choukri, *Jean Genet in Tangier*; Said, "On Jean Genet's Late Works"; Hankins, "Entretien avec Leila Shahid."
10 Michel Foucault's *The History of Sexuality, Vol. 1* is organized as a pointed riposte to the "repressive hypothesis." This tenant of popularized Freudo-Marxism, whose major intellectual figures were Herbert Marcuse and Wilhelm Reich, holds patriarchal capitalist culture to be founded on the repression of erotic desire, pleasure, and unalienated creativity. If for Freud, civilization is founded on repression, for gay liberationists, derepression was seen as opening the way to a new social order of revolutionary equality.
11 Holland, *The Erotic Life of Racism*, 9, emphasis in original. Similarly, Amber Jamilla Musser's work recentering race and gender difference to theories of masochism relies on understanding masochism "not as a mode of subversion, but as a symptom of the normative" (Musser, *Sensational Flesh*, 26).
12 See, for example, Bersani, *Homos*; Edelman, *No Future*; Tim Dean, *Unlimited Intimacy*. Queer psychoanalytic scholarship that *does* think racialization, and therefore, to some extent, history, as critical to the operations of desire includes Butler, "Passing, Queering"; Marriott, *Haunted Life*; Muñoz, *Disidentifications*; Scott, *Extravagant Abjection*; and Viego, *Dead Subjects*. I seek, in this chapter, to explicitly theorize the versions of history and temporality that inform racialized erotics.
13 Nyong'o, *The Amalgamation Waltz*, 10. The claim that race is a sociohistorical, rather than a natural or biological, formation is foundation to critical race theory. See Omi and Winant, *Racial Formation in the United States*.
14 Genet, *The Declared Enemy*, 132–33. "Ce qui est plus difficilement avouable, c'est que les Panthers sont des Noirs américains, les Palestiniens sont des Arabes. J'aurais du mal à expliquer pourquoi les choses se font comme ça, mais ces deux groupements ont une charge érotique très forte. Je me demande si j'aurais pu adhérer à des mouvements révolutionnaires qui soient aussi justes que—je les trouve très justes, le mouvement des Panthers et le mouvement des Palestiniens—mais cette adhésion, cette sympathie, est-ce qu'elle n'est pas commandée en même temps par la charge érotique que représente le monde arabe dans sa totalité ou le monde noir américain, pour moi, pour ma sexualité?" (Genet, *L'ennemi déclaré*, 156).
15 Said, "On Jean Genet's Late Works," 239.
16 Said, "On Jean Genet's Late Works," 229–30.
17 Millett, *Sexual Politics*, especially 22, 356. Cixous wrote that the *only* French twentieth-century examples of *écriture féminine* that she had ever discovered were Colette, Marguerite Duras, and, the lone man, Genet (Cixous, "The Laugh of the Medusa," 282–83). Mercer, *Welcome to the Jungle*, 219.
18 Hayes, *Queer Nations*, 44, my emphasis.
19 "Pornographie postcoloniale"; "le socle d'un engagement politique contestataire"; "ouvre potentiellement la voie à un investissement politique outrepassant le cadre normatif de l'agenda gay et lesbien hégémonique" (Cervulle and Rees-Roberts, *Homo exoticus*, 146–47, my translation and emphasis).
20 Reid-Pharr, "Dinge," 213.
21 Nash, *The Black Body in Ecstasy*; Scott, *Extravagant Abjection*; Rodríguez, *Sexual*

Futures, Queer Gestures, and Other Latina Longings, 139–82; Nguyen, *A View from the Bottom*.

22 See, for example, hooks, "Eating the Other"; Holland, "'From This Moment Forth, We Are Black Lesbians'"; Morgensen, *Spaces between Us*; Montez, "'Trade' Marks."

23 Cervulle, "French Homonormativity and the Commodification of the Arab Body," 175, 176.

24 Shepard, "'Something Notably Erotic,'" 88. For more on the history of the European (homo)sexualization of the Arab world, see Boone, *The Homoerotics of Orientalism*; Aldrich, *Colonialism and Homosexuality*. For the effects of this (homo)sexualization on Arab literature and culture, see Massad, *Desiring Arabs*.

25 Shepard, "'Something Notably Erotic,'" 110.

26 Shepard, "'Something Notably Erotic,'" 113.

27 Genosko, "The Figure of the Arab in *Three Billion Perverts*," 62.

28 "Il est très facile pour un Occidental, jeune ou vieux, d'avoir des rapports homosexuels avec les 'Arabes,' est c'est là le fait fondamental. Il est plus facile de draguer un 'Arabe,' à Paris, ou en province, à Bruxelles, à Amsterdam, que de draguer un Européen. Presque tous les jeunes Arabes sont prêts à coucher avec des hommes" ("Le sexe 'arabe,'" 34); all translations of quotations from *Three Billion Perverts* are my own. One intent of this essay is to provide an ethnographic explanation of the context informing the controversial transcribed discussion, "The Arabs and Us," printed in the same special issue. For this author, the "central problem [*problème central*]" the discussion poses is that "what happens in the sexual encounter between young homosexual Europeans, from a Catholic culture, intellectuals, bourgeois, or leftists, and 'Arab' laborers, young and old, of Arab-Islamic culture, who are not homosexual, but who are ready, given their origin and their state of sexual frustration, to fuck European fags and, more rarely, to let themselves be fucked by their Western partners. From this situation, something develops that is a mixture of love and hatred, tenderness and violence, racism and revolutionary will"; [que se passe-t-il dans la rencontre sexuelle entre des jeunes homosexuels, européens, de culture catholique, intellectuels bourgeois ou gauchistes, et des ouvriers 'arabes,' jeunes et vieux, de culture arabo-islamique, qui ne sont pas des homosexuels, mais qui sont prêts, par leur origin et par leur situation, de misère sexuelle, à baiser des pédés européens et, plus rarement, à se laisser baiser par leurs partenaires occidentaux. A partir de ce fait-là, quelque chose se développe qui est un mélange d'amour et de haine, de tendresse et de violence, de racisme et de volonté révolutionnaire] ("Le sexe 'arabe,'" 36).

29 For a critique of the frequently reiterated European notion that Arab-Islamic cultures are tolerant and permissive of sex between men, see El-Rouayheb, *Before Homosexuality in the Arab-Islamic World*. El-Rouayheb notes that, before the influence of a Victorian sexual morality in the nineteenth century, a series of noncoincident codes regarding status and age differentials, active/passive roles, the distinction between anal sex and other, less gravely sinful erotic acts, and platonic versus sexual love governed the conditions under which male-male sexual contact might not gravely damage a man's status.

30 Shepard, "'Something Notably Erotic,'" 110.
31 "'code d'amour' islamique avec ses combinaisons à sense unique, ses repartitions des rôles enkuleur/enkulé" ("Kouche!" 46).
32 "Les Arabes et nous" and "Kouche!" The author of "Kouche!," a French tourist in postcolonial Morocco, begins his narrative with a reflection on the impossibility of having satisfying sex across both postcolonial and cultural divides, "It seemed impossible to avoid the traps of neocolonial or sexual tourist pederasty with its folklore and its price, impossible to escape the Islamic 'code of love' with its one-way combinations, its distribution of roles fucker/fucked [Il ne me semblait pas possible d'éviter les pièges de la pédérastie néo-coloniale ou touristique avec son folklore et ses tarifs, pas possible de sortir du 'code d'amour' islamique avec ses combinaisons à sense unique, ses repartitions des rôles enkuleur/enkulé]" ("Kouche!" 46). His hope, nevertheless, of having a tender sexual encounter with the handsome Hassam is dashed when Hassam orders "Couche!" and fucks him painfully and maniacally. This disappointing sexual encounter is partly attributed to Arab-Islamic hypervirility, transformed in French gay liberationists' analysis into a damaging commitment to phallocracy and rigid sexist roles. Unlike some other contributors to the chapter, however, this author also considers how ambivalence or rage directed at a privileged tourist from the former imperial power might play a role in his trick's perceived aggression.
33 "Les Arabes et nous."
34 "Le sexe 'arabe.'"
35 "Kouche!"
36 "La rue."
37 "La rue."
38 "Les Arabes et nous" and "Rue des Vertus."
39 "Sex-pol en act," allegedly penned by Gilles Deleuze, and "Les culs énergumènes," which appears in a later chapter of the same publication, critique and reflect on the racism of "Les Arabes et nous."
40 Ahmed, *The Cultural Politics of Emotion*, 91–92.
41 Ahmed understands the erasure of the history of repetition and circulation that makes emotions attach to figures as what turns these figures into fetishes—objects that seem to have an "intrinsic" emotional or, in this case, erotic force (Ahmed, *The Cultural Politics of Emotion*, 11).
42 Marx, "Commodities"; Freud, "Fetishism"; Bhabha, "The Other Question."
43 Pietz, "The Problem of the Fetish I," 14.
44 In Freud's canonical account, fetishism is a psychic defense against the traumatic knowledge of women's "castrated" state. The fetishist disavows the sexual difference of women by investing his desire for the woman's penis in a substitute object, which Freud proposes is the last object the fetishist saw prior to the traumatic sight of the woman's genital lack. The fetish is thus at once a memorial to the fetishists' triumph over castration and an enshrinement of the fetishist's divided belief, that is, his simultaneous knowledge that women do not have penises and belief that, nevertheless, they do (Freud, "Fetishism").
45 Bhabha, "The Other Question," 107; Eng, *Racial Castration*, 150.

46 See Sedgwick, "Paranoid Reading and Reparative Reading"; Wiegman, *Object Lessons*, 301–43.
47 Holland, *The Erotic Life of Racism*, 43.
48 Tim Dean, *Unlimited Intimacy*, 148.
49 Tim Dean, *Unlimited Intimacy*, 147–48.
50 Tim Dean, *Unlimited Intimacy*, 158.
51 Tim Dean, *Unlimited Intimacy*, 160.
52 Tim Dean, *Unlimited Intimacy*, 160.
53 Tim Dean, *Unlimited Intimacy*, 162.
54 Tim Dean, *Unlimited Intimacy*, 165.
55 Pietz has demonstrated that part of what rendered West African "fetishism" bizarre to Europeans was that it worked metonymically—by creating seemingly random, but efficacious links between practices and material objects—rather than metaphorically, as did European iconography, in which images represented a higher power (Pietz, "The Problem of the Fetish II"). I am not arguing that we should return to West African "fetishism" as the "true" meaning of fetishism, but I do think it crucial to question the Freudian account of fetishism *at its root*, that is, in its foundation of fetishism on metaphoric substitutions which always reference *the same* originary source of meaning and power—the penis or the phallus—rather than on decentered metonymic chains of meaning.
56 See Crimp, AIDS.
57 For an account of stereotyping's role in rendering difference identifiable and knowable, see Dyer, "The Role of Stereotypes."
58 Deleuze and Guattari use *assemblage* to describe a heterogeneous multiplicity without a generalizable principle of organization (Deleuze and Guattari, *A Thousand Plateaus*).
59 "Je veux qu'il n'y ait plus des personnes, des moi. Ce que je veux: c'est un fonctionnement qui produit du plaisir, et c'est incompatible avec la rencontre de deux personnes qui s'affrontent. Je ne veux pas être une personne" ("Les Arabes et nous," 21).
60 See Bersani, "Is the Rectum a Grave?" and *Homos*; Tim Dean, *Unlimited Intimacy*.
61 Hocquenghem, *Homosexual Desire*, 137–38. "Le mouvement homosexuel est sauvage en ce qu'il n'est pas le signifiant de ce quelque chose d'autre que serait une nouvelle 'organisation sociale,' une nouvelle étape de l'humanité civilisée, mais la faille dans ce que Fourier appelle 'le système de la fausseté des amours civilisées'" (Hocquenghem, *Le désir homosexuel*, 161).
62 See Robcis, *The Law of Kinship*. For a reading of how Hocquenghem must provisionally accept the thesis of the phallocratic and Oedipal basis of desire, identity, and society in order to imagine the revolutionary possibilities of homosexual anal sex, see Schehr, "Defense and Illustration of Gay Liberation."
63 On tensions between FHAR gays and lesbians, see Bonnet, "De l'émancipation amoureuse des femmes dans la cité"; Hocquenghem, *L'après-mai des faunes*. On the history of the FHAR as originally a predominantly lesbian group that became, after a mass exodus of lesbians, a predominantly gay male group, see Bonnet, "De

l'émancipation amoureuse des femmes dans la cité"; and Sibalis, "L'arrivée de la libération gay en France."
64 As Tim Dean acknowledges, "The antisocial thesis properly begins with neither Edelman nor Bersani but rather with Guy Hocquenghem" (Caserio et al., "The Antisocial Thesis in Queer Theory," 827). Prearo also suggests that late Hocquenghem and FHAR writings anticipate queer theory (Prearo, *Le moment politique de l'homosexualité*, 140).
65 Bersani, "Is the Rectum a Grave?"
66 In yoking Hocquenghem and Bersani together, I am primarily emphasizing an affective similarity—a resonance in tone as well as in their set of assumptions about what constitutes the value of queer sexuality (or the queerness of sexuality). This move has much in common with Amber Jamilla Musser's astute observation that, despite their disagreements on the politics of S/M, Bersani and Foucault actually articulate "parallel claims about pleasure producing a way to exist outside of subjectivity" (Musser, *Sensational Flesh*, 16). This desire, common to a number of otherwise opposed queer thinkers, to make sex and/or jouissance figure an "outside" to subjectivity, selfhood, and power, *is utopian*, even in its antisocial modes, and both inherits and disavows gay liberation's own "redemptive reinvention of sex." This is not to overstate the theoretical commonalities between Bersani and Hocquenghem. Whereas Bersani is very much working within the psychoanalytic tradition, Hocquenghem is counterpsychoanalytic; and while both are fascinated by the dissolution of selves during sex, Hocquenghem strikes a Deleuzian note to emphasize that such a dissolution is also a machinic connection, whereas Bersani remains focused on *dis*connection. Nevertheless, both pose sex as a privileged and unique practice whose value consists in its corrosion of social identities and challenge to the social order.
67 Edelman's position is more complex. However, in identifying queerness with jouissance and the death drive, each of which dissolve "fetishistic engagements, undoing the consistency of a social reality that relies on Imaginary identifications, on the structures of Symbolic law, and on the paternal metaphor of the name," he invests jouissance with the queer capacity to shatter the Imaginary and Symbolic orders alike, thereby signaling the inheritance of liberationist negativity (Edelman, *No Future*, 25).
68 Bersani, "Is the Rectum a Grave?," 25.
69 "Tu te sens nié, tué, par cet Arabe qui t'encule. Et c'est le pied" ("Les Arabes et nous," 16).
70 "Des bites qui bandent"; "l'envie de me sentir comme un trou"; "consommer du viril"; "On pense à se les mettre dans le cul, et c'est tout. Et ça s'arrête là" ("Les Arabes et nous," 15, 16, 14, and 16, respectively).
71 "*Moi*, je jouis intellectuellement à l'idée de me livrer. *Lui*, il baise, mais il n'a pas cette distance intellectuelle. *Nous*, on reste des intellectuelles qui jouent à se livrer à la sauvagerie, à la bête" ("Les Arabes et nous," 18, my italics).
72 "La bête arabe"; "la bête qui dort en moi" ("Les Arabes et nous," 18).
73 Genet, *The Thief's Journal*, 234–35, translation modified. "Doucement, le grand

nègre s'allongera sur mon dos. Le nègre, plus immense que la nuit, me recouvrira. Tous ses muscles sur moi auront cependant conscience d'être les affluents d'un virilité qui converge à ce point si dur, si violemment chargé, le corps entier tressaillant par ce bien et cet bonheur. Nous serons immobiles. Il s'enfoncera davantage. Une sorte de sommeil, sur mes épaules terrassera le nègre, sa nuit m'écrasant où peu à peu je me diluerai. Ma bouche ouverte, je le saurai engourdi, retenu dans cet axe ténébreux par son pivot d'acier. Je serai léger. Je n'aurai plus aucune responsabilité. Sur le monde je porterai le regard clair prêté par l'aigle à Ganymède" (Genet, *Journal du voleur*, 267).

74 This alignment of black Africans with timelessness is consistent throughout Genet's novels. The black Africans of *Our Lady of the Flowers* live in a mythically unnumbered world with neither time nor age (Genet, *Our Lady of the Flowers*, especially 166, 168; Genet, *Notre-Dame-des-Fleurs*, especially 173, 176).

75 Genet, *Our Lady of the Flowers*, 179, translation modified. "Il pleurait. Ses beaux yeux étaient gonflés de larmes qui coulaient jusqu'à sa bouche: 'Aïe! Aïe!' Mais moi, ici, tout seul, je ne me souviens plus que de ce muscle élastique qu'il enfonçait sans qu'il y mît la main, je me souviens de ce membre vivant auquel je voudrais élever un temple" (Genet, *Notre-Dame-des-Fleurs*, 192).

76 Fanon, *Black Skin, White Masks*, 91. "Un schéma historico-racial," "tissé de mille détails, anecdotes, récits" (Fanon, *Peau noire, masques blancs*, 90).

77 Fanon, *Black Skin, White Masks*, 92. "Une hémorragie qui caillait du sang noir sur tout mon corps" (Fanon, *Peau noire, masques blancs*, 91).

78 This is not to say that it cannot also be reclaimed, by racialized subjects, as a source of pleasure. Darieck Scott has argued that the abject self-shattering engendered by blackness as a historico-racial schema can be embraced as a strategy of ecstasy by black people living in racist societies with painful historical inheritances (Scott, *Extravagant Abjection*, especially 245).

79 Bersani himself is careful to underline the limits of jouissance as well as the ways in which it may rely upon an exercise of sexual power that reaffirms social structures of domination: "Masochistic jouissance is hardly a political corrective to the sadistic use of power, although the self-shattering I believe to be inherent in that jouissance, although it is the result of surrender to the master, also makes the subject unfindable as an object of discipline" (Bersani, *Homos*, 99).

80 Freeman, "Time Binds, or, Erotohistoriography."

81 Fanon writes that the black is both "locked in his body" and "a slave to the past," for the black's body is perceived through the imprisoning weave of history (Fanon, *Black Skin, White Masks*, 200). "Enfermé dans son corps"; "esclave du passé" (Fanon, *Peau noire, masques blancs*, 182).

82 Keeling, *The Witch's Flight*, 33.

83 Holland, *The Erotic Life of Racism*, 10.

84 Holland, *The Erotic Life of Racism*, 18. My readings also bear out Hiram Pérez's observation that "a gay cosmopolitan imagines an idealized primitive figure that functions both as an object of desire and as the repository of disowned projections cast temporally and spatially backward" (Pérez, *A Taste for Brown Bodies*, 25).

85 Linda Williams, "Skin Flicks on the Racial Border," 285.

86 Genet, *Prisoner of Love*, 298–99. "Encore au début de 70, le Parti avait souplesse et raideur qui évoquaient un sexe mâle—aux élections ils préféraient son érection. Si les images sexuelles reviennent, c'est qu'elles s'imposent, et que la signification sexuelle du Parti—érectile—paraît assez évidente. Ce n'est pas qu'il ait été composé d'hommes jeunes, baiseurs qui déchargeaient avec leurs femmes aussi bien le jour que la nuit, c'est plutôt que, même si elles paraissaient sommaires, les idées étaient autant de viols gaillards mettant à mal une très vieille, déteinte, effacée mais tenace morale victorienne" (Genet, *Un captif amoureux*, 351).

87 On the Panthers' health care activism, see Nelson, *Body and Soul*. Elaine Brown succeeded Huey Newton as chair of the party from 1974 to 1977, and during this period, an unprecedented number of women held leadership positions. In Bobby Seale's estimate, the party was 60 percent female by 1969 (Seale, *A Lonely Rage*, 177). On women in the Black Panther Party, see Brown, *A Taste of Power*; Jennings, "Why I Joined the Party"; Matthews, "'No One Ever Asks, What a Man's Place in the Revolution Is.'" This is not to deny that Panther women often confronted misogyny and masculinism within the Party, but only to point out that this was the condition of left activism in general at the time, not an issue specific to black organizations.

88 Genet, *Prisoner of Love*, 205. "Non seulement la transfiguration de mes fantasmes mais leur matérialisation m'attendant là, devant moi" (Genet, *Un captive amoureux*, 244).

89 On changing representations of the Palestinians in the U.S. media during this time period, see Zaharna, "The Palestinian Leadership and the American Media."

90 When analyzing phenomena, such as affect and politics that, though they may coinfluence one another, remain ontologically distinct or occupy vastly different scales, it may be useful for work on race, gender, and sexuality to shift from the spatial metaphor of intersectionality, which implies commensurability in a three-dimensional space, to that of a resonance, feedback, and/or interference across different levels. See Massumi, *Parables for the Virtual*, for examples of the analytic potential of the latter group of spatial metaphors.

91 Reid-Pharr, "The Shock of Gary Fisher," 137.

92 Omi and Winant, *Racial Formation in the United States*.

93 Holland, *The Erotic Life of Racism*, 44.

94 Freeman, "Time Binds, or, Erotohistoriography," 59.

95 Nash, *The Black Body in Ecstasy*, 109–10.

CHAPTER 4: PEDERASTIC KINSHIP

1 Nealon, *Foundlings*.
2 White, *Genet*, 258.
3 Genet, *The Declared Enemy*, 257–58. "Échappant à la famille, j'échappais aux sentiments que j'aurais pu avoir pour la famille et aux sentiments que la famille aurait pu avoir pour moi. Je suis donc tout à fait—et je l'ai été très jeune—tout à fait détaché de tout sentiment familial" (Genet, *L'ennemi déclaré*, 298).
4 White, *My Lives*, 319.

5 Davis, "Black Nationalism," 292.
6 Hocquenghem, *Homosexual Desire*, 111. "Château de cartes" (Hocquenghem, *Le désir homosexuel*, 120).
7 "Familles, je vous hais! Foyers clos; portes refermées; possessions jalouses du bonheur" (Gide, *Les nourritures terrestres*, 67, my translation).
8 Weeks, Heaphy, and Donovan, *Same Sex Intimacies*, 10.
9 Weston, *Families We Choose*, 116.
10 Weston understands the 1980s North American discourse of "chosen family" as a response to the perceived failures of the utopian 1970s discourse of gay "community." "Among political activists and the bar crowd alike the notion of community voiced during the 1970s resembled nothing so much as a Jeffersonian version of Victor Turner's *communitas*: an alternative, nonhierarchical, and undifferentiated experience of harmony and mutuality." With growing critiques of the inequalities and exclusions of gay community during the late 1970s, this ideal lost credibility during the 1980s. At that moment, chosen family was positioned as the historical carrier of the gay liberationist ideal of an egalitarian and conflict-free gay community. Though it reclaims family, which liberationists understood to be irreparably patriarchal and heterosexist, the discourse of chosen family preserves the gay liberationist injunction to create a sociality that provides an alternative to the heterosexual family. Gay and lesbian chosen family was supposed to be distant—in its egalitarianism and "unfettered creativity"—from heterosexual kinship (Weston, *Families We Choose*, 109).
11 D'Emilio, "Capitalism and Gay Identity," 475.
12 "Si un gosse s'attache à un adulte, disons qu'il le monte un petit peu au sommet. Pour lui, c'est vraiment un tout. C'est quelqu'un qu'il admire, le frère qu'il aimerait avoir, le père qu'il aimerait avoir, l'adult qu'il aimerait être." Thomas could be described as a pederast rather than a pedophile, given that he prefers boys ages twelve to fifteen years old. When the interviewer asks if the term *pédé* shocked him, Thomas responds, "Pedophile was prettier [*Pédophile, c'était plus joli*]," reflecting the fact that the word *pédophile*, which had rarely been used until then, was briefly reclaimed as a positive and fresh-sounding term, preferred by leftists to the old-fashioned *pédéraste*, during the 1970s (Hennig, "Thomas, 30 ans, Bruno, 15 ans, le nouveau couple Zig-Zag," 154, 151). This and all further translations from primary 1970s sources are my own. On the brief French leftist reclamation of pedophilia, see Verdrager, *L'enfant interdit*.
13 Thomas's first love was twelve-year-old Hervé, whose bourgeois father was often absent or traveling. He recounts, "The kid suffered his father's absence terribly. And he told me that for him, I was not the father, but rather the elder brother he never had, since he had a younger brother [le gosse souffrait terriblement de cette absence du père. Et il m'a dit que pour lui, c'était non pas le père, mais le frère aïné qu'il n'avait pas, puisqu'il avait un frère plus jeune]" (Hennig, "Thomas, 30 ans, Bruno, 15 ans, le nouveau couple Zig-Zag," 140).
14 See Weston, *Families We Choose*, 149; Weeks, Heaphy, and Donovan, *Same Sex Intimacies*, 104–9.
15 Rowley, *Tête-à-tête*, 310.

16 For scholarship that considers such colonial pederastic relations, see Lim, *Brown Boys and Rice Queens*; Boone, *The Homoerotics of Orientalism*; Aldrich, *Colonialism and Homosexuality*; Mack, "Untranslatable Desire."
17 Amin, "Against Queer Objects."
18 For example, Gunther quotes extensively from an article from the FHAR's journal *Antinorm* that argues, relying on the writings of Wilhelm Reich, that boys' sexuality begins in childhood and peaks in adolescence. The article blames the repression of children's and youths' sexuality for a range of psychological disorders, hypothesizes that the goal of sexual repression "is to produce an individual who fits into the authoritarian order and who will submit to it regardless of all the misery and degradation" and concludes that "socialism alone can realize sexual liberation" with youth at the vanguard (quoted in Gunther, *The Elastic Closet*, 51).
19 This summary is based on my reading of the FHAR's "Trois milliards de pervers." See also Gunther, *The Elastic Closet*.
20 Verdrager, *L'enfant interdit*. Leftist pro-pedophile authors tended to affirm the child's will, autonomy, maturity, and active consent, bringing the child in proximity to full adult agency, while emphasizing the child at the heart of every adult. For example, René Schérer, a major philosopher of pedophilia, emphasizes "those 'transitions' which, between the child and the adult, establish accords, brief or durable, affective and carnal [ces 'transitions' grâce auxquelles, entre l'enfant et l'adulte, s'établissent des ententes, brèves ou durables selon les cas, à la fois affectives et de corps]" (Schérer, "A propos de la pédophilie," 90). Guy Hocquenghem, who coauthored *Co-ire*, one of the two special issues of *Recherches* on pedophilia published during the 1970s, with his former lover and professor René Schérer, theorizes child sexuality differently—as a chaotic and perverse energy of jouissance that disaggregates the social body as well as the "individuals" that compose it. Though "L'enfant interdit," like the other articles in the special issue, is unsigned, it bears Hocquenghem's theoretical stamp.
21 For example, the interview cited above with Thomas, who describes entering into idealized kinship relations with boys, was published in *Fous d'enfance*, a special issue of *Recherches* collecting leftist reflections on pedophilia.
22 Copies of the special issue of *Recherches* were seized and its editor, Félix Guattari, fined for an affronting public decency just after publication. In 2002, a password protected version adapted to the internet was published on the site of the French journal *Critical Secret*—this version was effectively censored, the "Pedophilia" chapter removed. See Genosko, "The Figure of the Arab in *Three Billion Perverts*," 62. The link on the website is currently inactive.
23 "A formé une commission de mineurs, qui ont commencé à dire: on ne veut pas être dragué par des types, être obligé de faire l'amour, comme si les mineurs étaient l'objet sexuel des pédérastes, pédérastie de type platonicien, pédagogique, très réationnaire, des types comme Montherlant, Peyrefitte: on a dit effectivement que ces types-là sont des pédérastes pédagogiques ancien style, alors la libération de l'école passe en même temps avec la libération contre ce genre de pédérastes" ("La pédophilie," 118).
24 "C'est ça qui est chiant, ce que tu appelles le pédéraste traditionnel, c'est qu'en fait

tu véhicules toute une partie répressive de la famille, famille pervertie puique tu y ajoutes la sexualité" ("La pédophilie," 126).

25 Quoted in Gunther, *The Elastic Closet*, 55, my italics.

26 Similarly, Hocquenghem and Schérer's theorization of a liberated pedophilia rejects the old hierarchical pederastic model: "As long as the separating structure functions, the compatibility between pederasty and pedagogy benefits only the pedagogical poison [La compatibilité entre pédérastie et pédagogie, tant que la structure separative fonctionne, profite seulement au poison pédagogique]" (Schérer and Hocquenghem, "Co-ire," 62).

27 Carolyn Dean, *The Frail Social Body*, 130–72. On pederastic masculinism's political heterogeneity, see Eribon, *Réflexions sur la question gay*, 331.

28 Gide, *Corydon*. Interestingly, Gide himself expressed contrary views of the relation between family and pederasty. In *The Fruits of the Earth* (*Les nourritures terrèstres*) (1896), the pederast, figured by the character Ménalque whom Gide based on Oscar Wilde, lures the youth to a poetic wandering away from his bourgeois home and family. Nevertheless, when penning a public defense of pederasty, Gide chooses a neoclassical masculinist vision of pederasty as cementing the social order. For an excellent reading of Gide's contradictory politics of pederasty, see Eribon, *Réflexions sur la question gay*, 302–43.

29 Hewitt, *Political Inversions*.

30 Verdrager, *L'enfant interdit*, 96–100.

31 "Famille pervertie" ("La pédophilie," 126).

32 Weston, *Families We Choose*, 48.

33 On the "ethnic peoplehood" model of gay community, see Epstein, "Gay Politics, Ethnic Identity."

34 Weston, *Families We Choose*.

35 Freeman, "Queer Belongings," 304.

36 Weston's informants tend to understand coming out according to U.S. tropes of seeking recognition as an autonomous adult, growing up to become a unique individual set against society, and moving out of the parental home. As many have argued, such understandings of coming out may not apply outside the United States or to immigrant families within the United States. See, for example, Manalansan, *Global Divas*; Provencher, *Queer French*.

37 I thank Rostom Mesli for these insights.

38 Ferguson, *Aberrations in Black*. Work in Queer Indigenous Studies has positioned Native American cosmologies of kinship, gender, and sexuality as queer in relation to white settler heteropatriarchy. See, for example, Rifkin, *When Did Indians Become Straight?*

39 Rodríguez, *Sexual Futures, Queer Gestures, and Other Latina Longings*, 36–37.

40 Scholars have scarcely begun to map versions of kinship based on same-sex sexuality prior to gay liberation. Weston does mention the existence of nonsexual relations between camp "sisters" or between older gay men and younger mentors that they introduced into "the life" during the 1950s and 1960s. She argues that midcentury North American queer kinship excluded sexual relationships (Weston, *Families We Choose*, 120–22). George Chauncey has remarked on the use of fictive

kinship terms such as *sister, auntie, mother, husband,* and *wife* in late nineteenth- and early twentieth-century U.S. gay male, and particularly fairy culture. He notes how gendered kinship terms were often used to define endogamous and exogamous relations, such that, for example, neither "sisters" nor men would have sex with one another, and "aunties" and "mothers" were often removed from the field of potential sexual partners (Chauncey, *Gay New York,* 290–91).

41 André Baudry referred to Arcadie, the French homophile group that he founded in the 1950s, as "a spiritual family" (Jackson, *Living in Arcadia,* 135). However, it was not until the late 1970s and early 1980s that identity and community became the basis of a mass homosexual movement for the first time in France (Prearo, *Le moment politique de l'homosexualité*).

42 Nealon, *Foundlings,* 1–2.

43 Halberstam, *In a Queer Time and Place,* 6.

44 Robcis, *The Law of Kinship,* 262. See also Fassin, "Same-Sex Marriage, Nation, and Race"; Fassin, "Entre famille et nation."

45 Genet, "Fragments..." (2003), 24. "La notion de rupture" (Genet, "Fragments..." [1990], 79).

46 Women are similarly essentialized within the thought of neoclassical pederastic masculinists. See Hewitt, *Political Inversions,* 120–29.

47 Genet, "Fragments..." (2003), 24. "Accumulant, à mesure qu'elle s'élabore, des gestes et des réflexions perverties par les notions de rupture, de fini, de discontinu, elle ne construit que d'apparents tombeaux" (Genet, "Fragments..." [1990], 79).

48 Genet, "Fragments..." (2003), 26. "Est-il possible que mes fureurs érotiques constamment braquées sur moi-même ou sur ce granit que sont mes amants, que ces fureurs ayant pour fin ma seule volupté accompagnent un order, une morale, une logique liés à une érotique conduisant à l'Amour?" (Genet, "Fragments..." [1990], 81).

49 In *Corydon,* Gide contrasts pathologized inverts with healthy, masculine pederasts. Many pederastic masculinists sought to distance themselves from stigmatized, feminized inverts and Uranists, although Hewitt underlines that some pederastic masculinists, such as John Henry MacKay, sought to form coalitions with Uranists, while critiquing Uranists such as Magnus Hirschfeld for sacrificing pederasts to criminal law. See Hewitt, *Political Inversions,* 143; and Carolyn Dean, *The Frail Social Body,* 130–72. For a fascinating study of the shifting and embattled lexicon for homosexuality in France during the early twentieth century, see Lucey, *Never Say I,* 29–54.

50 "Is it merely a question of a simple anecdote reducible to this: a pederast becomes infatuated with a boy who deceives him? The pederast despairs, becomes enraged, attacks. Ironic and sovereign, the child thinks he is strong. He tricks and is tricked. He is subtle and cruel with indifference. Those are the simple givens. The game is banal and easy" (Genet, "Fragments..." [2003], 30, translation modified). "S'agit-il donc d'une simple anecdote réductible à ceci: un pédéraste s'amourache d'un jeune garçon qui le berne? Le pédéraste se désole, enrage, s'enfonce. Ironique et souverain, l'enfant se croit fort. Il trompe et se trompe. Il est subtil et cruel par indifférence. Voilà des données simples. Le jeu en est banal et facile" (Genet, "Fragments..." [1990], 89).

51 According to David Halperin, it is not until homosexuality is no longer structured by compulsorily polarized roles, including those of man and boy that "Exclusive, lifelong, companionate, romantic, and mutual homosexual love becomes possible for both partners" (Halperin, *How to Do the History of Homosexuality*, 133–34). Likewise, in an oral interview, Grégoire (alias), a former member of the homophile group Arcadie, recalls that "back in the 1950s, the idea of a stable, lifelong partnership with someone his own age was not part of his personal homosexual identity" and goes on to relate this to the unavailability of a homosexual identity distinct from pederasty before the 1980s (Gunther, *The Elastic Closet*, 43).

52 For example, the narrative climax of John Henry Mackay's 1926 novel *The Hustler* (*Der Puppenjunge*) is when the main character, during a revelatory conversation with his aunt (whose deceased husband was himself a pederast), realizes that he could no longer love his youthful object of affection, the eponymous hustler, if the latter were to grow a mustache. By contrast, Genet's relationships with younger men were at times quite long-term, and often began after his beloved was capable of growing facial hair.

53 Genet's deliberately shocking novel *Funeral Rites* (*Pompes funèbres*) perversely mourns his dead lover, the French Resistance fighter Jean Decarnin, by praising Hitler and the collaborationist French Militia as exemplars of evil and betrayal.

54 Genet, *The Declared Enemy*, 125–26, translation modified. "Je vous rappelle que je n'ai ni père ni mère, que j'ai été élevé par l'Assistance publique, que j'ai su très jeune que je n'étais pas français, que je n'appartenais pas au village. J'étais élevé dans le Massif central. Je l'ai su d'une façon bête, niaise, comme ça: le maître d'école avait demandé d'écrire une petite rédaction, chaque élève devant décrire sa maison, j'ai fait la description de ma maison; il s'est trouvé que ma description était, selon le maître d'école, la plus jolie. Il l'a lue à haute voix et tout le monde s'est moqué de moi en disant: 'Mais c'est pas sa maison, c'est un enfant trouvé,' et alors il y a eu un tel vide, un tel abaissement. J'étais immédiatement tellement étranger, oh! le mot n'est pas fort, haïr la France, c'est rien, il faudrait plus que haïr, plus que vomir la France, enfin je . . . et . . . le fait que l'armée française, ce qu'il y avait de plus prestigieux au monde il y a trente ans, ait capitulé devant les troupes d'un caporal autrichien, eh bien ça m'a ravi . . . Quand une nation est à ce point soumise aux vertus militaires, on est obligé de dire que la France a été humiliée et je ne pouvais qu'adorer celui qui avait mis en œuvre l'humiliation de la France. Ensuite, je ne pouvais me retrouver que dans les opprimés de couleur et dans les opprimés révoltés contre le Blanc. Je suis peut-être un Noir qui a les couleurs blanches ou roses, mais un Noir. Je ne connais pas ma famille" (Genet, *L'ennemi déclaré*, 149).

55 For a perspicacious reading of Genet's lifelong hatred of France and impossible effort to "de-Francize himself [se *défranciser*]" through his admiration of Hitler, his flight from France, and his identification with stateless peoples, see Neutres, *Genet sur les routes du Sud*, 36–63.

56 Rodríguez, *Sexual Futures, Queer Gestures, and Other Latina Longings*, 44.

57 See Anderson, *Imagined Communities*.

58 In nineteenth- and early twentieth-century France, adoption, which was rather rare, was primarily a conduit for childless elderly individuals to designate an inher-

itor. As such, adoptees had to be over twenty-one, which was the age of majority, and adopters over fifty. It was not until the 1920s (Genet was born in 1910) that married couples were permitted to adopt minors, largely to deal with the large population of children orphaned by World War I. In 1972 all legal distinctions between "legitimate" (born in wedlock) and "natural" (bastard) children were eliminated. See Robcis, *The Law of Kinship*, 159–61.

59 For a famous reading of Genet's estrangement, as a foster child, from family, land, property, and village morality, see Sartre, *Saint Genet, comédien et martyr*, 13–19.
60 Shah, *Stranger Intimacy*, 262.
61 Genet was born in 1910, father unknown, to Camille Genet, who is believed to have been a prostitute, and who entrusted him to the Public Welfare Service.
62 Mercer, "The Panthers and Genet." Jean-Paul Sartre famously celebrated Genet as an existential hero who actively assumed his social position as a pariah, criminal, and pederast (Sartre, *Saint Genet, comédien et martyr*).
63 Genet, *The Thief's Journal*, 86–87. "Abandoné par ma famille il me semblait déjà naturel d'aggraver cela par l'amour des garçons et cet amour par le vol, et le vol par le crime ou la complaisance au crime. Ainsi refusai-je décidément un monde qui m'avaient refusé" (Genet, *Journal du voleur*, 97).
64 Genet, *The Declared Enemy*, 128. "Les Panthères mettaient en jeu toute une affectivité qui nous manque, et cette affectivité ne venait pas du fait qu'ils étaient d'origine africaine, qu'ils sont noirs ; mais simplement, ils sont bannis, ils étaient au ban et depuis quatre siècles, ils se retrouvaient dans l'expression Brothers (Frères)" (Genet, *L'ennemi déclaré*, 151).
65 Genet, *Prisoner of Love*, 421. "Les jours et les nuits passés sous les forêts d'Ajloun, de Salt à Irbid, aux bords du Jourdain, étaient une fête quand la définition de ce mot est celle-ci: le feu qui nous chauffe les joues d'être ensemble malgré les lois qui nous espèrent dans la déréliction; ou encore une autre: s'échapper de la communauté afin de rejoindre un lieu où, contre elle nous retrouverons des complices" (Genet, *Un captif amoureux*, 494).
66 For a use of the term *sideways* to indicate lateral motions that do not move progressively toward the adult futurity suggested by the verticality of the Anglophone metaphor of "growing up," see Stockton, *The Queer Child*.
67 I use *affect* here to signal a feeling that has not yet been socialized as an emotion by being named or assigned a particular narrative. This distinction resonates with Raymond Williams's definition of "structures of feeling" "as social experiences *in solution*, as distinct from other social semantic formations which have been *precipitated* and are more evidently and more immediately available" (Raymond Williams, *Marxism and Literature*, 133–34).
68 "Que signifiait ma présence blanche et rose au milieu d'eux? Encore ceci: pendant deux mois j'aurai été le fils de David. Mon père était noir et il avait trente ans de moins que moi. Mon ignorance des problèmes américains, peut-être ma fragilité et ma candeur m'obligeaient à rechercher en David une référence, mais lui-même se conduisait avec beaucoup de prudence à mon égard comme si ma débilité m'avait rendu cher" (Genet, *Un captif amoureux*, 352–53).
69 White, *Genet*, 522.

70 Mercer, "The Panthers and Genet."
71 Genet, *Prisoner of Love*, 96–97, translation modified. "Les Panthères Noires avaient, au lieu d'un enfant, découvert un vieillard abandonné, et ce vieillard était un Blanc ... Je réalisais là probablement un très vieux rêve enfantin, où des étrangers—mais au fond plus semblables à moi que mes compatriotes—m'ouvriraient à une vie nouvelle. Cet état d'enfance, et presque d'innocence m'avait été imposé par la douceur des Panthères, une douceur qui ne m'était pas accordée par privilège, mais de laquelle je bénéficiais puisqu'elle était, me semblait-il, la nature même des Panthères. Or, déjà vieillard, redevenir un enfant adopté, était très agréable puisque c'est grâce à cela que je connaissais une véritable protection et une éducation affectueuse, les Panthères se reconnaissant donc à leurs qualités pédagogiques" (Genet, *Un captif amoureux*, 116).
72 Freeman, "Queer Belongings," 304, 298.
73 Genet, *Prisoner of Love*, 299. "Tu es une mère pour moi" (Genet, *Un captif amoureux*, 351).
74 Genet, "Fragments ... ," 2003, 175n9. "Signification de la passion pédérastique: c'est la possession d'un objet qui n'aura d'autre destin que le destin exigé par l'amant. L'aimé devient objet chargé, dans ce mode, de représenter le mort (l'amant)" (Genet, "Fragments ... ," 1990, 90n1).
75 See Edelman, *No Future*. "Fragments ... " also foreshadows, however, the more upbeat understanding of pederasty as a form of kinship that Genet will later develop, when the narrator realizes that one beloved is "solar, in harmony with the order of the world. When I saw this, it was too late, I loved him. Helping him to realize himself in himself and not in me, little by little, subtly, the order of the world was to change my morality." Genet, "Fragments ... " (2003), 28. "Solaire, en accord avec l'order du monde. Quand je m'en aperçus, c'etait trop tard, je l'aimais. L'aidant à se réaliser en lui-même non en moi peu à peu, d'une façon subtile, l'order du monde altéra ma morale" (Genet, "Fragments ... " [1990], 86).
76 Genet, *The Declared Enemy*, 14, translation modified. The references to pederasty are rendered as "homosexuality" and its cognates in the English translation. "côté pédagogique." "Il est bien entendu que j'ai fait l'amour avec tous les garçons dont je me suis occupé. Mais je ne me suis pas occupé seulement de faire l'amour. J'ai cherché à refaire avec eux l'aventure que j'ai vécue dont le symbole est la bâtardise, la trahison, le refus de la société et enfin l'écriture, c'est-à-dire le retour à la société mais par d'autres moyens. Est-ce une attitude qui tient à moi seulement? La pédérastie, parce qu'elle met le pédéraste hors la loi, l'oblige à une remise en question des valeurs sociales et s'il décide de s'occuper d'un jeune garcon, il ne s'en occupera pas d'une façon plate. Il le mettra au fait des incohérences, à la fois de la raison et du cœur, qui s'imposent dans une société normale" (Genet, *L'ennemi déclaré*, 24).
77 Sinfield, *On Sexuality and Power*, 27.
78 See White, *Genet*, 463–65.
79 Genet, *The Declared Enemy*, 16. "Dans chaque cas, avec les jeunes gens, il m'a fallu inventer, tenir compte de leurs temperaments, de leurs caractères et de leurs goûts,

chaque fois faire quelque chose qui ressemble à l'acte créateur" (Genet, *L'ennemi déclaré*, 26).

80 Quoted in White, *Genet*, 517.
81 Freeman, "Queer Belongings," 299.
82 Genet's friend, the author Mohamed El Choukri, considered Genet responsible for Bentaga's suicide. See Choukri, *Jean Genet in Tangier*. On the final years of Genet's relationship with Bentaga, see White, *Genet*, 455–73.
83 Mercer, "The Panthers and Genet."
84 Genet, *Prisoner of Love*, 96–97, translation modified. "Un très vieux rêve enfantin"; "m'ouvriraient à une vie nouvelle" (Genet, *Un captif amoureux*, 116).
85 Ongiri, "Prisoner of Love."
86 Davis, "Black Nationalism," 292.
87 For an elaboration of the queer possibilities of moving *athwart*, see Sedgwick, *Tendencies*, xii. For an argument in favor of analyzing the "intimate and complicit gesture of moving *athwart*" rather than *against* normativity in queer theory, see Wiegman and Wilson, "Introduction," 11. Analogously, Butler argues that butch/femme lesbian genders are not reducible to heterosexual norms, yet cannot have life apart from them in Butler, "Afterword."
88 Rodríguez, *Sexual Futures, Queer Gestures, and Other Latina Longings*, 61.

CHAPTER 5: ENEMIES OF THE STATE

1 See White, *Genet*, 77.
2 See White, *Genet*; Neutres, *Genet sur les routes du Sud*; Sandarg, "Jean Genet and the Black Panther Party," for the details of Genet's travels to the United States and the Middle East and his late activism with the Palestinians and the Black Panthers. See Hankins, "Entretien avec Leila Shahid" for Shahid's account of Genet's involvement with the Palestinians and witnessing of the aftermath of the massacre of Palestinians at Shatila.
3 Genet, *The Declared Enemy*, 235. "Je suppose que vous admettez très bien que des Anglais aillent aider Israël qui était en danger. Pourquoi me demandez-vous pour quelle raison j'ai été aider un peuple qui est en danger? Entre les Juifs anglais et Israël il y avait des affinités. Il y a entre les Palestiniens, les Panthères et la Fraction armée rouge et moi des affinités. Et il est normal que j'aille les aider" (Genet, *L'ennemi déclaré*, 273).
4 "Des organisations qu'il a soutenues, Genet se souvient en premier lieu de ce qui les rend indéfendables aux yeux de l'opinion publique occidentale: le terrorism" (Neutres, *Genet sur les routes du Sud*, 253). This and all further translations of Neutres are my own.
5 Jones, "The Political Repression of the Black Panther Party 1966–1971," 415–16.
6 Jones, "The Political Repression of the Black Panther Party 1966–1971"; Morgan, "Media Culture and the Public Memory of the Black Panther Party."
7 Newton, *Revolutionary Suicide*, 109.
8 See Ogbar, "'Culture Is a Weapon in Our Struggle for Liberation.'"

9 The Popular Front for the Liberation of Palestine, which was responsible for the airplane hijackings of the late 1960s and early 1970s, is, after Fatah, the second largest group that forms the Palestinian Liberation Organization.
10 Zaharna, "The Palestinian Leadership and the American Media."
11 See Neutres, *Genet sur les routes du Sud*, 272–73.
12 Neutres reads Genet's admiration of Hitler, travels outside France, and identification with stateless peoples as animated by his lifelong hatred of France and impossible effort to rid himself of his Frenchness (*se défranciser*) (Neutres, *Genet sur les routes du Sud*, 36–63).
13 Genet, *The Declared Enemy*, 126. "Un conflit à l'intérieur du monde blanc" (Genet, *L'ennemi déclaré*, 149).
14 Genet, *The Declared Enemy*, 235. "Évidemment, j'ai été vers les peuples qui se révoltaient" (Genet, *L'ennemi déclaré*, 272).
15 On the state's monopoly on "legitimate" violence, see Weber, "Politics as a Vocation"; Reddy, *Freedom with Violence*.
16 Genet, *Prisoner of Love*, 383, translation modified. "Le janissaire du colon" (Genet, *Un captif amoureux*, 449).
17 See Puar, *Terrorist Assemblages*. On the related terms *homonormativity* and *queer liberalism*, respectively, see Duggan, "The New Homonormativity"; Eng, *The Feeling of Kinship*.
18 On homonationalism and pinkwashing, see, for example, Puar, "Citation and Censorship"; and Ben Daniel, "Zionist Geographies." For an exploration of queer politics in the context of the Palestine/Israel conflict, see the special issue of GLQ edited by Gil Hochberg, "Queer Politics and the Question of Palestine/Israel."
19 For instance, Scott Gunther argues that, after World War I, in the absence of a French homosexual political movement like those that had formed in Britain and Germany, the public image of male homosexuality was primarily constructed by doctors and the police, "who portrayed homosexuals as criminals and as potential traitors to the French nation" (Gunther, *The Elastic Closet*, 24). Vernon Rosario II argues that while German and British sexologists typically sought to separate homosexuality from other criminalized sexual perversions in order to bring it under the purview of medical pathology instead of that of law, French medical experts such as Tardieu, Charcot, and Magnan tended to lump homosexuality along with the other sexual perversions in order to emphasize its seriousness as a severe sign of congenital degeneracy that the criminal and legal systems ought to address (Rosario, "Pointy Penises, Fashion Crimes, and Hysterical Mollies," 157).
20 Peniston, *Pederasts and Others*, 3. *Pederasts and Others* was named after the ledger, "Pédérastes et autres," kept by a brigade of eight officers in Paris charged expressly with performing surveillance, harassing, gathering information on, and ideally arresting men who had sex with men from 1873 to 1879. The ledger records the names of 1818 individuals who were arrested, questioned, and investigated. Peniston's book demonstrates the salience of the construction of "la pédérastie" as a sign of criminality in late nineteenth-century France.
21 In Peniston's analysis, the 1791 penal codes "reflected a new view of sexual behavior

that restricted its public expression and limited it to the private sphere. They also expressed a new concern for the child as an innocent victim of sexual predators. They were, therefore, used extensively against men who had same-sex sexual relations in public or with minors" (Peniston, *Pederasts and Others*, 22). Paradoxically, the *same* penal codes that decriminalized homosexuality produced the figure of the "pederast" as a criminal who endangered youth and who brought both sex and deviant cross-class and extrafamilial liaisons dangerously into public space.

22 By the nineteenth century in France, "pederasty [*la pédérastie*]" was the most popular term for any form of sex between men. Peniston documents that though it continued to be popularly associated with the idea of an adult man corrupting an adolescent boy or an aristocrat exploiting a working-class youth, arrests that conformed to such patterns were in the minority. Although the traditional pederastic pattern of adult men with adolescents was common in this subculture, particularly among prostitutes, who were mostly adolescents, and their clients, the subculture as a whole reflected a shift to age-differentiated relations between older and younger adult men, and, less commonly, sex between adult men of roughly the same age. See Peniston, *Pederasts and Others*, 9, 111–19.

23 On the extralegal repression of men who had sex with men, see Sibalis, "The Regulation of Male Homosexuality in Revolutionary and Napoleonic France"; and Peniston, *Pederasts and Others*.

24 Peniston, *Pederasts and Others*, 2.

25 Pederasty and man/boy love are part of this history of depathologization and decriminalization. They were left behind by 1970s gay and lesbian rights-oriented strategies, largely because they could not be easily cleansed of the pathologies of sickness and crime. See chapter 1.

26 Hocquenghem, *Homosexual Desire*, 67; Hocquenghem, *Le désir homosexuel*, 30.

27 "Il existe un rapport très net, chez Genet par exemple, entre homosexualité et criminalité . . . c'est cette relation entre pédés et délinquants qui fait des homosexuels un groupe d'irrécupérables pour la société, un mouvement révolutionnaire assez étonnant" (Hocquenghem, *L'après-mai des faunes*, 174).

28 The 1960 Mirguet amendment, which was designed to combat "social scourges" such as homosexuality, prescribed a higher penalty for homosexual than for heterosexual affronts to public decency (sex acts in public). For more on the amendment, see Gunther, *The Elastic Closet*, 35–38.

29 Stanley, "Fugitive Flesh," 3.

30 Stanley, "Fugitive Flesh," 2, my emphasis.

31 For Genet's account of Hilliard's arrest, see Genet, *L'ennemi déclaré*, 48; Genet, *The Declared Enemy*, 34–35.

32 The principal purpose of Genet's 1970 trip to the United States was to raise funds and build public support for getting Bobby Seale, Huey Newton, and the Panther 21 out of prison. Even after leaving the United States, Genet would continue to work toward the liberation of incarcerated Panthers and their supporters, writing articles to alert the French public about Angela Davis's incarceration, and, upon invitation, penning the introduction to *Soledad Brother*. See "Angela and Her Brothers" and "Angela Davis Is in Your Clutches" in Genet, *The Declared Enemy* ("Angela

et ses frères" and "Angela Davis est entre vos pattes" in Genet, *L'ennemi déclaré*), as well as Genet's introduction to George Jackson, *Soledad Brother*.

33 See Genet, *Prisoner of Love*, 250; Genet, *Un captif amoureux*, 295; and Genet's introduction to George Jackson, *Soledad Brother*.

34 For example, in a pivotal 1970 speech, Newton remarked on the striking similarities between the repression of the Detroit riots of 1967 and the Vietnam War (Newton, *To Die for the People*, 36).

35 I borrow this term from Stoler, "Developing Historical Negatives."

36 Foster parents received a stipend from the French Assistance Publique for taking in a foster child until age twelve. Genet's foster parents, the Regniers, took him in to replace the stipend they had been receiving for Lucie Wirtz, their foster child who, at twelve, was leaving to become a farmworker (White, *Genet*, 11).

37 The charges that led to Genet's incarceration at Mettray were vagrancy and riding a train without a valid ticket. Before being sent to Mettray, Genet was sent to apprentice as a typographer at the École d'Alembert, transferred to the Hospice for Welfare Children in Paris, placed to work in the home of the blind composer René de Buxeuil, subjected to neuro-psychiatric treatment at Le Patronage de l'Enfance et de l'Adolescence, held at the panoptic Petite-Roquette Prison for adolescents, paroled on a farm in the Somme region, and held at a jail in Meaux. See White, *Genet*, xxii–xxiii.

38 Genet, *The Declared Enemy*, 258. "Mettray servait à former des marins" (Genet, *L'ennemi déclaré*, 299).

39 See White, *Genet*, 84.

40 See White, *Genet*, 72, 85.

41 Genet, *Prisoner of Love*, 383, translation modified. "Le janissaire du colon" (Genet, *Un captif amoureux*, 449). For a reading of the colonizer's janissary as a figure for the contradictions of colonialism, see Neutres, *Genet sur les routes du Sud*, 153–60.

42 Genet, *Prisoner of Love*, 382–86; Genet, *Un captif amoureux*, 449–53.

43 Foucault, *Discipline and Punish*, 297. "La plus célèbre de toute une série d'institutions qui bien au-delà des frontières du droit criminel ont constitué ce qu'on pourrait appeler l'archipel carcéral" (Foucault, *Surveiller et punir*, 347).

44 The research documents collected at the Genet archives at IMEC indicate that he consulted a varied set of texts, including histories of the French reformatories for minors, letters from administrators to entrepreneurs and luminaries, formal administrative reports, and texts such as Medlsheim's and Détrimont's 1846 *Projet de colonisation d'une partie de l'Algérie par les condamnés libérés, les pauvres et les orphelins*. Preparatory documents for Jean Genet, "Le langage de la muraille."

45 Foucault, "The Lives of Infamous Men," 158. "Sécheresse" (Foucault, "La vie des hommes infâmes," 238).

46 "Le but caché, que j'ai découvert dans les documents dont vous aurez toutes les photocopies, était la culture de six cents hectares de terre par une main-d'œuvre jamais payée; la transformation d'une jeunesse un peu anarchique en escadrons rompus à la discipline, déjà préparés pour l'autorité militaire, pour les coups d'éclat aux Colonies (en Algérie d'abord), à travers le monde, soit comme marins, fantassins, cultivateurs" (Genet, Letter to Bernard Tavernier).

47 "La courbe descendante de la France" (Genet, Letter to Bernard Tavernier).
48 "Nous avons les mêmes colonies en Grande-Bretagne et en Sud-Africa: celà rapporte moins que nos nègres cependant!" (Genet, "Le langage de la muraille").
49 Genet may also be referencing the process by which Christian boys were selected to be enslaved and conscripted into the Janissary Army during the Ottoman Empire. Boys were first made to strip so that they could be examined for bodily defects as well as overall beauty (Yilmaz, "Becoming a *Devsirme*," 122).
50 "Pas ému" (Genet, "Le langage de la muraille").
51 Genet, *The Declared Enemy*, 35. "On ne m'a pas touché parce que je suis Blanc et que je ne fais courir aucun danger à la société américaine" (Genet, *L'ennemi déclaré*, 48).
52 I borrow the term *archive fever* from Derrida, *Archive Fever*.
53 Hesford, *Feeling Women's Liberation*, 105.
54 Jonathan Flatley uses the phrase *affective mapping* to describe how emotional associations with elements of the social world allow one to navigate that world and, potentially, to imagine its political transformation (Flatley, *Affective Mapping*). See also Gould, *Moving Politics*, on how shifting a collective "emotional habitus" can correspondingly shift the "political horizon" of collective action.
55 On the response to "Violence and Brutality," see White, *Genet*, 598; Genet, *The Declared Enemy*, 346–55; and Genet, *L'ennemi déclaré*, 384–92.
56 Genet, *The Declared Enemy*, 171. "Le grain de blé qui germe et fend la terre gelée, le bec du poussin qui brise la coquille de l'œuf, la fécondation de la femme, la naissance d'un enfant relèvent d'accusation de violence" (Genet, *L'ennemi déclaré*, 199).
57 "Violence transparente" (Neutres, *Genet sur les routes du Sud*, 262).
58 Genet, *The Declared Enemy*, 173. "Ses arguments politiques, étouffés il est vrai par une action violente nommée ici 'terrorisme' (parenthèse: un mot encore, celui de 'terrorisme' qui devrait être appliqué autant et davantage aux brutalités d'une société bourgeoise)" (Genet, *L'ennemi déclaré*, 202).
59 Genet, *The Declared Enemy*, 172. "L'architecture des H.L.M., la bureaucratie, le remplacement du mot—propre ou connu—par le chiffre, la priorité, dans la circulation, donnée à la vitesse sur la lenteur des piétons, l'autorité de la machine sur l'homme qui la sert, la codification des lois prévalant sur la coutume, la progression numérique des peines..." (Genet, *L'ennemi déclaré*, 200).
60 On governmentality, see Foucault, *Security, Territory, Population*.
61 Chandan Reddy argues that "freedom" in the high-security post-9/11 United States is increasingly defined as freedom from the threat of arbitrariness. See Reddy, *Freedom with Violence*, 38. Julian Reid refers to this removal of arbitrariness from the domain of life as "logistical life" (Reid, *The Biopolitics of the War on Terror*, 12–13).
62 S.v. "brute, adj., and n. 1" and "brutality, n." *Oxford English Dictionary* online, http://www.oed.com.proxy.library.stonybrook.edu/view/Entry/24012?rskey=siG1U9&result=2&isAdvanced=false#eid, http://www.oed.com.proxy.library.stonybrook.edu/view/Entry/24007?redirectedFrom=brutality#eid.
63 Genet, *The Declared Enemy*, 171. "Le procès fait à la violence c'est cela même qui est la brutalité" (Genet, *L'ennemi déclaré*, 199).
64 For similar arguments, see Foucault, *"Society Must Be Defended"*; Benjamin, "Critique of Violence."

65 See Genet, *The Declared Enemy*, 348–49; Genet, *L'ennemi déclaré*, 386.
66 Genet, *L'ennemi déclaré*, 171, translation modified. "L'hypocrisie profonde et la barbarie de la bourgeoisie s'étalent impunément sous nos yeux, que nous regardions vers les métropoles où sa domination a revêtu des formes respectables, civilisées, ou vers les colonies où elle est brutale" (Genet, *L'ennemi déclaré*, 199).
67 Genet, *Prisoner of Love*, 118, translation substantially modified. "Cette séance fut sans doute enchantée par la présence dans la nuit d'une jeunesse buveuse de thé et de jus d'orange, écoutant et enseignant un vieux Français, soudainement posé sous les branches d'un hiver qui débuta en Septembre Noir, au milieu des terroristes rieurs sans cynisme, moqueurs, capable de trouvailles verbales, un peu dévergondés mais avec autant de retenue que des séminaristes de dix-sept ans, des terroristes dont le nom faisait trembler comme une feuille la page des journaux. A terre et en plein ciel leurs exploits y étaient rapportés avec effroi et dégoût, un dégoût sur le visage et dans les mots assez bien imité" (Genet, *Un captif amoureux*, 140).
68 Genet, *Prisoner of Love*, 118. "Les doux terroristes" (Genet, *Un captif amoureux*, 141).
69 Genet, *Prisoner of Love*, 374. "Le mot terroriste montre des dents métalliques, sa mâchoire, la gueule rouge du monstre"; "faire la chasse à Israël n'indique pas qu'on soit adversaire ni ennemi, mais terroriste, le mot disant alors que le terrorisme distribue indifféremment la mort et qu'il doit être détrui où qu'on le trouve" (Genet, *Un captif amoureux*, 439).
70 As Jasbir Puar has influentially argued, "Queerness is always already installed in the project of naming the terrorist; the terrorist does not appear as such without the concurrent entrance of perversion, deviance" (Puar, *Terrorist Assemblages*, xxiv).
71 Genet, *Prisoner of Love*, 184. "Les journaux du monde entier décrivirent cet assassinat que nul ne nomma terrorisme sur un territoire souverain. Il fut considéré comme l'un des Beaux-Arts" (Genet, *Un captif amoureux*, 220).
72 Neutres, *Genet sur les routes du Sud*, 61–62.
73 Genet, *Prisoner of Love*, 99. "La terre manque aux Noirs comme elle manque aux Palestiniens. Les deux situations—Noirs américains et Palestiniens—ne sont pas les mêmes en tout point, mais en cela que les uns et les autres sont sans terre. Proprement martyrisés, à partir de quel territoire vont-ils préparer la révolte?" (Genet, *Un captif amoureux*, 118–19).
74 Genet, *Prisoner of Love*, 14, translation modified. "Si la terre entière est le royaume de la terreur nous savons à qui le devoir, vous distribuez la terreur en vous terrant. Les terroristes d'aujourd'hui et de qui je parle exposent volontairement leurs corps, la différence est là" (Genet, *Un captif amoureux*, 21).
75 Genet, *Prisoner of Love*, 15, translation modified. "Le détrius de nations 'assises'" (Genet, *Un captif amoureux*, 22).
76 Reddy, *Freedom with Violence*, 225.
77 Asad, *On Suicide Bombing*, 35. The discourse of "human shielding," which the Israeli government employed extensively during 2014 Operation Protective Edge, is one example of a "liberal" state using the argument of its adversary's failure to value the lives of its civilians in order to justify killing those very civilians. One

Israeli Defense Force advertisement features two panels. One reads "Israel Uses Weapons to Protect Its Civilians," and the other, "Hamas Uses Civilians to Protect Its Weapons." A caption under both panels concludes "Hamas Puts Palestinian Civilians in the Line of Fire." The implication of this advertisement and of the discourse on "human shielding" is that, given its barbaric failure to value civilian life, Hamas, not Israel, is responsible for deaths of Palestinian civilians killed by Israeli airstrikes targeting civilian buildings in a conflict that disproportionately claimed Palestinian lives.

78 Asad, *On Suicide Bombing*, 38.
79 See Said, *The Question of Palestine*.
80 Medovoi, "Global Society Must Be Defended," 72. Reddy argues that we might understand asymmetrical warfare against racialized threats as "race wars" in which "the kind of disproportionate force that the military uses is predicated on and justified by the position that the racial enemy is outside the terms of sovereignty, the nation-state, civility, rationality, and political society" (Reddy, *Freedom with Violence*, 234, 235).
81 Foucault locates the first form of state racism in the European discourse of degeneracy (Foucault, "*Society Must Be Defended*"). Ann Stoler has convincingly argued that empire may have informed the language and imagery of racial degeneracy as often as the other way around (Stoler, *Race and the Education of Desire*, 123). Alexander Wehiliye has critiqued Foucault for embracing an ontological difference between ethnic and biopolitical racism and ignoring the former (Weheliye, *Habeas Viscus*).
82 Puar, *Terrorist Assemblages*, 35.
83 Stewart and McGregor, "Jean Genet's Psychiatric Examination in 1943."
84 Genet, *Miracle of the Rose*, 246. "Je n'aime pas les opprimés. J'aime ceux que j'aime, qui sont toujours beaux et quelquefois opprimés mais debout dans la révolte" (Genet, *Miracle de la rose*, 318).
85 For Raymond Williams, "structures of feeling" are collective rather than individual. In claiming *enemies of state* as a structure of feeling, I am speculatively suggesting that it may have powered not only Genet's political feelings, but also those of others constituted as criminal-queers, racialized criminals, and terrorists (Raymond Williams, *Marxism and Literature*, 128–35).
86 Genet, *The Declared Enemy*, 42–43. "Si je suis sincère, je dois dire que ce qui m'a touché d'abord, ce n'est pas leur souci de recréer le monde. Bien sûr, ça viendra et je n'y suis pas insensible, mais ce qui m'a fait me sentir proche d'eux immédiatement, c'est la haine qu'ils portent au monde blanc, c'est leur souci de détruire une société, de la casser. Souci qui était le mien très jeune mais je ne pouvais pas changer le monde tout seul. Je ne pouvais que le pervertir, le corrompre un peu" (Genet, *L'ennemi déclaré*, 55–56).
87 A well-known passage from *Prisoner of Love* depicts the Palestinians becoming terrorist "stars," striking a pose for photographers from Western journals. Genet may have been reflecting, in this passage, on the mediatized representations that animated *his own* attraction to the Palestinians (Genet, *Prisoner of Love*, 12–14; Genet, *Un captif amoureux*, 19–21).

88 Hochberg, *Visual Occupations*, 69.
89 Genet, *Prisoner of Love*, 205, translation modified. "Ornés"; "non seulement la transfiguration de mes fantasmes mais leur materialization" (Genet, *Un captif amoureux*, 244). Hochberg, *Visual Occupations*, 84.
90 As a number of thinkers of coalition have remarked, coalition rarely feels unproblematically comfortable and always requires dedication and work. See Reagon, "Coalition Politics"; Cohen, "Punks, Bulldaggers, and Welfare Queens." On the "emotion work" of ACT-UP, see Gould, *Moving Politics*, 213–66.
91 Genet was far from the only white person to route his revolutionary desires through black and Third World movements. For an account of the range of U.S. white leftists who started revolutionary terrorist groups in imagined solidarity with black and Third World movements, see Burrough, *Days of Rage*. Unlike most of the white leftists Burrough studies, Genet joined the Panthers and Palestinians directly rather than starting a white solidarity group.
92 Halperin writes, "As the very word implies, 'queer' does not name some national kind or refer to some determinate object; it acquires its meaning from its oppositional relation to the norm. Queer is by definition *whatever* is at odds with the normal, the legitimate, the dominant" (Halperin, *Saint Foucault*, 62). Cohen, "Punks, Bulldaggers, and Welfare Queens," 438, my emphasis.
93 Cohen, "Punks, Bulldaggers, and Welfare Queens," 438.
94 Ferguson, *Aberrations in Black*, 137.
95 For an argument that an antinormative sensibility defines queer theory as a field, see Wiegman and Wilson, "Introduction." I understand the "sensibility" of antinormativity within Queer Studies as affectively encoding the defiant reclamation of "queer" and the oppositional, in-your-face attitude of 1990s AIDS activism in the United States. See Gould, *Moving Politics*, 256.
96 On glimpsing utopian futurity, see Muñoz, *Cruising Utopia*. Cohen originally offered her thoughts on a coalition of those marginalized in relation to intersectional forms of dominant power as a modest "framework from which the *difficult work* of coalition politics can begin" (Cohen, "Punks, Bulldaggers, and Welfare Queens," 462, my emphasis). However, in some recent queer scholarship, instead of a starting point, queer coalition has instead become *the endpoint* of analysis and *the answer* to the problem of single-axis identity politics being diagnosed.
97 See, for example, Warner, *The Trouble with Normal*; Hong and Ferguson, *Strange Affinities*; Shah, *Stranger Intimacy*; Muñoz, *Disidentifications*; Stanley, "Fugitive Flesh."
98 Genet, *The Declared Enemy*, 42. "La haine qu'ils portent au monde blanc" (Genet, *L'ennemi déclaré*, 56).
99 Gould, *Moving Politics*, 328–94.
100 Ahmed, *The Cultural Politics of Emotion*, 50.
101 Genet, *The Declared Enemy*, 132, my emphasis. "Est-ce que vous pouvez dire quelle serait votre révolution politique?" "Non"; "la révolution ne me permettrait probablement pas la révolte, c'est-à-dire la révolte individuelle"; "mon point de vue est très égoïste. Je voudrais que le monde, mais faites bien attention à la façon dont je

le dis, *je voudrais que le monde ne change pas pour me permettre d'être contre le monde*" (Genet, *L'ennemi déclaré*, 156, my emphasis).
102 Dollimore, *Sexual Dissidence*, 319.
103 Jakobsen, "Queer Is? Queer Does?," 522.
104 Genet's preference for the present of oppositionality and revolt over either the desired future of nation-statehood or the tradition of Islamic religious teachings led him, at times, to diminish the import of land, nation-statehood, and Islam in the Palestinian struggle: "When I looked at the Palestinian revolution from a viewpoint higher than my own, it was never desire for territory, for land more or less derelict and unfenced kitchen gardens and orchards, but a great movement of revolt, a challenge over rights which reached to the limits of Islam, not only involving territorial boundaries but also calling for a revision, probably even a rejection, of a theology as soporific as a Breton cradle" (Genet, *Prisoner of Love*, 103). "De plus haut que moi-même quand je la contemplais, la revolution palestinienne ne fut jamais désir de territoires, presque terrains perdus, jardins potagers ou vergers sans clôture, mais un grand mouvement de révolte d'une contestation cadastrale jusqu'aux limites du monde islamique, non seulement limites territoriales mais révision et probablement négation d'une théologie aussi endormeuse qu'un berceau breton" (Genet, *Un captif amoureux*, 123).
105 Genet, *The Declared Enemy*, 244, translation modified. "Écoutez: le jour où les Palestiniens seront institutionalisés, je ne serais plus de leur côté. Le jour où les Palestiniens deviendront une nation comme une autre nation, je ne serais plus là"; "Je crois que c'est là que je vais les trahir. Ils ne le savent pas" (Genet, *L'ennemi déclaré*, 282).
106 See Edelman, *No Future*.
107 For a positive reading of the ethics of betrayal in Genet's relation to the Palestinians, see Penny, "Genet among the Palestinians."
108 In an essay on Eve Sedgwick and reparative reading, Love writes, "Recognizing that it is not only reparation but damage at work in Sedgwick's late essays will let us begin the hard work of deidealization. And that's love too" (Love, "Truth and Consequences," 240). I am interested in thinking through the implications of deidealization as not only a critical practice, but also a means of living with queer scholarly attachments that cannot fulfill the outsized hopes we invested in them.

EPILOGUE: HAUNTED BY THE 1990S

1 Eng, Halberstam, and Muñoz, "Introduction," 1.
2 Eng, Halberstam, and Muñoz, "Introduction," 1.
3 Eng, Halberstam, and Muñoz, "Introduction," 2.
4 Heather Love has discussed this introduction in relation to what she calls "Queer Theory's Everything Problem," that is, the field's "universalizing ambitions" and implicit dismissal of sexuality as "small-scale, private, trivial." I thank her for generously allowing me to read and cite this oral paper.

5 Eng, Halberstam, and Muñoz, "Introduction," 1.
6 Butler, "Critically Queer," 19.
7 As Love puts it in her reading of this passage, "The work of 'queering' is never done" (Love, *Feeling Backward*, 18).
8 Sedgwick, *Tendencies*, xii.
9 On the institutional reasons for queer theory's early appeal, see Jagose, "The Trouble with Antinormativity," 34.
10 Much queer scholarship produced during the 1990s and early 2000s focused precisely on this set of issues. For an argument in favor of considering the 1980s "sex wars" as part of a feminist genealogy of Queer Studies, see Love, "Introduction." Gayle Rubin offers a fuller account than I can here of the context of sexual politics in the 1980s and 1990s (Rubin, "Afterword to 'Thinking Sex'").
11 Deborah Gould argues that *queer* emerged around 1990 as "a new sensibility" that combined "fury and pride about gay difference and about confrontational activism, antipathy toward heteronormative society, and aspirations to live in a transformed world" (Gould, *Moving Politics*, 256).
12 Sedgwick, *Tendencies*, xii.
13 Warner, "Introduction," xxvi; Love, "Queer Theory's Everything Problem."
14 Eng, Halberstam, and Muñoz, "Introduction," 1.
15 Wiegman, *Object Lessons*, 122.
16 Jagose, "The Trouble with Antinormativity," 34.
17 Pérez, "You Can Have My Brown Body and Eat It, Too!," 172; Puar, *Terrorist Assemblages*, 22–23. Pérez's essay is part of the "What's Queer about Queer Studies Now?" special issue. My analysis of the rhetoric of the introduction of the special issue is not intended as a critique of essays included in that issue.
18 Chen, *Animacies*, 64, 68–69.
19 Martin, "Extraordinary Homosexuals and the Fear of Being Ordinary."
20 For the argument that the ontologization of queer as sheer productivity, particularly by scholarship on new materialisms, reproduces the logics of finance capital, see Rosenberg, "The Molecularization of Sexuality." Still, we lack a full-scale exposé of the relation between the queer discourse of fluidity, flexibility, and mobility and the demands of neoliberal capital.
21 Chen, *Animacies*, 83.
22 Chen, *Animacies*, 78.
23 Annamarie Jagose demonstrates that although gay barebacking, anal fisting, and erotic vomiting have been worthy of queer theoretical interest, orgasm has not. See Jagose, *Orgasmology*, 175–215.
24 Ahmed, *The Cultural Politics of Emotion*, 91.
25 Brad Epps critiqued the "fetish of fluidity" in queer theory as early as 2001. Epps, "The Fetish of Fluidity."
26 For example, Tim Dean advocates in favor of "affirmatively forgetting" both the context and the fetishized authors of queer theory's U.S. emergence in the 1990s so that queer might do new work in other languages and geopolitical contexts. Tim Dean, "Queer Theory without Names," 428.
27 Although I agree with Christopher Castiglia and Christopher Reed that queer

theory was institutionalized at the cost of the history of 1970s–80s U.S. gay culture in general and of the AIDS crisis in particular, I disagree strongly with their monocausal focus on only these particular historical sites as the sites of relevance for Queer Studies. Castiglia and Reed, *If Memory Serves*.
28 Hilderbrand, "Retroactivism," 303.
29 Muñoz, *Cruising Utopia*, 27.
30 Muñoz, *Cruising Utopia*, 22.
31 Muñoz, *Cruising Utopia*, 35.
32 Eng, *The Feeling of Kinship*; Puar, *Terrorist Assemblages*, xxvii.
33 Puar, *Terrorist Assemblages*, 221.
34 Arondekar and Patel, "Area Impossible," 152.
35 Ahmed, *The Cultural Politics of Emotion*, 202.
36 Cvetkovich, *An Archive of Feelings*.

bibliography

Abelove, Henry. "New York City Gay Liberation and the Queer Commuters." In *Deep Gossip*, 70–88. Minneapolis: University of Minnesota Press, 2005.
Abraham, Nicolas, and Maria Torok. "Mourning *or* Melancholia: Introjection *versus* Incorporation." In *The Shell and the Kernel: Renewals of Psychoanalysis*, vol. 1, 125–38. Chicago: University of Chicago Press, 1994.
Adam, Barry. "Age Preferences among Gay and Bisexual Men." *GLQ: A Journal of Lesbian and Gay Studies* 6, no. 3 (2000): 413–33.
———. "Age, Structure, and Sexuality: Reflections on the Anthropological Evidence on Homosexual Relations." *Journal of Homosexuality* 11, nos. 3–4 (1986): 19–33.
Ahmed, Sara. *The Cultural Politics of Emotion*. New York: Routledge, 2004.
Aldrich, Robert. *Colonialism and Homosexuality*. London: Routledge, 2003.
Al-Kassim, Dina. "Epilogue: Sexual Epistemologies, East in West." In *Islamicate Sexualities: Translations across Temporal Geographies of Desire*, edited by Kathryn Babayan and Afsaneh Najmabadi, 297–339. Cambridge, MA: Harvard University Press, 2008.
Alloula, Malek. *The Colonial Harem*. Translated by Myrna Godzich and Wlad Godzich. Minneapolis: University of Minnesota Press, 1986.
Ambroise-Rendu, Anne-Claude. *Histoire de la pédophilie: XIXe–XXIe siècle*. Paris: Fayard, 2014.
Amin, Kadji. "Against Queer Objects." *Feminist Formations* 28, no. 2 (2016): 101–11.
Anderson, Benedict. *Imagined Communities*. New York: Verso, 2006.
"Les arabes et nous." In "Trois milliards de pervers: Grande encyclopédie des homosexualités." Special issue, *Recherches* 12 (1973): 10–24.
Arondekar, Anjali, and Geeta Patel. "Area Impossible: Notes toward an Introduction." *GLQ: A Journal of Lesbian and Gay Studies* 22, no. 2 (2016): 151–71.
Asad, Talal. *On Suicide Bombing*. New York: Columbia University Press, 2007.
Ben Daniel, Tallie. "Zionist Geographies: Neoliberal San Francisco, Pinkwashing, and Gay Palestine." *Spaces and Flows: An International Journal of Urban and Extra Urban Studies* 1, no. 4 (2011): 49–57.
Benjamin, Walter. "Critique of Violence." In *Reflections: Essays, Aphorisms, Auto-*

biographical Writings, edited by Peter Demetz, translated by Edmund Jephcott, 277–300. New York: Schocken, 1978.

Ben-Moshe, Liat, Che Cossett, Nick Mitchell, and Eric Stanley. "Critical Theory, Queer Resistance, and the Ends of Capture." In *Death and Other Penalties: Philosophy in a Time of Mass Incarceration*, edited by Geoffrey Adelsberg, Lisa Guenther, and Scott Zeman, 266–96. New York: Fordham University Press, 2015.

Berlant, Lauren. *Cruel Optimism*. Durham, NC: Duke University Press, 2011.

Bersani, Leo. *Homos*. Cambridge, MA: Harvard University Press, 1995.

———. "Is the Rectum a Grave?" *October*, no. 43 (1987): 197–222.

Bhabha, Homi. "The Other Question: Stereotype, Discrimination, and the Discourse of Colonialism." In *The Location of Culture*, 94–120. New York: Routledge, 1994.

Bonnet, Marie-Jo. "De l'émancipation amoureuse des femmes dans la cité: Lesbiennes au XXe siècle." *Les temps modernes*, no. 598 (1998): 85–112.

Boone, Joseph. *The Homoerotics of Orientalism*. New York: Columbia University Press, 2014.

Brown, Elaine. *A Taste of Power: A Black Woman's Story*. New York: Pantheon, 1992.

Burrough, Bryan. *Days of Rage: America's Radical Underground, the FBI, and the Forgotten Age of Revolutionary Violence*. New York: Penguin Press, 2015.

Butler, Judith. Afterword to *Butch/Femme: Inside Lesbian Gender*, edited by Sally Munt, 225–30. London: Cassell, 1998.

———. "Critically Queer." *GLQ: A Journal of Lesbian and Gay Studies* 1, no. 1 (1993): 17–32.

———. *Gender Trouble: Feminism and the Subversion of Identity*. New York: Routledge, 1999.

———. "Passing, Queering: Nella Larsen's Psychoanalytic Challenge." In *Bodies That Matter: On the Discursive Limits of "Sex,"* 122–38. New York: Routledge, 1993.

Califia, Pat. Introduction to *Doing It for Daddy*, edited by Pat Califia, 9–16. New York: Alyson Books, 1994.

Caserio, Robert, Lee Edelman, Judith Halberstam, José Esteban Muñoz, and Tim Dean. "The Antisocial Thesis in Queer Theory." *PMLA* 121, no. 3 (2006): 819–28.

Castiglia, Christopher, and Christopher Reed. *If Memory Serves: Gay Men, AIDS, and the Promise of the Queer Past*. Minneapolis: University of Minnesota Press, 2012.

Cauchy, Jean-Christophe, Francis Lacombe, and Eric Lamien. "Qui a peur des pédophiles?" *Gai pied hebdo*, no. 455 (January 31, 1991): 52–61.

Cervulle, Maxime. "French Homonormativity and the Commodification of the Arab Body." *Radical History Review*, no. 100 (2008): 170–79.

Cervulle, Maxime, and Nick Rees-Roberts. *Homo exoticus: Race, classe et critique queer*. Paris: Armand Colin, 2010.

Chauncey, George. *Gay New York: Gender, Urban Culture, and the Making of the Gay Male World, 1890–1940*. New York: Basic Books, 1994.

Chen, Mel. *Animacies: Biopolitics, Racial Mattering, and Queer Affect*. Durham, NC: Duke University Press, 2012.

Choukri, Mohamed. *Jean Genet in Tangier*. Translated by Paul Bowles. New York: Ecco, 1974.

Cixous, Hélène. "The Laugh of the Medusa." In *The Signs Reader: Women, Gender, and*

Scholarship, edited by Elizabeth Abel and Emily K. Abel, 297. Chicago: University of Chicago Press, 1983.

Cohen, Cathy. "Punks, Bulldaggers, and Welfare Queens: The Radical Potential of Queer Politics?" *GLQ: A Journal of Lesbian and Gay Studies* 3 (1997): 437–65.

Crimp, Douglas, ed. *AIDS: Cultural Analysis, Cultural Activism*. Cambridge, MA: MIT Press, 1998.

"Les culs énergumènes." In "Trois milliards de pervers: Grande encyclopédie des homosexualités." Special issue, *Recherches* 12 (1973): 130–69.

Cvetkovich, Ann. *An Archive of Feelings: Trauma, Sexuality, and Lesbian Public Cultures*. Durham, NC: Duke University Press, 2003.

Danan, Alexis. *Maisons de supplices*. Paris: Denoël et Steele, 1936.

Davis, Angela. "Black Nationalism: The Sixties and the Nineties." In *The Angela Y. Davis Reader*, edited by Joy James. Oxford: Blackwell, 1998.

Dean, Carolyn. *The Frail Social Body: Pornography, Homosexuality, and Other Fantasies in Interwar France*. Berkeley: University of California Press, 2000.

Dean, Tim. "Queer Theory without Names." *Paragraph* 35, no. 3 (2012): 421–34.

———. *Unlimited Intimacy: Reflections on the Subculture of Barebacking*. Chicago: University of Chicago Press, 2009.

Delany, Samuel. *Times Square Red, Times Square Blue*. New York: New York University Press, 1999.

Deleuze, Gilles, and Félix Guattari. *A Thousand Plateaus: Capitalism and Schizophrenia*. Minneapolis: University of Minnesota Press, 1987.

D'Emilio, John. "Capitalism and Gay Identity." In *The Lesbian and Gay Studies Reader*, edited by Henry Abelove, Michèle Aina Barale, and David Halperin, 467–76. New York: Routledge, 1993.

Derrida, Jacques. *Archive Fever: A Freudian Impression*. Translated by Eric Prenowitz. Chicago: University of Chicago Press, 1998.

Dinshaw, Carolyn. *Getting Medieval: Sexualities and Communities, Pre- and Postmodern*. Durham, NC: Duke University Press, 1999.

Dinshaw, Carolyn, Lee Edelman, Roderick A. Ferguson, Carla Freccero, Elizabeth Freeman, Judith Halberstam, Annamarie Jagose, Christopher Nealon, and Nguyen Tan Hoang. "Theorizing Queer Temporalities: A Roundtable Discussion." *GLQ* 13, nos. 2–3 (2007): 177–95.

Dollimore, Jonathan. *Sexual Dissidence: Augustine to Wilde, Freud to Foucault*. Oxford: Clarendon, 1991.

Duggan, Lisa. "The Discipline Problem: Queer Theory Meets Lesbian and Gay History." In *Sex Wars: Sexual Dissent and Political Culture*, edited by Lisa Duggan and Nan Hunter, 10th anniv. ed., 179–91. New York: Routledge, 2006.

———. "The New Homonormativity." In *Materializing Democracy: Toward a Revitalized Cultural Politics*, edited by Russ Castronovo and Dana Nelson, 175–94. Durham, NC: Duke University Press, 2002.

Durham, Scott. "Editor's Preface: In the Language of the Enemy." In "Genet: In the Language of the Enemy." Special issue, *Yale French Studies*, no. 91 (1997): 1–6.

Dyer, Richard. "The Role of Stereotypes." In *Media Studies: A Reader*, 245–51. New York: New York University Press, 2000.

Edelman, Lee. *No Future: Queer Theory and the Death Drive*. Durham, NC: Duke University Press, 2004.

El-Rouayheb, Khaled. *Before Homosexuality in the Arab-Islamic World, 1500–1800*. Chicago: University of Chicago Press, 2005.

Eng, David L. *The Feeling of Kinship: Queer Liberalism and the Racialization of Intimacy*. Durham, NC: Duke University Press, 2010.

———. *Racial Castration*. Durham, NC: Duke University Press, 2001.

Eng, David L., Judith Halberstam, and José Esteban Muñoz. "Introduction: What's Queer about Queer Studies Now?" *Social Text* 23, nos. 3–4 (2005): 1–17.

Epps, Brad. "The Fetish of Fluidity." In *Homosexuality and Psychoanalysis*, edited by Tim Dean and Christopher Lane, 412–31. Chicago: University of Chicago Press, 2001.

Epstein, Steve. "Gay Politics, Ethnic Identity: The Limits of Social Construction." *Socialist Review* 17, nos. 3–4 (1987): 9–54.

Eribon, Didier. *Réflexions sur la question gay*. Paris: Fayard, 1999.

———. *Une morale du minoritaire: Variations sur un thème de Jean Genet*. Paris: Fayard, 2001.

Fanon, Frantz. *Black Skin, White Masks*. New York: Grove, 1967.

———. *Peau noire, masques blancs*. Paris: Seuil, 1952.

Fassin, Éric. "Entre famille et nation: La filiation naturalisée." *Droit et société* 72, no. 2 (2009): 373–82.

———. "Same-Sex Marriage, Nation, and Race: French Political Logics and Rhetorics." *Contemporary French Civilization* 39, no. 3 (2014): 281–301.

Féray, Jean-Claude. *Grecques, les moeurs du hanneton? Histoire du mot pédérastie et de ses dérivés en langue française*. Paris: Quintes-feuilles, 2004.

Ferguson, Roderick. *Aberrations in Black: Toward a Queer of Color Critique*. Minneapolis: University of Minnesota Press, 2004.

———. *The Reorder of Things: The University and Its Pedagogies of Minority Difference*. Minneapolis: University of Minnesota Press, 2012.

Fischel, Joseph. "Against Nature, against Consent: A Sexual Politics of Debility." *differences: A Journal of Feminist Cultural Studies* 24, no. 1 (2013): 55–103.

———. *Sex and Harm in the Age of Consent*. Minneapolis: University of Minnesota Press, 2016.

Fishman, Sarah. *The Battle for Children: World War II, Youth Crime, and Juvenile Justice in Twentieth-Century France*. Cambridge, MA: Harvard University Press, 2002.

Flatley, Jonathan. *Affective Mapping: Melancholia and the Politics of Modernism*. Cambridge, MA: Harvard University Press, 2008.

Flaubert, Gustave. *A Sentimental Education*. Oxford: Oxford University Press, 2008.

Foucault, Michel. *Abnormal: Lectures at the Collège de France, 1974–1975*. New York: Picador, 2003.

———. "De l'amitié comme mode de vie." In *Dits et Écrits II, 1976–1988*, 982–86. Paris: Gallimard, 2001.

———. *Discipline and Punish: The Birth of the Prison*. Translated by Alan Sheridan. New York: Vintage Books, 1979.

———. "Friendship as a Way of Life." In *Ethics: Subjectivity and Truth*, edited by Paul Rabinow, translated by Robert Hurley, 135–40. New York: New Press, 1997.

———. *The History of Sexuality: An Introduction*. New York: Vintage, 1990.
———. "The Lives of Infamous Men." In *Power: Essential Works of Foucault, 1954–1984*, edited by James Faubion, 157–75. New York: New Press, 2000.
———. "La loi de la pudeur." In *Dits et Écrits II, 1976–1988*, 763–77. Paris: Gallimard, 2001.
———. "Nietzsche, Genealogy, History." In *The Foucault Reader*, edited by Paul Rabinow, 76–100. New York: Pantheon, 1984.
———. "Nietzsche, la généalogie, l'histoire." In *Dits et Écrits II, 1970-1975*, 136–56. Paris: Gallimard, 1985.
———. *Security, Territory, Population: Lectures at the Collège de France, 1977–78*. Edited by François Ewald, Alessandro Fontana, and Michel Senellart. Translated by Graham Burchell. New York: Palgrave Macmillan, 2007.
———. "Sexual Morality and the Law." In *Politics, Philosophy, Culture: Interviews and Other Writings, 1977–1984*, edited by Lawrence Kritzman, 271–85. New York: Routledge, 1988.
———. *"Society Must Be Defended": Lectures at the Collège de France, 1975–1976*. New York: Picador, 2003.
———. *Surveiller et punir: Naissance de la prison*. Paris: Gallimard, 1975.
———. "La vie des hommes infâmes." In *Dits et écrits II, 1976–1988*, 237–53. Paris: Gallimard, 2001.
Freccero, Carla. *Queer/Early/Modern*. Durham, NC: Duke University Press, 2005.
Freeman, Elizabeth. "Queer Belongings: Kinship Theory and Queer Theory." In *A Companion to Lesbian, Gay, Bisexual, Transgender, and Queer Studies*, edited by George E. Haggerty and Molly McGarry, 295–314. Oxford: Blackwell, 2007.
———. "Time Binds, or, Erotohistoriography." *Social Text* 23, nos. 3–4, 84–85 (2005): 57–68.
———. *Time Binds: Queer Temporalities, Queer Histories*. Durham, NC: Duke University Press, 2010.
Freud, Sigmund. "Fetishism." In *The Standard Edition of the Complete Psychological Works of Sigmund Freud*, edited by James Strachey, 21:152–59. London: Hogarth, 1974.
———. "Mourning and Melancholia." In *Standard Edition of the Complete Psychological Works of Sigmund Freud*, edited by James Strachey, 14:243–58. London: Hogarth Press, 1957.
Gaillac, Henri. *Les maisons de correction 1830–1945*. Paris: Editions Cujas, 1991.
Genet, Jean. "Les bonnes." In *Oeuvres complètes*, 4:137–76. Paris: Gallimard, 1968.
———. *Un captif amoureux*. Paris: Gallimard, 1986.
———. *Un chant d'amour*. DVD. Los Angeles, CA: Cult Epics, 2007.
———. *The Declared Enemy: Texts and Interviews*. Edited by Albert Dichy. Translated by Jeff Fort. Stanford, CA: Stanford University Press, 2004.
———. *L'ennemi déclaré: Textes et entretiens*. Edited by Albert Dichy. Paris: Gallimard, 1991.
———. "Fragments . . ." In *Fragments . . . et autres textes*, 67–98. Paris: Gallimard, 1990.
———. "Fragments . . ." In *Fragments of the Artwork*, edited by Werner Hamacher, translated by Charlotte Mandell, 19–35. Stanford, CA: Stanford University Press, 2003.

———. *Funeral Rites*. New York: Grove, 1969.
———. *Journal du voleur*. Paris: Gallimard, 1949.
———. "Le langage de la muraille." Film manuscript, 1981–82, Jean Genet Archive, Institut Mémoires de l'Édition Contemporaine.
———. "Le langage de la muraille." Preparatory documents for Jean Genet, film manuscript, 1981–82, Jean Genet Archive, Institut Mémoires de l'Édition Contemporaine.
———. Letter to Bernard Tavernier. Preparatory documents for "Le langage de la muraille," film manuscript, 1981–82, Jean Genet Archive, Institut Mémoires de l'Édition Contemporaine.
———. *The Maids and Deathwatch: Two Plays by Jean Genet*. Translated by Bernard Frechtman. New York: Grove, 1961.
———. *Miracle de la rose*. Paris: Gallimard, 1946.
———. *Miracle of the Rose*. Translated by Bernard Frechtman. New York: Grove, 1966.
———. *Notre-Dame-des-Fleurs*. Paris: Gallimard, 1948.
———. *Our Lady of the Flowers*. Translated by Bernard Frechtman. New York: Grove, 1991.
———. *Pompes funèbres*. Paris: Gallimard, 1953.
———. *Prisoner of Love*. Translated by Barbara Bray. New York: New York Review of Books, 2003.
———. *The Thief's Journal*. New York: Grove, 1964.
Genosko, Gary. "The Figure of the Arab in *Three Billion Perverts*." *Deleuze Studies* 1, no. 1 (2007): 60–78.
Gide, André. *Corydon*. Translated by Richard Howard. New York: Farrar, Straus and Giroux, 1983.
———. *Les nourritures terrestres suivi de Les nouvelles nourritures*. Paris: Gallimard, 1936.
Gill, Michael. *Already Doing It: Intellectual Disability and Sexual Agency*. Minneapolis: University of Minnesota Press, 2015.
Gordon, Avery. *Ghostly Matters: Haunting and the Sociological Imagination*. Minneapolis: University of Minnesota Press, 1997.
Gould, Deborah. *Moving Politics: Emotion and ACT UP's Fight against AIDS*. Chicago: University of Chicago Press, 2009.
Gunther, Scott. *The Elastic Closet: A History of Homosexuality in France, 1942–Present*. New York: Palgrave Macmillan, 2009.
Halberstam, Judith. *Female Masculinity*. Durham, NC: Duke University Press, 1998.
———. *In a Queer Time and Place: Transgender Bodies, Subcultural Lives*. New York: New York University Press, 2005.
———. *The Queer Art of Failure*. Durham, NC: Duke University Press, 2011.
Hale, C. Jacob. "Leatherdyke Boys and Their Daddies: How to Have Sex without Women or Men." *Social Text* 15, nos. 3–4 (1997): 223–36.
Halperin, David. *How to Do the History of Homosexuality*. Chicago: University of Chicago Press, 2002.
———. *One Hundred Years of Homosexuality: And Other Essays on Greek Love*. New York: Routledge, 1990.
———. *Saint Foucault: Towards a Gay Hagiography*. Oxford: Oxford University Press, 1995.

Hankins, Jérôme, ed. "Entretien avec Leila Shahid." In *Genet à Chatila*. Paris: Solin, 1992.

Harkins, Gillian. "Foucault, the Family and the Cold Monster of Neoliberalism." In *Foucault, the Family, and Politics*, 82–117. New York: Palgrave Macmillan, 2012.

Hart, Lynda, and Joshua Dale. "Sadomasochism." In *Lesbian and Gay Studies: A Critical Introduction*, edited by Sally Munt and Andy Medhurst, 341–55. New York: Continuum International, 1997.

Hayes, Jarrod. *Queer Nations: Marginal Sexualities in the Maghreb*. Chicago: University of Chicago Press, 2000.

Heaney, Emma. "The New Woman: Sexology, Literary Modernism, and the Trans Feminine Remainder." *Genre* 48, no. 1 (2015): 1–33.

Hekma, Gert. "The Drive for Sexual Equality." *Sexualities* 11, nos. 1–2 (2008): 46–50.

Hennig, J.-L. "Thomas, 30 ans, Bruno, 15 ans, le nouveau couple Zig-Zag." In "Fous d'enfance." Special issue, *Recherches*, no. 37 (1979): 137–65.

Hesford, Victoria. *Feeling Women's Liberation*. Durham, NC: Duke University Press, 2013.

Hewitt, Andrew. *Political Inversions: Homosexuality, Fascism, and the Modernist Imaginary*. Stanford, CA: Stanford University Press, 1996.

Hilderbrand, Lucas. "Retroactivism." *GLQ: A Journal of Lesbian and Gay Studies* 12, no. 2 (2006): 303–17.

Hilliard, David, and Lewis Cole. *This Side of Glory*. Boston: Little, Brown, 1993.

Hochberg, Gil, ed. "Queer Politics and the Question of Palestine/Israel." Special issue, *GLQ: A Journal of Lesbian and Gay Studies* 16, no. 4 (2010).

Hochberg, Gil. *Visual Occupations: Violence and Visibility in a Conflict Zone*. Durham, NC: Duke University Press, 2015.

Hocquenghem, Guy. *L'après-mai des faunes*. Paris: Grasset et Fasquelle, 1974.

———. *Le désir homosexuel*. Paris: Éditions Universitaires, 1972.

———. "L'enfant interdit." In "Co-ire: Album systématique de l'enfance." Special issue, *Recherches*, no. 22 (1976): 45–60.

———. *Homosexual Desire*. Translated by Daniella Dangoor. Durham, NC: Duke University Press, 1993.

Holland, Sharon Patricia. *The Erotic Life of Racism*. Durham, NC: Duke University Press, 2012.

———. "'From This Moment Forth, We Are Black Lesbians': Querying Feminism and Killing the Self in Consolidated's Business of Punishment." In *Raising the Dead: Readings of Death and (Black) Subjectivity*, 124–48. Durham, NC: Duke University Press, 2000.

Hong, Grace Kyungwon, and Roderick A. Ferguson, eds. *Strange Affinities: The Gender and Sexual Politics of Comparative Racialization*. Durham, NC: Duke University Press, 2011.

hooks, bell. "Eating the Other: Desire and Resistance." In *Media and Cultural Studies: KeyWorks*, edited by Meenakshi Gigi Durham and Douglas M. Kellner, 366–80. Oxford: Blackwell, 2006.

Jablonka, Ivan. *Les vérités inavouables de Jean Genet*. Paris: Éditions du Seuil, 2004.

Jackson, George. *Soledad Brother: The Prison Letters of George Jackson*. New York: Coward-McCann, 1970.

Jackson, Julian. *Living in Arcadia: Homosexuality, Politics, and Morality in France from the Liberation to AIDS.* Chicago: University of Chicago Press, 2009.

Jagose, Annamarie. *Orgasmology.* Durham, NC: Duke University Press, 2013.

———. "The Trouble with Antinormativity." *differences: A Journal of Feminist Cultural Studies* 26, no. 1 (2015): 26–47.

Jakobsen, Janet R. "Queer Is? Queer Does?: Normativity and the Problem of Resistance." *GLQ: A Journal of Lesbian and Gay Studies* 4, no. 4 (1998): 511–36.

Jennings, Regina. "Why I Joined the Party: An Africana Womanist Reflection." In *The Black Panther Party (Reconsidered),* edited by Charles E. Jones, 257–65. Baltimore: Black Classic Press, 1998.

Johnson, Colin. *Just Queer Folks: Gender and Sexuality in Rural America.* Philadelphia: Temple University Press, 2013.

Jones, Charles E. "The Political Repression of the Black Panther Party 1966–1971: The Case of the Oakland Bay Area." *Journal of Black Studies* 18, no. 4 (June 1988): 415–34.

Keeling, Kara. *The Witch's Flight: The Cinematic, the Black Femme, and the Image of Common Sense.* Durham, NC: Duke University Press, 2007.

Khanna, Ranjana. *Dark Continents: Psychoanalysis and Colonialism.* Durham, NC: Duke University Press, 2003.

Klein, Melanie. *Love, Guilt, and Reparation: And Other Works 1921–1945.* New York: Delacorte, 1975.

"Kouche!" In "Trois milliards de pervers: Grande encyclopédie des homosexualités." Special issue, *Recherches* 12 (1973): 45–49.

Kunzel, Regina. *Criminal Intimacy: Prison and the Uneven History of Modern American Sexuality.* Chicago: University of Chicago Press, 2008.

Lapie, Victor. *Saint-Florent-la-Vie.* Paris: Vigot Frères, 1946.

Larique, Marius. "Mettray-Eysses, ligne directe I." *Détective,* no. 443 (April 22, 1937): 12–16.

Le Breton, Auguste. *Les hauts murs.* Paris: Rocher, 1999.

Leeming, David. *James Baldwin: A Biography.* New York: Alfred A. Knopf, 1994.

Léger, Raoul. *Souvenirs d'un colon 1922–1927: Punir pour éduquer? Suivis de contributions historiques.* Edited by Jacques Bourquin. Paris: Éditions L'Harmattan, 1997.

Levine, Judith. *Harmful to Minors: The Perils of Protecting Children from Sex.* Minneapolis: University of Minnesota Press, 2002.

Lim, Eng-Beng. *Brown Boys and Rice Queens: Spellbinding Performance in the Asias.* New York: New York University Press, 2013.

Love, Heather. "Doing Being Deviant: Deviance Studies, Description, and the Queer Ordinary." *differences: A Journal of Feminist Cultural Studies* 26, no. 1 (2015): 74–95.

———. *Feeling Backward: Loss and the Politics of Queer History.* Cambridge, MA: Harvard University Press, 2007.

———. "Introduction: Rethinking Sex." In "Rethinking Sex." Special issue, *GLQ: A Journal of Lesbian and Gay Studies* 17, no. 1 (2011): 1–14.

———. "Queer Theory's Everything Problem." Paper presented at the Thinking Feminism at the Limits Conference, Institute for Research on Women and Gender, Columbia University, March 8, 2013.

———. "Truth and Consequences: On Paranoid Reading and Reparative Reading." *Criticism* 52, no. 2 (2010): 235–41.
Lucey, Michael. *Never Say I: Sexuality and the First Person in Colette, Gide, and Proust.* Durham, NC: Duke University Press, 2006.
Mack, Mehammed Amadeus. "Untranslatable Desire: Interethnic Relationships in Franco–Arab Literature." *Comparative Literature Studies* 51, no. 2 (2014): 321–43.
Mackay, John Henry. *The Hustler: The Story of a Nameless Love from Friedrichstrasse.* Translated by Hubert Kennedy. Boston: Alyson, 1985.
Malgorn, Arnaud. *Jean Genet: Portrait d'un marginal exemplaire*. Paris: Gallimard, 2002.
Manalansan, Martin. *Global Divas: Filipino Gay Men in the Diaspora*. Durham, NC: Duke University Press, 2003.
Mao, Douglas, and Rebecca Walkowitz, eds. *Bad Modernisms*. Durham, NC: Duke University Press, 2006.
Marriott, David. *Haunted Life: Visual Culture and Black Modernity*. New Brunswick, NJ: Rutgers University Press, 2007.
Martin, Biddy. "Extraordinary Homosexuals and the Fear of Being Ordinary." *differences: A Journal of Feminist Cultural Studies* 6, nos. 2–3 (1994): 100–125.
Marx, Karl. "Commodities." In *Capital*, vol. 1: *A Critique of Political Economy*, edited by Friedrich Engels, translated by Samuel Moore and Edward Aveling, 41–96. Mineola, NY: Dover, 2011.
Massad, Joseph. *Desiring Arabs*. Chicago: University of Chicago Press, 2007.
Massumi, Brian. *Parables for the Virtual: Movement, Affect, Sensation*. Durham, NC: Duke University Press, 2002.
Matthews, Tracye. "'No One Ever Asks, What a Man's Place in the Revolution Is': Gender and the Politics of the Black Panther Party 1966–1971." In *The Black Panther Party (Reconsidered)*, edited by Charles E. Jones, 267–304. Baltimore: Black Classic Press, 1998.
Medovoi, Leerom. "Global Society Must Be Defended: Biopolitics without Boundaries." *Social Text* 25, no. 91 (2007): 53–79.
Mercer, Kobena. "The Panthers and Genet." Paper presented at The Late Genet: Symposium 3, Nottingham Contemporary, Nottingham, UK. September 30, 2011.
———. *Welcome to the Jungle: New Positions in Black Cultural Studies*. New York: Routledge, 1994.
Millett, Kate. *Sexual Politics*. Urbana: University of Illinois Press, 2000.
Montez, Ricardo. "'Trade' Marks: LA2, Keith Haring, and a Queer Economy of Collaboration." *GLQ: A Journal of Lesbian and Gay Studies* 12, no. 3 (2006): 425–40.
Morgan, Edward. "Media Culture and the Public Memory of the Black Panther Party." In *In Search of the Black Panther Party: New Perspectives on a Revolutionary Movement*, edited by Jama Lazerow and Yohuru R. Williams. Durham, NC: Duke University Press, 2006.
Morgensen, Scott. *Spaces between Us: Queer Settler Colonialism and Indigenous Decolonization*. Minneapolis: University of Minnesota Press, 2011.
Muñoz, José Esteban. "Cruising the Toilet: LeRoi Jones/Amiri Baraka, Radical Black Traditions, and Queer Futurity." *GLQ* 13, nos. 2–3 (2007): 353–67.

———. *Cruising Utopia: The Then and There of Queer Futurity*. New York: New York University Press, 2009.
———. *Disidentifications: Queers of Color and the Performance of Politics*. Minneapolis: University of Minnesota Press, 1999.
Musser, Amber Jamilla. *Sensational Flesh: Race, Power, and Masochism*. New York: New York University Press, 2014.
Nash, Jennifer. *The Black Body in Ecstasy: Reading Race, Reading Pornography*. Durham, NC: Duke University Press, 2014.
Nealon, Christopher. *Foundlings: Lesbian and Gay Historical Emotion before Stonewall*. Durham, NC: Duke University Press, 2001.
Nelson, Alondra. *Body and Soul: The Black Panther Party and the Fight against Medical Discrimination*. Minneapolis: University of Minnesota Press, 2011.
Neutres, Jérôme. *Genet sur les routes du Sud*. Paris: Fayard, 2002.
Newton, Huey P. *Revolutionary Suicide*. New York: Harcourt Brace Jovanovich, 1973.
———. *To Die for the People: The Writings of Huey P. Newton*. New York: Random House, 1972.
Nguyen, Hoang Tan. *A View from the Bottom: Asian American Masculinity and Sexual Representation*. Durham, NC: Duke University Press, 2014.
Nyong'o, Tavia. *The Amalgamation Waltz: Race, Performance, and the Ruses of Memory*. Minneapolis: University of Minnesota Press, 2009.
Ogbar, Jeffrey O. G. "'Culture Is a Weapon in Our Struggle for Liberation': The Black Panther Party and the Cultural Politics of Decolonization." In *In Search of the Black Panther Party: New Perspectives on a Revolutionary Movement*, edited by Jama Lazerow and Yohuru R. Williams. Durham, NC: Duke University Press, 2006.
Omi, Howard, and Michael Winant. *Racial Formation in the United States*. 3rd ed. New York: Routledge, 2015.
Ongiri, Amy Abugo. "Prisoner of Love: Affiliation, Sexuality, and the Black Panther Party." *Journal of African American History* 94, no. 1 (2009): 69–86.
"La pédophilie." In "Trois milliards de pervers: Grande encyclopédie des homosexualités." Special issue, *Recherches* 12 (1973): 116–28.
Peniston, William A. *Pederasts and Others: Urban Culture and Sexual Identity in Nineteenth-Century Paris*. New York: Routledge, 2007.
Penny, James. "Genet among the Palestinians: Sex, Betrayal, and the Incomparable Real." In *Comparatively Queer: Interrogating Identities across Time and Cultures*, edited by Jarrod Hayes, Margaret Higonnet, and William Spurlin, 193–214. New York: Palgrave Macmillan, 2010.
Pérez, Hiram. *A Taste for Brown Bodies: Gay Modernity and Cosmopolitan Desire*. New York: New York University Press, 2015.
———. "You Can Have My Brown Body and Eat It, Too!" *Social Text* 23, nos. 3–4 (2005): 171–91.
Pietz, William. "The Problem of the Fetish I." *RES: Anthropology and Aesthetics* 9 (1985): 5–17.
———. "The Problem of the Fetish II: The Origin of the Fetish." *RES: Anthropology and Aesthetics* 13 (1987): 23–45.

Prearo, Massimo. *Le moment politique de l'homosexualité: Mouvements, identités et communautés en France*. Lyon: Presses universitaires de Lyon, 2014.
Provencher, Denis. *Queer French: Globalization, Language, and Sexual Citizenship in France*. Burlington, VT: Ashgate, 2007.
Puar, Jasbir. "Citation and Censorship: The Politics of Talking about the Sexual Politics of Israel." In *The Imperial University: Academic Repression and Scholarly Dissent*, ed. Sunaina Maire and Piya Chatterjee. Minneapolis: University of Minnesota Press, 2011.
———. *Terrorist Assemblages: Homonationalism in Queer Times*. Durham, NC: Duke University Press, 2007.
Reagon, Bernice Johnson. "Coalition Politics: Turning the Century." In *Home Girls: A Black Feminist Anthology*, edited by Barbara Smith, 343–56. New Brunswick, NJ: Rutgers University Press, 2000.
Reddy, Chandan. *Freedom with Violence: Race, Sexuality, and the U.S. State*. Durham, NC: Duke University Press, 2011.
Reid, Julian. *The Biopolitics of the War on Terror: Life Struggles, Liberal Modernity, and the Defense of Logistical Societies*. Manchester, UK: Manchester University Press, 2006.
Reid-Pharr, Robert. "Dinge." In *The Routledge Queer Studies Reader*, edited by Donald Hall and Annamarie Jagose, 212–19. New York: Routledge, 2012.
———. "The Shock of Gary Fisher." In *Black Gay Man: Essays*, 135–49. New York: New York University Press, 2001.
Revenin, Régis. *Une histoire des garçons et des filles: Amour, genre et sexualité dans la France d'après-guerre*. Paris: Vendémiaire, 2015.
Rifkin, Mark. *When Did Indians Become Straight? Kinship, the History of Sexuality, and Native Sovereignty*. Oxford: Oxford University Press, 2011.
Robcis, Camille. *The Law of Kinship: Anthropology, Psychoanalysis, and the Family in France*. Ithaca, NY: Cornell University Press, 2013.
Rodríguez, Juana María. "Queer Sociality and Other Sexual Fantasies." *GLQ: A Journal of Lesbian and Gay Studies* 17, nos. 2–3 (2011): 331–48.
———. *Sexual Futures, Queer Gestures, and Other Latina Longings*. New York: New York University Press, 2014.
Rohy, Valerie. *Anachronism and Its Others: Sexuality, Race, Temporality*. Albany: State University of New York, 2009.
Rosario, Vernon A., II. "Pointy Penises, Fashion Crimes, and Hysterical Mollies: The Pederasts' Inversions." In *Homosexuality in Modern France*, edited by Jeffrey Merrick and Bryant T. Ragan Jr., 146–76. Oxford: Oxford University Press, 1996.
Rosenberg, Jordana. "The Molecularization of Sexuality: On Some Primitivisms of the Present." *Theory and Event* 17, no. 2 (2014), https://muse.jhu.edu/.
Roubaud, Louis. *Les enfants de Caïn*. Paris: Bernard Grasset, 1925.
Rowley, Hazel. *Tête-à-tête: Simone de Beauvoir and Jean-Paul Sartre*. New York: HarperCollins, 2005.
Rubin, Gayle. "Afterword to 'Thinking Sex: Notes for a Radical Theory of the Politics of Sexuality.'" In *Deviations: A Gayle Rubin Reader*, 182–93. Durham, NC: Duke University Press, 2011.
———. "Blood under the Bridge: Reflections on 'Thinking Sex.'" *GLQ: A Journal of Lesbian and Gay Studies* 17, no. 1 (2011): 15–48.

———. "Geologies of Queer Studies: It's Déjà Vu All Over Again." In *Deviations: A Gayle Rubin Reader*, 347–56. Durham, NC: Duke University Press, 2011.

———. "The Leather Menace: Comments on Politics and s/m." In *Deviations: A Gayle Rubin Reader*, 109–36. Durham, NC: Duke University Press, 2011.

———. "Thinking Sex: Notes for a Radical Theory of the Politics of Sexuality." In *Deviations: A Gayle Rubin Reader*, 137–81. Durham, NC: Duke University Press, 2011.

"La rue." In "Trois milliards de pervers: Grande encyclopedia des homosexualités." Special issue, *Recherches* 12 (1973): 38–44.

"Rue des vertus." In "Trois milliards de pervers: Grande encyclopédie des homosexualités." Special issue, *Recherches* 12 (1973): 25–27.

Said, Edward. "On Jean Genet's Late Works." In *Imperialism and Theater: Essays on World Theater, Drama and Performance*, edited by J. Ellen Gainor. London: Routledge, 1995.

———. *The Question of Palestine*. New York: Routledge and Kegan Paul, 1980.

Sandarg, Robert. "Jean Genet and the Black Panther Party." *Journal of Black Studies* 16, no. 3 (1986): 269–82.

Sartre, Jean-Paul. *Saint Genet: Actor and Martyr*. Minneapolis: University of Minnesota Press, 1963.

———. *Saint Genet, comédien et martyr*. Paris: Gallimard, 1952.

Schehr, Lawrence. "Defense and Illustration of Gay Liberation." *Yale French Studies* 90 (1996): 139–52.

Schérer, René. "A propos de la pédophilie." In "Fous d'enfance." Special issue, *Recherches*, no. 37 (1979): 87–95.

Schérer, René, and Guy Hocquenghem. "Co-ire: Album systématique de l'enfance." Special issue, *Recherches*, no. 22 (1976).

Scott, Darieck. *Extravagant Abjection: Blackness, Power, and Sexuality in the African American Literary Imagination*. New York: New York University Press, 2010.

Seale, Bobby. *A Lonely Rage: The Autobiography of Bobby Seale*. New York: Times Books, 1978.

Sedgwick, Eve Kosofsky. "Afterword." In *Gary in Your Pocket*, 273–91. Durham, NC: Duke University Press, 1996.

———. *Between Men: English Literature and Male Homosocial Desire*. Gender and Culture. New York: Columbia University Press, 1985.

———. "Paranoid Reading and Reparative Reading, or, You're So Paranoid, You Probably Think This Essay Is about You." In *Touching Feeling: Affect, Pedagogy, Performativity*, 123–52. Durham, NC: Duke University Press, 2003.

———. *Tendencies*. Durham, NC: Duke University Press, 1993.

"Le sexe 'Arabe.'" In "Trois milliards de pervers: Grande encyclopédie des homosexualités." Special issue, *Recherches* 12 (1973): 32–37.

"Sex-pol en act." In "Trois milliards de pervers: Grande encyclopédie des homosexualités." Special issue, *Recherches* 12 (1973): 28–31.

Shah, Nayan. *Contagious Divides: Epidemics and Race in San Francisco's Chinatown*. Berkeley: University of California Press, 2001.

———. *Stranger Intimacy: Contesting Race, Sexuality, and the Law in the North American West*. Berkeley: University of California Press, 2011.

Shepard, Todd. "'Something Notably Erotic': Politics, 'Arab Men,' and Sexual Revolution in Post-Decolonization France, 1962–1974." *Journal of Modern History* 84, no. 1 (2012): 80–115.

Sibalis, Michael. "L'arrivée de la libération gay en France: Le Front Homosexuel d'Action Révolutionnaire (FHAR)." Translated by Nathalie Paulme. *Genre, Sexualité & Société*, no. 3 (June 1, 2010).

———. "The Regulation of Male Homosexuality in Revolutionary and Napoleonic France, 1789–1815." In *Homosexuality in Modern France*, edited by Jeffrey Merrick and Bryant T. Ragan Jr., 80–101. Oxford: Oxford University Press, 1996.

Sinfield, Alan. *On Sexuality and Power*. New York: Columbia University Press, 2004.

Stanley, Eric. "Fugitive Flesh: Gender Self-Determination, Queer Abolition, and Trans Resistance." In *Captive Genders: Trans Embodiment and the Prison Industrial Complex*, edited by Nat Smith and Eric Stanley. Oakland, CA: AK Press, 2011.

Stanley, Eric, and Chris Vargas. *Criminal Queers*. DVD. San Francisco: TKRC Films, 2012.

Stewart, Harry E., and Rob Roy McGregor. "Jean Genet's Psychiatric Examination in 1943." *French Review* 62, no. 5 (1989): 793–802.

Stockton, Kathryn Bond. *The Queer Child: or, Growing Sideways in the Twentieth Century*. Durham, NC: Duke University Press, 2009.

Stoler, Ann Laura. "Developing Historical Negatives." In *Along the Archival Grain: Epistemic Anxieties and Colonial Commonsense*, 105–40. Princeton, NJ: Princeton University Press, 2009.

———. *Race and the Education of Desire: Foucault's History of Sexuality and the Colonial Order of Things*. Durham, NC: Duke University Press, 1995.

Torok, Maria. "The Illness of Mourning and the Fantasy of the Exquisite Corpse." In *The Shell and the Kernel: Renewals of Psychoanalysis*, vol. 1, 107–24. Chicago: University of Chicago Press, 1994.

Tout! Special issue, no. 12 (1971).

"Trois milliards de pervers: Grande encyclopédie des homosexualités." Special issue, *Recherches* 12 (1973).

Uvslokk, Geir. *Jean Genet: Une écriture des perversions*. Amsterdam: Rodopi, 2011.

Valentine, David. *Imagining Transgender: An Ethnography of a Category*. Durham, NC: Duke University Press, 2007.

Verdrager, Pierre. *L'enfant interdit: Comment la pédophilie est devenue scandaleuse*. Paris: Armand Colin, 2013.

Viego, Antonio. *Dead Subjects: Toward a Politics of Loss in Latino Studies*. Durham, NC: Duke University Press, 2007.

Warner, Michael. "Introduction." In *Fear of a Queer Planet: Queer Politics and Social Theory*, vii–xxxi. Minneapolis: University of Minnesota Press, 1993.

———. "Normal and Normaller: Beyond Gay Marriage." *GLQ: A Journal of Lesbian and Gay Studies* 5, no. 2 (1999): 119–71.

———. *The Trouble with Normal: Sex, Politics, and the Ethics of Queer Life*. Cambridge, MA: Harvard University Press, 2000.

Warner, Michael, and Lauren Berlant. "Sex in Public." In *Publics and Counterpublics*, 187–208. New York: Zone Books, 2002.

Weber, Max. "Politics as a Vocation." In *The Vocation Lectures*, edited by David Owen and Tracy B. Strong, translated by Rodney Livingstone, 32–93. Indianapolis: Hackett, 2004.

Weeks, Jeffrey. "Inverts, Perverts, and Mary Annes: Male Prostitution and the Regulation of Homosexuality in England in the Nineteenth and Early Twentieth Centuries." *Journal of Homosexuality* 6, nos. 1–2 (1981): 113–34.

Weeks, Jeffrey, Brian Heaphy, and Catherine Donovan. *Same Sex Intimacies: Families of Choice and Other Life Experiments*. London: Routledge, 2001.

Weiss, Margot. "The Epistemology of Ethnography: Method in Queer Anthropology." *GLQ: A Journal of Lesbian and Gay Studies* 17, no. 2 (2011): 649–64.

Weheliye, Alexander. *Habeas Viscus: Racializing Assemblages, Biopolitics, and Black Feminist Theories of the Human*. Durham, NC: Duke University Press, 2014.

Weston, Kath. *Families We Choose: Lesbians, Gays, Kinship*. New York: Columbia University Press, 1991.

White, Edmund. *Genet: A Biography*. New York: Alfred A. Knopf, 1994.

———. *My Lives: An Autobiography*. New York: HarperCollins, 2006.

Wiegman, Robyn. *Object Lessons*. Durham, NC: Duke University Press, 2012.

Wiegman, Robyn, and Elizabeth Wilson. "Introduction: Antinormativity's Queer Conventions." *differences: A Journal of Feminist Cultural Studies* 26, no. 1 (2015): 1–25.

Williams, Linda. "Skin Flicks on the Racial Border: Pornography, Exploitation, and Interracial Lust." In *Porn Studies*, edited by Linda Williams, 271–308. Durham, NC: Duke University Press, 2004.

Williams, Raymond. *Marxism and Literature*. Oxford: Oxford University Press, 1977.

Wilson, Elizabeth. *Gut Feminism*. Durham, NC: Duke University Press, 2015.

Wood, Naomi. "Creating the Sensual Child: Paterian Aesthetics, Pederasty, and Oscar Wilde's Fairy Tales." *Marvels and Tales* 16, no. 2 (2002): 156–70.

Yilmaz, Gulay. "Becoming a *Devsirme*: The Training of Conscripted Children in the Ottoman Empire." In *Children in Slavery through the Ages*, ed. Gwyn Campbell, Suzanne Miers, and Joseph C. Miller, 119–34. Athens: Ohio University Press, 2009.

Zaharna, R. S. "The Palestinian Leadership and the American Media: Changing Images, Conflicting Results." In *The Middle East and the American Media*, edited by Y. Kamalipour, 37–49. Chicago: Greenwood, 1995.

index

Adam, Barry, 197–98n36
adoption: Genet's fantasy of himself as the adopted foundling of the Black Panther Party, 16–17, 112, 130, 136; and Genet's intimate relationships to heterosexual households, 110–11; in nineteenth- and early twentieth-century France, 126, 220–21n58; Simone de Beauvoir's legal adoption of Sylvie Le Bon, 115. *See also* foundling; rupture from kinship/belonging
affective histories of *queer*: and the field of Queer Studies, 17, 182–87; and historical disposition to the past, 16, 47–48, 68, 71–75; and the multitemporal form of collective memory, 106; and nonlinear queer time, 105–8. *See also* structures of feeling
age-differentiated male same-sex sexuality: and across-class relationships, 22–23, 29, 32, 40–41; Ancient Greek pederasty, 20, 38–40, 198n46, 199–200n67, 200n69; "backwardness" associated with, 29, 33, 36, 40; as a dominant male same-sex relational form, 24–25, 225n22; erotic relations between uncles and nephews, 114; Genet's *reversal* of the pederastic age differential, 129–31, 137–38; in late nineteenth-century Paris, 39, 225n22; and lifelong partnership, 220n51; and social power, 29, 36; and sodomy laws in France, 147–48, 224–25nn20–21; and sodomy prosecutions in the early twentieth-century U.S., 34, 201n82; and the structuration of Genet's relations, 5. *See also* Daddy/Boy play; pederastic kinship relations; pedophile-child relations

Ahmed, Sara, 211n41; on hatred, 173; on how emotions "open up futures," 189; on "stickiness," 89, 184
AIDS: eroticization of "the bug" of HIV, 92–93; and the ethical values identified with queer political culture, 7; and the in-your-face attitude of 1990s AIDS activism, 185, 230n95; Reagan administration's nonresponse to, 180
anti-identitarianism: political potential of, demonstrated by Genet, 150, 168–71, 189; and Queer Studies, 30–31, 181–82, 186. *See also* self-shattering
Anzaldúa, Gloria, 183
Arcadie, 219n41, 220n51
Arondekar, Anjali, and Geeta Patel, 188
Asad, Talal, 165, 166–67
attachment genealogy: and failure in the face of the ideals of politicized scholarship, 13–14, 44; Genet's nostalgia for prison pederasty, 1, 15–16, 48, 64–68, 72; and the interdisciplinary future of Queer Studies, 17, 177, 187–90; and liberationist negativity, 78–80; and objects of unease in queer theory, 14–15, 30–32, 188–90; and pederastic modernity, 15, 32–33; productively disturbing role of pederastic kinship relations, 114–15, 139–40

backwardness: and age-differentiated male same-sex sexuality, 29, 33, 36, 40; and Genet's *Miracle of the Rose*, 47–48; of old-style colonialist pederasty, 77–78; pederasty as a retrograde mode, 12, 26–29; queer relations *made retrograde*, 12, 24–29, 33–36; in relation to political futurity, 29–30, 47–48, 84

Baldwin, James, 25, 46, 73–74

Baudry, André, 219n41

BDSM subculture: and consent, 23, 26, 199n53; and erotic egalitarianism, 35; and the ethics of power, 25–26; persecution of, 23. *See also* Daddy/Boy play

Benjamin, Walter, 178

Bentaga, Abdallah: Genet's alliance with the Panthers as a tribute to him, 136; Genet's enthusiasm for his career as a high-wire artist, 135; Genet's prose poem "The Tightrope Walker" written for, 135, 136; his suicide, 135, 223n82; mourning of him related to Genet's political activism with the Panthers, 136, 138

Berlant, Lauren, 13

Bersani, Leo: on Genet as a transgressive performer, 3; Hocquenghem's anticipation of his psychoanalytic queer negativity, 94–96, 213n64, 213n66; on jouissance, 214n79; and queer exceptionality, 193n37; "The Gay Daddy," 27

Bhabha, Homi, 90

Black Panthers: and the black stud stereotype, 102–4; criminalization and imprisonment shared with Genet, 150–51; criminalized by the U.S. government, 142–44; female membership of, 215n87; Genet's activism with, 80–82, 136–38, 230n91; Genet's fantasy of himself as the adopted foundling of, 16–17, 112, 130, 136; Genet's fund-raising for the liberation of incarcerated Panthers, 225–26n32; individual members. *See* Hilliard, David; Newton, Huey P.; Seale, Bobby

Blüher, Hans, 118

Bonnet, Marie-Jo, 208n6

Boone, Joseph, 200n71

Boy Scouts: *détournements* of comics and illustrations from French Boy Scout novels, 86; homosocial male hierarchy of, 53–54, 56–57; rehabilitation of juvenile delinquents through participation in, 53

Burrough, Bryan, 230n91

Butler, Judith: on butch/femme lesbian genders and heteronormativity, 8, 223n87; on the political charge of *queer* as a product of historical conditions, 179–80; theory of gender performativity, 61, 205n48

Califia, Patrick, 109–10, 114

Cervulle, Maxime, 85; and Nick Rees-Roberts, 82

Chauncey, George, 40–41, 200n74, 218–19n40

Chen, Mel, 181, 182–83

child sexuality: and abuses in correction houses for minors, 46–47, 49, 202n12; psychological disorders blamed on the repression of, 217n18; sex panic around pedophilia as a threat to children's innocence, 22, 35; theorized by Hocquenghem and Schérer, 217n20. *See also* age-differentiated male same-sex sexuality; pederastic kinship relations; pedophile-child relations

chosen families: denigration of traditional role of families by, 119–20; and Genet's life practices of affiliation, 110–12, 118–19, 121; perceived failures of the utopian discourse of, 216n10; and queer reparative aspirations, 109–10, 112–14; relation to queerness, 15, 17, 119–21

Choukri, Mohammad, 78

Cixous, Hélène, 81, 209n17

coalitional solidarity: and the divergent temporalities of the political and the erotic, 80; of the FHAR, 76–77; principle of "different identities, same goals," 174; and queer coalitional oppositionality, 17, 147, 150, 171–75, 230n96; and Queer Studies, 4–9, 13, 17, 76. *See also* erotic coalition

Cohen, Cathy, 35, 171–72

Comité d'urgence anti-répression homosexuelle (CUARTH), 148, 194n8

consent: equalization of homosexual and heterosexual ages of, 34, 194–95n8; and sexual majority in France, 195n9; and

sodomy laws in France, 147–48, 195n9, 224–25nn20–21
Coviello, Peter, 65

Daddy/Boy play, 197–98nn36–37; and gay leather culture, 27–28, 196–97n32, 197n37; and the linguistic use of Daddy in sexual play, 197n35; pederasty distinguished from, 25–29; and queer families of choice, 109–10, 114
Danan, Alexis, 47, 49, 51, 72, 201–2n11
Davis, Angela, 16–17, 46, 112, 137, 225–26n32
Dean, Carolyn, 203n34
Dean, Tim, 100, 213n64; "affirmatively forgetting" advocated by, 232n26; queer theory of fetishism, 80, 91, 106
Deleuze, Gilles, and Félix Guattari, *Anti-Oedipus*, 94, 212n58
D'Emilio, John, 113–14
Dinshaw, Carolyn, 14, 30, 193n39
Dollimore, Jonathan, 173

Edelman, Lee: on liberationist negativity, 95, 193n37, 213n67; "no future" of, 33–34, 132, 174, 198n48
El-Rouayheb, Khaled, 210n29
Eng, David L., Judith Halberstam, and José Esteban Muñoz, 177–82, 188
erotic coalition: defined, 78; Hocquenghem's championing of, 208n8
erotic egalitarianism, 35–38, 42, 199n65

Fanon, Frantz, 46, 100–101, 214n81
Ferguson, Roderick, 120, 171–72
fetishism: Dean's queer theory of, 80, 91–93, 106; and the eroticization of "the bug" of HIV, 92–93; Freudian framework of, 90, 211n44, 212n55. *See also* racial fetishism
FHAR. *See* Front homosexuel d'action révolutionnaire (Homosexual Front of Revolutionary Action)
Fischel, Joseph, 35, 197n34, 198n51, 199n65
Flatley, Jonathan, 227n54
forgetting: and the illness of mourning, 69–71; and the multitemporal form of collective memory, 106; of queer adolescent yearnings, 64–68; by Queer Studies of the U.S. scene of the 1990s, 184, 232n26

Foucault, Michel: affect and emotion in his historical methodology, 29–30; on the French penal code's age of consent, 195n9; Freudian repressive hypothesis addressed by, 209n10; "Friendship as a Way of Life," 15, 19–22, 193n1, 194n5; unease associated with uninstitutionalized relations by, 19–22
foundling: Genet's identification as, 48, 56, 121, 125–29; Nealon on, 109, 121–23, 125; "sideways" structure of feeling of, 121n66, 128–29. *See also* adoption
"Fragments . . .": homosexualized pederasty in, 128; liberationist pederasty imagined in, 123–25, 128
Freeman, Elizabeth, 14; concept of erotohistoriography, 16, 68–69, 101
Freud, Sigmund: erotic fetish of, 90, 211n44, 212n55; on mourning, 69, 206n67; repressive hypothesis, 209n10
Freudo-Marxism: derepression advocated by, 93–94, 209n10; and gay liberationist ideals of erotic coalition, 77–78
Friedlaender, Benedict, 118
Front homosexuel d'action révolutionnaire (Homosexual Front of Revolutionary Action; FHAR), 217n18; radical, coalitional politics of, 76–77; tensions between FHAR gays and lesbians, 208n6, 212–13n63; *Three Billion Perverts (Trois milliards de pervers)*, 86–87, 93–94, 116, 210n28, 217n22
Funeral Rites (Pompes funèbres), 68, 69, 220n53

Genet, Jean: birth to and abandonment by Camille Genet, 126–27, 221n59, 221n61; contemporary subcultural iconicity of, 1; on the development of pederastic virility, 59–61, 205n48; estrangement from and hatred of the French state, 125–28, 138–39, 144, 161, 169, 221n59; film scripts (*see* "The Language of the Wall"); foster family placement of, 151, 226n36; funds raised for liberation of incarcerated Panthers, 225–26n32; his practice of deidealization, 11–12, 15; Hitler perversely admired by, 125–26, 127, 144–45, 169, 220n53, 220n55, 224n12; homophobia of, 111, 193n33;

Genet, Jean (*continued*)
as an ideal object for Queer Studies, 4–7, 9–10, 13, 176–77; identification as an "outlaw" and "antihero," 2–3, 82, 135, 145–46, 157, 159–60; queer exemplarity of, 15; racialized sexuality of, 82–84; and the Red Army Faction (RAF), 17, 142, 144, 145, 147, 150, 160–64, 169, 170; relationship with Bentaga (*see* Bentaga, Abdallah); relationship with Jacky Maglia, 110, 133, 135; relationship with Mohammed El Katrani, 110; works (*see* "Fragments . . ."; *Funeral Rites*; "The Language of the Wall"; *Miracle of the Rose*; *Our Lady of the Flowers*; *Prisoner of Love*; *A Song of Love*; *Thief's Journal*; "Violence and Brutality")
Gide, André: defense of pederasty, 112, 117, 200n76, 219n49; pederasts distinguished from inverts, 124; and the sexual tourism industry in colonial French North Africa, 200n71
Gill, Michael, 35
Gordon, Avery, 5
Gould, Deborah, 173, 191n12, 227n54, 232n11
Guattari, Félix, *Three Billion Perverts* (*Trois milliards de pervers*), 86–87, 93–94, 116, 210n28, 217n22
Gunther, Scott, 21, 194–95nn7–8, 198n50, 217n18, 224n19

Haden, Patricia, 158
Halberstam, Jack (Judith), 14, 107–8, 122; "What's Queer about Queer Studies Now?" special issue, 177–82, 188
Hale, C. Jacob, 196–97n32
Halperin, David, 171, 181, 220n51, 230n92; on the possibility of lifelong, companionate mutual partnership, 37–38, 220n51
Harkins, Gillian, 32, 195n19
Hart, Lynda, and Joshua Dale, 199n53
Hayes, Jarrod, 82
Heaney, Emma, 200n69
Hekma, Gert, 35
Hesford, Victoria, 158
Hewitt, Andrew, 117–18, 219n49
Hilderbrand, Lucas, 185
Hilliard, David: and Genet's eroticized fantasy of kinship, 129–31, 136, 137; intuition that the Panthers could trust Genet, 150–51
Hochberg, Gil, 170
Hocquenghem, Guy: child sexuality theorized by, 217n20; on the criminal constitution of homosexuality, 149, 150; on the elimination of age of sexual majority in the French penal code, 195n9; erotic coalition championed by, 208n8; legal sexual consent as a concern, 195n9, 197n34; liberated pedophilia theorized by, 218n26; liberationist negativity of, 78–79, 94–95, 213n64, 213n66; radical opposition to the Oedipal family, 112
Holland, Sharon Patricia, 11; on antinormative autonomy, 35, 79; critique of queer time, 102, 106–7; dictum that "there is no raceless course of desire," 90
homonationalism: defined by Jasbir Puar, 146; and Genet's embodiment of the queer romance of the alternative, 2, 17, 146–47, 159–60; and *queer*'s affective histories, 13, 15, 186–87
homophobia: and AIDS, 181; FHAR's response to French forms of, 76–77; Genet's, 111, 193n33; and historical identification of homosexuality with crime, 148–49; pederasty associated with internalized forms of, 24, 32–33; queer time's entanglement with the disempowering history of, 108
homosexuality, criminalization of, 147–50, 224n19, 225n28

Jablonka, Ivan, 47
Jagose, Annamarie, 232n9, 232n23
Jakobsen, Janet R., 173
Johnson, Colin, 40–41
Johnson, E. Patrick, 183
Jones, Charles E., 143

Keeling, Kara, 101
kinship relations: exclusion of nonnormative raced and classed families from neoliberal types of, 120–21; French familialist idealist version of, 95, 122–23; Genet's professed detachment from familial feeling, 110–11; and neoliberal discourse of

choice, 119–20. *See also* adoption; BDSM subculture; chosen families; Daddy/Boy play; pederastic kinship relations
Klein, Melanie, 11
Kunzel, Regina, 34, 40–41, 50–51, 65

"The Language of the Wall" ("Le langage de la muraille"): compared to his other unrealized film scripts, 153; French disciplinary and penal institutions addressed in, 17, 145, 147; and Genet's preparatory letter to Bernard Tavernier, 154; on Mettray's role in French projects of social management and imperial exploitation, 153–57
Lapie, Victor: as the pen name of Henri Joubrel, 53; *Saint-Florent-Life* (*Saint-Florent-la-Vie*), 52–53, 56, 203n24
Le Breton, August, 52, 54
Lim, Eng-Beng, 25, 42–43
Love, Heather, 11, 14, 30, 108, 231n4; *Feeling Backward*, 14, 74, 108, 193n39; on the work of queering, 232n7

Mackay, John Henry, 118, 220n49, 220n52
Malcolm X, 46
Manalansan, Martin, 32
Mapplethorpe, Robert, 81–82, 180
Martin, Biddy, 181–82
Medovoi, Leerom, 158
Mercer, Kobena, 81–82, 127, 129, 136
Mettray: and August Le Breton's *The High Walls* (*Les hauts murs*), 52, 54, 202n21; founding of, 54–55; Genet's incarceration at, 16, 57–68, 226n37; and Genet's nostalgia for imprisonment, 46–47, 71–75; its "secret purpose" exposed in Genet's letter to Bernard Tavernier, 154; and the pederastic patterning of Genet's relations, 137–38; released inmates as potential pederasts, 205n54
Middleton, Donna, 158
Millett, Kate, 81
Miracle of the Rose (*Miracle de la rose*): Deloffre's orgasm of mourning in, 68, 69–71; Genet's masculine development at Mettray described in, 57–64; queer historical disposition toward the past described in, 16, 47–48, 68, 71–75

Mirguet amendment, 149, 225n28
mourning: of Bentaga related to Genet's political activism with the Panthers, 136, 138; Deloffre's orgasm of mourning in the *Miracle of the Rose*, 69–71; and erotic response, 68–71; Freud on, 69, 206n67
Muñoz, José Esteban, 30, 71, 177–78, 185; "What's Queer about Queer Studies Now?" special issue, 177–82
Musser, Amber Jamilla, 193n37, 209n11, 213n66

Nash, Jennifer, 83, 107–8
Nealon, Christopher: on "foundlings," 109, 121–23, 125; term *affect-genealogies*, 28
Neutres, Jérôme, 82, 142, 144, 166, 224n12
Newton, Huey P., 215n87, 225n32, 226n34
Nguyen, Hoang Tan, 83
Nyong'o, Tavia, 79

Ogbar, Jeffrey O. G., 143
Ongiri, Amy Abugo, 137
orphans. *See* adoption; foundling; queer historical orphanage
Our Lady of the Flowers (*Notre-Dame-des-Fleurs*), 1, 7, 58–59, 68; racial fetishism portrayed in, 93, 99–100, 214n74; street queen Divine and her pimp Darling in, 1, 7

Palestinians: Genet's activism with the Palestinian Liberation Organization, 80–84, 164–65, 168–71; goals of statehood and sovereignty not supported by Genet, 174–75, 231n104. *See also* Popular Front for the Liberation of Palestine (PFLP)
pederastic kinship relations: as a challenge to the Oedipal family and social structure, 115–18; capacity to move *athwart* social categories, 12, 22, 25, 139; eroticized differences as the base of, 118–21; former boy-beloved Albert on, 116, 119; and Genet's life practices of affiliation, 110–12, 119–21, 134–39; as a productively disturbing attachment genealogy, 114–15, 139–40; as a threat to parental and state jurisdiction over minors, 35. *See also* BDSM subculture; Daddy/Boy play

pederastic modernity: critical dimension of, 42–44; Genet's *reversal* of the pederastic age differential as a form of, 129–31, 137–38; hierarchical and exploitative structure of modernity revealed by, 10, 23, 42–44; kinship relations, 111–15; and lifelong, companionate, romantic and mutual love, 37–38, 220n51; and the native boy/white man dyad, 42–43

pederasty: and *caïdisme*, 50; and European views of Arab-Islamic sexuality, 29, 40, 87–88, 96–97, 210nn28–29, 211n32; homosexuality identified with, 37–38, 41, 124, 148, 194n8, 195n11; as an object for politicized scholarship, 44; as the outcome of Genet's maternal abandonment, 127; released inmates of Mettray as potential pederasts, 205n54; as a retrograde mode, 12, 25–29; as a virile culture-building and nation-sustaining form of homosociality, 117–18. *See also* consent

pedophile-child relations: 1970s vision of it as ethical, 23–24, 33, 115–16; and abuse of power, 128–29, 203n34; and the conceptual invention of pedophilia, 24, 32–33, 198n45; parent-child relations compared with, 115–16

Peniston, William A., 39, 40, 148

Pérez, Hiram, 214n84

Pietz, William, 90, 212n55

pimps: Darling from Genet's *Our Lady of the Flowers*, 1, 7; disavowal of their queer adolescent passions, 64, 66–67; virile heterosexuality of, 63, 67, 205n54

pinkwashing, 15, 146

Popular Front for the Liberation of Palestine (PFLP): airplane hijackings, 144; and the PLO, 224n9

Prearo, Massimo, 213n64

Prisoner of Love (*Un captif amoureux*): and Genet's eroticized fantasy of kinship in, 129–30; history of sixties nationalism revealed in, 16–17, 112, 137; sexualized imagery of Panthers in, 103–4

Puar, Jasbir: on antinormative autonomy, 35, 186–87; bifurcated reception of Foucault critiqued by, 168; homonationalism defined by, 146; ideal state of "freedom from norms," 181; on queerness installed in the naming of terrorists, 228n70

queer: definitional openness of, 178–82, 183; emergence of key concepts of, from a U.S. political context, 187–88

queer historical orphanage: connection to foundling reaffiliation, 127–28, 190; pederastic kinship as a response to, 134–35; rupture from kinship/belonging, 123–24, 127, 130. *See also* foundling

racial fetishism: of "Arab men" by the FHAR, 16, 88–89; and the black stud stereotype, 102–4; in Genet's writing, 82, 93, 99–100, 214n74; political potency of, 101–5, 215n90; of the white bottom, 14, 16, 87–89, 96–102, 105–6, 214n78. *See also* whiteness

Reddy, Chandan, 227n61, 229n80

Reid, Julian, 227n61

Reid-Pharr, Robert, 83, 105–6

reparation: deidealization as an expanded understanding of, 11, 192n31, 231n108; and the ideal of chosen families, 109–10, 112–14; of liberationist pederasty, 124; Sedgwick on, 10–11, 192n31, 231n108

Robcis, Camille, 95, 122

Robinson, Patricia, 158

Rodríguez, Juana María: on Daddy play, 197n35; on the exclusion of nonnormative raced and classed families from neoliberal kinship, 120–21; on the "futural register of consent," 197n34; on self-racialization, 83; on sexual contracts and forms of coercion, 140

Rosario, Vernon A., II, 224n19

Roubaud, Louis, 48, 52, 201–2n11

Rubin, Gayle, 22, 23, 25, 195n17, 195n19, 232n10

rupture from kinship/belonging: Genet's estrangement from and hatred of the French state, 126–28, 144, 161, 221n59; Genet's professed detachment from familial feeling, 110–11; rupture from time related to, 121–23, 132–34. *See also* queer historical orphanage

Said, Edward, 78, 81, 82
Sartre, Jean-Paul: admiration of Genet, 2–3, 221n62; difficulty with *Miracle*, 47; *Tout!* edited by, 76–77
Schérer, René, 217n20, 218n26
Scott, Darieck, 11, 83, 214n78
Seale, Bobby, 215n87, 225n32
Sedgwick, Eve Kosofsky: and the capacity of pederasty to move *athwart* social categories, 12, 22, 139; on "hygienic dislinkages" between sadomasochistic play and real social power, 34; on *queer* as inextinguishable, 180; on reparation and damage, 10–11, 192n31, 231n108
self-shattering: deidealization of the value of, 93, 100–101; and queer negativity, 16, 30, 78–79, 94–96, 193n37; racialization of, 96–102, 214n78
sexual tourism, 32, 40, 200n71, 211n32
Shahid, Leila, 78, 141
Shah, Nayan, 126–27, 192n26, 201n82
Shepard, Todd, 80, 85–89
Sinfield, Alan, 25, 36, 44, 114, 133–34, 199n64, 200n79
Solanas, Valerie, 158
A Song of Love (*Un chant d'amour*), visual citations in *Criminal Queers*, 45–46
Stanley, Eric, and Chris Vargas, *Criminal Queers*, 45–46
Stanley, Eric, and Nat Smith, *Captive Genders*, 149–50
Stoler, Ann Laura, 152, 229n81
structures of feeling: defined, 201n8, 221n67; enemies of state as, 147, 169, 229n85; and Genet's foundling longings, 48, 56, 128–29. *See also* affective histories of *queer*

Thief's Journal (*Journal du voleur*): Genet's relationship to Armand in, 199–200n67; pederasty portrayed as the outcome of maternal abandonment in, 127; racial fetishism portrayed in, 93, 98–99
Thomas (self-identified pedophile interviewed for *Fous d'enfance*), 114, 216nn12–13, 217n21
Torok, Maria, 69–71

unease: and age-differentiated sex within Queer Studies, 5, 15, 25, 33–38, 43; associated with uninstitutionalized relations by Foucault, 19–22; attachment genealogy used to confront the object of, 14–15, 30–32, 188–90; as a generative heuristic for politicized scholarship, 9–10
Uvslokk, Geir, 199–200n67

Verdrager, Pierre, 115–16
"Violence and Brutality," 17, 147, 160–64

Warner, Michael, 7, 179, 181
Weeks, Jeffrey, 40–41, 200n75; and Brian Heaphy and Catherine Donovan, 37, 113
Weheliye, Alexander, 229n81
Weston, Kath, 113, 119, 216n10, 218n36, 218–19n40
White, Edmund, 110, 111, 129, 133, 138, 193n33
whiteness: French masculinity associated with, 48, 57, 85–87; and Genet's exceptionalism, 81–84; native boy/white man dyad, 25, 42–43, 77; and the porno-trope of the non-white hypersexual stud, 85; and the racialization of self-shattering, 16, 96–102, 214n78; white supremacy, 5. *See also* racial fetishism
Wiegman, Robyn, 8, 181, 192n29
Wilde, Oscar, 25, 41, 196n27, 200n76
Williams, Linda, 102–3
Williams, Raymond, 201n8, 221n67, 229n85

Zaharna, R. S, 144

www.ingramcontent.com/pod-product-compliance
Lightning Source LLC
Chambersburg PA
CBHW070322240426
43671CB00013BA/2336